Windows® Game Programming with Visual Basic and DirectX

Wayne S. Freeze

Que®

201 W. 103rd Street
Indianapolis, Indiana 46290

WINDOWS® GAME PROGRAMMING WITH VISUAL BASIC AND DIRECTX

Copyright © 2002 by Que

International Standard Book Number: 0-7897-2592-4

Library of Congress Catalog Card Number: 2001096458

Printed in the United States of America

First Printing: December 2001

05   04   03   02   4   3   2   1

Trademarks

Warning and Disclaimer

Publisher
David Culverwell

Executive Editor
Candace Hall

Acquisitions Editor
Michelle Newcomb

Development Editor
Howard Jones

Managing Editor
Thomas F. Hayes

Senior Editor
Susan Ross Moore

Copy Editor
Kate O. Givens

Indexer
Angie Bess

Proofreaders
Marcia Deboy
Maribeth Echard

Technical Editor
Micheal McDonald

Team Coordinator
Cindy Teeters

Media Developer
Michael Hunter

Interior Designer
Ruth Harvey

Cover Designers
Dan Armstrong
Ruth Harvey

Page Layout
Susan Geiselman
Brad Lenser
Michelle Mitchell

TABLE OF CONTENTS

ABOUT THE AUTHOR

Wayne S. Freeze started working with computers in 1975 and he hasn't stopped yet. Along the way, he's held nearly every computer-related job available in a large computer organization. Before he started writing full-time, he was the technical support manager at the University of Maryland at College Park, where he was responsible for a large IBM mainframe and a diverse collection of smaller computers.

This is his tenth computer book and his first for Que. Until now, he's spent most of his time writing about Visual Basic, databases, or some combination thereof. He also writes magazine articles for several different magazines on topics ranging from how to create Office macros to digging into the guts of the Common Runtime Library in Microsoft's new .NET framework.

Now, Wayne works out of his house in rural South Dakota with his lovely wife Jill (who also writes computer books) and his two children, Christopher (age 8) and Samantha (age 6). Jill, whom Microsoft crowned an "Internet zealot," is a prize-winning beta tester and has worked extensively with products like Microsoft Office and Internet Explorer. Her books are aimed at consumers and her *Sams Teach Yourself Computer Basics in 24 Hours, Third Edition* (Sams, 2001, ISBN: 0-672-32301-X) has received rave reviews from her readers. Chris is only eight years old, but is one of the sharpest game players Wayne knows. He can easily beat kids twice his age with most computer games. Wayne rarely plays multi-player computer action games with Chris anymore, simply because he consistently beats him! Chris was the only person in the state of South Dakota to win a prize in Gateway and Microsoft's nationwide computer game contest, and he ranked in the top 200 players in his age range in the country! When Wayne was looking for a beta tester for Swim Mall, Chris was a natural choice, and made countless valuable suggestions for the game's improvement.

Like Chris, Wayne's daughter Sammy is also a whiz with computers, though given a choice between playing with her computer and dancing, she'll pick dancing every time.

DEDICATION

In memory of Deb Falkinburg.

ACKNOWLEDGMENTS

I want to remember a special lady who is no longer with us. About a dozen years ago, she was a major influence in my life, along with her husband Tim. Both of them helped me through a very difficult time in my life. Time and distance has separated us recently, but she has been in my thoughts a lot lately. I will really miss you, Deb.

There is a long story behind this book, but the short version is that I was supposed to write it for a different publisher and after a long string of broken promises I decided it wasn't worth my sanity to write the book. Then one day while I was talking to Candace Hall at Que, I described the book to her. Before I could think twice, I was digging the foundation for Swim Mall. Thanks, Candy.

Along the way, I was able to work with some extraordinary people, such as Michelle Newcomb, who was very patient when I missed deadline after deadline, and Howard Jones, who seemed to fill several different roles in this book in addition to the one he was hired for.

Without the help of a number of people at Caligari, Syntrillium, and Adobe, this book would not have been possible. I want to thank Roman Ormandy and Kristine Gardner from Caligari Corporation and Hart Shafer at Syntrillium Software Corporation for copies of their software, plus permission to include copies of trueSpace and Cool Edit on the CD-ROM. I also want to thank Will Saso from Adobe Systems Incorporated for his help with getting copies of Photoshop and Illustrator for use with this book.

I want to acknowledge the support my agent Laura Belt has given me while this book unfolded. She's worth her weight in gold (or is that goldens). She helps to keep my friendly neighborhood banker happy, which in turns helps me keep a roof over my head.

I also want to mention some of my friends: Rick, who believes there isn't anything I can't program; Shaun, who has some misguided views of Java; Ian, for telling me about Cool Edit; and Bob K., who I thought about when I was discussing the probability theory in this book. I also want to mention Ariane, Elwyn, Dr. Bob, Veronica, Scott, Randy, and Vikki, all of whom I miss now that I live in the middle of nowhere.

A big thank-you needs to go to Bucky and Goose for helping out with so many things.

I haven't seen my Mom and Dad for over a year as I write this, and it makes me sad. Maybe one of these days I'll show up on your doorstep and surprise you. In the meantime, Mom, please get better.

Samantha is my little girl who wants to be a dancing veterinarian, who performs at the Olympics; I just want her to sit on my lap and be cute. I love you beans.

I want to say to my lovely wife Jill that I truly love you and I'm sorry about the Dummies book. I know you'll do well with your plan to create FP while you finish your great American novel.

Finally, I want to say thank-you to my son and beta tester, Christopher. It was your sense of humor that really made Swim Mall fun to write. It's time for bed, CJ. Third grade awaits you in the morning.

TELL US WHAT YOU THINK!

As the reader of this book, *you* are our most important critic and commentator. We value your opinion and want to know what we're doing right, what we could do better, what areas you'd like to see us publish in, and any other words of wisdom you're willing to pass our way.

As an Executive Editor for Que, I welcome your comments. You can fax, email, or write me directly to let me know what you did or didn't like about this book—as well as what we can do to make our books stronger.

Please note that I cannot help you with technical problems related to the topic of this book, and that due to the high volume of mail I receive, I might not be able to reply to every message.

When you write, please be sure to include this book's title and author as well as your name and phone or fax number. I will carefully review your comments and share them with the author and editors who worked on the book.

Fax: 317-581-4666

E-mail: feedback@quepublishing.com

Mail: Candace Hall
            Executive Editor
            Que Publishing
            201 West 103rd Street
            Indianapolis, IN 46290 USA

INTRODUCTION

In this introduction

I've been fascinated by computer games for years. Some of my first experiences date back to the late 1960s when I was in junior high school. I was allowed to skip math class once a week to use an old teletype terminal. I spent hours punching a tic-tac-toe game written in BASIC onto paper tape so that I could play it when I connected to the mainframe.

In college, I was hooked on a Star Trek game written in BASIC that ran on a Hewlett Packard 2000 timesharing computer. I spent many hours playing the game and discussing strategy with my classmates. One summer, a few friends and I created a more advanced version of the game based on a source code listing we found in *Creative Computing*, one of the first hobbyist computer magazines ever created.

Later, I spent a lot of time playing Adventure (also known as The Colossal Cave), which was created by a pair of MIT students, Willie Crowther and Don Woods, on a mainframe computer. This game used phrases like "You are standing at the end of a road before a small brick building" to create images in your mind. It was the first of an entire genre of computer games now known as Interactive Fiction.

Back then, I didn't care much for labels, I just wanted to beat the game. I created lots of notes but wasn't able to beat it. Fortunately, the source code for the game was readily available. I studied the source code and eventually defeated it with a perfect score.

The first time I saw SimCity, I thought the entire premise for the game seemed dumb. My wife, on the other hand, thought it was an interesting concept, so she bought it anyway. She asked me to install in on our computer early the next morning. Eight hours later she found me still at the computer, playing the game. I hadn't left my seat! Ever since then, I've always been first in line each time a new version of SimCity came out.

CREATING A COMPUTER GAME

By now you may have guessed that I'm hooked on computer games. I don't really want to know how much money I've spent on games over the years, not to mention computers and other hardware to support the games I played.

However, playing computer games is a far cry from building computer games. It's my belief that the hardest type of computer program to write today is a game. Writing an operating system is a close second. Fifteen years ago anyone could build a computer game in his or her spare time. Today it takes teams of specialists many months or even years to build a computer game.

Even though building a high-end commercial computer game is next to impossible for anyone outside a handful of specialists, that doesn't mean you can't learn some of the fundamental principles and have a little fun at the same time.

If you want to create your own computer game, you need to make a few initial decisions, such as the type of game you want to create, the programming language you want to use, and the operating system API you want to use.

TYPES OF GAMES

There are many different types of computer games. The key types are listed here:

- **Action games** were first made popular by such titles as Doom and Tomb Raider. The premise is that you control the actions of a 3D character as you wander around trying to solve a set of puzzles. A subset of these games are known as first person shooters, where a major part of the action involves killing everything in sight.

- **Adventure games** are similar to the original Adventure game in that you guide one or more characters on a quest. These games are sometimes known as role playing.

- **Arcade games** are generally simple 2D games that involve manipulating an object trough a maze to avoid a series of traps or firing at objects to prevent being destroyed. Classic examples of this type of game include PacMan, Centipede, and Space Invaders.

- **Driving/flying games** generally place you behind the wheel while you drive a car or fly an airplane. The classic example of this type of game is the Microsoft Flight Simulator series of games.

- **Platform games** are essentially 2D games where you guide a character through a maze to solve a puzzle. Their name comes from the fact that in most of the games your character walks or jumps from platform to platform while solving the puzzle. Mario Brothers for the Nintendo console is probably the most famous game of this type.

- **Puzzle games** exist solely to solve puzzles. Examples of these games include the Solitaire game included with Windows and the Incredible Machine.

- **Simulation games** attempt to simulate a particular environment. You are not allowed to directly control the game, rather you must indirectly control the game by modifying various game parameters. These parameters in turn influence how the simulator controls the details of the game. The defining example of this game type is the SimCity series of games from Maxis.

- **Sports games** provide a way to play games such as football, baseball, or hockey on your computer.

- **Strategy games** provide you with resources that you can directly control. These resources can be devoted to creating other resources, expanding to reach a goal or engaging in warfare. My favorite strategy game is Civilization.

It is often difficult to classify a game as a specific type, because it may have characteristics that span multiple types.

VISUAL BASIC

The first programs I ever wrote were in a computer language known as BASIC, and although I have used many programming languages over the years, somehow I keep returning to it. Microsoft's Visual Basic is the most popular form of the language today and it is used by more than 3,000,000 programmers, making it the most popular programming language in the world.

I like Visual Basic for many reasons, but the biggest reason is that it is the easiest language to use when you want to write an application for Microsoft Windows. Visual Basic includes excellent debugging tools and many of the problems that drive C++ programmers crazy are automatically handled for you. Because I'm also known as "The Lazy Programmer," the less time I spend writing and debugging programs means that much more time to spend with my family (or more time to play computer games).

DirectX

DirectX refers to a collection of objects you can incorporate in a program to build a game. DirectX includes many separate components that address various aspects of game programming. In its latest version, DirectX 8 has evolved to become the primary API for game developers. Here are some of the key components of DirectX 8.

- **DirectDraw** is a high-performance interface that makes it practical for a programmer to create 2D graphics. Although DirectDraw is still included in DirectX 8, it hasn't been enhanced since DirectX 7. It continues to exist for compatibility reasons.
- **Direct3D** is the 3D graphics interface. It uses the hardware assists found in many video cards to create 3D displays that were impossible only a few short years ago.
- **DirectInput** provides a unified approach to handing input from the user. This means your program need not know if the input is coming from a joystick, mouse, or keyboard.
- **DirectMusic** allows you to play many different music formats on your computer, including MIDI and MP3.
- **DirectSound** allows you to create or play various types of sounds in your computer, which are typically saved in .WAV files.
- **DirectPlay** makes it easier to coordinate communications between multiple computers in a multiplayer game.

Introducing Swim Mall

I had been thinking about building a simulation game, but I didn't want to duplicate any of the games already in the marketplace. This ruled out any games based on city management, airline/airport management, fast food restaurants, and many other things.

Then one day I happened to be walking through a shopping mall and was thinking how it resembled a small city and the name Swim Mall popped into my head. From there, the rest was easy.

Swim Mall is simply a simulation of an underwater shopping mall. Your job as the player is to manage the mall's growth from a shrimpy little shopping mall to a whale of a place to shop. You'll have to attract new stores to the mall and make it a nice place to visit. You'll also have to worry about various problems, ranging from cleaning the trash left on the floor to crime to responding to major emergencies. Managing a shopping mall on the ocean floor is a tough, thankless job!

My original intent for Swim Mall was to use 2D graphics along the lines of the original SimCity game. However, when I started working with DirectX 8, I decided to abandon the 2D approach and go with 3D graphic images. I'm sure that the appearance of the game is much better with 3D graphics. At the same time, using Direct3D simplified the code needed to generate graphics.

YOUR CHALLENGE

As you read this book, you may want to keep a running list of ideas of changes that you would like to make to the game. These changes can range from minor code improvements to additional game objects or brand new features not implemented in the original game.

When you're finished with the book, your challenge is to implement these changes using the source code provided on the CD-ROM and submit them to my Web site at www.JustPC.com. I'll collect the changes and post them so that other readers can download them. Once each month, I'll review the submissions with my panel of judges and select the best one. That person will win a small prize. A complete set of rules and instructions will be posted on the Web site, so stop by, take a look, and send me your code.

WHO SHOULD READ THIS BOOK

This book is aimed at someone who already has a working knowledge of Visual Basic. If you have six months to a year experience, you should do fine. I use Class modules extensively in the program, so you should be familiar with how they work, including how to define properties, methods, and events.

Be warned, DirectX is not for the faint of heart. It is probably the most complex API in Microsoft's suite of application programming interfaces. I will lead you though enough of the API to build the game, but I'll try to avoid the features that aren't absolutely necessary to keep the complexity to a minimum.

You should also know a little bit about mathematics, particularly matrix operations. Some of the 3D functions require computing things by adding and multiplying matrixes. I'll try to explain enough of the math so you'll understand what I'm doing, but if you can't follow the math, don't worry. You should be able to plug the numbers into the code to get the results you want without the math.

I'll also demonstrate how to create the 3D graphics using a reasonably priced, 3D design tool called trueSpace. However, knowing a 2D graphics tool like Adobe Photoshop or PaintShopPro may also prove useful in this book.

SYSTEM REQUIREMENTS

Creating a game using 3D graphics requires a relatively substantial computer system. If your computer doesn't have 3D accelerator video card, you may as well forget about trying to run it. Also, don't try to run this game in anything less then a 500Mhz processor. I suggest a minimum of 128MB of memory and recommend at least 256.

I developed this system on a 600MHz computer running Windows 2000 with 384MB of memory. Windows 98 or Windows Me should also be acceptable, though be prepared to reboot your computer frequently, as some mistakes will cause your computer to lock up. Don't assume that Windows 2000 is the perfect solution either; I managed to crash my system several times while debugging parts of the game.

You'll need a copy of Visual Basic 6 and the DirectX 8 software development kit (SDK). You can use any edition of Visual Basic, including the Learning Edition, because the user interface elements come from the DirectX SDK, not the ActiveX controls you would typically use.

In addition to the DirectX 8 SDK, you'll need the Microsoft Speech SDK, version 5.1, to add the text to speech facilities used in the game.

I suggested earlier knowledge of Photoshop or PaintShopPro would prove useful, which means that it is only useful if you have access to the software. I've been using Photoshop for a long time and highly recommend it to anyone who needs to create 2D graphics.

On the other hand, designing 3D graphics is a true art form and using a 3D design package like trueSpace requires a lot of time and effort, but it can be done. You won't absolutely need trueSpace to run the game as it exists in this book. I've already created those images. However, if you wish to design a new 3D image for the challenge, you'll need a tool like trueSpace.

Finally, you'll need a tool such as Cool Edit to create and edit sound files used in the game. Among other things, you can use it to create .WAV files from a microphone, copy music CDs to .MP3 files, and edit and transform the contents of a sound file much like Photoshop edits and transforms an image.

For your convenience, I've included the DirectX and Speech SDKs on the book's CD-ROM. Also, I've included demo copies of both trueSpace and Photoshop on the CD-ROM.

WHAT THIS BOOK COVERS

This book covers the design and implementation of a simulation computer game called Swim Mall. The game relies on Direct3D to display the graphics and to DirectInput interact with the user. I'll cover enough about DirectSound and DirectMusic to create the sounds and music the game needs.

All source code, graphics, and other support files are included on the CD-ROM that comes with the book. This includes all of the configuration files, images, sound clips, and so on, though I have omitted my favorite MP3 files for copyright reasons. Each chapter has a directory containing the game or other sample files that were discussed in that chapter.

WHAT THIS BOOK DOESN'T COVER

As much as I wanted to cover how to build multiple types of games in this book, there simply wasn't enough room. Where there are many similar aspects among the various types of games, each type has its own unique aspects. For instance a driving or flying game needs far more complex 3D scenery, and it also requires a complex physics model to determine how the car or airplane will move.

Likewise, an adventure game requires a complex story behind the game to make it truly interesting. Of course, having detailed animation for this type of game is just as important and is probably even more difficult.

Also, this book doesn't cover the fundamentals of Visual Basic. If you don't understand the difference between a class and an event, set this book aside and go read *Sams Teach Yourself Visual Basic 6 in 24 Hours*, by Greg Perry (Sams, 1999, ISBN: 0-672-31533-5). It will be worth your time and save you a lot of frustration in the long run.

Although this book spends a lot of time talking about DirectX and 3D graphics programming, I barely scratch the surface on both topics. For more information about game programming check out *Tricks of the Windows Game Programming Gurus* by Andre Lamothe (Sams, 1999, ISBN: 0-672-31361-8). This book provides a lot of information about the theory of game programming that is worth reading despite the fact that it relies on C++ for its examples.

You can also learn more about DirectX by reading *Sams Teach Yourself DirectX 7 in 24 Hours* by Robert Dunlop (Sams, 1999, ISBN: 0-672-31634-X). Although it does a fair job of covering DirectX, it doesn't spend a lot of time working with Direct3D and most of the examples are written in C++.

CONVENTIONS USED IN THIS BOOK

This book uses various stylistic and typographic conventions to make it easier to use.

Note

When you see a note in this book, it indicates additional information that can help you better understand a topic or avoid problems related to the subject at hand.

Tip

Tips introduce techniques applied by experienced developers to simplify a task or to produce a better design. The goal of a tip is to help you apply standard practices that lead to robust and maintainable applications.

Caution

Cautions warn you of hazardous procedures (for example, actions that have the potential to compromise the security of a system).

QUESTIONS AND COMMENTS

You can visit my Web site at www.JustPC.com for the latest information about this book or information about my other books. You should also find a version of the game that you can download for your friends. Any reader submissions will also be posted to the Web site, so you may want to check back periodically for any updates.

The Web site also contains a collection of articles and other information that you may find useful. These are primarily articles I wrote for various magazines, plus a few articles I've written just for the Web.

If you have questions about Visual Basic and DirectX, you can visit Microsoft's news server at msnews.microsoft.com and check out the microsoft.public.vb.directx newsgroup or the other microsoft.public.vb newsgroups. There are a lot of friendly people there and I try to stop by as often as I can.

You should also feel free to send me email at WFreeze@JustPC.com if you have questions or comments about the book. If you find any bugs in the game or any of the sample programs, please let me know. Likewise if you have any ideas that you think would improve the game, let me know.

Although I promise to read all of the e-mail I receive, it may take awhile for me to respond. I try to answer short, simple questions quickly, while long and complex questions may sit around for a couple of weeks or more. Please understand that I make my living from writing, so you may not get a prompt or complete answer to your question. But don't let this scare you from writing; I really enjoy hearing from my readers.

OTHER RESOURCES

Fortunately, there are a lot of resources available for game programmers. Aside from the Microsoft newsgroups listed previously, there are a number of other DirectX groups like msnews.microsoft.com that provide more focused discussions on specific features of DirectX like graphics, sound, input devices, and video. Look for the newsgroups beginning with the microsoft.public.directx prefix. Be prepared, though, because nearly all of the discussions in these groups use C++.

The DirectX SDK documentation files and sample programs contain a wealth of information that shouldn't be ignored. Examples are provided for both Visual Basic and C++ and span the full range of topics from drawing a simple triangle to advanced topics like using programmable shaders, which go far beyond the scope of this book.

Don't forget the DirectX Web site on MSDN (`http://msdn.Microsoft.com/directx`). There are a number of articles and tips that are freely available for you to browse. This is also the place to look for updates and fixes to DirectX.

There are some Web sites that focus on Visual Basic game development. My favorite is DirectX 4 VB (`http://64.23.12.52/`), which has a large number of tutorials. You can also visit the VB Game Programming Web Ring at `http://vbgamersring.com/`, which contains likes to other game programming Web sites.

When browsing through Web sites, be careful. Many of them focus on DirectX 7, which is incompatible with DirectX 8. DirectX 7 is primarily a 2D graphics interface with some 3D features, while DirectX 8 is strictly a 3D graphics tool. Also note that some of these Web sites sell game engines for Visual Basic, which hide some of the complexity behind DirectX. Although these engines can simplify your game programming, they lock you into a particular technology which may or may not be around in a few years. I suggest learning DirectX first and then deciding whether you really want to use a different approach.

PART I: DIVING INTO THE GAME

DEVELOPING AN IDEA INTO A GAME

At one time or another, most computer gamers have wished they could change the way a game worked. Making the game easier to beat is probably the number one change on most people's lists. The second most popular change would be to make the game more challenging, and third is probably to customize the game by inserting information about people and places they know.

Changing a game is much easier than developing a game from scratch. For a new game, you have many details to resolve, such as the story behind the game, the conflict within the game, and which features should be included, not to mention something so basic as picking the type of game.

The goal of this chapter is to produce a simple blueprint, or *game design document*, for implementing Swim Mall. To get a feel for information that will go into the document, you need to get a feel for Swim Mall. Because the easiest way to get a feel of a piece of software is to play around with it a bit, I'm going to show you how to install the game and then walk you though some of the game's key features. Once you've done that, I'll present the design document I used to build this game.

DESIGNING THE GAME

Before you build a computer game you need to identify how it will work. It's not sufficient to say, "I'm going to build a game like SimCity, but base it underwater and use fish instead of people." You need to think through the game and identify all kinds of information—from the game's basic philosophy down to the details of the individual choices and actions the player can make during the game.

The game design document should focus on functional issues such as how the game will interact with the player and how the computer will respond. It should avoid implementation details, which will be resolved as the game is developed.

The game design document is in no way a substitute for the game's documentation. The information in the game design document is intended to guide the developer while he or she creates the game. Normally you wouldn't want the game players to have access to the document because it might allow them to work around some of the challenges presented by the game. It's far more fun for the player to determine how the game works by playing the game itself.

As you read through this document, any comments in *italics* are not part of the Game Design Document, but rather my thoughts and comments about what this section is supposed to accomplish.

GAME DESIGN DOCUMENT FOR SWIM MALL

Swim Mall is a simulation game where the player manages an underwater shopping mall. While many aspects of the game are similar to games such as SimCity and Roller Coaster Tycoon, humor is an important element of the game.

At the start of a game design document, all you really need is a short paragraph that introduces the basic concept behind the game. Making a comparison to existing games allows anyone reading the document to get a fast understanding of the type of game you're building.

PHILOSOPHY

The primary purpose of Swim Mall is to teach someone the concepts of game programming; therefore many aspects of the game need to be simplified to ensure that the basic concepts are easily understood.

Swim Mall also must be easily expandable to anyone with access to the source code. This provides the capability for someone to test his or her knowledge of the game by adding extensions—a new shopper, a new store, a unique emergency, and so on.

Performance is not a primary issue with this game. While this doesn't mean that performance will be ignored, it does imply that the game will not deliver the same level of performance that a commercial game of similar complexity would have. This is a direct result of keeping the game simple and understandable. Optimizing a game is a black art that involves a lot of experience and often makes the final product difficult to maintain.

As a side effect of focusing on technique rather than performance, all of the files used by the game will be unencrypted and uncompressed. This may waste some disk space, but it will make the inner workings of the game easier to understand.

A game need not be complex to be fun to play. Many classic games such as Solitaire, Asteroids, and SimCity are based on a relatively simple set of rules.

Humor such as puns, jokes, and funny visual elements are used throughout the game to help compensate for lack of complexity.

The philosophy section is important, because it establishes a set of rules that govern how the game will work. You will have to make many decisions not spelled out in the game design document while building the game. By stating the game's philosophy up front, you make the choice that best fits with the game's philosophy.

STORY

Swim Mall is a tale of the Oceanic Mall. Your job as the mall manager is to transform this small shopping center into the most successful undersea mall in existence. To increase your customer satisfaction, you must make your mall attractive to the customers in your neighborhood. Success often brings new competition, so if you are too successful, you can expect that the other mall managers will try to steal your customers.

Advertising is important when you need to attract customers to your mall. You need to worry about where to target your advertisements so they do the most good.

You also need to worry about which stores you have in the mall to make it as attractive as possible to your customers. You don't want a situation where your mall has five pet stores and six banks.

Each store has a lease agreement with the mall, however, if you set the rent too high you may drive the store out of business. Likewise if you set the rent to low, you may not make enough money to survive. Of course, you'd better remember to renew the leases before they expire or the store will be forced to leave the mall before the lease is up.

Every game has a story that sets the stage for the game. The storyline for a game like Duke Nukem is "Kill all of the aliens before they kill us." Most storylines are more complex than this because they need to introduce the game's characters and setting.

The story should also identify the major sources of conflict and competition in the game. In the end, all games revolve around conflict and competition, no matter if it's saving the Earth from invading space aliens or beating the rest of the cars in the race. Without conflict and competition, you don't have a game.

Like the game's philosophy, the story will provide a basis to decide many of the game's details. In this case, I couldn't include an invasion of rats as a disaster simply because the rats couldn't survive underwater. However, you can use a crusty crab to get the same results.

TECHNICAL FEATURES

To be appealing to the game player, the game contains these technical features.

These features communicate why the game is technically advanced. Think of them as advertising that would appear on the game's box under the heading Technical Features.

- **Real-time simulation engine**—Models the economics of the shopping mall based on the criteria outlined in this document.

- **3D graphics engine**—Displays the mall as a 3D image (based on Direct3D as implemented in DirectX 8). The graphics engine enables you to view the mall from several different directions as well as control the level of detail the player can see.
- **3D animation engine**—Displays the customers in the mall in real-time.
- **MP3 music player**—Provides background music for the game.
- **Speech Synthesizer**—Translates text messages into speech.
- **Extendibility**—Allows other game developers to modify the game's source code and objects to add new features and scenarios.

GAME OBJECTS

The game revolves around two main objects, customers and stores, plus a handful of other objects.

These objects are listed here mostly to help define words and concepts used when describing how the user controls the game and how the computer will respond.

CUSTOMERS

Each customer in the game has these characteristics.

- **Name**—A value that can be modified by the game's player.
- **Image**—An index into a table of images that will be displayed on the screen when the customer is present in the mall. Like names, images can be modified by the player.
- **Needs**—A list of needs that are satisfied by the stores in the mall.
- **Location**—The zone where the customer is located.
- **Satisfaction**—An index for each store in the mall that is a factor in choosing where to shop.
- **Type**—Specifies the general type of the customer.
- **Position**—Identifies the customer's position in the mall only when the customer is actually in the mall.

STORES

Like customers, each store has a set of characteristics that describe how they are used within the mall.

- **Name**—A value that uniquely identifies the store.
- **Image**—A 3D image of the store that will be displayed in the mall.

- **Needs**—A list of needs that satisfies customer needs.
- **Rent**—A method that determines the minimum and maximum rent values that the store is willing to pay.
- **Profit**—A method that determines how much profit the store will generate from each customer visit.
- **Service**—A method to determine the minimum and maximum number of customers that the store can service at any point in time.

OTHER OBJECTS

The other important objects included in the game are listed below.

- **Bank**—Holds money in the checking account for the mall. Also loans money to the mall based on the total value of the mall.
- **Neighborhood**—A high-level view of the area surrounding the mall. This is used primarily to direct advertising to a particular location and to spot the location of the other shopping malls with which you are competing. Note that characteristics of a neighborhood will change over time, which implies that the customers that shop at the player's mall will have different needs over time.
- **Raymond**—The assistant mall manager, who provides information and advice about how to play the game.
- **Mall Strait Journal**—The industry standard newspaper for catching the latest shopping news. It is also the best location to place ads to attract new stores to your mall.

USER INTERACTION

The user interacts with the game through a well-defined set of controls. There are three main areas of controls; the pre-game setup where the user selects the initial conditions for the game, the gameplay activities where the user is actively playing the game and the game options, where the player can tweak the way the game works.

PRE-GAME SETUP

In the pregame setup, the user can specify the following items. Note that in most cases the player doesn't have complete control over the item, but can merely select one item from a list of items.

- **Initial type of mall**—Choose from a predefined list of empty malls. Some variations include a strip mall where the stores are all arranged on one side, a single-story mall and a two-story mall. Note that the initial type of the mall will also determine the number of stores available.

- **Initial funding**—Choose the amount of cash and/or initial loan amount, plus the untapped credit limit. This determines the amount of money with which the player will start the game.

- **Size and type of neighborhood**—Choose from a predefined list of neighborhoods.

- **Number and type of competitors**—Choose the maximum number of other malls in the same neighborhood.

- **Winning condition**—Determine the criteria for winning.

GAMEPLAY ACTIVITIES

The user directly controls the following aspects of the game while the game is active.

This list should be fairly complete before you start building your game. Adding major features later could have a negative impact on the overall vision of the game.

- **Location of mall services**—Initial placement of mall managed facilities such as the entrances, food court, bathrooms, stairs, elevators, security offices, utility plant, benches, telephones, information desk, vending machines, trashcans, plants and the mall office.

- **Expansion and renovation**—Choose when and how to expand the mall to accommodate new stores and mall services. Also renovate various parts of the mall as they wear out.

- **Attract stores**—Place ads informing potential store owners that the mall is looking for particular types of stores.

- **Select stores**—From the set of stores that respond to the ad, select the appropriate mix of stores for the mall, negotiate contracts with the stores (fixed rent, percentage of profit, or a combination of the two), and choose the appropriate store size plus their store's placement in the mall. Also control carts in the hallways.

- **Attract customers by advertising**—Place advertising in local and regional newspapers, TV, and radio.

- **Attract customers by special promotions**—These are special events that the mall can hold to attract customers. Typically these are holiday themed events such as having Santa Claus available during December.

- **Manage mall employees**—Hire and fire janitors, security, and administrative workers, and set their priorities to help them perform their job more effectively.

- **Manage money**—Collect rents from stores, borrow and pay back money to the bank, pay bills including taxes, utilities, salaries, insurance, advertising, and promotions.

- **Respond to emergencies**—Determine the appropriate response to an emergency.

- **Reports from Raymond**—Displays information about how the mall is doing internally, including reports of emergencies, and other problems.

- **Read the Mall Strait Journal**—Displays the newspaper containing information about how the player's mall stacks up against the competition, enables you to place ads to attract stores, and provides other business tips.

GAME OPTIONS

The player can specify options that permit them to control these items.

- **Game speed**—Affects how fast the master clock runs relative to real time. The player can choose from several speed options and a pause mode that suspends the game's activity.

- **Save and restore games**—Gives the player a choice to save a currently running game or to restore a previously saved game.

- **Control sound and music**—A general switch that instructs the program to enable or disable sound effects and background music. Also contains a volume control to adjust the relative sound levels.

- **Location of music files**—Because no MP3 files will be distributed with the game, it will be the player's responsibility to supply the name of a directory where these files may be found.

SIMULATION ENGINE'S CONTROL

The computer will control most of the activities during the game in it's real-time simulation engine.

- **Master clock**—Controls the date and time of the simulation. Many calculations use date and time value.

- **Neighborhood**—Sets the number of the customers available in the neighborhood and their average distance from the mall. The neighborhood is broken into zones by average income.

- **Customers**—Determines how frequently customers will arrive at the mall. Each customer will be selected from a location in the neighborhood and then their needs and satisfaction will be evaluated to see if they will go to your mall or one of the competitors.

- **Disasters**—There are a number of possible disasters, such as an invasion of crusty crabs and shark attacks. Also watch out for fires, explosions, and invading aliens.

- **Raymond**—Shows up whenever there is good news or bad news.

- **Mall Strait Journal**—Periodically appears and announces various trends in shopping malls. Also it will announce prizes and awards.

GAME VARIABLES

Game variables track how well the player is doing in the game. These variables, along with the master clock, can be used to determine the winning conditions.

- **Customer satisfaction**—Describes the overall success of the shopping mall. A high level of customer satisfaction will attract customers to the mall, while a low level will drive customers away.

- **Cash**—Contains the amount of money you have to spend in improvements. In general more money is better than less, though may make negotiating rents with stores difficult.

- **Loans**—Contains the total amount of money that the player has borrowed from the bank. There is an upper limit on the amount of money that the bank is willing to lend the mall, based on the total value of the mall.

- **Value**—Contains the current value of the mall. Note that the individual stores aren't counted as part of the mall, because they represent individual businesses. However, their leases add value to the mall.

- **Interest rate**—Contains the current short-term interest rate. This affects the interest payment the player must make to the bank.

CHEAT CODES

No computer game will be complete without the capability to enter cheat codes. A list of cheat codes follows.

Cheat codes are really just another term for debugging aids. They provide shortcuts to allow someone testing the game to reach a certain stage in the game more quickly, where they can test a particular feature.

- **Congressperson**—Gives you lots of money.
- **Alan Greenspan**—Makes interest rates low.
- **Beach Boys Music**—Improves the mall's customer satisfaction level.
- **Income Taxes**—Reduces the mall's customer satisfaction level.
- **Mall Of America**—Attracts all of the stores in the game to the player's mall.
- **Porsche 944**—Displays frame rate, plus camera and viewpoint information on the screen.

EASTER EGGS

These are items hidden in the mall that the player might find while playing the game. These items can only be found after entering a cheat code.

- **Who is Chris?**—Displays a picture of Chris.
- **Electric Wayne**—Displays a funny picture of Wayne.

FINAL THOUGHTS

The game design document is a way to outline how the game will work. It defines the things the user will control and how the computer will respond. It's important to recognize that the game design document is not a complete design document—it merely outlines the major pieces of the game from a functional perspective. If the design starts to look like code, you've gone too far.

CHAPTER 2

INTRODUCING DIRECTX

If you want to build a game in Visual Basic you have only one real option, which is to use DirectX. Without DirectX, you might create a game using a combination of controls and clever code, but you'd have a difficult time doing animations, and even drawing simple pictures would take a lot of time and resources. Although DirectX can be complicated to use, it has the advantage of displaying graphical information much faster than the native VB tools and allows you deal with more complicated graphics than you might believe.

This chapter focuses on how to set up DirectX and draw some simple 3D graphics. The code in this chapter assumes that you've installed the DirectX SDK on your computer. Although in theory you need only install the DirectX runtime components, it is worthwhile to install the entire SDK, or at least the Visual Basic components if you're tight on disk space. There are many sample programs and other utilities that you'll find useful, especially the DirectX Documentation library.

Caution

Bumpy road ahead

When I say DirectX can be difficult to use, believe it! While debugging the code in this chapter, you can expect your computer to crash, even if you're running Windows 2000. I recommend saving your changes frequently and not running any other applications while you're debugging. After this block of code is stable, you shouldn't have nearly as many problems.

UNDERSTANDING DIRECTX

DirectX is an application programming interface (API) that provides low-level access to the computer's hardware to create games and other multimedia applications. In addition to providing support for 2D and 3D graphics, it also provides a standard way to access input devices, play music and sounds, and coordinate play between multiple players over a network.

WHY DIRECTX?

DirectX was developed as a low-level, high performance replacement for using Win32 APIs to display information on a screen. Although Win32 APIs in Windows have a lot of capability, they are very slow when displaying graphics on the screen. Thus for many years, most game developers chose to stick with DOS because DOS allowed them to access video cards directly to give their games the best possible performance.

The downside to using DOS was that the game developer needed a different set of video drivers for each video card on the market. This meant that some games might not run on a particular video card because the card wasn't sufficiently popular enough for the game developer to develop a video driver or the video card was released after the game.

Because Microsoft wanted to encourage game developers to switch from DOS to Windows, it needed to provide an alternate way to display graphics that met the needs of game developers. They came up with an approach that provided a low-level, no frills access to developers, called DirectX.

DirectX eliminated the need for game developers to write drivers for each video card. Instead, video card manufacturers were required to supply drivers to standards developed by Microsoft. Then calls to DirectX would be translated into calls to the video card driver.

PART

1

CH

2

Although DirectX offered many advantages for the game developer, the early versions weren't well accepted by game developers. However, Microsoft persisted and after awhile most game developers began to use DirectX. DirectX version 5 was the first version of DirectX that was really popular with the game developer community and most games after that point were developed for DirectX.

Even though each new version of DirectX added new capabilities that didn't exist in previous versions, Microsoft was careful to preserve the functionality from previous releases. This ensures that if your game ran properly on DirectX 5, it will run properly on DirectX 6, 7, 8, and beyond.

Until DirectX version 7, it wasn't practical for Visual Basic programmers to use DirectX. Prior to DirectX 7, only a C-style interface was provided. If you wanted to access DirectX from Visual Basic, you needed a special program that acted as a COM wrapper. It provided a way to translate COM calls into DirectX calls. In DirectX version 7, Microsoft added a COM interface to DirectX that allowed Visual Basic direct access to DirectX.

Microsoft made major changes to DirectX 8, including merging the 2D graphics support into the 3D graphics support. This really means that if you want to develop 2D graphics, you should stick with the DirectX 7 interfaces. However, Microsoft added many new functions in DirectX 8 that make it a lot easier to create 3D graphics, as you'll see in this chapter.

DIRECTX SERVICES

DirectX is a collection of COM components organized into four main functional services: graphics, input management, audio programming, and networking support (see Figure 2.1). Graphics services are further broken into DirectDraw and Direct3D, whereas DirectX Audio is broken into DirectMusic and DirectSound.

- **DirectX** is the root of all of the DirectX components. It provides the environment in which the rest of the services operate.

- **DirectDraw** displays 2D graphics. Although this service has been stabilized with DirectX 7 and is no longer enhanced, you can continue to use it in DirectX 8 without change.

- **Direct3D** displays 3D graphics. To use Direct3D, you need a 3D accelerator video card to ensure adequate performance. Version 8 of Direct3D includes a rich collection of tools that make 3D programming much easier than it was in the past.

- **DirectInput** provides a unified collection of objects for managing input devices. It allows your program to treat the input as coming from a single device-independent source rather than discrete devices such as the keyboard, mouse, or joystick.

- **DirectMusic** allows you to create and play music on your computer using a variety of formats including, MIDI, WAVE, and MP3. It is capable of playing both music and sound files through a unified architecture.

- **DirectSound** allows you to play complex sounds on the computer. It is an older interface that has been partially replaced by the DirectMusic interface, however DirectSound is still the preferred service when you want to capture complex sounds.

- **DirectPlay** contains the interfaces that allow two or more computers running the same game to exchange both game information and messages between the players, including both text messages and voice messages.

Figure 2.1
The DirectX object model provides four main services.

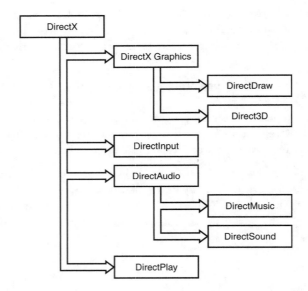

COM-municating with Windows

COM stands for Component Object Model. This is a technique used by Microsoft to provide Windows programmer with a reusable object model. COM components typically reside in a .DLL file, which can be shared by many different applications. Many operating system functions, including DirectX are made available to Visual Basic programmers using COM.

INTRODUCING 3D GRAPHICS

Swim Mall makes extensive use of Direct3D graphics. Believe it or not, this simplifies much of the programming required to display the graphics. If you try to present a 3D appearance using 2D graphics, you have to develop complex algorithms to determine which object is in front of another and then hide the parts of the objects that aren't visible. With Direct3D, you simply draw your graphics using a 3D coordinate system and Direct3D does the rest.

THE 2D COORDINATE SYSTEM

Visualizing 2D graphics is pretty easy because everything is placed according to two axes (see Figure 2.2). A coordinate of (3,2) means that this point is located 3 units down the X-axis, and 2 units down the Y-axis.

Figure 2.2
The location (3,2) is easy to visualize in a 2D coordinate system.

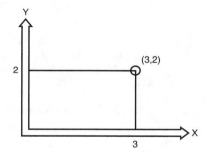

The values of a coordinate increase as you move to the right on the X-axis and up on the Y-axis. The location where the X- and Y-axes touch is known as the *origin* and has the coordinate value (0,0). Values to the left of the origin along the X-axis or down from the origin along the Y-axis are negative.

You can define a 2D shape such as a rectangle by specifying the coordinates for each corner of the rectangle. For instance, in Figure 2.2 you can see a rectangle formed by using the following coordinates: (3,2), (3,0), (0,0), and (0,2).

THE 3D COORDINATE SYSTEM

The 3D coordinate system introduces a new axis, called the Z-axis. This axis represents depth (see Figure 2.3). As you move away from the origin, values along the Z-axis increase. Thus, the coordinate (3,2,1) can be located by counting 3 units to the right on the X-axis, 2 units up on the Y-axis and 1 unit back on the Z-axis. This system is known as the *left-hand coordinate system*. It is also called the *3D space*.

Figure 2.3
The location (3,2,1) is harder to visualize in a 2D coordinate system.

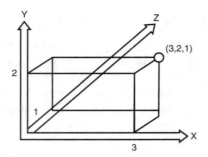

Like the 2D coordinate system, values below and to the left of the origin use negative numbers. Likewise, values along the Z-axis mean that the coordinate is closer to you than the origin.

On the other hand

Because I'm taking a practical approach to this book, I'm going to sidestep a lot of the math wherever practical. You should know that there is a right-hand coordinate system where values along the Z-axis increase as they come toward you and decrease as they go away from you. The right-hand coordinate system is typically used in mathematics and other sciences, but makes graphics programming more difficult.

To define a 3D shape such as a box, you need to define the coordinates for each corner of the box. Because a box has eight corners you need to define eight coordinates. Using the box shown in Figure 2.3, you have the following coordinates: (3,2,1), (3,2,0), (3,0,0), (3,0,1), (0,2,0), (0,2,1), (0,0,1), and (0,0,0).

If you select any four coordinates, you basically have the four corners of a square. For instance the coordinates (3,2,0), (3,0,0), (0,0,0), and (0,2,0) define the side of the box that is facing you. In fact, if you look at the coordinates you should notice that they are essentially the same as the square shown in Figure 2.1, except that they include a Z-axis value of 0. So another way of looking at the box is that it's merely composed of six rectangles.

THE WORLD IS MADE OF TRIANGLES

As you might expect, 3D objects in Direct3D are created by drawing smaller objects and connecting them together. The fundamental object in Direct3D is the triangle. Any 3D object can be approximated by using a series of triangles, including objects with curved surfaces like spheres, cylinders, and cones.

A simple object with flat surfaces can be represented exactly by using triangles. Consider the box shown in Figure 2.4. Each of the three sides you can see is represented by two triangles. Thus, the entire box could be represented by 12 triangles.

Figure 2.4
You can draw a three-dimensional box using 12 triangles.

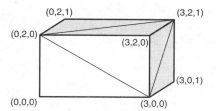

More complex objects can be drawn with triangles. For instance, in Figure 2.5 you can see how a circle can be approximated by using a collection of triangles. In the first example, six triangles are arranged with their points together in the center of the circle. In the second example, eight triangles are used. Finally in the third example, 16 triangles are used, giving a fairly close approximation of a circle. If 16 triangles don't yield a smooth enough circle, you can always add more until you get the circle you want.

Figure 2.5
The more triangles you add, the rounder your circle will look.

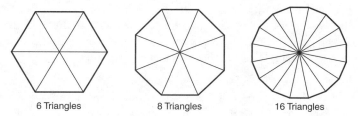

The same technique can be applied to nearly any shape. If you use enough triangles you can approximate anything from a sphere to a fish or even a human.

DRAWING LOTS OF TRIANGLES

Because each corner of a triangle is known as a vertex, you can specify any triangle by specifying the coordinates of each vertex. In turn, if you provide DirectX with a list of vertexes, you can display a lot of triangles with a single call. The list of vertexes is known as a *vertex buffer*.

Note

Vertices and vertexes

You can use either *vertices* or *vertexes* when referring to more than one vertex.

One of the biggest limitations of graphics is moving data around. Let's assume that your 3D object contains 2,000 triangles (which isn't a lot for some objects). If you use three *single* values to store the coordinates of each vertex, you have 72,000 bytes of information to move (2,000 triangles×3 vertexes per triangle×3 coordinate values for each vertex×4 bytes for each *single* value in the coordinate). This is a lot of data, especially if you store other information for each vertex.

However, when you're drawing shapes, nearly all of the triangles share at least one vertex with another triangle. This is very obvious if you look at Figure 2.5 again. Rather than storing each triangle explicitly, DirectX allows you to store triangles as either strips or fans (see Figure 2.6).

Figure 2.6
Using triangle strips and fans can save a lot of resources.

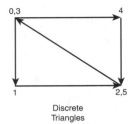

Discrete
Triangles

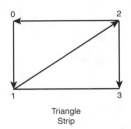

Triangle
Strip

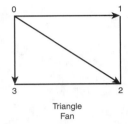

Triangle
Fan

To draw a regular square with discrete triangles requires six vertexes. However, with a triangle strip, you need only four. The key behind a triangle strip is that after the first triangle, each new vertex uses the last two vertexes to draw a triangle. In theory, this means that you need only n+2 vertexes to draw a sequence of n triangles. Of course you can't use triangle strips everywhere, but even they can make a big difference.

Triangle fans are very useful for drawing curved shapes. The first vertex value is the center of the shape. The next two vertexes define a triangle using the center vertex. The fourth vertex defines another triangle by using the previous vertex and the center vertex. Like triangle strips, triangle fans are very efficient.

COLORS

If you are familiar with Web programming, you may have seen how to specify a color value using a combination of red, blue, and green values. You can specify a value for each of the colors in the range of 0 to 255, where 0 means that none of the color is included and 255 is the maximum.

Colors in DirectX have four components. Like Web colors, you have red, blue, and green components. However in DirectX, the possible values for the colors range between 0.00 and 1.00, where 0.00 means no color and 1.00 means maximum color.

The fourth component of a DirectX color controls the transparency of an object. This value is known as alpha. Like red, blue, and green, this value ranges from 0.00 (totally transparent) to 1.00 (totally opaque).

LIGHTS AND VIEWPOINTS

A 3D object only appears to be a 3D object because there is a light to create shadows. This is a very important concept. Without lights and shadows a sphere would appear as a simple circle. Likewise you need a light to know where you are looking to determine what you're going to see. The front and back of a 3D object depends on the viewpoint.

There are two main kinds of lights in DirectX: direct and ambient. An *ambient* light illuminates everything equally whereas a *direct* light is used to cast shadows on your 3D objects.

Ambient lighting doesn't have a direction and shows up uniformly on your object. Through the use of ambient lighting, you can see all sides of your 3D objects. Keep in mind that relying totally on ambient lighting means that your objects won't have a light side and a dark side, so some 3D effects are lost.

The location of a direct light is specified as a 3D coordinate value. A simple direct light is unidirectional, meaning that it will shine on the surfaces that are directly in line with the light. One problem with using triangles to represent an object is determining which side of the triangle is up. A triangle has two sides; a front and a back. The back of the triangle shouldn't be visible, whereas the front is supposed to reflect light.

To address this problem, DirectX computes a normal vector that describes which way the face is pointing. It does this by using the three vertexes of the triangle to determine the vector, which is at right angles to the surface of the triangle. The amount of direct light that will appear on the object is determined by the angle between the normal vector and the vector that points from the surface in the direction of the light. The smaller the angle, the more light will fall onto the surface. If angle is greater than 90 degrees, the surface will not receive any light.

A viewpoint requires two 3D coordinate values. The first one marks the location of the viewer, whereas the second marks the location of where the viewer is looking. This establishes the direction of view. You will see any 3D objects that are in the direction of view.

In addition to the viewpoint vector, you also need to specify the field of view. The field of view can range from wide angle to telephoto just like a zoom lens on a camera. If you choose to use a wide angle or telephoto field of view, you may get some distortion so it is a good idea to leave the field of view alone and simply move the location of the viewer to see an object up close.

I'M A LITTLE TEAPOT

To demonstrate how to use Direct3D to display graphics, I've created a simple program that displays a 3D image on your screen that you can play with. Don't worry if some of the concepts discussed in this program seem a little strange, you will understand them before long. Playing around with this program will give you a better context with which to understand them.

This program consists of four modules; the Form1 module containing the main form, a Global module that contains global constants and definitions and two class modules, Debugger, and DXGraphics. Most of the work by this program is done by the two class modules Debugger and DXGraphics. The Debugger class provides a convenient way to capture debugging information. I'll use this class throughout the book to record various pieces of information while the program is running. This information will prove invaluable when attempting to debug the program.

The DXGraphics class (see Table 2.1) deals with the DirectX graphics routines and does most of the work in this program. The main form merely collects commands that set various DXGraphics properties or call the appropriate DXGraphics method.

TABLE 2.1 DXGRAPHICS PROPERTIES AND METHODS

Name	Description
CreateTeapotMesh	Method that creates a teapot mesh that can be displayed by the Render method.
DebugObject	Property containing an object reference to a valid Debugger object.
hWnd	Property containing a handle to the window to be displayed.
InitDX	Method that initializes the class so that it may display 3D graphics.
ResetView	Method to restore the viewpoint and the camera to the default location.
Render	Method to display the 3D objects on the screen.
ShowFrameRate	Property that, when True, causes the frame rate and other useful information to be displayed on the graphics screen.
View	Method to shift the camera and viewpoint locations by the specified amount.
Zoom	Method to move the camera closer or further from the viewpoint location.

Note

It's up to you

The entire source code for this program is found on the CD-ROM in VBGame\Chapter02. You should take some time to load the program into Visual Basic and run it. Also, please take the time to examine all of the code in this program.

INSTALLING DIRECTX

Before you develop programs with DirectX 8, you need to install the DirectX 8 Software Development Kit (SDK) on your computer. A copy of the SDK is on the book's CD-ROM in the \Microsoft\DirectX8 directory. Simply run the program dx8a_sdk.exe to install the SDK. As you follow the steps in the Installation Wizard, make sure that you install the documentation, the utilities, and the sample programs for Visual Basic. These will prove extremely helpful for writing your own DirectX programs.

Tip

DirectX without the SDK

I've included a copy of the standard DirectX installation file (dx80eng.exe) so you don't have to install the full SDK to get DirectX 8 on your other computers. Although these versions of DirectX are current as of when the book went to press, you should check `http://msdn.Microsoft.com/` to find the latest versions of the software, along with other advice about how to develop DirectX programs.

After installing the SDK, you need to add the DirectX library to your Visual Basic application. You can do this by choosing Project, References from Visual Basic's main menu. After a few moments, a dialog box like the one shown in Figure 2.7 will appear. Simply place a check mark next to the line `DirectX 8 for Visual Basic Type Library`. This will add all of the DirectX definitions to your application.

Figure 2.7
Adding the DirectX 8 type library to your application.

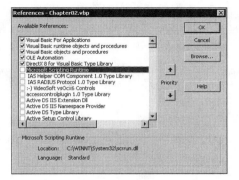

STARTING THE PROGRAM

In `Form1`, these three key module level variables contain information critical to the programs operation. The `dx` object contains a reference to the `DXGraphics` class that manages the Direct3D resources used to draw information on the screen. The `GameDebugger` object contains a reference to the `Debugger` class that will be used throughout the program to output useful status information to a debugging file. The `GameActive` variable controls the execution of the main program.

```
Dim dx As DXGraphics
Dim GameDebugger As Debugger
Dim GameActive As Boolean
```

When `Form1` loads, these statements are executed, which starts everything in motion. By executing `Me.Show` and the `DoEvents` routine, the main form is displayed on the screen before the `Form_Load` event completes. Then the `InitGame` routine is used to initialize all of the objects and variables needed to run the game, whereas the `PlayGame` routine actually runs the main game.

```
Me.Show
DoEvents
InitGame
PlayGame
```

When the user closes the form, `GameActive` will be set to `False` and the game will be shut down nicely.

The `InitGame` routine is shown in Listing 2.1. It begins by creating and enabling a new instance of the `Debugger` object. Then it calls the `InitGraphics` routine to initialize DirectX. If the `InitGraphics` encounters an error, the `InitGame` routine will end the program by calling `Unload Me`. Finally I set `GameActive` to `True` to indicate that I'm ready to run the game.

LISTING 2.1   FORM1.INITGAME

```
Sub InitGame()

Dim Result As Long

Set GameDebugger = New Debugger
GameDebugger.Enable

Result = InitGraphics
If Result <> 0 Then
    MsgBox "Can't initialize DirextX graphics! Ending program!"
    Unload Me

End If

GameActive = True

End Sub
```

The `InitGraphics` function is shown in Listing 2.2. This function instantiates the `DXGraphic` class and sets various property values in the new object before calling the `InitDX` method to initialize the object. If `InitDX` returns a non-zero result, some sort of error occurred while initializing DirectX and the error needs to be passed back to the calling routine. Then assuming everything is fine, it creates an object that will be displayed on the screen and return zero to indicate that this routine worked properly.

LISTING 2.2   FORM1.INITGRAPHICS

```
Function InitGraphics() As Long

Dim Result As Long

Set dx = New DXGraphics
Set dx.DebugObject = GameDebugger

dx.hWnd = Picture1.hWnd
dx.ShowFrameRate = True

Result = dx.InitDX
```

LISTING 2.2 CONTINUED

```
If Result <> 0 Then
    GameDebugger.WriteLong "dxInit failed", Result
    InitGraphics = Result

End If

dx.CreateTeapotMesh

InitGraphics = 0

End Function
```

Note

I'm lazy, that's why

If you read through these listings, you may have noticed that I'm treating this code like a game, even though it's not. That's because these routines will eventually evolve into the logic that manages the game. Because I'm essentially lazy, I decided to build the code once and reuse it throughout the book.

INITIALIZING DIRECTX OBJECTS

After starting the program, I've worked my way down to the DXGraphics class, which I'm going to use to manage the DirectX graphics calls. The InitDX method shown in Listing 2.3 controls the initialization process. The routine begins by turning off error detection with the On Error Resume Next statement to prevent a runtime error. This allows me to capture the error number and pass it back to the calling routine. I'll use this technique throughout the program whenever there is a chance that I could get a runtime error.

LISTING 2.3 DXGRAPHICS.INITDX

```
Public Function InitDX() As Long

On Error Resume Next

Dim Result As Long

Result = InitDXObjects()
If Result <> 0 Then
    DXDebugger.WriteLine "Can't Initialize DX Objects!"
    InitDX = Result
    Exit Function

End If

Result = InitDXDevice()
If Result <> 0 Then
    DXDebugger.WriteLine "Can't Initialize DX Device!"
    InitDX = Result
```

LISTING 2.3 CONTINUED

```
    Exit Function

End If

InitDXLights

SetDeviceState

Result = InitDXFonts()
If Result <> 0 Then
    DXDebugger.WriteLine "Can't Initialize DX Fonts!"

End If

InitDX = Result

End Function
```

Five main steps are performed. First the InitDXObject function is called to initialize the DirectX objects that provide the framework for performing DirectX calls. Then the InitDXDevice function is called to create the graphics display devices. Then the lights that will make the object visible are initialized by calling InitDXLights and the initial device state is set by calling SetDeviceState. Next, I'll initialize the game's fonts using the InitDXFonts method. After this is complete, the method will return the calling program.

In the InitDXObjects function, new instances of the three main DirectX objects are created; DirectX8, Direct3D8, and D3DX8 for graphics. These are declared at the module level. Note that each object ends with an 8. This means that the definition of the object is unique to version 8 of DirectX and this technique ensures that when Microsoft releases DirectX version 9 that your game won't be adversely impacted by a new implementation of the DirectX object.

```
Private dx As DirectX8
Private d3d As Direct3D8
Private d3dx As D3DX8
```

Note

Five, six, seven, eight

You may notice that many of the DirectX COM components include an 8 at the end of the object. This 8 comes from the version number associated with DirectX. Although you may find this somewhat unusual, it is necessary to ensure that your application continues to run without change under any future version of DirectX.

I start the InitDXObjects routine (see Listing 2.4) by using the same technique I used in the InitDX routine to disable the default error handler. Then I create an instance of the DirectX8 object by using the Set New statement.

LISTING 2.4 DXGRAPHICS.INITDXOBJECTS

```
Private Function InitDXObjects() As Long

On Error Resume Next
Err.Clear

Set dx = New DirectX8
DXDebugger.WriteErr "Create DirectX8:", Err
If Err.Number <> 0 Then
    InitDXObjects = Err.Number
    Exit Function

End If

Set d3d = dx.Direct3DCreate()
DXDebugger.WriteErr "Create Direct3D:", Err
If Err.Number <> 0 Then
    InitDXObjects = Err.Number
    Exit Function

End If

Set d3dx = New D3DX8
DXDebugger.WriteErr "Create Direct3DX:", Err

InitDXObjects = Err.Number

End Function
```

After I have a valid DirectX8 object, I need to create the Direct3D8 object using the
Direct3DCreate method of the DirectX8 object. This object allows you to display and
manipulate 3D objects. Finally I create a new instance of the D3DX8 object, which contains
helper routines and objects to simplify Direct3D programming.

Tip

Don't Dim As New

You may have noticed that the Dim As New statement hadn't been used to create a
new instance of an object. Although this may be simpler to code, it forces Visual Basic
to add code to each reference to the object to see if the object has been created and to
create it if the object doesn't exist. Although this extra overhead isn't noticed by many
applications, it might make a difference in a simulation game that can use every CPU
cycle it can get.

INITIALIZING DIRECT3D

To display your 3D graphics on the screen, you need to open a Direct3DDevice. This
device is responsible for translating your software requests into hardware requests that are
sent to the video card.

Direct3D supports three main types of devices: hardware, reference, and software. The hardware device type (also called a *HAL* device—HAL stands for Hardware Abstraction Layer) uses hardware to display your 3D images on the screen. The reference device type (also known as a *REF* device) performs the same functions by using a standard software package written by Microsoft. The software device type is a custom written software package that works like Microsoft's. In practice you'll never use a software device type.

Although Direct3D will display the 3D images using a REF device type, the performance is so bad as to make your game unusable. Using REF, your game may run as much as 100 times slower than if you use a HAL device. Thus if your application displays 25 frames per second using a HAL device, it may only update the display every 2 to 4 seconds with a REF device. A game that displays less then 10 frames per second is unplayable, whereas anything over 30 frames per second is considered very good.

Note

HAL 9000

The HAL specifically uses the hardware accelerator to perform rasterization and shading. *Rasterization* is the process of converting a series of 3D coordinates into 2D coordinates, whereas *shading* is the process of computing how the lights and shadows would appear on the 3D object.

Because I'm going to use the Direct3DDevice object throughout the DXGraphics class, I'm going to declare it as the module level. In addition, I'm going to declare a few other values associated with the device at the module level because it will be helpful to have them available to other routines in this class:

```
Private d3dDevice As Direct3DDevice8
Private d3dWindow As D3DPRESENT_PARAMETERS
Private d3dDispMode As D3DDISPLAYMODE
```

In Listing 2.5, I begin by declaring a few local variables and turning off error checking. Then I use the GetDeviceCaps method to get some information about your video card. I instruct the method to use your default adapter (remember Windows can support multiple displays) and specify the HAL device type. The routine will return the information about the adapter in the variable, Caps. If this routine fails, you know that the video adapter is not a HAL device.

LISTING 2.5   DXGRAPHICS.INITDXDEVICE

```
Private Function InitDXDevice() As Long

Dim Caps As D3DCAPS8
Dim DevType As CONST_D3DDEVTYPE
Dim DevBehaviorFlags As Long

On Error Resume Next
```

LISTING 2.5   CONTINUED

```
Err.Clear

d3d.GetDeviceCaps D3DADAPTER_DEFAULT, D3DDEVTYPE_HAL, Caps
If Err.Number = D3DERR_NOTAVAILABLE Then
    DXDebugger.WriteLine "HAL is not available, using " & _
        "software vertex processing"
    DevType = D3DDEVTYPE_REF
    DevBehaviorFlags = D3DCREATE_SOFTWARE_VERTEXPROCESSING

Else
    DevType = D3DDEVTYPE_HAL
    DXDebugger.WriteLong "VertexProcessingCaps=", _
        Caps.VertexProcessingCaps

    If Caps.VertexProcessingCaps = 0 Then
        DXDebugger.WriteLine "HAL is available, " & _
            "using software vertex processing"
        DevBehaviorFlags = D3DCREATE_SOFTWARE_VERTEXPROCESSING

    ElseIf Caps.VertexProcessingCaps = &H4B Then
        DXDebugger.WriteLine "HAL is available, " & _
            "using hardware vertex processing"
        DevBehaviorFlags = D3DCREATE_HARDWARE_VERTEXPROCESSING

    Else
        DXDebugger.WriteLine "HAL is available, " & _
            "using mixed vertex processing"
        DevBehaviorFlags = D3DCREATE_MIXED_VERTEXPROCESSING

    End If

End If

d3d.GetAdapterDisplayMode D3DADAPTER_DEFAULT, d3dDispMode
DXDebugger.WriteDispMode d3dDispMode
DXDebugger.WriteLine "Using windowed mode"

d3dWindow.Windowed = 1
d3dWindow.SwapEffect = D3DSWAPEFFECT_DISCARD
d3dWindow.BackBufferFormat = d3dDispMode.Format
d3dWindow.BackBufferCount = 1
d3dWindow.hDeviceWindow = hWnd
d3dWindow.EnableAutoDepthStencil = 1
d3dWindow.AutoDepthStencilFormat = D3DFMT_D16

Err.Clear
Set d3dDevice = d3d.CreateDevice(D3DADAPTER_DEFAULT, _
    DevType, hWnd, DevBehaviorFlags, d3dWindow)
DXDebugger.WriteErr "Create Direct3D Device:", Err

InitDXDevice = Err.Number

End Function
```

Just because you have a HAL device doesn't mean that all of the functions needed by DirectX can be performed in hardware. Some functions may still have to be performed by software. You need to examine the Caps variable to all of the details you can perform in hardware. Of all the fields in Caps the one that is most important is the VertexProcessingCaps field. Each bit in this field has a specific meaning, but there are only two values you really need to worry about. Zero means that the video card has no capabilities beyond the basic HAL, so you'll need to use software vertex processing. If all the defined bits were set, you would have the hex value 4B, which means you can use hardware vertex processing. If it isn't one of these two values, you need to specify mixed vertex processing.

The next step is to define the presentation parameters I store in the variable d3dWindow. Before I do that, I need to get the current display mode using the GetAdapterDisplayMode method. Then I can begin to define the individual fields in d3dWindow. In this application I'm going to assume that the display will only be a windowed application, so I will set the Windowed field to 1. If I wanted to use a full screen display, I'd have to set the Windowed field to 0 and define a few other fields that aren't used for a windowed application.

> **Note**
>
> **Windowed versus Full-Screen**
>
> Don't confuse the Windowed field with the WindowState property of a Visual Basic form. When Windowed is set to 0, the game will hide the Windows desktop and display the graphics directly to the display. When Windowed is set to 1, the graphics are displayed as a window on the desktop using the Visual Basic Form object. You can use the Form object's WindowState property to control whether this window is minimized, maximized or shown as a normal window.

The hWnd field needs a valid handle to a window. If you're familiar with Win32 API programming, this should make sense, otherwise, this value needs to come from the hWnd property of a Form object or a Picture control, which is what I did when I initialized the key properties for this class.

Finally, after doing all of this work, I can call the CreateDevice method using the values I defined earlier. If everything works, I should have a valid device I can use to display 3D graphics. If not, there is probably some sort of compatibility problem with the hardware. Here is where the debug log will come in handy. However, this routine is sufficiently robust that it should work, no matter what type of video card you have.

Tip

It's too big

One of the biggest problems with writing a computer book involves reformatting listings to fit within the width of a page. In Visual Basic this involves breaking the statement at the appropriate location (you can't break it in the middle of a string for instance) and adding a space and an underscore character to the end of the line. This enables me to simply continue the statement on the next line. Normally I update the sample programs so that they look like the text you see in the book. However in this book, I decided not to update the sample programs because it made them much harder to read. You'll see that they don't break in the same place that lines do in the book.

SETTING LIGHTS

You need to enable at least one light to properly view a 3D object. The light will determine how the shadows are rendered on the display. DirectX supports three types of lights—directional, spot, and point. *Directional* and *point* lights illuminate the entire object, whereas a *spot* light illuminates only a small portion of the object. The only difference between a point light and a directional light is that you can specify the position of a point light, whereas a directional light is assumed to be an infinite distance away so that the entire scene is illuminated evenly.

Note

Illuminating lighting

Even though lighting appears to be simple, it is perhaps one of the most complex features in DirectX. Designing effective lighting is one of those things that separates a high end commercial game from other games. This topic goes beyond the scope of this book. You can refer to the DirectX SDK documentation for more information about this topic.

Direct3D gives you quite a few options to tweak when you define a light, including the color, position, and direction. In this program I'm using a single directional white light to keep things simple. You should try other values to see their effect on the teapot.

In Listing 2.6, I begin by declaring some temporary variables that I use to hold values I want to pass the light methods associated with the Direct3D device I created in Listing 2.5. I set the red, green, blue, and alpha properties of the Col variable to 1. Unlike Web pages, colors in DirectX are specified as a floating-point number ranging from 0 to 1. Thus, the RGB value (1,1,1) specifies the color white just like the value FFFFFF would specify white in a Web page. A value of (1,0,0) means red, while a value of (1,1,0) is the color blue.

LISTING 2.6 DXGRAPHICS.INITDXLIGHTS

```
Private Sub InitDXLights()

Dim d3dLight As D3DLIGHT8
Dim Mtrl As D3DMATERIAL8
Dim Col As D3DCOLORVALUE

DXDebugger.WriteLine "Initializing lights"

Col.a = 1
Col.r = 1
Col.g = 1
Col.b = 1

d3dLight.Type = D3DLIGHT_DIRECTIONAL
d3dLight.diffuse = Col
d3dLight.Direction = vec3(-1, -1, -1)

Mtrl.Ambient = Col
Mtrl.diffuse = Col
d3dDevice.SetMaterial Mtrl

d3dDevice.SetLight 0, d3dLight
d3dDevice.LightEnable 0, 1

End Sub
```

Next, I initialize d3dLight by setting the Type property to D3DLIGHT_DIRECTIONAL, which makes it a directional light, setting the diffuse property to the color variable I just initialized and setting the Direction property to point in direction of –1, –1, –1 using the vec3 helper function, which simply converts the three coordinated into a D3DVECTOR. Here is the code for vec3.

```
Private Function vec3(x As Single, y As Single, Z As Single) As D3DVECTOR

vec3.x = x
vec3.y = y
vec3.Z = Z

End Function
```

After the characteristics of the light have been defined, you need to define a material for the Direct3D device. Even though these statements may not make a lot of sense, they are necessary to define the light. Finally, I can use the SetLight method to define and enable the light information in d3dLight as light 0.

> **Tip**
>
> ### Type not object
>
> The D3DLIGHT8 reference is not a COM component, but a Visual Basic Type value, containing a number of individual fields. This means that you don't have to create an instance of it to use it. DirectX usually uses types to pass a lot of complex information to and from various methods. To make it easy to separate types from COM components, the name of a type is written in uppercase letters, whereas the name of a COM component uses mixed case.

CREATING A 3D OBJECT

In many ways, 3D graphics programming can be really hard. If you had to compute all of the triangles yourself and then position them in the 3D space, you'd probably go nuts or become a full-time game programmer. Fortunately, Direct3D includes a utility library that contains a number of classes and functions that will make your life easier. This library is accessed through the D3DX8 object I created at the same time I created the other DirectX objects.

The first step to create a simple 3D object is to declare an object variable to hold it. A D3DXMesh like the one that follows is one method to hold all of the information related to a 3D object.

```
Private TeaPot As D3DXMesh
```

In Listing 2.7, I use the CreateTeapot method to create a 3D object. If you think this seems too easy, you're right. The teapot that is created by this process has a lot of limitations, but for the purposes of this particular sample program it is ideal. It allows you to debug the Direct3D initialization and display logic, knowing that you have a valid image to display.

LISTING 2.7   DXGRAPHICS.CREATETEAPOT

```
Public Sub CreateTeapotMesh()

Set TeaPot = d3dx.CreateTeapot(d3dDevice, Nothing)

End Sub
```

DISPLAYING GRAPHICS

All of the work done so far in this chapter has been to prepare DirectX to display 3D graphics. The PlayGame routine in Listing 2.8 contains a tight loop that calls the Render method from DXGraphics to display the 3D object on the screen. Because displaying graphics is rather CPU intensive, I call DoEvents to give other activities in the system a chance at the CPU.

LISTING 2.8 FORM1.PLAYGAME

```
Sub PlayGame()

Do While GameActive
    dx.Render
    DoEvents

Loop

EndGame

Unload Me

End Sub
```

The loop will continue until GameActive becomes False. Closing the window or pressing the Exit button will set GameActive to False and stop the loop. Then I can call the EndGame routine to clean up after the game and then call Unload Me to close the form and end the program.

RENDERING THE SCENE

Displaying graphics in a game is somewhat different than displaying graphics as part of a normal program. In a normal program, you simply display the graphics as you create them. Windows takes care of the rest of the details. Because DirectX gives you low-level access to the graphics hardware, you have to do a lot more for yourself.

DirectX uses two buffers to hold the graphics. The front buffer is used to display the graphics while the back buffer is used as a temporary storage area for the graphics being rendered. When the back buffer has been filled, the two buffers are swapped and the process repeats itself. This is a very powerful technique that enables you to create a frame of graphics in memory and then present the completed frame very quickly.

This technique also enables you to animate the objects on the screen. Remember that a television set displays still images on the screen about 30 times per second. As long as you can swap your buffers at the same speed, your objects will appear to move realistically.

Listing 2.9 contains the routine that actually displays the graphics on the screen. Before I can display any graphics, I need to identify three transformations that describe how Direct3D will display the graphics. All of these transformations are computed using matrix arithmetic. If you don't understand matrixes, don't worry, the code works and you can use it anyway.

LISTING 2.9   DXGRAPHICS.RENDER

```
Public Function Render() As Long

On Error Resume Next

Dim matProj As D3DMATRIX
Dim matView As D3DMATRIX
Dim matWorld As D3DMATRIX
Dim matTemp As D3DMATRIX
Dim matTrans As D3DMATRIX

D3DXMatrixIdentity matWorld
d3dDevice.SetTransform D3DTS_WORLD, matWorld

D3DXMatrixRotationY matView, Rotation
D3DXMatrixLookAtLH matTemp, CameraPoint, ViewPoint, _
    vec3(0, 1, 0)
D3DXMatrixMultiply matView, matView, matTemp
d3dDevice.SetTransform D3DTS_VIEW, matView

D3DXMatrixPerspectiveFovLH matProj, pi / 4, 1, 0.1, 500
d3dDevice.SetTransform D3DTS_PROJECTION, matProj

d3dDevice.Clear 0, ByVal 0, _
    D3DCLEAR_TARGET Or D3DCLEAR_ZBUFFER, &H404040, 1#, 0

d3dDevice.BeginScene

TeaPot.DrawSubset 0

If ShowFrameRate Then
    DrawFrameRate
    DrawViewPoint

End If

d3dDevice.EndScene

Err.Clear
d3dDevice.Present ByVal 0, ByVal 0, 0, ByVal 0
If Err.Number <> 0 Then
    DXDebugger.WriteErr "Presentation error", Err
    Render = Err.Number

End If

End Function
```

The first transformation (D3DTS_WORLD) describes where the current origin of the world is located, along with how the world is scaled and rotated. In this case, I just want to display things as they are, so I initialize matWorld to the identity matrix and call SetTransform.

The second transformation describes how to view the world (D3DTS_VIEW). It essentially places the camera relative to the world. I compute a rotation matrix by using the D3DXMatrixRotationY function, which describes where the camera should be located by rotating the camera around the center of the world by using value in Rotation. Then I compute the viewpoint by using the D3DXMatrixLookAtLH routine, which takes the location of the camera and the position in space you want to look at, plus a vector that describes which axis is up (vec3(0,1,0)). Then I can multiply the two matrixes together to get the true view transformation.

The third transformation describes how to project the information on the screen. The D3DXMatrixPerspectiveFovLH routine creates a matrix that takes into consideration the field of view (FOV), the aspect ratio, plus values for near and far. The FOV describes whether to render the scene and is typically expressed as Pi/x, where x=4 will give a normal view, x<4 gives a wide angle view or x>4 gives a telephoto view. Note that value doesn't zoom the data, but merely controls how distorted the resulting image will be.

The value or aspect should be one if you are displaying on a screen with identical heights and widths. Otherwise you should use the screen's height to width ratio (Height/Width). If you don't make this adjustment, your images could appear to be short and fat or tall and thin depending on the sizes of your screen.

Finally the last two values determine when something is too close to be displayed or too far away to be displayed. These values are really relative to how your world is scaled and you may have to pick different values depending on your world.

After these transformations are set, the real work begins. The first step is to clear the back buffer using the Clear method. Of the parameters listed here, the most interesting is the value &H404040, which describes the default color to be displayed—in this case a dark gray. If I didn't clear the back buffer, any information already in the back buffer would remain, which could cause problems if the position of some of the objects in the display have changed.

Immediately after clearing the display, I call BeginScene to mark the start of the operations against the back buffer. Next I call DrawSubset, which displays the teapot on the buffer. If there were other objects to be displayed, they would also be put here. Next I make calls to DrawFrameRate and DrawViewPoint to display this information on the screen while the program is running. These values can be useful to see how fast your teapot is being displayed. Finally, when all of the objects have been displayed, I call EndScene to mark the end of the updates to the back buffer.

The last step of rendering the display is to flip the front and back buffers. This is done by calling the Present method. This frees the old front buffer so that you can begin drawing a new set graphics on it for the next flip.

PART

I

CH

2

> **Note**
>
> **Matrixes and vectors**
>
> Throughout this chapter I've referred mathematical concepts known as vectors and matrixes. A vector is simply the line that starts with the first point and goes through the second point. A matrix is a two dimensional array with a number of standard operations. In DirectX, a matrix containing four rows and four columns is used to represent to describe the location of one object relative to another. You can use matrix operations to change the size of an object or rotate an object. While a detailed knowledge of how matrixes and vectors work is useful, the code supplied will take care of all of the detail work. For more information about how vectors and matrixes are used with 3D graphics programming, see *Tricks of the Windows Game Programming Gurus* by Andre LaMothe (Sams, 1999, ISBN: 0-672-31361-8).

Figure 2.8
Running the teapot program.

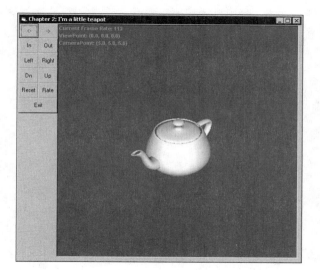

FINAL THOUGHTS

The goal of this program is to give you something to play with. If DirectX worked like a normal, high-level Visual Basic control, you'd simply drag the 3D teapot control onto your form and you'd be done. Instead, DirectX is a low level control and this means that there is a lot of code that is complex, convoluted, and cryptic. Fortunately, most of this code can be treated as boilerplate and once it works properly, you can forget about it.

This program contains a lot of code that I didn't go over. Some of it, particularly the Debugger class, is pretty straightforward and really didn't need any explanation. It's more important to look at the information in the Debug.Log file after you run the program to see how things happened in this program.

I strongly suggest that you load this program and run it. After you see how the program works, you should try changing values such as the color of the light to see how the teapot will look or how changing the aspect ratio and FOV will distort the 3D image. Experimentation is the best way to learn how DirectX works.

CREATING 3D GRAPHICS

In this chapter

Now that you can display a simple pre-generated graphic like the teapot on the screen, it's time to look into building your own graphics. The last chapter discussed how it is possible to build any 3D graphic from the right set of triangles. However, it also mentioned that this was hard work. While hard work has its place, it's better to avoid it if at all possible. Fortunately there is a better alternative: Caligari trueSpace.

In addition to a 3D graphics design tool, you'll also find that you need some tools to create 2D graphics. My favorite tools are Adobe Photoshop and Illustrator. I find them invaluable any time I'm dealing with graphics. I'll talk about these tools in Chapter 4, "Turning 2D Graphics into 3D Graphics."

Note

On the CD-ROM

I've included a demo copy of the trueSpace5.1 software on the CD-ROM to let you try the software. If you like it, you can purchase it from the Caligari Web site at `http://www.Caligari.com`.

INTRODUCING CALIGARI TRUESPACE

3D design tools are used in many different industries, ranging from special effects companies making movies and television shows to Web designers looking to create cutting edge logos. They are even used to develop scenery and objects in 3D games. Without a good 3D design tool, building a computer game is simply not practical.

There are a number of 3D design tools in the marketplace today. However, many of them start in the $2,000 to $3,000 range and end up costing almost twice that by the time you get all of the necessary add-on packages. This is well beyond the budget of the beginning game developer. Fortunately, there is an inexpensive alternative that provides most of the features found in the high-priced applications, and it has an affordable price tag.

The Caligari company has been developing 3D graphics software since the late 1980s. In 1994, they released the first in a series of products called trueSpace. With each new version, a host of new capabilities are added and the latest version, trueSpace5.1, compares favorably with products costing over 10 times its price.

I'm using Caligari trueSpace5.1 in this book because one of its key features is the capability to export files that are compatible with DirectX. Besides support for exporting DirectX files, it includes the capability to create animations, including people that walk, creating VRML worlds that can be viewed over the Internet, and integrating 3D sound into your creations.

Unlike most software companies, Caligari continues to actively market versions of its older software at a price attractive to people new to the 3D graphics market. In many cases, the beginning game developer isn't prepared to use all of the capabilities of the newer versions of the software, so using an older version of the software isn't a big deal. Support for

DirectX mesh files was introduced starting with trueSpace3.1. However, I recommend using trueSpace4.0 or newer because of the better DirectX support.

INTRODUCING ADOBE PHOTOSHOP AND ILLUSTRATOR

While trueSpace is a powerful tool, its strengths are in its capability to create and manipulate 3D objects. However, a computer game programmer will often use 2D graphics in many places, including in their 3D graphics.

Although you have even more choices for 2D design tools, I tend to stick with Adobe Photoshop and Illustrator. I've used these tools for years and while I've tried other tools over time, I keep coming back to them. While neither Photoshop nor Illustrator is particularly cheap, once you make the initial investment, you'll find it pays for itself over time. Upgrades are reasonably priced, making it easy to stay current. I've included an evaluation copy of Photoshop on the CD-ROM, in the \Adobe directory.

CONSTRUCTING 3D GRAPHICS

Building 3D graphics is relatively easy. You take standard shapes like cubes, cylinders, and spheres and combine them to form the shape you want. As you combine the shapes, you can paint them or wrap them with a 2D image. The final result is an object that you can load into your Direct3D application and manipulate at a high level without having to know that the object you see in your display is really just a collection of triangles with different colors.

BASIC CONCEPTS

When you start trueSpace, you have a work area known as a *scene*. A scene contains a series of objects. An object can be a primitive object such as a cube, a cylinder, a sphere, a cone, a torus (a donut-shaped object), or a plane. An object can also be a complex object composed of a series of one or more primitive objects.

When using trueSpace to create graphics for DirectX, you want to create objects, not scenes. If you can save the object in DirectX format, your game will be able to load the object using a relatively short block of code. Then you have the capability to manipulate the object as a single unit even though the object may be fairly complex visually.

As with the teapot in Chapter 2, "Introducing DirectX," lights provide the effects necessary to view a 3D object. You can add or reposition the lights in trueSpace to make the design process easier. However, it is important to note that the lights are not coupled to the object you're designing. Although the lights are part of the scene, they are not part of the object. When you display the object in your game, you'll have to place your own lights using DirectX.

The 3D coordinate system used by trueSpace involves X-, Y-, and Z-axes that I talked about in Chapter 2. And like the teapot program in Chapter 2, you are free to zoom, rotate, and move the viewpoint (note that in trueSpace, the viewpoint is referred to as an eye). This will not affect the object you create, but it will make it easier to see what you are doing.

When you add a primitive object to the scene, it has a default color. You can easily change the color; however, you probably want to do something more than simply color the object. You have the option to paint an object with a texture. A texture is simply an image file that is displayed on the surface of the object, much like wallpaper is pasted onto a wall. Textures make your objects appear more realistic and are an important part of any 3D game.

Tip

Reading room

While there are very few books on trueSpace and none on trueSpace5, you might try reading *Inside trueSpace4* by Frank A. Rivera (New Riders, 1999, ISBN: 1-562-05957-2). While it is a little out of date, it does a good job of teaching you how to create 3D graphics using trueSpace.

USING TRUESPACE

To say that trueSpace has a unique user interface may be putting it a bit mildly (see Figure 3.1). Rather than putting the title bar and menu items at the top of the window, Caligari chooses to put them at the bottom of the window. Also, the user interface relies heavily on icons that are displayed around the edges of the user interface.

Figure 3.1
trueSpace has an unconventional user interface.

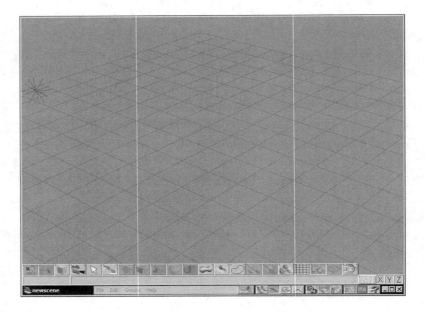

Tip

Flipping back

If you prefer the menu items listed at the top of the window, you can easily change this by choosing File, Preferences and then placing a checkmark beside TopMenu in the Preferences dialog box.

Also unlike most Windows applications, the functions performed by the toolbar icons are not duplicated by those listed in the main menu. In fact there are very few main menu commands in trueSpace. To select a visible icon, simply move the mouse pointer over the desired button and click the left mouse button.

Many tools are part of a group of similar tools. This is indicated by a small blue triangle in the upper left corner of the icon. If you press and hold the left mouse button while hovering the mouse pointer over an icon, a flyout will be displayed containing the other tools available. To select one of these tools, continue to hold the left mouse button down and move the mouse pointer over the icon you want to use. Then release the mouse button to select the icon. This will both select the desired tool and display the tool's icon as the default icon for the flyout.

Many of the tools available in trueSpace also have an associated dialog box that controls various settings for the tool. Any tool that has a property dialog box displays a small red triangle in the upper-right corner of the icon. To display the dialog box, simply right-click the tool's icon. If this user interface seems complex, it really isn't. After a few days of exposure you should be fairly comfortable using it. If you can't remember what a particular button will do, simply move the mouse pointer over the button. A description of the button will be displayed in the area above the main menu.

trueSpace Tools

In Figure 3.2, I've expanded all of the toolbars to show most of the tools available in trueSpace. While the number of tools may seem overwhelming, I'm going to stick with these tools to create the simple 3D models used in this book.

PART

I

CH

3

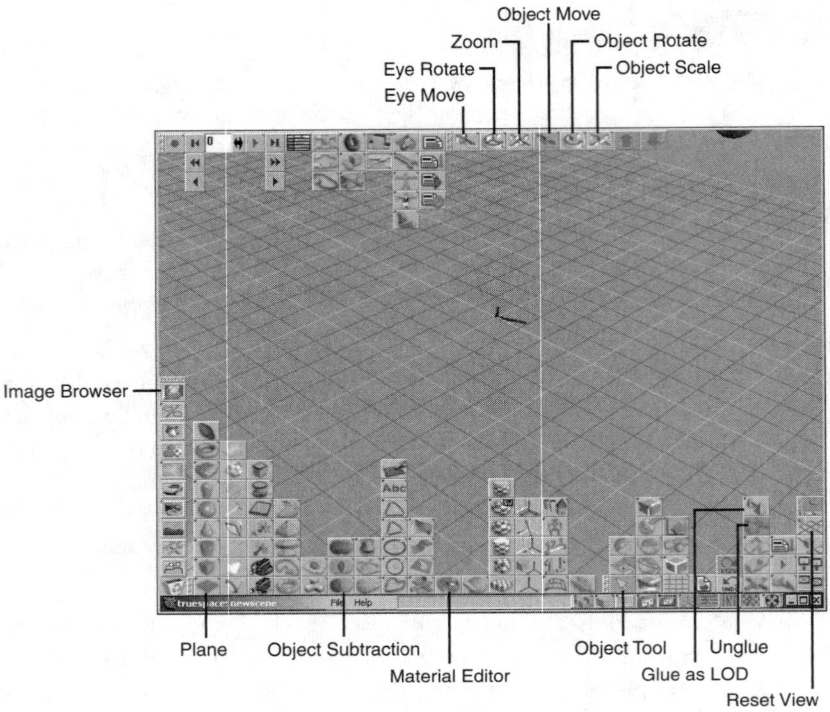

Figure 3.2
Selected tools in
trueSpace5.1.

- **Eye Move**—Used to change the location of the camera relative to the object by using the mouse.
- **Eye Rotate**—Used to rotate the camera around the object by using the mouse.
- **Zoom**—Used to change the field of view of the object using the mouse.
- **Object Move**—Used to drag the object around the scene using the mouse.
- **Object Rotate**—Used to rotate the object around its center using the mouse.
- **Object Scale**—Used to increase or decrease the size of an object.
- **Image Browser**—Used to select a texture to be painted on an object.
- **Plane**—Used to draw a plane in the scene.
- **Object Subtraction**—Used to subtract the currently selected object from the scene, including the parts of any other objects that may overlap it.
- **Material Editor**—Used to select and apply colors or textures to an object.
- **Object Tool**—Used to select an object. Right-clicking the icon will display information about the object.
- **Glue as Level of Detail**—Used to join an object to the currently selected object.
- **Unglue**—Used to separate the currently selected object glued object into two or more independent objects.
- **Reset View**—Used to restore the current view of the scene to the default view.

CREATING A MALL

Creating a shopping mall is really a three-step process. The first step is designing the basic mall. The second step is constructing an empty mall using the graphics tools I've discussed. The third step is creating the stores and other objects that can be placed inside the mall by the user.

It is important to remember at this stage of the development process that it is desirable to build as much flexibility into things as practical, while at the same time keeping the design easy enough to implement. One way to accomplish this is to create the independent 3D graphics files that can be loaded into the game. This gives me the flexibility to design a simple mall to use while building the game and allows me to create more complex malls later. Then the players can choose the mall they want to use in their game.

DESIGNING A MALL

If you take the time to look at a typical shopping mall, you'll notice that the mall is really constructed from a series of similar objects. Most stores are the same basic size, typically 20 to 25 feet wide and 40 to 50 feet deep. I call this a standard store.

Larger stores within the mall are generally allocated the space that would normally hold two or three standard stores. Anchor stores (big name department stores, usually) are typically located outside the mall proper with one or more doors connecting the anchor store to a hallway.

If the mall has a food court, you'll find a collection of small spaces allowed for the food vendors. The size of these spaces can vary greatly because the food court is often located in an out-of-the-way place in the mall, but this isn't a requirement. Some food courts are located in the space that would normally be occupied by three or four standard stores.

Located near the food court you'll find public restrooms. There are at least two, one for men and one for women. However, there is a trend nowadays to include a special restroom for families There you will often find a telephone or two, plus a drinking fountain.

Most malls today include a series of kiosks in the center of the hallways that permit small vendors to sell items like cell phones and jewelry. These kiosks often make for a crowded hallway, so they are generally located only in hallways that are fairly wide. Also located in the hallway are various objects like benches, ATM machines, telephones, drinking fountains, plants, and so on. Some malls even include an information desk where shoppers can ask questions, have gifts wrapped, rent strollers, and so on.

Outside the mall proper, but attached to the main mall, is a mechanical area that holds the heating and air conditioning equipment to heat and cool the mall. You may also find other equipment in this area, such as trash bins and storage for the lawn and garden equipment used to maintain the space outside the mall.

Not all of the mall's facilities are located outside. Most malls have a main office where the mall's management and staff work. Also, most malls have a separate security office where security officers can monitor security cameras that watch the public areas of the mall.

Figure 3.3 shows a design of one of the malls I'm going to use in this game. It is a relatively simple floor plan allowing for eight standard stores plus one anchor store. There is a food court with four food vendors (marked with an F on the diagram), restrooms for men and women (marked M and W), a mall office (marked O), a security office (marked S) and a mechanical area. This arrangement leaves a very open hallway for kiosks, benches, plants, and other things that you may want to add to the mall.

Figure 3.3
The design of a simple shopping mall for Swim Mall.

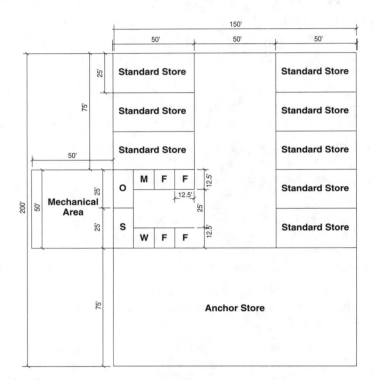

CREATING AN EMPTY MALL

To turn the diagram in Figure 3.2 into a 3D object is to map the dimensions in the diagram into dimensions understood by trueSpace and DirectX. In general, dimensions for 3D objects are specified in meters. In practice, it really doesn't matter. As long as you are consistent you can choose any mapping you want.

In this case, I'm using the scale that 1 unit in the 3D object corresponds to 12 1/2 feet. Because the mall shown in Figure 3.2 is roughly 200 by 200 feet, the 3D object will be 16 by 16 in size.

The mall itself will be constructed using the Plane object. I'll use the Plane object for the floor of the mall and the walls. The mall is broken into several main areas: the anchor store, the hallway, the group of five standard stores, the group of three standard stores, the mechanical area, and the food court. Each of these areas will need to be constructed independently to control how the particular section will appear in the game.

Note

On the CD-ROM

The steps in this chapter will require access to files from the CD-ROM in the \VBGame\Chapter03 directory. You should copy them to your hard disk into a working directory so that you can modify them as necessary to create your own mall.

To create this shopping mall, follow these steps:

1. Start trueSpace.
2. Select the Plane tool and move the mouse pointer over the floor of the scene. Left click and drag the mouse point to create a square to create the floor of the mall (see Figure 3.4). Don't worry about the size of the plane, as it will be adjusted shortly.

Figure 3.4
Building the mall begins with adding a plane to the trueSpace scene.

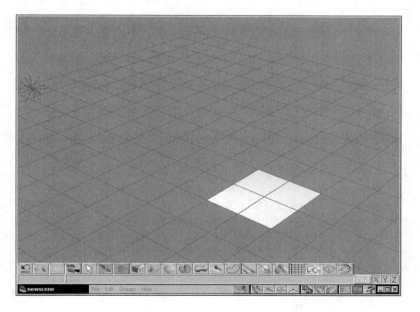

3. Move the mouse pointer to the Object Tool button (the big white arrow) and click the right mouse button. This will display detailed information about the plane you just added (see Figure 3.5). Notice that information in this window reflects the plane you just drew. The X, Y, and Z values refer to the center of the plane relative to the center of the scene (also known as the origin). The rotation X, Y, and Z values represent the

PART

I

CH

3

angle in degrees that the plane is rotated from it's initial position. Since the plane hasn't been rotated, these values are zero. Finally the size values reflect the size of the plane you just drew.

Figure 3.5
Viewing details about the plane.

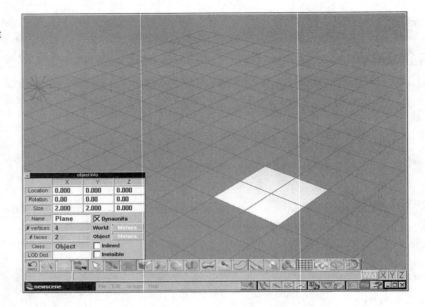

4. To convert this plane into the foundation for the anchor store, I need to resize and relocate the plane. The easiest way to do this is to change the values in the object info window. Because the anchor store is 75 by 150 feet or 6 by 12 squares in 3D coordinate units, simply enter the 12 and 6 into the boxes for the X- and Y-coordinates. Then enter –2 and 6 for the X and Y location coordinates. At the same time, you should change the name of the object from Plane,1 to Anchor Foundation (see Figure 3.6).

5. Because you can't see all of the anchor store foundation, you may want to change the level of zoom on the screen. Click on the Zoom button and move the mouse pointer to the display area. Press and hold the left mouse button and drag the mouse pointer down to zoom out and see more of the mall. If you drag the mouse upwards, you zoom in on a particular part of the mall. Remember that you can always use the Reset View tool to restore the view to the default.

6. You can also change the relative position of the mall within the display by clicking the Eye Move button and using the mouse to reposition the objects in the display. Click on the display area and drag the mouse to the left to move the scene to the right.

Figure 3.6
Resizing the plane floor to the size of the anchor store.

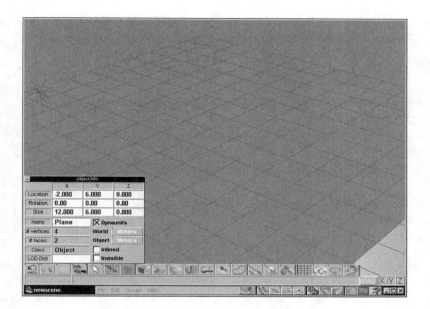

Tip

Screen size simplifies seeing stuff

All of the screenshots in this book are sized to fit on a monitor whose resolution is 800×600 . When working with trueSpace, having a larger screen resolution is better. I recommend using a minimum screen resolution of 1024×768, while 1280×1024 is close to perfect. This enables you to see more of your object in the screen without zooming and moving the eye around.

7. To create the foundation for the group of five standard stores, create a new plane object and change its X and Y size values to 4 and 10 and its X and Y location values to –6 and –2. Give this plane a name of 5 Store Foundation.

Tip

Demolishing your mistakes

If you get an object totally messed up and want to start over again without disturbing the rest of your scene, simply press the Delete key. This will delete the currently active object. If the object you wish to delete isn't the current object, select the Object Tool and click on the object you want to delete to make it the current object.

8. The main hallway can be created the same way, by creating a new plane and using X and Y size values of 4 and 10 and X and Y location values of –2 and –2. You can name this plane Main Hallway. The group of three stores (3 Store Foundation) needs yet another plane with X and Y size values of 4 and 6 and X and Y location values of 2 and

–4. The mechanical area's plane (Mechanical Area) has X and Y size values of 4 and 4 and X and Y location values of 6 and 1. After creating these planes, your mall should look like Figure 3.7.

Figure 3.7
Laying out the major areas in the mall.

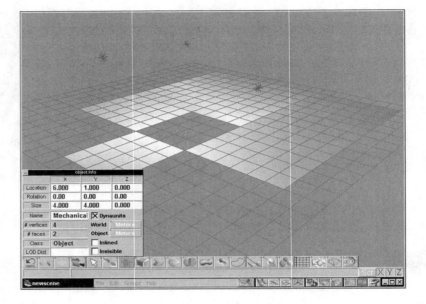

9. If you look closely at Figure 3.7, you will notice that there is a hole in the middle of the mall where the food court and offices will be placed. I'll talk about how to create these objects shortly, but first I want to apply some textures to the foundation to make it easier to understand how the mall is organized. A texture is simply a 2D image that will be displayed on the 3D object. To apply a texture to an object in the mall, click on the Material Editor tool. This will display the property window shown in Figure 3.8. The sphere in the center of this window displays how the texture will look wrapped around a sphere. Clicking on the sphere will show you how the texture looks on other types of objects.

10. Next, click on the Image Browser icon to display the image browser and press on the Folder icon to choose the location of your image files. In this case, the image files can be found in \VBGame\Chapter03 directory of the CD-ROM). Click and drag the image that looks like concrete over to the sphere and drop it. The sphere will now look like it's wrapped in concrete (see Figure 3.9).

Figure 3.8
Choose the directory containing the image files you wish to use as textures.

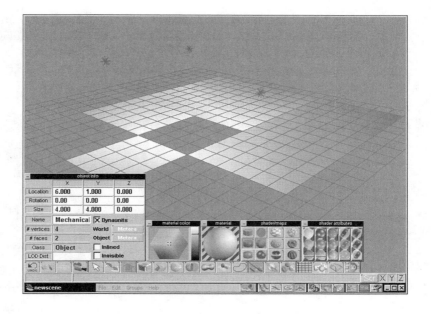

Figure 3.9
Drag the concrete image over to the sphere in the Material Editor properties window.

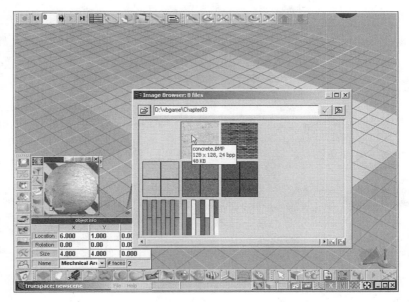

Tip

Tippy tools

If you hold the cursor over an image in the Image Browser, you'll see a tool tip that includes additional information about the image file, including the file name, the size of the image, the number of bits per pixel and the approximate size of the image.

11. Close the Image Browser window and choose the Paint Face tool from the list of icons to the right of the sphere in the Material Editor. The Paint Face tool is located with several other painting tools in the third flyout from the top. Move the mouse pointer to the mall foundation and click each part of the foundation except for the hallway (see Figure 3.10).

Figure 3.10
Turning the foundation into concrete.

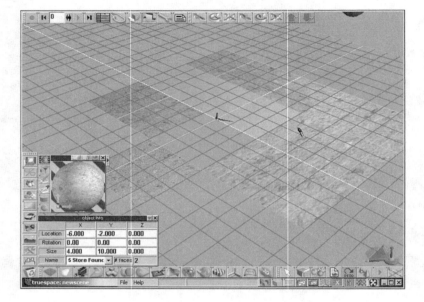

12. Following the same process described in step 10, choose another texture for the hallway. In this example, I'm going to use `Browntiles.BMP`, but there are other textures in the directory that you may want to use. As before, to apply a texture to an object, simply click the object—but make sure that the Paint Face button is selected.

Tip

Saving your sanity

You should periodically save your scene using the File, Scene, Save As command. This will provide a checkpoint from which you can recover your object if you make a mistake. Saving also makes it easy to change the object once you create it.

13. One of the problems with applying a texture to an object is that the texture is resized to fit the entire object. In the case of `Browntiles.BMP`, the image file contains only four tiles. This doesn't look very good. However, you can repeat the image multiple times by changing the values for the U Repts and V Repts in the Texture Map window. Press the Color: Texture Map button at the top of the Material Editor window (the first button on the left, which contains a color gradient) to display the Color: Texture Map window. The default values for U Repts and V Repts are 1 and 1, which means that the

texture will be repeated one time horizontally and one time vertically across the entire plane. Set U to 4 and V to 10 to match the size of the hallway, then use the Paint Face tool to replace the existing texture with the new texture (see Figure 3.11). If you want, you can also repeat the same process using the concrete texture, however I didn't bother because the concrete texture will not be visible once the mall has some stores in it.

Figure 3.11
Adding tiles to the hallway makes the mall more interesting.

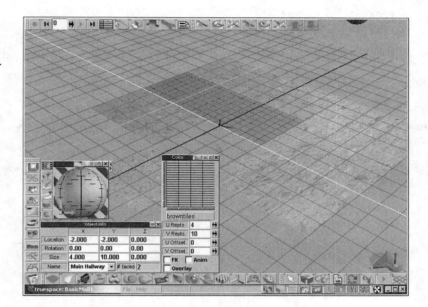

PART

I

CH

3

Tip

Undoing your mistakes

trueSpace maintains an undo list just like most Windows applications. Clicking the Undo button will remove the most recent change. Clicking the Undo button again will remove the previous change.

14. To finish the mall's foundation, I'm going to add the hallway in the food court area (Food Court Hallway). Because the brown tiles are currently selected (you can verify this by looking in the Color: Texture Map window) any new objects will automatically be created with this texture. You should adjust the U Repts and V Repts to 3 and 2 before creating the new plane so that the texture will be properly displayed. Then you should use 3 and 2 for the X and Y size parameters and 1.5 and 1 for the X and Y location parameters. Notice that the food court's hallway matches the main hallway . Of course you can always repaint the hallway after you create the plane to get the proper values for U and V.

15. There are two sets of food court stores (Food Court 1 and Food Court 2), both of which have X and Y size values of 3 and 1. The location of the first is 1.5 and –0.5, while the location of the second is 1.5 and 2.5. The mall office and the security office (Offices Foundation) can be created using size values of 1 and 4 and location values of

3.5 and 1. Remember to switch back to the Concrete.BMP texture file or these areas will be painted with the brown tiles texture.

16. Now that the foundation is poured, it's time to start working on the walls. Again, I'm going to use the plane object, however this time I need to rotate it so that it is in a vertical position rather than a horizontal position. Because I want the walls unpainted, you need to right click over the sphere in the Material Editor and select Reset All from the popup menu. Use the Plane tool to add a new plane to the scene. Set the X and Y location to –2 and 9 and set the X and Y size 12 and 1. To put the wall vertical you need to set the Y rotation to 90. This gives you the perfect wall, except that half of it is below ground, so you need to set the Z location to 0.5 to allow the wall to rest on the surface (see Figure 3.12).

Figure 3.12
Building the first wall in the mall.

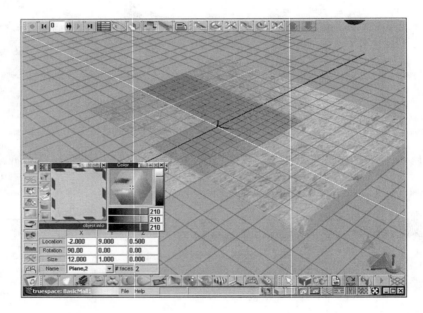

17. The next wall is somewhat tricky. You should create the plane with an X and Y size of 16 and 1 and an X, Y, and Z location of –8, 1, and 0.5; and X and Y rotations of 90 degrees. While you could simply use a Y rotation of 90 degrees and change the X and Y size to 1 and 16, any texture you apply to the wall will be rotated 90 degrees. Although this won't make a difference with a texture such as the brown tiles or concrete, it will make a big difference if you use a tile that has a strong horizontal or

vertical direction such as bricks or wood. Just remember if the object looks right with only a Y rotation, you still need an X rotation.

18. You can continue to draw walls around the perimeter of the mall. The next wall has an X, Y, and Z location of 4, 1, and 0.5, X and Y rotation values of 90 and 90, and an X and Y size of 16 and 1. The walls around the maintenance area have an X, Y, and Z location of 6, 3, and 0.5, an X rotation value of 90, and an X and Y size of 4 and 1; an X, Y, and Z location of 8, 1, and 0.5, X and Y rotation values of 90, and an X and Y size of 1 and 4; and an X, Y, and Z location of 6, –1, and 0.5, an X rotation value of 90, and an X and Y size of 4 and 1. Remember to give each wall a meaningful name such as Wall6 so that you can identify the wall later if you decide to edit the mall again.

Tip

Dragging objects

Although it is easy to enter the information directly in the Object Info window, you can also drag an object around in the scene by selecting the Object Move button. Click on the object you want to move and drag it to the new location. You can also choose the Object Rotate button to rotate the object and the Object Scale button to change the size of the object. In both cases, you simply click the object you want to change and drag the mouse around on the screen. If you aren't happy with the change, remember you can always click the Undo button.

---

19. At this point all of the walls around the mall are erected, except for the wall at the front of the mall. Because the front of the mall is at the back of the mall, you should click the Eye Rotate button and drag the mouse from side to side until the front of the mall is at the front of the display (see Figure 3.13).

Figure 3.13
Rotating the mall to make the front more visible.

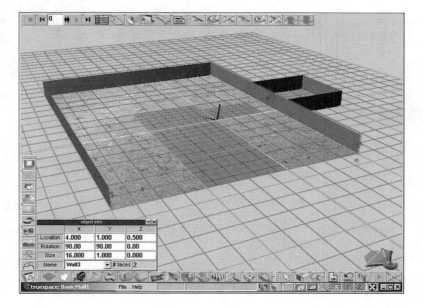

20. The front wall needs to be created in three segments. All three will have an X rotation of 90, an X and Y size of 4 and 1, and a Y and Z location of –7 and 0.5. The first segment has an X location of –6. The second segment has an X location of –2. The third segment has an X location of 2. The segment in the middle I'll refer to as the entrance. Note that while the scene has been rotated in the previous step, the coordinates remain the same. Now that the back of the mall is closest to the eye, the coordinates remain negative.

21. The next step in creating the mall is to apply a texture to all of the walls. In this case I want to use the `Redbrick.BMP` file and apply the texture to both sides of the walls except for the entrance. You can do this by selecting the `Redbrick.BMP` file in the Texture Map window and selecting the Use Texture Map button in the Shader/Maps window. Select the Paint Object button to paint both sides of the object at the same time. When you're finished, the mall should look like Figure 3.14.

Figure 3.14
Painting red bricks over most of the walls in the mall.

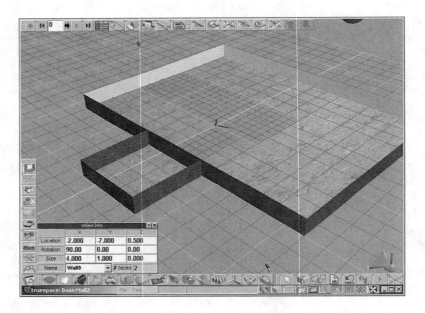

Tip

Moving lights

The red stars on the screen represent lights that provide illumination and shadows. Sometimes it can be helpful to move them to a different location to make your textures easier to see. Simply select the Object Move button and click the light. The red star will become white. You can then drag the light around on the scene until it lights up the part of the scene you need.

22. At this point, the empty mall is complete except for the entrance. I saved the entrance to the mall for last because it needs holes cut into it to allow customers to enter and exit. The easiest way to do this is to create an object the size of the hole you want to make, place it where you want the hole, and then use the Object Subtraction tool to delete the new object, including any places where it overlaps the old object. To protect your investment in the mall at this point, you should save the entire scene to disk. That way, if you make a mistake in cutting the holes, you can simply load the scene and start over again. Choose File, Save As, Scene from the main menu, enter the filename BasicMall, and click OK.

Tip

Selecting stuff

If you double-click an object in the scene after selecting the Object Tool, all other objects in the scene will be displayed as a wire frame. If trueSpace can't determine which object you selected, the entire collection of objects will be displayed normally. When this happens, try moving your mouse slightly and double-click until you select the object you want.

23. Click the Cube button (on the same flyout as the Plane tool) and add a cube to the scene. Change the object's info so that the X, Y, and Z location is –3.3, –7, 0.3 and the X, Y, and Z size is 0.6, 0.6, and 0.6. This creates a cube that is placed exactly where I want the first door (see Figure 3.15). Next click the plane that forms the entrance wall. You can verify that you selected the proper object by checking the name in the Object Map. Finally click the Object Subtraction button and click the cube. If you did everything correctly, you'll end up with a hole in the door (see Figure 3.16).

Figure 3.15
Creating a box that occupies the same space as a door.

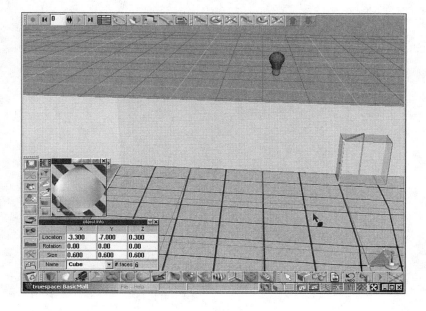

Figure 3.16
Subtracting the box
leaves an opening in
the wall.

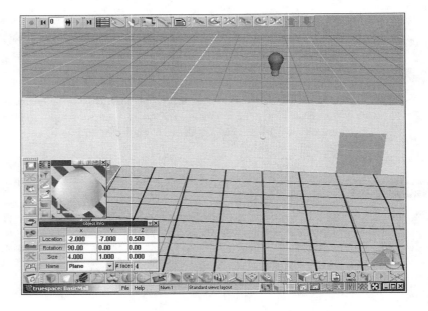

24. Repeat this process three more times for each entrance but use the following values for the X location of the cube: –2.5, –1.5, and –0.7. Then you can apply a new texture to this surface using the Paint Object tool. I suggest using Aluminum.BMP file. This will result in an entrance that looks like Figure 3.17.

Figure 3.17
Finishing the entrance
allows customers to
enter and exit the
mall.

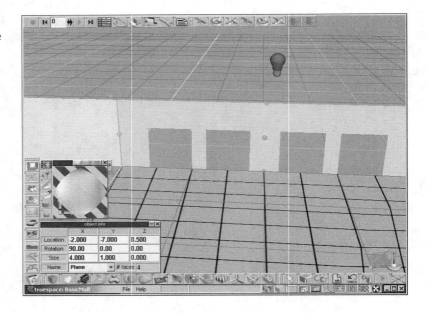

25. At this point your mall is a collection of objects that aren't connected together. For DirectX to display them, they must be glued together. Once you glue them together it will be hard to edit your mall, so you should save your scene to disk again before starting the following operations. This will allow you to easily edit the mall in the future.

26. Use the Object Tool to select one of the primitive objects comprising the object. Then select the Glue as LOD button. This changes the mouse pointer to a glue bottle. Click the other pieces of your object to glue them to the first piece. When you glue the first piece, the current object will be fully displayed, while the remaining objects will be displayed using a wire frame, which makes it easier to identify the objects that haven't been glued. You can also use the Object Info window to verify the names of the object as you glue them together.

27. Next you need to save your mall as an object that you can use in DirectX. Choose File, Save Object As from the main menu and specify the name `BasicMall`. Choose DirectX `.X` as the file type and put a checkmark in the ASCII check box. Clicking Save will save your mall (see Figure 3.18).

PART

I

CH

3

Figure 3.18
Saving your mall as a
DirectX .

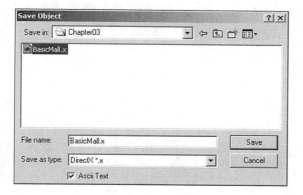

FINAL THOUGHTS

Creating the objects you can manipulate in your program using a tool like trueSpace is much easier than trying to write code to generate the graphics. This is the way most professional game developers create 3D graphics, though they will typically use more advanced tools and in some cases they'll build their own tools that will help automate creating graphics.

The same techniques I used to build the mall can be used to build the rest of the objects in the mall.

CHAPTER 4

TURNING 2D GRAPHICS INTO 3D GRAPHICS

In this chapter

In the last chapter, I showed you how to create 3D graphics using trueSpace. While trueSpace works with 3D meshes, you need to wrap 2D images over them to make them look realistic. When dealing with 2D graphics, you have a number of different tools you can use. Because I've used Adobe's Photoshop for years, I'm going to focus on this tool. However, other tools like Adobe's Illustrator and Paint Shop Pro are just as useful for creating textures.

CREATING 2D GRAPHICS

There are two main approaches to creating 2D graphics. The first is obvious; you start with a blank screen and simply draw them using a tool like Illustrator. However, unless you are a talented artist, or are trying to create a relatively simple image, you will probably want to avoid this approach. It is much harder than it looks.

The second approach involves creating a picture outside the computer by drawing it on paper or building a model or finding a real-life object and taking its photograph. You can scan the paper or photograph into the computer or use a digital camera to capture the image. Once the image is on the computer, you can easily modify it to meet your needs with a tool like Photoshop.

Note

Respect copyrights

There are many Web sites on the Internet that display artwork. While it might be tempting to use this artwork in your game, be certain that you are not violating any copyrights. Much of the material is made available for non-commercial use, typically in someone's personal Web site. However, your game may or may not fall into this category. So before you use someone else's artwork, you need to verify two things: that they hold the copyright on the material and that your use of their material will not violate their copyright. In the long run, you may find it better simply to create your own artwork.

TWEAKING IMAGES WITH PHOTOSHOP

Photoshop is a very complex tool. Don't expect to become an expert in it overnight. I'm still finding new tricks after using Photoshop for years.

It's very easy to think of Photoshop as just a powerful paint program. All of the tools you find in Microsoft Paint are there, including pencils, brushes, color palettes, paint buckets, erasers, and so on. However, this represents only a small part of what Photoshop can do.

One of the interesting features in Photoshop is its filters. Using filters, you can change how an image looks. For instance, you use the Sharpen filter to make the image look less fuzzy or you can use the Stained Glass filter to translate your image into a stained glass work of art.

Other tools in Photoshop allow you to edit the image by cropping it, resizing it, and changing how the colors appear. Photoshop also contains powerful tools that allow you to extract part of an image so that you can copy it and paste it in another image.

INTRODUCING PHOTOSHOP

At first glance, Photoshop has a rather complicated looking interface (see Figure 4.1) due to the number of tools and information it displays. The tools are split between the floating toolbar on the left side of the Photoshop window and the floating information windows found on the right side.

Figure 4.1
The Photoshop user interface looks complicated at first.

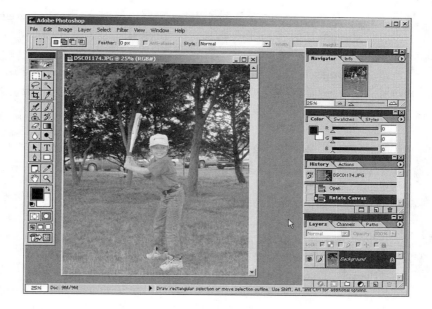

The toolbar contains a number of different tools for changing an image. Many of the buttons on the toolbar represent a tool selected from a list of tools. You can select a different tool by right-clicking the button and selecting the new tools from the pop-up menu. Some of the tools you'll find useful are

- **Marquee tool**—Selects part of an image. You can choose from a rectangle, ellipse, single row, and single column.
- **Move tool**—Repositions selections and layers on an image.
- **Lasso tool**—Makes selections by drawing a freehand shape, a polygonal shape, or snapping to the nearest edge on the image.
- **Magic wand tool**—Selects similarly colored areas.
- **Crop tool**—Eliminates unwanted parts of an image.
- **Airbrush tool**—Draws a line with a fuzzy edge.

- **Brush tool**—Draws a line with soft edges using the foreground color. The pencil tool draws a line with a hard edge.
- **Eraser tool**—Removes newly drawn pixels and restores the image to a previously saved state.
- **Paint Bucket tool**—Fills an area with the selected foreground color.
- **Gradient tool**—Fills an area with a blended set of colors based on the pattern selected.
- **Type tool**—Adds text to the image using the current foreground color.
- **Eyedropper tool**—Changes the foreground color to the selected image color.

Below the individual tools is a pair of squares that contain the current foreground and background colors. You can swap the current foreground and background colors by clicking the curved arrow that points at the two colors.

Often when you select a particular tool, it will have a set of options that refines how the tool works. These options are displayed in the Tool Options bar, which is located immediately below the main menu.

The floating information windows on the right side of the Photoshop main window provide a lot of information about the current state of the image you are working on, including:

- **Navigator**—Displays a thumbnail copy of the current image. The area currently visible is outlined with a red rectangle and you can control the current zoom factor by using the slider bar beneath the image.
- **Color/Swatches**—Contains information about the current foreground color. You can adjust the sliders to choose a different color on the Color tab. The Swatches tab displays a series of colors you can choose for the foreground color.
- **History**—Documents each change you made to the image. Clicking on an entry will display how the image looked after that change was made and optionally create a snapshot of that image. You can also selectively delete changes made to the original image.
- **Layers**—Lists each layer that is part of the current image. You can insert new layers into the stack to achieve the appropriate effect or delete existing layers as desired.

> **Tip**
>
> **Bigger is better**
> Like trueSpace, Photoshop is much easier to use when it has a big window. I recommend using a 1024×768 or larger screen resolution. Although you can get away with a smaller screen resolution when you are editing only a single image, you'll quickly find the larger area useful when you have opened multiple images.

EDITING IMAGES

Photoshop supports all the most common image types including .JPG, .GIF, and .BMP, plus it supports a number of other useful image types like .TGA (Targa) and .TIFF (Tagged-Image File Format). As you might expect, you can use the normal File, Open command to open the file. However, Photoshop also includes a File, Open As command that lets you open an existing file and assign it a new name. This command is useful because Photoshop will not let you open the same file twice.

You can also import an image into Photoshop using a scanner or other TWAIN-compliant device. However, I generally find it faster to use the scanner's tools to create an image file and then load the image into Photoshop.

Once you have loaded an image into Photoshop you can change the size and shape of the image using the Cropping tool and the image size command. The Cropping tool enables you to mark a rectangular area on the image that you want to save and discard the rest. Note that this process reduces the size of the image, so be careful to make sure that you end with an acceptable size.

Tip

The power of two

Ultimately, you will want your images to have a length and width that is a power of two, such as 64×64, 128×128, or 256×256 if you plan to use them to as textures for your meshes. While you can use other sizes, not all video cards will support them.

To use the cropping tool, simply click the tool and move the mouse pointer to one of the corners of the rectangle you want to save. While holding the left mouse button down, move the mouse to show the rectangle you want to save. After you release the left mouse button, the areas you will discard are shown dimmer than the area you will save (see Figure 4.2).

Figure 4.2
The crop tool dims the areas you want to delete from the image.

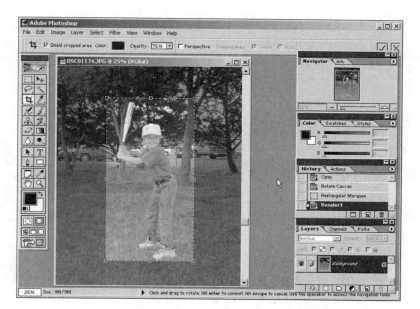

If you made a mistake, you can move the sides of the rectangle until you have identified the area you want to save from the image. Right-click the image and select Crop to discard the unwanted part of the image or Cancel to remove the cropping rectangle.

Although cropping an image will change the size of the image, the Image, Image Size command will also change the size of the image. However, unlike the Cropping tool, Image Size changes the size of the whole image. Although you can increase the size of the image, the larger image will seem blocky because Photoshop has to analyze the image to create the new pixels. This is something you won't do very often.

On the other hand, shrinking an image is a very common Photoshop task. I generally shoot pictures or scan images at a relatively high resolution. Then I'll use the Image Size command to reduce the image to a more manageable size. When Photoshop reduces the size of an image, it analyzes a groups of pixels to determine the color of each new pixel in the reduced image. This approach means that the smaller image is better than it would have been if you originally scanned or photographed the original image at the smaller size.

For instance, if I plan to scan an image for use as a 128×128 pixel texture, I'll probably scan the image to create an intermediate image of 1024×1024 or 2048×2048. Then I can try to resize the image to 128×128. If the smaller image looks a little strange because too much information was lost, I may use the various tools in Photoshop to retouch the intermediate image to make the smaller image look better.

Other useful tools in Photoshop are the Transform tools (choose Edit, Transform). These tools allow you to stretch and compress the image in several different ways by using these commands: Scale, Rotate, Skew, Distort, and Perspective. There are also some shortcuts for common tasks such as flipping an image and rotating an image 90 degrees.

USING LAYERS

Images in Photoshop are composed of a series of one or more layers. The final image you see is really just the combination of all the individual layers stacked on top of one another. For the most part, each layer is transparent with some individual part of the final image on it.

Perhaps the easiest way to understand how layers work is to imagine how a cartoon is created. The artist draws a complete background image. Then on top of the background image, the cartoonist places various objects that can move, such as the characters. If the objects overlap one another, the object farthest away from the camera is placed on the background. This process is repeated until the object closest to the camera is placed on top.

In Photoshop, each layer is manipulated independently. You can apply a filter to a level or draw on the level using any of the standard drawing tools. You can also cut or copy part of a layer and paste it on another layer.

The bottom layer of the image is called the *background*. Typically this is a complete image that was digitized using a scanner or taken with a digital camera.

Each layer above the bottom layer is transparent until you put something on the image. Thus if you add some text to a layer, only the text is visible on the layer. The rest of the layer is still transparent. This allows the background to show through everywhere but where the text is placed. The layers are documented in the Layers information window (see Figure 4.3).

Figure 4.3
You can see all of the layers in your current image.

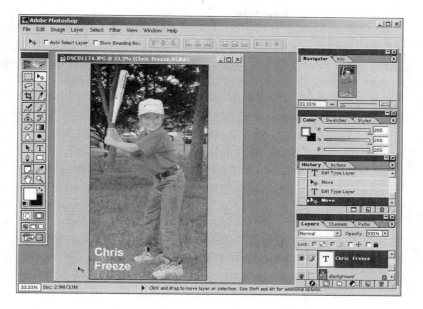

You can create a new layer by choosing Layer, New, Layer from the main menu. Some of the tools will automatically create a new layer. For instance, the Text tool always places its text on a new layer. Any time you paste something from the Clipboard, it will be placed on a new layer. This makes it easy to use the Move tool to adjust the position of the layer relative to the background image. Note that the Brush, Pencil, Eraser, and Paint Bucket tools all work on the currently selected layer.

To delete a layer, all you have to do is right-click the layer in the Layer information window and choose delete from the pop-up menu. Alternatively, you can click the layer and drag it to the trashcan at the bottom of the Layer information window. You can move a layer up or down in the stack of layers by clicking on the layer and dragging it to its new location.

You can combine two adjoining layers by selecting the upper layer and choosing Layer, Merge Down from the main menu. You can merge all layers, including the background, by choosing Layer, Flatten Image from the main menu.

PART

I

CH

4

Tip

Saving twice saves time
Only the Photoshop file format (.PDD) will save a complete copy of the image, including the individual layers. To use any other file format, you need to flatten the image, so it's probably a good idea to save your image using both the Photoshop file format (.PDD), as well as the format you want to use. This will save you time if you want to edit the image later.

In addition to the layer's transparency, you can control the transparency of the objects on a layer by tweaking the layer's opacity. By default, opacity is set to 100%, meaning that any object on a layer will completely hide any objects beneath it. To change the opacity, simply select the desired layer in the Layers information window and change the opacity value.

If you set the layer's opacity to 50% percent the objects on that layer will be blended with the layers below it. This makes the objects on the layer partially transparent. If you set the opacity for a layer to 0%, the objects on that layer will no longer be visible.

EXTRACTING PARTS OF AN IMAGE

Photoshop is an MDI application, meaning that you can have multiple images open at the same time. You'll find having multiple images open to be very useful because one of the most common ways to construct an image is to take a piece from one image and paste it onto another image.

Probably the most common reason for extracting part of an image is to use the extracted part as an overlay on top of another image. You might copy the extracted image as a new layer in an image you're creating in Photoshop or save the image with a transparent background for use as an overlay in your game.

The most common way to select the part of the image is to copy. You can use several tools discussed earlier including the Marquee, Lasso, and Magic Wand tools. With the Marquee and Lasso tools, you simply move the tool over the part of the image you want to select. With the Magic Wand tool, you touch it to the area of similar colored pixels you want to select.

Once the part of the image is selected, you can use the Move tool to move the selected part of the image. Note that the selected part of the image remains part of the current layer and as soon as the part of the image is deselected, it will be saved as part of the layer. If you moved part of the selected part of the image outside the edges of the image, these parts will be lost once the selected part is deselected.

Selecting part of an image will also restrict where a particular tool will work. For instance, if you select part of the image and pour the Paint Bucket into the selected area, the Paint Bucket's color will be restricted to the selected area.

The Select main menu command includes some other useful tools for choosing part of an image or layer. Select, Deselect will remove any selection marks from the image. If the selected area was changed by moving it or using the pencil, brush, or other tools, the changes will be committed to the image or layer affected.

The Select, Inverse command selects any unselected pixels, while deselecting any selected pixels. This is a very useful trick when combined with the Magic Wand. Because it's often hard to select the foreground part of an image with the Magic Wand, simply select the background parts and use the Select, Inverse command to get the foreground part of the image.

One of the most powerful ways to select part of an image is the Image, Extract command. This will display the window shown in Figure 4.4. To use this function, simply use the highlighter to mark over the edge of the area you want to select. You don't need to be very careful other than to ensure that the actual edge is covered by the highlighter. Then using the Paint Bucket tool, you fill the area that you want to extract.

Figure 4.4
The Extract window makes it easy to extract part of the image.

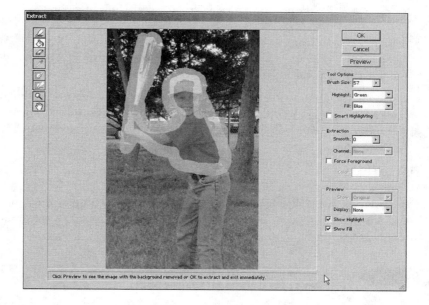

Pressing the Preview button causes Photoshop to find the edge of the image and display the results to you. Then you can use other tools such as the Cleanup tool and the Edge Touchup tool to tweak edges so that they are nice and sharp.

RUNNING FILTERS AND MORE

Photoshop includes a large number of tools that allow you to change how an image looks. These tools are known as *filters*. A filter distorts how an image looks. Here are some of the more interesting filters for a game programmer:

- **Sharpen**—Looks for edges (places where there is a distinct difference in colors) and increases the contrast of the adjacent pixels. The net effect is that the image looks crisper and more in focus.

- **Diffuse**—Makes the image look less focused.

- **Diffuse Glow**—Leaves a glowing edge surrounding an image. This works best with an extracted image that is sitting on top of a single color background.

- **Clouds**—Creates a cloud-like image that replaces the current layer.

- **Noise**—Replaces pixels in the image with randomly distributed color levels. This is useful when creating textures or providing a more realistic look to a heavily retouched area.

- **Find Edges**—Identifies edges in the image and creates a relatively interesting special effect.

- **Mosaic Tiles**—Creates an interesting effect, especially when used with the Noise filter.

- **Grain**—Adds texture to an image with different kinds of graininess.

These filters represent a small number of the filters available in Photoshop. Not all of them will be useful to game programmers, but as with any creative activity, you should take the time to try each of them to see what results you can get.

Along with the filters, you can change the existing colors using several different adjustments found on the Image, Adjust menu. Some of the commands such as Color Balance and Brightness/Contrast are pretty straightforward. However, my favorite tool is Hue/Saturation.

In the Hue/Saturation dialog box (see Figure 4.5), you see a series of sliders that enable you to adjust Hue, Saturation, and Lightness. By playing with these sliders you can change the base color of an image. Thus you can turn a brown object purple, green, or red just by moving a few sliders. You can also restrict the changes to a particular color for even more control over the image.

Tip

Twice the textures for half the work

There will be situations in your game where you will want to use a texture that differs only in color from another texture. The Hue/Saturation tool allows you to take your artwork that you have already created and make it a different color. Thus you can create white walls, blue walls, and brown walls all from the same basic texture.

Figure 4.5
The Hue/Saturation dialog box changes the colors in your image.

CREATING A STORE

The steps to build a store are similar to those used to build the mall. Of course, the store is simpler because the store has only four walls, plus a door and window. However, to make each store a little different, I need a wider assortment of textures for each one.

CREATING A SIMPLE TEXTURE WITH PHOTOSHOP

Each store needs two basic textures. One texture will be placed on the outside wall of the store facing into the mall, which will contains the store's name. The other texture will line the interior walls of the store.

Generally textures must be square—their height and width must be the same. Also, the dimension of a texture must be a power of 2, such as 128 or 256. Although some video adapters support textures as large as 1,024×1,024, it is much more practical to stick with 128×128 or 256×256. These values are supported by nearly all video adapters and they make more efficient use of video memory.

The storefront texture has two basic areas. The top 40% of the space is available for the store's sign or logo. This space is available all of the way across. The bottom 60% of the space represents the space used by the door and windows into the store. You can construct this texture by using the following steps.

Although the texture is 128×128 pixels wide, the store front has a width of 2 and a height of 1. This means that you must either use only the top half of the texture, stretch it horizontally so that it fits across the store front, or tile it so that the same texture is used twice.

For this store, I'm going to use a single texture and stretch it across the entire front. This means that the image will look a little funny in Photoshop, but is will be okay when it's displayed in the game.

1. Start Photoshop. Select File, New from the main menu to display the New dialog box (see Figure 4.6). Enter **128** pixels for the Width and Height fields and enter **64** pixels/inch for the Resolution. Select RGB Color as the Mode and set Contents to Transparent. Enter a name for the image and click OK.

Figure 4.6
Creating a new image in Photoshop.

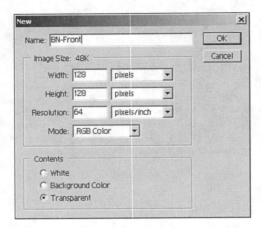

2. To make viewing the image you're creating easier, choose View, Show Rulers and View, Show, Grid from the main menu. This will add horizontal and vertical rulers around your new image, and draw grid lines at each one inch mark. To make the grid lines more useful, choose Edit, Preferences, Guides & Grid, which will display the Preferences dialog box. Change the field Gridline Every 1 inch to .25 inch.

3. Because the image is relatively small, you should zoom level to 300% using the Navigator information window. You can also zoom in by choosing View, Zoom In three times from the main menu or pressing Ctrl++ on the keyboard three time (see Figure 4.7).

4. The first thing I want to do with the new image is to create a background. Select pure white as the foreground color by setting the sliders to 255 for each color in the Color information window. Then use the Paint Bucket tool to fill the image.

5. To make the background more interesting, use the Filter, Noise, Add Noise command and specify a value of 7% for the amount of noise. Select Uniform distribution and leave the Monochromatic check box unchecked.

6. Change the foreground color to dark green (red 0, green 100, and blue 0). Swap the foreground color with the background color and change the new foreground color to medium red (red 192, green 0, blue 0).

7. Now select the Text tool and choose the Arial, Bold, 24 point, Crisp, Left Justify from the tool options bar. Switch the foreground color back to green.

Figure 4.7
Adding gridlines and rulers makes the image easier to edit.

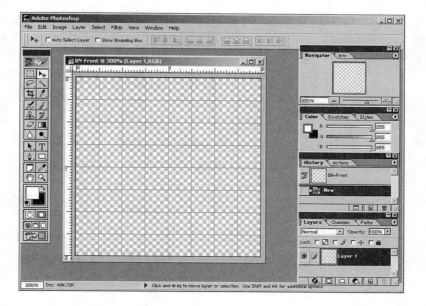

8. Position the text cursor somewhere over the image and type **Barnacles**. Press the Enter key and switch the foreground color to red. Type an &, followed by a space. Switch the foreground color back to green and type **Noble**.

9. After entering the text, switch to the Move tool and reposition the text so that the text is in the upper-left corner of the image (see Figure 4.8). You should leave a little gap between the text and the edges of the image so that it will look more like a real sign on a store front.

PART

I

CH

4

Figure 4.8
Drawing the name of the store on the texture.

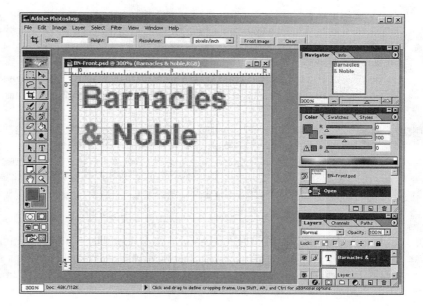

10. Use the Layer, Flatten Image command to merge all of the layers together to form a single image.

11. Finally, use the File, Save As command to save the image. Choose the .BMP format and enter a filename. Click OK to save the file. Another dialog box will ask you to specify OS/2 or Windows format and the color depth. Choose Windows and 24-bit, respectively, and click OK. Photoshop will flatten all of the layers and save the file.

CREATING A COMPLEX TEXTURE WITH PHOTOSHOP

Creating a texture from scratch is hard, especially if you want to include a lot of detail in the image. Fortunately, there are other ways to create textures for your game. My favorite way is to find something similar to what I need in the game, and then use a digital camera to take a picture of it.

Like the store front texture, the interior texture is 128×128 pixels. However, the interior walls are different sizes. The side walls are four units wide by one unit tall, while the back wall is two units wide. Rather than simply stretch the texture as I did for the store front, I'm going to tile these textures like I did with the brick walls in the shopping mall in the last chapter.

Note

On the CD-ROM

A sample image file taken directly from a digital camera can be found on the CD-ROM as \VBGame\Chapter04\BNRawInterior.JPG.

1. After taking the picture, copy it to your hard disk and load it into Photoshop.

2. When shooting a photograph of an object you want to use as a texture, it makes sense to center the image so that you can crop the excess later. So to crop the image, select the Crop tool and choose the part of the image you want use as the basis for your texture. Although you don't have to ensure that the cropped image is square, it will be helpful later, especially if you want to minimize distortion. Both the gridlines and rules will be helpful to you if you want to make the image square (see Figure 4.9).

Tip

Straight and level

It is very important to make sure that any pictures you take are straight and level. Although Photoshop can rotate an image until it is level, the rotated image will not have the same quality as the original.

3. Even after you cropped the image, most likely the image is still much larger than you want. Because the image you've loaded is relatively large when compared to the size of the texture, the next step is to reduce the size of the image. Choose Image, Size and

specify 128 pixels for the height and width. Note that if your cropped image wasn't square, you should uncheck the Constrain Proportions check box; otherwise you won't be able to create a square image.

Figure 4.9
Loading an external created image into Photoshop.

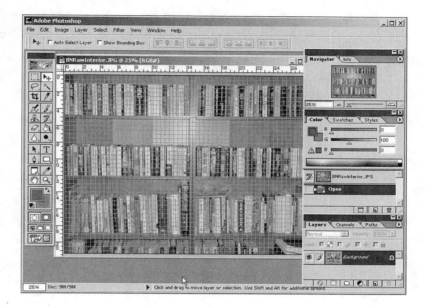

4. Assuming you are satisfied with the image, you can simply save the image to disk using the .BMP format. However, you can continue to manipulate the image to create the look you want.

CREATING AN EMPTY STORE WITH trueSpace

After creating the new textures, creating the store is a relatively simple process. The only real issue is that the store must be slightly smaller than the area reserved for the store; otherwise, the walls of the store would overlap the walls of the mall.

1. Start trueSpace or select File, New, Scene from the main menu to create a new object.

2. Select the Add Plane tool and create a new plane. Right click on the Object tool to display the Object Info window and set the X and Y sizes to 1.95 and 3.9, respectively. Label this plane Floor.

3. Click the Material Editor icon to display the Material Editor window. Then click the Image Browser icon to display the Image Browser window. Change directories until you locate the copy of the files from the CD-ROM associated with this chapter (see Figure 4.10).

Figure 4.10
Locating a texture in trueSpace.

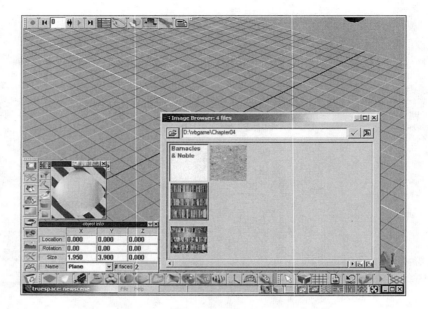

4. Drag the Concrete.BMP texture from the Image Browser window to Material Editor window and close the Image Browser window.

5. Click the Color icon in the title bar of the Material Editor to display the Color information window. Adjust the U and V values to 2 and 4.

6. Repeat the Concrete.BMP texture two times in the X direction and four times in the Y direction.

7. Select the Replace Material tool on the left side of the Material Editor window and use it to paint the plane you just created.

8. Use the Image Browser window to switch the current texture to BNInterior.BMP. Switch U and V to 4 and 2, respectively.

9. Add another plane to the store. Set its X and Y size properties to 1.95 and 1.0, the X rotation property to 90, and Y and Z location properties to –1.95 and 0.5. Label this plane BackWall. Note that the texture will automatically be applied to the plane.

10. Create the front wall using the same parameters as the back wall, except set the X location property to 1.95 and the Z rotation to 180. Label this plane as FrontWall.

11. Set the U and V values to 8 and 2. Then add another plane for the first side wall using these values: location X=-0.975 and Z=0.5; rotation X=90 and Y=90; size X=3.9 and Y=1. Create the second side wall with the same values, except set the X location to 0.975. Label these walls SideWall1 and SideWall2.

12. Use the Image Browser to replace the current texture with BNFront.BMP.

13. To create a doorway in the store, create a cube with the following X, Y, and Z location: –0.4, 2, and 0.3 and the following X, Y, and Z size: 0.6, 0.6, and 0.6. Then use the Object Tool to select the store and then use the Object Subtraction tool to remove the cube and create the doorway.

14. To create a window in the store, create a cube with the following X, Y, and Z location: 0.45, 2, and 0.35 and the following X, Y, and Z size: 0.8, 0.3, and 0.5. Then select the store using the Object Tool and remove the cube using the Object Subtraction tool.

Figure 4.11
Subtracting a cube from a plane leaves an open window into the store.

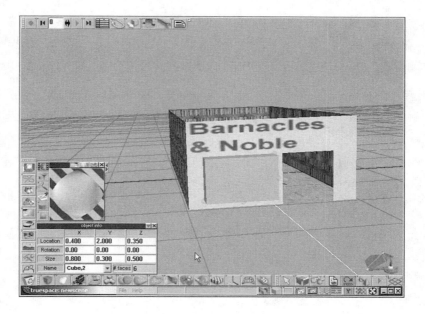

15. Choose File, Save As, Scene from the main menu and specify a filename of `BarnaclesNoble`. If you want to make changes to the store later, such as changing the textures, simply load this scene and make any edits you desire, complete the remaining steps to convert the store to a DirectX .X file.

16. Select the Object Tool and select the floor. Then choose the Glue As Sibling tool and click each of the walls to create a single object. If you don't do this and attempt to save your design as an object, only the currently selected plane will be saved. You should not need to save the scene again even though you have made changes to it.

17. Choose File, Save As, Object As from the main menu and choose DirectX .X as the file type. Also put a check mark in the ASCII checkbox. Specify the name `BarnacleNoble.X` and click OK to save the object.

18. Exit trueSpace. Do not save the scene again or you will replace the scene containing the individual components with one that contains a single glued together object, which will be much harder to edit.

FINAL THOUGHTS

Creating interesting textures is probably the hardest part of developing a game—at least for most programmers. It takes a special talent to create artwork from scratch, whether using a tool like Illustrator or Photoshop or simply drawing something by hand. My preference is to find real objects and use a digital camera to take a picture. Then I can use Photoshop to modify the image.

Learning to use Photoshop effectively can take a long time. Just when you think you've mastered it, you'll find a new feature or trick that you can use to tweak your images.

One tool in Photoshop I didn't discuss is the Liquify tool. This tool allows you to stretch and distort images by dragging pixels around on the screen. The best way to describe the effect is that it allows you to create a melted version of the original image. While you probably don't want to use the Liquify tool to make major changes to an image, you can use it to exaggerate parts of an image to make it a little more interesting.

LOADING MALL INFORMATION

In this chapter

After creating the 3D graphics for the shopping mall and some stores, it's time to jump back into Visual Basic and talk about how to get this information into the computer so DirectX can display it on the screen.

DESIGN DETAILS

Like most computer games, Swim Mall needs to keep track of a lot of information related to the 3D objects displayed in the game. This information can be broken into two main categories; disk-based structures and memory-based structures.

DISK-BASED STRUCTURES

Disk-based structures represent permanent information about the game. This information is broken into two broad categories, *static information*, which includes 3D object files and information files about the objects; and *dynamic information*, which represents transient information such as saved games.

Rather than keep most of this information in the game's root directory, I choose to separate this information into a series of directories listed in Table 5.1. Only a few files are contained in the root directory, such as the game's executable file and startup parameters file. The source code to the game will also be stored in the root directory while the game is in development. In the packaged version of the game, the source code will be omitted.

TABLE 5.1 GAME DIRECTORIES

Name	Description
.	Contains the game's executable files, plus other key files for the game. It also contains the other directories listed in this table. This directory is also referred to as the game's root directory.
Anchors	Contains the DirectX .X files, texture files, and .SMS files for anchor stores.
Customers	Contains the DirectX .X files for the customers that walk around in the mall.
Foods	Contains the DirectX .X files, texture files, and .SMS files for food court vendors.
Malls	Contains the DirectX .X files, texture files, plus the mall information files for all of the shopping malls available in the game.
Media	Contains any sound files that can be played during the game.
Music	Contains music files that will be played during the game.
Objects	Contains the DirectX .X files, texture files, plus the object information files for all 3D objects in the game except for malls and stores.
SavedGames	Directory containing the information about saved game.
Scenarios	Contains standard starting scenarios.
Stores	Contains the DirectX .X files, texture files, plus the store information files for all of the stores available in the game.

The `Anchors`, `Foods`, `Malls`, `Objects`, and `Stores` directories hold static information about the 3D objects in the game. This structure permits you to add as many objects to the game as you want by copying the files to the appropriate directory.

The `SavedGames` directory has one file for each saved game, which represents the current state of the shopping mall. The same is true for the `Scenarios` directory. Because the same information is kept about a scenario as the saved game, a player can create his or her own scenario by copying a saved game to the `Scenarios` directory.

The `Music` and `Media` directories will be discussed later in the book when I discuss DirectMusic and DirectSound. The `Customers` directory will be discussed when I add customers to the mall.

Note

Write never files

The SavedGames directory is the only directory the Swim Mall program will ever update. All of files in the rest of the directories will never be updated while the game is running. This leaves open the option to run the game from CD-ROM, but mostly it ensures that the game doesn't change anything by accident that might adversely affect the game. Of course, if you want to install additional objects in the game, you will need to update some or all of these directories.

In addition to the directories, Swim Mall uses a number of different file types (see Table 5.2). Chapter 3, "Creating 3D Graphics," showed you how `.BMP` files and `.X` files are used. The `.SMG` file is used in three ways. First, it holds the current state of a game and is stored in the `SavedGames` directory. Second, it is used to hold game scenarios in the `Scenarios` directory. Third, the file called `SwimMall.SMG` contains the initial startup parameters for the game. Unlike normal saved game files, this file resides in the root directory of the game.

TABLE 5.2   FILE TYPES IN SWIM MALL

Name	Description
.BMP	Bitmap file containing a texture that will be displayed on a 3D object.
.MID	Contains a MIDI file that can be played in the background while the game is played.
.MP3	MP3 file containing music that can be played during the game.
.SMG	Swim Mall Game file containing saved game information.
.SMM	Swim Mall Mall file containing information about a particular shopping mall.
.SMO	Swim Mall Object file containing information about a particular object in a mall.
.SMS	Swim Mall Store file containing information about a particular store.
.WAV	Wave file containing sound information that is played during key events during the game.
.X	DirectX mesh file containing a 3D object that can be displayed on the screen.

The .SMM file contains information about a particular shopping mall, while the .SMO and .SMS contain information about general objects and stores respectively.

> **Note**
>
> **Stores, stores and more stores**
>
> Even though anchor stores, food court vendors, and regular stores all have separate directories, they all use the same fundamental information and use the same data structures. The separate directories are mostly a matter of connivance. It allows me to keep the various types of stores separate, which simplifies some of the later programming.

The game also uses .MP3 and .MID files to provide mall music and .WAV files to provide specific sound effects for special events in the mall. I'll cover how these files are used later in the book when I discuss DirectAudio in Chapter 14, "Attention, Shoppers."

SWIM MALL FILE FORMAT

All of the Swim Mall files use the same basic format to make things easier to parse. This means that I can use a single class to read and write all of the different types of files.

When it came to designing the file format for these files I though about using XML for a moment and then discarded it almost immediately. Although XML is a powerful tool for defining data, it's overkill for this application. It would take far more code to load and extract the data from the XML document than to write some simple code that loads the content of a simple text file.

I finally settled on using a simple format for the file, as shown in Listing 5.1. This format is composed of a key, followed by an equal sign (=), followed by a data value. Each key/data pair must fit onto a single line and must not contain an equal sign in the key or the value. This approach allows me to read a single line of the file and parse it quickly using the Split function.

LISTING 5.1   SWIMMALL.SMG (ABBREVIATED LISTING)

```
Type=Saved Game
Mall=BasicMall.SMM
Name=The Oceanic Mall
```

This approach has two main advantages. First because I'm using a simple text file, you can easily edit it with any text editor like Write or Notepad. A more complicated structure would require a custom editor program. Second, you can easily add more information to the end of the file. Thus as the game evolves, you can include additional information about an object with minimal effort.

In addition to identifying the type of information kept in the file, the Type key allows me to verify that the file is in the proper format. If this key/data pair is not in the first line of the file, the class used to read the file will return an error code to its caller.

There is one minor limitation to this format and that is how to handle collections of information. Consider the information that is necessary to place a store in a mall. For each store, you need the X and Y location, plus the size of the store you can place there. You also need to know how to turn the store so that the opening of the store will face front. Listing 5.2 contains the complete listing for the SwimMall.SMG file.

LISTING 5.2   SwimMall.SMG (Complete Listing)

```
' The Swim Mall initialization file
Type=Saved Game
Name=The Oceanic Mall
Mall=BasicMall.SMM
Viewpoint\x=0.0
Viewpoint\y=0.0
Viewpoint\z=0.0
Camera\x=5.0
Camera\y=5.0
Camera\z=5.0
Zoom=1
Rotation=0
Anchor\1=
Food\1=
Food\2=
Food\3=
Food\4=
Store\1=BarnaclesNoble.SMS
Store\2=
Store\3=
Store\4=
Store\5=
Store\6=
Store\7=
Store\8=
```

Although the information for the basic mall is still arranged as key=data, I've extended the meaning of key to allow a multilevel hierarchy using backslashes (\) between each key level. This allows me to uniquely identify the attributes associated with a particular store's location in the mall.

Caution

Text files aren't secure

The primary drawback to text files is the same as one of their advantages—they are easy to read and change. If someone wanted, they could easily change the information in a file to make the game easier to beat. Swim Mall is an open game—if you cheat, you cheat only yourself. However, if you are developing a commercial game, you should spend some time and develop binary file structures to hold the information your game uses and the tools to edit them to protect your data. You may even want to develop an encryption routine to prevent someone from changing the game. You might consider looking for a commercial routine that allows you to zip and unzip information from inside your program. This would allow you to easily access multiple files at run time, while preventing the user from looking at the data by using an encryption key.

MEMORY-BASED STRUCTURES

Storing data on the hard disk is fine, but you need to move it into memory before you can use it. Although you can store everything using simple variables or arrays, I'm going to use a series of classes that not only hold the information, but provide a set of common operations that I would perform against the information.

Each of the four main types of files (.SMG, .SMM, .SMO, and .SMS), will have a class associated with it. These classes are Game, Mall, MallObject, and Store. Because there is more than one Store in a mall, I'll create a Stores class for the set of stores in the mall. I'll also create a MallObjects class to do the same thing for the MallObject class. These classes will be linked to the mall object.

LOADING A SAVED GAME

When Swim Mall starts, it needs to load a saved game to get the initial information to be displayed. The player will also have the capability to load a saved game while playing the game. Thus the same tools to load a saved game also are responsible for initializing the game at startup.

THE GAME CLASS

The saved game file contains basic information about a shopping mall, including the stores and other items in the mall. It also holds other information about the game such as the amount of money the player has and statistics about the stores and mall. Because we don't really have a game at this point, the saved game file really just holds information about how to display the shopping mall on the screen. As we work through the book, we'll expand the information kept in the saved game file to include the other information that is necessary to restore a game already in progress.

Because there are a number of different types of items in the game, I've developed an object model that assigns a different class to each of the key items (see Figure 5.1). The Game class contains overall game information. In this chapter, it is merely responsible for loading the saved game information.

Figure 5.1
Modeling the items in shopping mall using different classes.

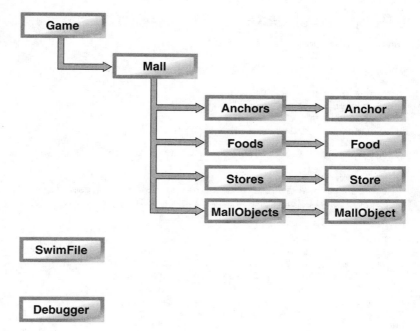

In many ways, the Mall class is merely a container for the other items in the shopping mall: Anchors, Foods (food court vendors), Stores, and MallObjects. Because each of these items is really a collection of items, I've included classes for both the specific item and the collection of items.

Finally, there are two other utility classes that are used in this part of the game, the Debugger class and the SwimFile class. The Debugger class was introduced in Chapter 2, "Introducing DirectX," and writes formatted debugging information to the Debug.Log file. The SwimFile class is a low-level class designed to read and parse the information in a Swim Mall formatted file.

USING THE GAME CLASS

I like to create classes that do most of the work in the application. This means that the code in the Form object does little more than create the objects necessary for the application and run the main application loop. In Swim Mall, this class is known as the Game class.

In Form1 (see Listing 5.3), I defined a module level variable called GameObj that contains an instance of the Game class. Then I call the InitGame function to initialize the game. In

Chapter 2, when we looked at this function, it merely initialized the DirectX graphics. Now it creates a new instance of the Game object and uses the LoadGame method to restore the SwimMall.SMG file in the root directory of the application. If the saved game file was successfully restored, the DirectX classes will be initialized by the InitGraphics function.

LISTING 5.3 FORM1.INITGAME

```
Function InitGame() As Long

Dim Result As Long

Set GameDebugger = New Debugger
GameDebugger.Enable

Set GameObj = New Game
Set GameObj.DebugObject = GameDebugger
Result = GameObj.LoadGame(App.Path & "\" & "SwimMall.SMG")

If Result <> 0 Then
   GameDebugger.WriteLine "Can't load the Swim Mall game file."
   MsgBox "Can't load the Swim Mall game file."

Else
   Result = InitGraphics
   If Result <> 0 Then
      GameDebugger.WriteLine "Can't initialize DirectX graphics!"
      MsgBox "Can't initialize DirectX graphics!"

   End If

End If

GameActive = (Result = 0)

InitGame = Result

End Function
```

MODULE VARIABLES IN THE GAME CLASS

One of the main concepts behind a class is to encapsulate information and provide properties and methods to access this data, which is why the module level variables in the class are very important. Listing 5.4 shows the variables associated with the Game class.

LISTING 5.4 MODULE LEVEL VARIABLES IN THE GAME CLASS

```
Private GameDebugger As Debugger
Private xName As String
Private xMallFileName As String
Private xViewPoint As D3DVECTOR
Private xCameraPoint As D3DVECTOR
Private xZoom As Single
```

LISTING 5.4   CONTINUED

```
Private xRotation As Single

Private AnchorFiles() As String
Private FoodFiles() As String
Private MallObjectFiles() As String
Private StoreFiles() As String

Private MallObj As Mall
```

The `GameDebugger` object is merely an object reference to the same `Debugger` object defined in the main program. The `xName` and `xMallFileName` variables contain the name of the mall and the `.SMM` filename in the `Malls` directory containing details of the mall. The `xViewPoint`, `xCameraPoint`, `xZoom`, and `xRotation` variables hold information that controls how the player will see the mall on the screen. Finally, the `MallObj` variable holds a reference to a `Mall` object that contains details of the mall. All of these variables are exposed using `Property Get` routines, while the `GameDebugger` object can also be set using a `Property Set` routine.

The `AnchorFiles`, `FoodFiles`, `MallObjectFiles`, and `StoreFiles` arrays hold references to the files in the `Stores` and `Objects` directories containing details about the stores and other objects in the mall. These variables are placed at the module level simply because they are accessed from multiple routines. These values are not used outside this class.

INSIDE THE LoadGame METHOD

The `LoadGame` method of the `Game` class is a high-level routine that loads all of the data stored on disk related to a game (see Listing 5.5). It uses the `SwimFile` class to read and extract information from the saved game file.

LISTING 5.5   GAME.LOADGAME

```
Public Function LoadGame(Filename As String) As Long

Dim k1 As String
Dim k2 As String
Dim k3 As String
Dim d As String
Dim RC As Long
Dim GameFile As SwimFile

GameDebugger.WriteLine "Loading game file: " & Filename

Set GameFile = New SwimFile

RC = GameFile.OpenInFile(Filename)
If RC = 0 Then
   Do While Not GameFile.AtEndOfStream
      GameFile.GetData k1, k2, k3, d
      SetData k1, k2, k3, d

   Loop
```

LISTING 5.5   CONTINUED

```
      GameFile.CloseFile

End If

PostGameLoadProcessing

GameDebugger.WriteLong "Game load complete.", RC

LoadGame = RC

End Function
```

The LoadGame routine begins by using the Debugger object to mark the start of the load process. Then I instantiate a copy of the SwimFile class that I'll use to read in the information from the saved game file. The GetData method returns the three key values in k1, k2, and k3, while the data is returned in d. I use the SetData subroutine to process each line returned from the GetData routine. I'll cover the SetData routine after I finish this one, but for now, you can assume that SetData just sets values in the module level variables for processing later.

Next I check to see if the saved game file includes a filename for the mall. If it does, I create a new Mall object and load the information from the file associated with the mall.

Finally, I call the PostGameLoadProcessing routine to load the information for the various stores and objects in the mall. Note that I can't perform some of these actions until after I've loaded all of the game's information because some of these values will override the default values supplied in the game's definition files.

EXTRACTING DATA FROM THE SAVED GAME FILE

The SetData routine is simply a place to process a line of data from the saved game. It uses the three key values to identify the operation to perform and then performs it using the data value. If you think this sounds like a big Select statement, you're right (see Listing 5.6).

LISTING 5.6   GAME.SETDATA

```
Private Sub SetData(Key1 As String, Key2 As String, _
   Key3 As String, Data As String)

Select Case Key1
   Case "name"
      xName = Data

   Case "mall"
      xMallFileName = Data

   Case "viewpoint"
      SetLocation xViewPoint, Key1, Key2, Data

   Case "camera"
```

LISTING 5.6   CONTINUED

```
        SetLocation xCameraPoint, Key1, Key2, Data

    Case "rotation"
        SetNumber xRotation, Key1, Data

    Case "zoom"
        SetNumber xZoom, Key1, Data

    Case "anchor"
        SetFilename AnchorFiles, Key1, Key2, Data

    Case "food"
        SetFilename FoodFiles, Key1, Key2, Data

    Case "object"
        SetFilename MallObjectFiles, Key1, Key2, Data

    Case "store"
        SetFilename StoreFiles, Key1, Key2, Data

    Case Else
        GameDebugger.WriteLine "Unknown key value: " & Key1 & _
            " \ " & Key2 & " \ " & Key3 & " = " & Data

End Select

End Sub
```

Because the saved game file doesn't contain a lot of information at this stage of the development process, this routine is relatively short. Basically I use the first key from the saved game file to identify a particular key value, and then I process the data accordingly.

In the case of a single key with a string value (such as Name), I merely assign the value in data to the appropriate module level variable. In the case of a simple numeric value (such as Rotation), I call a routine called SetNumber, which verifies that the value is numeric before saving it in the appropriate module level variable.

The code to handle multilevel keys, such as Viewpoint\x, is a bit more complex, which is why I placed it in a separate subroutine. The keys for the filenames associated with a store like Store\1 or other mall object have a numeric index, which indicates their relative placement in the mall. These indexes are specified as the second key in the data file. The easiest way to store this information is in a string array.

PART

I

CH

5

Tip

When does CameraPoint match camerapoint?

One of the problems with parsing data from an input file is trying to ensure that your program checks for the proper form of the identifier. By default, Visual Basic will return `False` if you compare `CameraPoint` and `camerapoint`. Most programmers avoid this problem by converting both strings to lowercase before comparing them. However, if you include `Option Compare Text` at the start of your module, strings will be compared in a case-insensitive manner and there is no need to convert to lowercase.

In Listing 5.7, I pass the string array which will hold the final value, along with the first two key values and the data value. Although the first key value isn't really necessary, if there is an error in the conversion process, having the complete key is useful when outputting debug information.

LISTING 5.7   GAME.SETFILENAME

```
Private Sub SetFilename(fn() As String, Key1 As String, _
   Key2 As String, Data As String)

Dim i As Long

If IsNumeric(Key2) Then
   i = CLng(Key2)

   If i > UBound(fn) Then
      ReDim Preserve fn(i)

   End If

   fn(i) = Data

Else
   GameDebugger.WriteLine "Illegal filename key value: " & _
      Key1 & "/" & Key2 & " = " & Data

End If

End Sub
```

The `SetFilename` routine is relatively straightforward. I begin by verifying that the second key value containing the index of the object is numeric and if so I will save it to the appropriate index value. To make sure that I don't have a subscript error, I check the index against the upper bound of the array and use the `ReDim` statement with the `Preserve` option to ensure that the upper bound of the array is as large as the index value.

Caution

Minimal error checking

Note that I don't bother to see if there is already data at that position in the array. Although I don't mind taking the time to ensure that a runtime error doesn't occur by verifying that the string key has a numeric value, it is really up to the programmer to ensure that the proper data is loaded. You should treat the Swim Mall files as an extension of the application itself and treat errors in the Swim Mall files just like you would treat errors in the program.

READING DATA USING THE SwimFile CLASS

The SwimFile class is designed to simplify reading files formatted using the key/data format. One of the problems with dealing with a text file is finding a way to skip all of the crud like blank lines and comments that inevitably creep in. By isolating all of the code to deal with these problems in this class, I don't have to deal with them throughout the code.

SwimFile uses the FileSystemObject from the Microsoft Scripting Runtime library for I/O rather than traditional Visual Basic file I/O statements, because I like the object-oriented approach. There are two main methods in this class that I used in the Game class, OpenInFile, which opens the Swim Mall File, and the GetData method, which returns the next block of data.

I also expose the AtEndOfStream property through a custom property class that allows the code using this class to determine when there is no more data to be processed. I also provide a CloseFile method, which calls the text stream's Close method.

The OpenInFile method opens the specified file as an input file and verifies that the file is a Swim Mall file by verifying that the first key in the file contains the word type (see Listing 5.8). It starts by declaring some local variables and specifying On Error Resume Next because I want to handle my own error checking.

LISTING 5.8   SWIMFILE.OPENINFILE

```
Public Function OpenInFile(FileName As String) As Long

Dim k1 As String
Dim k2 As String
Dim k3 As String
Dim d As String

On Error Resume Next

Set txt = fso.OpenTextFile(FileName, ForReading, _
     False, TristateUseDefault)
If Err.Number = 0 Then
   GetData k1, k2, k3, d
   If LCase(k1) <> "type" Then
      OpenInFile = -1

   Else
```

LISTING 5.8   CONTINUED

```
        FileType = d
        OpenInFile = 0

   End If

Else
   OpenInFile = Err.Number

End If

End Function
```

The work really begins when I try to open the file for reading as a text stream object
(TextStream). If I don't have an error, I'll use the GetData routine to extract the first line
from the file. If the first key value isn't type, I'll return an error, otherwise I'll save the key's
data into a Public module level variable called FileType so that any program that uses this
class can determine the file type.

In Listing 5.9, I assume that the txt object contains a value text stream and use the ReadLine
method to return the next line from the file. Note that I use the Trim function to ensure that
the first non-blank character is in the first position in the string.

LISTING 5.9   SWIMFILE.GETDATA

```
Sub GetData(Key1 As String, Key2 As String, _
   Key3 As String, Data As String)

Dim l As String
Dim k() As String

l = Trim(txt.ReadLine)
Do While ((Left(l, 1) = "'") Or Len(l) = 0) And _
      Not txt.AtEndOfStream
   l = Trim(txt.ReadLine)

Loop

If Len(l) > 0 Then
   k = Split(l, "=", 2)

   If UBound(k) > 0 Then
      Data = Trim(k(1))

   End If

   If UBound(k) > 0 Then
      k = Split(k(0), "\")

   End If

   If UBound(k) > 1 Then
```

LISTING 5.9   CONTINUED

```
        Key3 = Trim(k(2))

    End If

    If UBound(k) > 0 Then
        Key2 = Trim(k(1))

    End If

    Key1 = Trim(k(0))
Else
    Key1 = "SwimFile"
    Key2 = "Error"
    Data = "Unexpected end of file found!"

End If

End Sub
```

Notice the tight loop that will discard blank lines and lines that begin with a single apostrophe ('). This allows you to include comments in your file. Unlike Visual Basic however, only leading apostrophes are permitted. If the apostrophe appears anywhere after the first character, it is treated as part of the key or the data value.

After I have a line of data, I verify that the discard empty lines loop didn't end early by checking the length of the input string. If the length is zero, I'll return an error message in the keys and data arguments. Otherwise, I'll use the Split function to break the input string into a maximum two pieces. The first piece will hold the key or keys from the line, while the second piece if present will hold the value associated with the keys. Each piece will be in a separate element of the k array. So if UBound of k is 1, I have a piece of data to return in the argument Data.

Next, I Split the first element of k into the individual keys associated with this line of text. Then it is merely a matter of examining the upper bound of k to see if the key is present and get its value.

LOADING MALL AND STORE INFORMATION

At the end of the LoadGame routine, I call the PostGameLoadProcessing after I have finished reading the SwimMall.SMG file. This routine creates all of the objects that hold the information about the mall and overrides the default values from the initialization files with those values found in the saved game file (see Listing 5.10).

The first step is to create the mall object and use the mall object's LoadMall method to load the information for the mall. Note that I have to pass along the GameDebugger object, so I can write debug information. This method will create all of the objects for the stores and other items in the mall.

PART

I

CH

5

LISTING 5.10   GAME.POSTGAMELOADPROCESSING

```
Private Sub PostGameLoadProcessing()

Dim i As Integer

If Len(xMallFileName) > 0 Then
    Set MallObj = New Mall
    Set MallObj.DebugObject = GameDebugger
    MallObj.LoadMall App.Path & "\malls\" & xMallFileName

End If

For i = 1 To UBound(AnchorFiles)
    If Len(AnchorFiles(i)) > 0 Then
        MallObj.Anchors(i).LoadAnchor App.Path & _
            "\Anchors\" & AnchorFiles(i)

    End If

Next i

For i = 1 To UBound(FoodFiles)
    If Len(FoodFiles(i)) > 0 Then
        MallObj.Foods(i).LoadFood App.Path & _
            "\Foods\" & FoodFiles(i)

    End If

Next i

For i = 1 To UBound(MallObjectFiles)
    If Len(MallObjectFiles(i)) > 0 Then
        MallObj.MallObjects(i).LoadMallObject App.Path & _
            "\Objects\" & MallObjectFiles(i)

    End If

Next i

For i = 1 To UBound(StoreFiles)
    If Len(StoreFiles(i)) > 0 Then
        MallObj.Stores(i).LoadStore App.Path & _
            "\Stores\" & StoreFiles(i)

    End If

Next i

End Sub
```

After the LoadMall method has finished, I loop through all of the filenames loaded from the saved game file and use the appropriate load routine to override any existing values in these objects with new values from the new files.

CREATING STORES AND OTHER MALL ITEMS

The `LoadMall` method is very similar to the `LoadGame` method. It uses the `SwimFile` object to load the information in the mall's .SMM file. `LoadMall` calls its own version of `SetData`, which is shown in Listing 5.11. Like the other `SetData` routine, this one is essentially one really large `Select` statement.

LISTING 5.11   MALL.SETDATA

```
Private Sub SetData(Key1 As String, Key2 As String, _
   Key3 As String, Data As String)

Dim an As Anchor
Dim fd As Food
Dim mo As MallObject
Dim st As Store
Dim k As String

Select Case Key1
   Case "name"
      xName = Data

   Case "dxfilename"
      xdxFileName = Data

   Case "anchor"
      k = Key1 & "\" & Key2

      If AnchorsObj(k) Is Nothing Then
         Set an = New Anchor
         an.Name = k
         Set an.DebugObject = MallDebugger
         AnchorsObj.Add an

      End If

      Select Case Key3
         Case "Depth"
            AnchorsObj(k).Depth = CSng(Data)
         Case "Rotation"
            AnchorsObj(k).Rotation = CSng(Data) / 180 * pi
         Case "Width"
            AnchorsObj(k).Width = CSng(Data)
         Case "X"
            AnchorsObj(k).X = CSng(Data)
         Case "Y"
            AnchorsObj(k).Y = CSng(Data)
         Case "Z"
            AnchorsObj(k).Z = CSng(Data)
         Case Else
            MallDebugger.WriteLine "Unknown anchor value: " _
               & Key2 & "\" & Key3 & " = " & Data

      End Select
```

PART

I

CH

5

LISTING 5.11   CONTINUED

```
    Case "food"
       k = Key1 & "\" & Key2

       If FoodsObj.Item(k) Is Nothing Then
          Set fd = New Food
          fd.Name = k
          Set fd.DebugObject = MallDebugger
          FoodsObj.Add fd

       End If

       Select Case Key3
          Case "Depth"
             FoodsObj(k).Depth = CSng(Data)
          Case "Rotation"
             FoodsObj(k).Rotation = CSng(Data) / 180 * pi
          Case "Width"
             FoodsObj(k).Width = CSng(Data)
          Case "X"
             FoodsObj(k).X = CSng(Data)
          Case "Y"
             FoodsObj(k).Y = CSng(Data)
          Case "Z"
             FoodsObj(k).Z = CSng(Data)
          Case Else
             MallDebugger.WriteLine "Unknown food value: " _
                & Key2 & "\" & Key3 & " = " & Data

       End Select

    Case "object"
       k = Key1 & "\" & Key2

       If MallObj(k) Is Nothing Then
          Set st = New MallObject
          mo.Name = k
          Set mo.DebugObject = MallDebugger
          MallObj.Add mo

       End If

       Select Case Key3
          Case "Depth"
             MallObj(k).Depth = CSng(Data)
          Case "Rotation"
             MallObj(k).Rotation = CSng(Data) / 180 * pi
          Case "Width"
             MallObj(k).Width = CSng(Data)
          Case "X"
             MallObj(k).X = CSng(Data)
          Case "Y"
             MallObj(k).Y = CSng(Data)
          Case "Z"
             MallObj(k).Z = CSng(Data)
```

LISTING 5.11   CONTINUED

```
        Case Else
            MallDebugger.WriteLine "Unknown mall object value: " _
                & Key2 & "\" & Key3 & " = " & Data

        End Select

    Case "store"
        k = Key1 & "\" & Key2

        If StoresObj(k) Is Nothing Then
            Set st = New Store
            st.Name = k
            Set st.DebugObject = MallDebugger
            StoresObj.Add st

        End If

        Select Case Key3
            Case "Depth"
                StoresObj(k).Depth = CSng(Data)
            Case "Rotation"
                StoresObj(k).Rotation = CSng(Data) / 180 * pi
            Case "Width"
                StoresObj(k).Width = CSng(Data)
            Case "X"
                StoresObj(k).X = CSng(Data)
            Case "Y"
                StoresObj(k).Y = CSng(Data)
            Case "Z"
                StoresObj(k).Z = CSng(Data)
            Case Else
                MallDebugger.WriteLine "Unknown store value: " _
                    & Key2 & "\" & Key3 & " = " & Data

        End Select

    Case Else
        MallDebugger.WriteLine "Unknown key value: " & _
            Key1 & "\" & Key2 & "\" & Key3 & " = " & Data

End Select

End Sub
```

Although this listing is long, notice that the Case clauses associated with each four types of mall objects (anchors, foods, mall objects, and stores) are nearly identical. They differ only in terms of the objects used to hold the information. Because of this, I'm only going to discuss how to load the anchor's information.

When I begin processing an anchor, I create a temporary key value that combines the first two keys from the file. This value will be used in multiple places in this block of code, so this will save a little code as well as saving a little typing. As a bonus, it also helps the code to fit on a single line in the book.

Next, I check the AnchorsObj collection to see if there is a member in the collection with a Name property with a value contained in k. If the collection returns Nothing, I need to create a new Anchor object and add it to the collection before I can process any of its properties. Before I add the new Anchor property to the collection, I set its Name property to k and create an object reference to the Debugger object used throughout this program. Then I can use the AnchorObj collection's Add method to add the newly created object to the collection.

After the object exists, I can process the value associated with Key3 using yet another Select statement. This one is much simpler, however, and simply assigns the value to the appropriate property. The only tricky part here is that internally DirectX uses radians to measure angles, whereas trueSpace uses degrees. Because most people think in terms of degrees, I decided to leave the value in the initialization file in degrees. Thus I have to convert the value to radians by dividing it by 180 and multiplying it by pi.

ANCHOR PROPERTIES

At this point, the Anchor object is little more than a collection of standard properties, plus a very simple version of the same LoadData and SetData routines that initialize selected values from the specified .SMS file in the Anchors directory.

Rather than go into detail about the code, I'll just run through the key properties that are stored in the object (see Listing 5.12). With the exception of the Location property, all of the properties are simple Public variables. The Depth, Height, and Width properties describe the size of the store. X, Y, and Z describe the location of the center of the store, while Rotation describes how to turn the store so that the front of the store faces the mall's hallway. The DXFilename contains the name of the DirectX .X file that contains the 3D object as drawn in trueSpace. Name contains the name of the store's location in the mall and is generally written as Anchor\1.

LISTING 5.12 ANCHOR MODULE LEVEL DECLARATIONS

```
Private AnchorDebugger As Debugger
Private xLocation As D3DVECTOR

Public Depth As Single
Public DXFilename As String
Public Filename As String
Public Height As Single
Public Name As String
Public Rotation As Single
Public Width As Single
Public X As Single
Public Y As Single
Public Z As Single
```

MANAGING COLLECTIONS OF ANCHORS

One of the most useful Visual Basic tricks I've learned over the years was how to build my own collection of objects that will work with the For Each statement. The Anchors, Foods, MallObjects, and Stores collections use this technique.

The actual data for the collections are stored in a `Collection` object. The class uses five methods: `Count`, `Remove`, `Item`, `Add`, and `NewEnum`. The count method simply returns the `Count` property from the `Collection` object. The `Add` method simply calls `Collection.Add`, while the `Remove` method calls `Collection.Remove`. This leaves only the `Item` and `NewEnum` methods to be looked at closely.

The `Item` method is tricky for two reasons. First, I've marked this method as the default method for the object. This means that if you access the `Anchors` object without explicitly specifying a method, the `Item` method will be assumed.

To mark a method as default, you need to modify its procedure attributes. Select Tools, Procedure Attributes from the main menu to display the Procedure Attributes dialog box. Choose the Item routine in the drop-down box labeled Name and click the Advanced button to see all the options available (see Figure 5.2). Choose `(Default)` for the `Procedure ID` to make this method the default method for the class.

Figure 5.2
Setting the procedure attribute to Default for the `Item` method.

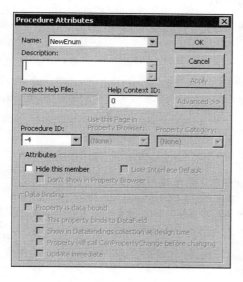

The other trick I use is to suppress error checking within the routine (see Listing 5.13). If an error occurs, I'll return Nothing to the calling program rather than generating a run-time error. This is a quick way to see if the object exists in the collection without having to build a special search method.

LISTING 5.13   ANCHORS.ITEM

```
Public Function Item(Key As Variant) As Anchor

On Error Resume Next

Set Item = xAnchors.Item(Key)
```

LISTING 5.13   CONTINUED

```
If Err.Number <> 0 Then
    Set Item = Nothing

End If

End Function
```

The real trick to making your own collection work properly is the `NewEnum` method. This method must be defined as shown in Listing 5.14. Then you must use the Procedure Attributes tool to specify a value of `-4` for the Procedure attribute. Without this magic number, the `For Each` statement can't be used with this collection.

LISTING 5.14   ANCHORS.ITEM

```
Public Function NewEnum() As IUnknown

Set NewEnum = xAnchors.[_NewEnum]

End Function
```

The `NewEnum` method returns the next object in the collection. It simply calls an undocumented method in the `Collections` object, that returns the next object in `Collections` object. So in this case, I merely call the `NewEnum` method in the `xAnchors` object to get the next object managed by the `Anchors` class.

> **Note**
>
> **I'm lazy; you don't have to be**
>
> Most Visual Basic programmers don't know about the Procedure Attributes tool. You can specify a short description for the method that will show up in the object browser by entering a value in the Description box. If you put a check mark in the Hide This Member check box, you can prevent the member from being seen in the object browser. If you're into database programming, you can use this tool to create data-bound properties.

FINAL THOUGHTS

This chapter featured a lot of complex code. Some of it will be used in the next chapter, when I discuss how to load the 3D graphics created in trueSpace and display them on your screen. However, I could have written a much simpler initialization tool to do that.

The reason I created such a complex process is that eventually it will be needed to support the simulation part of the game. Because the player can choose from a collection of stores and other mall objects, there is a lot of information that will be associated with each individual item that need not be loaded unless the player wants to use the item.

DISPLAYING 3D GRAPHICS

In this chapter

After creating the 3D graphics for the shopping mall and some stores and loading a bunch of initialization files, it's time to jump back into DirectX so that you can display them on the screen.

INITIALIZING GRAPHICS INFORMATION

After the mall has been loaded into memory, it's time to load the graphics into memory using the initialization information loaded into the objects discussed in Chapter 5, "Loading Mall Information." These objects contain the filenames of the 3D objects that need to be displayed, along with their relative location in the world.

Because I want to keep the graphics isolated from the rest of the game, I use a different set of objects to store the actual objects that will be drawn on the screen. Using the DXGraphics class from Chapter 2, "Introducing DirectX," I've defined six new classes that will hold the actual graphics data (see Figure 6.1).

Figure 6.1
Graphics information is stored in a collection of Visual Basic classes.

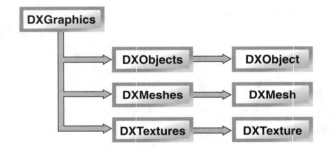

The mall is broken into a set of graphics objects designed independently using a 3D modeling tool like trueSpace. These graphics objects include the mall itself, the stores, food court vendors, and anything else that will be displayed inside the mall. Each of the graphics objects are stored in a Visual Basic class called DXObject.

DXObject contains all the information needed to display the graphics object on the screen. This includes the information from the DirectX .x file, also known as a *mesh*, plus the textures that will be displayed on the meshes. To minimize the resources needed, the meshes and textures are loaded only once and stored in their own object classes. This allows you to create a single object that can be used in multiple places in the mall, while avoiding a lot of overhead to load each new copy individually.

Meshes are stored in the DXMesh class, along with the materials and filenames associated with the textures that are displayed on each face of the mesh. The DXMeshes collection is similar to the collection classes discussed in Chapter 5 (Anchors, Foods, MallObjects, and Stores) and exists solely to manage the set of meshes.

Like meshes, each individual texture is stored in its own DXTexture object and the collection of textures are contained in the DXTextures object. To retrieve a texture, you just need to know the filename of the texture. This imposes a slight limitation on the way you design your graphics. Because the filename must be unique within the collection, you can't create two textures that are stored in different directories with the same name, unless they hold the same image.

For example, you can't use a texture called `BlueStripes.BMP` that has vertical stripes in the `Stores` directory and another texture called `BlueStripes.BMP` that has diagonal strips in the `Anchors` directory. The first copy loaded will be used, while the second copy will be assumed to be a duplicate of the first copy.

LOADING YOUR MALL

Displaying DirectX graphics has two distinct phases. First the graphics must be loaded into memory and then the graphics must be rendered to the screen. Loading the graphics is a relatively complex process, yet when boiled down to its essential elements, it really isn't all that bad.

INITIALIZING DIRECTX

In `InitGame`, the graphics subsystem was initialized by calling `InitGraphics` (see Listing 6.1). `InitGraphics` is responsible for two things. First, it must create a new instance of the `DXGraphics` class and call the `InitDX` method to initialize the Direct3D device. Second, it must load the `.X` files from the initialization information that we just loaded.

LISTING 6.1 FORM1.INITGRAPHICS

```
Function InitGraphics() As Long

Dim Result As Long
Dim a As Anchor
Dim f As Food
Dim m As MallObject
Dim s As Store

Set dx = New DXGraphics
Set dx.DebugObject = GameDebugger

dx.Windowed = True
dx.hWnd = Picture1.hWnd
dx.ShowFrameRate = True
dx.Height = Picture1.Height / Screen.TwipsPerPixelY
dx.Width = Picture1.Width / Screen.TwipsPerPixelX
dx.DefaultCameraPoint = GameObj.CameraPoint
dx.DefaultViewpoint = GameObj.Viewpoint
dx.DefaultRotation = GameObj.Rotation

Result = dx.InitDX
If Result <> 0 Then
   GameDebugger.WriteLong "dxInit failed", Result
```

LISTING 6.1   CONTINUED

```
    Unload Me

End If

With GameObj.Mall
    dx.LoadMeshFromDisk App.Path & "\Malls", _
        .DXFilename, .Location, .Rotation, DXObjectMall

End With

For Each a In GameObj.Mall.Anchors
    dx.LoadMeshFromDisk App.Path & "\Anchors", _
        a.DXFilename, a.Location, a.Rotation, dxobjectanchor

Next a

For Each f In GameObj.Mall.Foods
    dx.LoadMeshFromDisk App.Path & "\Foods", _
        f.DXFilename, f.Location, f.Rotation, dxobjectfood

Next f

For Each m In GameObj.Mall.MallObjects
    dx.LoadMeshFromDisk App.Path & "\Objects", _
        m.DXFilename, m.Location, m.Rotation, dxobjectfood

Next m

For Each s In GameObj.Mall.Stores
    dx.LoadMeshFromDisk App.Path & "\Stores", _
        s.DXFilename, s.Location, s.Rotation, dxobjectstore

Next s

End Function
```

The InitGraphics routine begins by creating a new DXGraphics object, setting various properties, and calling the InitDX method from the DXGraphics class. Unlike the version of this routine in Chapter 2, there is now a Windowed property that controls whether the program is displayed in a window (True) or in full screen mode (False).

Note

Don't use full screen mode

Although the version of DXGraphics supports full screen mode, I don't recommend using it because the only user interface controls exist outside of the DirectX managed display area, which leaves you no way to control the program.

You can now include values for Viewpoint, CameraPoint, and Rotation, which are loaded from the saved game file. Also you can specify the Height and Width of the screen in pixels, which is very important for determining the perspective displayed on the screen in a resizable window and also for properly determining the size of a full screen display.

Assuming that DirectX was initialized properly with the call to InitDX, the individual DirectX .x files can be loaded. Use a For Each loop that runs through the collection of individual items in the mall and call the LoadMeshFromDisk method to load the 3D object into memory.

When the object is loaded into memory, there are three items of information beyond the filename that are needed to display the object properly. The first is the object's location within the mall. This includes the object's X and Z properties, how to rotate the object from its default orientation to the way it must be placed in the mall, and the type of mall object.

Note

Why Z?

One issue you will encounter when creating objects in trueSpace and displaying them with DirectX is that the Y- and Z-axes are swapped. In trueSpace the Z-axis points straight up, whereas in DirectX the Y-axis points straight up. This means that you need to swap the Y and Z coordinates when you translate a coordinate value from trueSpace to DirectX.

LOADING A 3D OBJECT INTO MEMORY

The LoadMeshFromDisk method (see Listing 6.2) loads a 3D object created with trueSpace into memory so that it can be displayed later. This routine takes a number of parameters, including the name of the mesh, the location in the 3D world space where the mesh will be displayed, how the mesh needs to be rotated to fit into the shopping mall, and the type of object that is being displayed. All of this information will be saved into a DXObject and added to the collection of DXObjects maintained by the DXGraphics object.

LISTING 6.2   DXGRAPHICS.LOADMESHFROMDISK

```
Public Function LoadMeshFromDisk(MeshPath As String, _
    MeshFile As String, Location As D3DVECTOR, _
    Rotation As Single, Typ As DXObjectTypes) As Long

Dim mtrlbuffer As D3DXBuffer
Dim i As Long
Dim fname As String
Dim o As DXObject
Dim m As DXMesh
Dim t As DXTexture
Dim nMaterials As Long
Dim MeshMat As D3DMATERIAL8

On Error Resume Next

If Len(MeshFile) = 0 Then
    LoadMeshFromDisk = 0
```

Listing 6.2 Continued

```
    Exit Function

End If

fname = MeshPath & "\" & MeshFile

DXDebugger.WriteLine "Loading mesh: " & fname
Set o = New DXObject
o.Name = MeshFile
o.mType = TexturedMesh
o.oType = Typ
o.Location = Location
o.Rotation = Rotation
o.MeshFilename = MeshFile

If DXmshs(MeshFile) Is Nothing Then
    Set m = New DXMesh
    Set m.Mesh = d3dx.LoadMeshFromX(fname, _
        D3DXMESH_MANAGED, d3dDevice, Nothing, _
        mtrlbuffer, nMaterials)
    If m.Mesh Is Nothing Then
        DXDebugger.WriteDXErr "Can't load mesh", Err
        LoadMeshFromDisk = Err.Number
        Exit Function

    End If

    m.Name = MeshFile
    m.Materials = nMaterials
    For i = 0 To nMaterials - 1
        d3dx.BufferGetMaterial mtrlbuffer, i, MeshMat
        MeshMat.Ambient = MeshMat.diffuse
        m.MeshMaterials(i) = MeshMat
        fname = d3dx.BufferGetTextureName(mtrlbuffer, i)
        m.MeshTextures(i) = fname

        If Len(fname) > 0 Then
            If DXtexs(fname) Is Nothing Then
                Set t = New DXTexture
                Set t.Texture = d3dx.CreateTextureFromFile(_
                    d3dDevice, MeshPath & "\" & fname)
                t.Name = fname

                DXtexs.Add t

            End If

        End If

    Next i

    DXmshs.Add m

End If
```

LISTING 6.2 CONTINUED

```
DXobs.Add o

LoadMeshFromDisk = 0

End Function
```

The first thing to do is verify the filename isn't blank. If it is, exit the routine without attempting to load anything. Then echo the filename to the Debug.LOG file. Next construct a complete filename by appending MeshFile and MeshPath together and create a new instance of the DXObject to hold the new mesh. In the new instance of DXObject, set its properties to the values associated with this particular 3D object.

Next, pass the mesh's filename to the DXmshs object to see if you need to load the mesh file from disk. Because the default method for this class is the Item method, you need not specify it to use it. Thus if DXmshs(MeshFile) returns Nothing, you know that you have to load the mesh. If the mesh is already loaded, you can just add the new DXObject to the DXObjects collection and return to the calling program.

To load the mesh, create a new instance of the DXMesh object. Then use the LoadMeshFromX to load the .X file into memory. This method takes several parameters beside the name of the file to be loaded. The D3DXMESH_MANAGED means that the data will be loaded into Direct3D managed memory, which will help improve overall performance. The mtrlbuffer and the nMaterials contain information about how each face in the mesh will be displayed.

> **Tip**
>
> **It didn't work right!**
>
> The most common error when loading an .x file is trying to load a non-existent file. So if you don't see the 3D object displayed on screen, the first place you should check is the Debug.LOG file. As each mesh is loaded, the filename is added to the log file and if there is a problem, the error information should be written immediately afterwards.

After the mesh has been loaded, you need to extract some information from the material buffer, mtrlbuffer. Specifically, you need to get the texture filename using the BufferGetTextureName method and the lighting information using the BufferGetMaterial method. The mtrlbuffer contains an array of values, so you have to supply an index to identify which value you want.

After getting the lighting information, you want to change the Ambient property to the same value as diffuse. This helps to ensure that the colors show up properly using Ambient lighting. Then you can save this information into the MeshMaterials property in the DXMesh object.

PART
I

CH
6

In the same loop, you can also get the filename associated with the texture. Then you can check in textures collection (DXtexs) to see if you've already loaded the texture. If not, create a new instance of the DXTexture object and use the CreateTextureFromFile method to get the texture. Then You can then add the texture to the DXTextures object and repeat the process until all of the information in mtrlbuffer has been processed.

Finally, add the DXObject to the DXObjects collection, set a return value of zero to indicate that everything worked fine, and exit the method.

Note

It works, but it's not fast

Although this technique works it will take a lot of time to initially process all the files associated with the mall. There are many techniques that you can use to speed up this process, but you'll always have some sort of delay when loading the graphics. This is why most games display some sort of splash screen or movie at the start of the game. This helps to distract users while a lot of work is being done in the background.

DISPLAYING GRAPHIC INFORMATION

The process of displaying Direct3D graphics is relatively simple in theory. First you define your environment using three matrixes—world, view, and projection. Second, you clear the display and add each of your 3D objects to the world. Third, you display your graphics. Although this process sounds simple, it can be extremely messy in practice.

The *world matrix* describes where the origin of your world is located. This is usually the simplest of the three matrixes—at least in terms of initialization. However, this value will change as you add new objects to your world.

The *view matrix* describes the location of the camera that looks at your world. The camera is similar to the eye used by trueSpace, but unlike trueSpace, where the location of the eye is fixed and you move the world around to view it, the camera represents a point in 3D space, while the viewpoint represents the particular place in 3D space the camera is looking at.

The *projection matrix* describes how your world's coordinates are mapped to screen coordinates. This process controls whether your world will be viewed with either a telescopic or wide angle effect or whether objects in your world will be displayed as tall and skinny or short and fat. These values represent the extremes of a range of choices. Making the proper ones will make your game far more interesting.

You also have to worry about the placement of lights. Remember the red stars in trueSpace that you had to move occasionally so that you could better see what you were doing? They have the same effect in DirectX. In addition to having independent lights, you can always use ambient lighting so that all sides of your 3D objects are illuminated equally. While this makes your objects more visible, it also means that they will lose some of their 3D effect, since the object will no longer have a light and dark side.

RENDERING YOUR MALL

Now that all of the information has been loaded into the mall, you need to display it. This means that you need to take the graphics information you loaded earlier with the `LoadMeshFromDisk` method and display it on the screen. In addition, you also need to address how to move the viewpoint around on the screen and control other aspects of managing your game's display.

THE MAIN LOOP

The `PlayGame` routine (see Listing 6.3) is the main processing loop in this program. This loop simply calls the `Render` method from the `DXGraphics` class and then calls the `DoEvents` routine to allow Windows to perform any other processing in your system. Without the call to `DoEvents`, your game may prevent any other program from running, which could eventually lead to crashing your computer system.

LISTING 6.3   FORM1.PLAYGAME

```
Sub PlayGame()

Do While GameActive
   dx.Render
   DoEvents

Loop

End Sub
```

RENDERING DIRECT3D GRAPHICS

The `Render` method is another routine that looks rather nasty at first glance (see Listing 6.4). In practice, however, it's really not all that bad. The routine begins by declaring a bunch of temporary variables and disabling error checking, meaning that it's up to the programmer to check for possible errors.

LISTING 6.4   DXGRAPHICS.RENDER

```
Public Function Render() As Long

On Error Resume Next

Dim matTemp As D3DMATRIX
Dim matTrans As D3DMATRIX
Dim vecTemp As D3DVECTOR
Dim vp As D3DVIEWPORT8
Dim mm As D3DMATERIAL8
Dim o As DXObject
Dim i As Long

D3DXMatrixIdentity matWorld
```

PART

I

CH

6

LISTING 6.4   CONTINUED

```
d3dDevice.SetTransform D3DTS_WORLD, matWorld

D3DXMatrixIdentity matView
D3DXMatrixRotationY matView, Rotation
D3DXMatrixLookAtLH matTemp, CameraPoint, _
    Viewpoint, vec3(0, 1, 0)
D3DXMatrixMultiply matView, matView, matTemp
d3dDevice.SetTransform D3DTS_VIEW, matView

D3DXMatrixPerspectiveFovLH matProj, pi / 4, _
    Height / Width, 0.1, 100
d3dDevice.SetTransform D3DTS_PROJECTION, matProj

D3DXVec3Subtract vecTemp, CameraPoint, Viewpoint
d3dDevice.GetViewport vp
D3DXVec3Unproject vecLight, vecTemp, vp, matProj, _
    matView, matWorld
D3DXVec3Scale vecLight, vecLight, -1
d3dLight.Direction = vecLight
d3dDevice.SetLight 0, d3dLight
d3dDevice.LightEnable 0, 1

d3dDevice.Clear 0, ByVal 0, D3DCLEAR_TARGET Or _
    D3DCLEAR_ZBUFFER, &H404040, 1#, 0

d3dDevice.BeginScene

For Each o In DXobs
    D3DXMatrixIdentity matTemp
    D3DXMatrixRotationY matTemp, o.Rotation
    D3DXMatrixTranslation matTrans, -o.Location.X, _
        -o.Location.Y, -o.Location.Z
    D3DXMatrixMultiply matTemp, matTemp, matTrans
    d3dDevice.SetTransform D3DTS_WORLD, matTemp

    If o.mType = SimpleMesh Then
       DXmshs(o.Name).Mesh.DrawSubset 0

    ElseIf o.mType = TexturedMesh Then
       With DXmshs(o.MeshFilename)
          For i = 0 To .Materials - 1
             d3dDevice.SetMaterial .MeshMaterials(i)
             d3dDevice.SetTexture 0, _
                DXtexs(.MeshTextures(i)).Texture
             .Mesh.DrawSubset i

          Next i
       End With

    ElseIf o.mType = SelectedMesh Then
       With DXmshs(o.MeshFilename)
          For i = 0 To .Materials - 1
             mm.Ambient.a = 1
             mm.Ambient.r = 1
             mm.Ambient.b = 0.5
```

LISTING 6.4   CONTINUED

```
                mm.Ambient.g = 0.5
                mm.diffuse = mm.Ambient
                d3dDevice.SetMaterial mm
                d3dDevice.SetTexture 0, _
                   DXtexs(.MeshTextures(i)).Texture
                .Mesh.DrawSubset i

         Next i

      End With

   End If

Next o

If ShowFrameRate Then
   DrawFrameRate
   DrawViewPoint

End If

d3dDevice.EndScene

Err.Clear
d3dDevice.Present ByVal 0, ByVal 0, 0, ByVal 0
If Err.Number <> 0 Then
   Render = ResetDX

End If

End Function
```

DEFINING TRANSFORMS

The first real step in displaying the graphics is to define an initial world matrix. I use the D3DXMatrixIdentity routine to define an identity matrix and use the SetTransform method to assign this value to the world matrix. This will set the origin to (0, 0, 0), which is always a good place to start.

Setting the view is somewhat more complex. Start out by assigning the view to the identity matrix. Then use the value of the Rotation to determine how to turn the view around on the Y-axis. Rather than go through the complex mathematics involved to determine how to rotate the view, simply use the D3DXMatrixRotationY routine to spin the view matrix around. Remember that rotation values are specified in radians, not degrees.

PART
I

CH
6

Tip

A full circle with two pi

A full circle has 360 degrees, or 2 pi radians. So to convert a value in degrees to radians, simply multiply the value by pi/180. To convert a value in radians to degrees, simply multiply by 180/pi.

Next create a temporary matrix using the `D3DXMatrixLookatLH` routine that uses the current `CameraPoint` and `Viewpoint` values with a special vector that indicates which axis is pointing up `vec3(0, 1, 0)`, which in this case is the Y-axis. Then you can use the `D3DXMatrixMultiply` function to multiple these matrixes together to create the final matrix that describes the current view.

You can create the projection matrix by using the `D3DXMatrixPerspectiveFovLH` routine. This creates a matrix containing the appropriate perspective, including the proper field of view. The field of view is typically specified as a value of pi divided by some value. `Pi/4` gives a normal view, which is equivalent to a 50mm lens on a 35mm camera. Smaller values such as `pi/x`, where x is greater than 4, will give you a telescopic effect, as you might experience with a 200mm or larger camera lens. Larger values such as `pi/x` where x is less than 4 give you a wide angle lens effect. Note that any value other than `pi/4` will distort your 3D object, so use them with care.

The `Height/Width` ratio here helps to compensate for a display that is not square. If you set this parameter to 1 and your display's width is greater than its height, your image will be stretched horizontally, making the objects appear short and fat. If your display window is taller than wider, the images would appear as tall and skinny. By using the proper ratio here, DirectX can compensate and show your objects in the way you designed them.

The last two parameters, `.1` and `100`, instruct DirectX where to clip your view of the scene. Anything closer to the camera than `.1` will not be shown, and anything farther away than `100` will not be shown.

POSITIONING THE LIGHT

Positioning the light is a little bit complicated because it relies on a series of vector and matrix mathematical functions to compute the location of the light. Start by subtracting the `CameraPoint` vector from the `Viewpoint` vector and saving it into a temporary vector. Then use the `D3DXVec3Unproject` routine to convert this temporary vector into a vector that describes where the light should be placed by using the view transform that was set earlier.

Then you can use this value to set where the light should be pointing by setting the `Direction` property of a light object. Next, use the `SetLight` method to add this light to the world space as light `0` and use the `LightEnable` method to turn it on.

By adding the light so that it is shining away from the camera's location, it will ensure that whatever the player is looking at will be properly illuminated.

DISPLAYING THE SCENE

Based on the way I've initialized the Direct3DDevice, there are two buffers containing your graphics. The one buffer is actively being displayed, while the second buffer is available to be loaded with data to be displayed. After you've loaded all of your objects into the second buffer, you can quickly swap them. Then the buffer you just loaded will become the active display buffer, while the buffer was the active display buffer is available for your program to update with new data to be displayed on the screen.

The display process begins with a call to the Direct3Ddevice's Clear method. This statement erases the information that existed previously in the buffer. If you omit this step, the old information will remain in the display. One of the useful functions in this display is the capability to set the background to a specific color. Although I use dark gray (&H404040), you can specify any color value you want.

Tip

What color is my background?

Colors can be specified as an RGB value, where R is red, G is green, and B is blue. Each value can range from 0 to 255 decimal or 00 to FF in hex. The way I usually determine a color is to choose a color in Photoshop using either the color swatches tool or the color sliders. Then I just translate the values from each color field into hex and insert them into the color constant.

The second step in this process is to call the BeginScene method. This step merely marks the beginning of your local processing. Note that each call to BeginScene must have a corresponding call to EndScene or your program will generate an error.

After you have started your scene, you can add your 3D objects to the buffer. In this case use a For Each statement to iterate through the collection of DXObject values in the Dxobs collection.

To display an object, you must adjust the origin of the world. This is necessary because each of the objects was created with an origin of (0, 0, 0) in 3D space. By moving the origin of the world to a new location, the object can be correctly drawn. I like to think of this as moving the world to suit the object rather than moving the object to suit the world.

Moving the world's origin involves nothing more than computing a new world origin using the same basic technique used to create the view. First create an identity matrix and use the D3DXMatrixRotation routine to spin the origin into the proper location based on the rotation value supplied in the initialization file. Next compute an offset from the real origin of the world using the location information also supplied in the initialization information for the object. Finally, use the SetTransform method to reposition the word's origin.

DXObject supports three different types of 3D objects. The first type is a simple mesh (SimpleMesh) without texture or material information. This is basically the teapot object that was used in Chapter 2. Both of the other two types of objects (TexturedMesh and SelectedMesh) enable you to display 3D objects with textures. The only difference between these two objects is that a SelectedMesh object will be displayed with a red tint that makes it easy for the player to determine which object in the mall has been selected.

An object with textures has multiple parts, which must be drawn separately. Each part of your object that has a different texture or color must be handled independently from the rest. Displaying each piece is merely a matter of using a For loop to go through the list of materials and using the SetMaterial and SetTexture method to make them the active components and then calling the DrawSubset method to draw the particular part of the subset containing the texture.

When it comes time to draw a selected mesh, use the same basic process, however before you call SetMaterial, change the material's attributes slightly. By changing the color information in the Ambient and diffuse properties, the 3D object will be displayed with a red tint. This is a great technique for highlighting a particular 3D object.

The color properties in DirectX contain the typical red, blue, and green colors, plus a transparency factor called alpha. Like normal DirectX colors, this value is a Single that can range from zero to one. Zero means that the material is totally transparent, while one means that the material is solid. Normally the alpha, red, blue, and green attributes would all be set to one, meaning that the texture is painted over a white surface. However by setting the blue and green components to one half, the texture will be painted over a reddish surface, which will display the texture with a reddish tint.

Tip

With a little help

The With statement can be extremely useful when using objects that are nested within other objects. It establishes a temporary pointer to the object you are using and any reference that starts with a period (.) will automatically use that temporary object. This can lead to less typing, but more importantly, it can help to improve performance because you avoid the overhead of locating the object each time you use it. Typically you will use the With statement when dealing with deeply nested objects or collections of objects. Note that only the innermost With statement will be active if you nest With statements. Visual Basic must be able to associate the property or method with the appropriate object, which is impossible if you had more than one active With statement.

After displaying all of the 3D objects, you can display frame rate and viewpoint information if desired. Then you can end the scene with the EndScene method.

The most likely place for an error to occur is when you present the information to the display using the Present method. Although this can fail for any number of reasons, the typical remedy is to reinitialize the Direct3D device and related objects. This is handled by the ResetDX routine. This routine merely calls the InitDX method to rebuild all of the DirectX information.

DISPLAYING TEXT ON THE SCREEN

One of the things I find useful is the capability to display text on the Direct3D screen while the program is running and one of the most interesting things to display this way is the frame rate. DirectX makes this easy to do through a method called DrawText. However, as with most things in DirectX, you must initialize an object containing information about the text you want to display before you can use DrawText.

Displaying text relies on a special object called the D3DXFont object that contains the information about the character font and the font's attributes. In the module level of DXGraphics, I defined a D3DXFont object called GameFont that I can use in this class. Listing 6.5 shows the code to initialize this font. (A call to this routine is included in the InitDX routine.)

LISTING 6.5   DXGRAPHICS.INITDXFONTS

```
Private Function InitDXFonts() As Long

Dim FntDesc As IFont
Dim Fnt As StdFont

Set Fnt = New StdFont
Fnt.Name = "Arial"
Fnt.Size = 8
Fnt.Bold = True
Set FntDesc = Fnt
Set GameFont = d3dx.CreateFont(d3dDevice, FntDesc.hFont)

DXDebugger.WriteErr "Initializing GameFont", Err

InitDXFonts = Err.Number

End Function
```

To initialize the D3DXFont object, you must first create a StdFont object to hold all of the information about the font. In this case, I chose an 8 point, Arial font in bold to display information. After defining the StdFont object, assign it to an IFont object, which you then pass along to the CreateFont method. It is important to do it this way because the StdFont object doesn't include the hFont handle that the CreateFont method needs, but the FntDesc object can't be initialized properly using Visual Basic.

The DrawFrameRate routine (see Listing 6.6) computes the current frame rate and displays it on the screen. It uses the GetTickCount Win32 API routine to return a Long value containing the number of milliseconds since your computer was started. If more than a second (1,000 milliseconds) has elapsed since the last time the information was captured, it will save the current time into LastTimeCheckFPS and save the current value of FramesDrawn into a variable called FrameRate. It then sets the frames drawn to zero.

PART

I

CH

6

LISTING 6.6   DXGRAPHICS.DRAWFRAMERATE

```
Private Sub DrawFrameRate()

Dim TextRect As RECT

If GetTickCount - LastTimeCheckFPS >= 1000 Then
    LastTimeCheckFPS = GetTickCount
```

LISTING 6.6 CONTINUED

```
    FrameRate = FramesDrawn
    FramesDrawn = 0

End If

FramesDrawn = FramesDrawn + 1

TextRect.Top = 1
TextRect.Left = 1
TextRect.bottom = 16
TextRect.Right = 200
d3dx.DrawText GameFont, &HFFFF0000, _
    "Current Frame Rate: " & FrameRate, TextRect, _
    DT_TOP Or DT_LEFT

End Sub
```

After you update the frame rate information add one to FramesDrawn to keep track of the number of frames drawn during this interval of time. Remember this routine is called only once for each frame displayed.

To display the frame rate on the screen, you need to define a rectangle containing the onscreen coordinates in pixels where the text can be displayed. Use a RECT structure to hold this information and set the Top, Left, Bottom, and Right properties so that the data will be displayed in the upper-left corner of the screen.

Call the DrawText method using the GameFont object defined earlier and specify a color/alpha combination of &HFFFF0000. This hex value means the characters should be drawn using a solid color and that the color should be red. The first two hex digits contain the alpha value in the range of 00 to FF, while the remaining six digits contain the color using two hex digits each for red, green, and blue.

Next specify a text string using the FrameRate value computed earlier, the RECT structure containing the onscreen location for the text, and positioning information. In this case, instruct the method to display the text aligned with the left and top edges of the rectangle.

Note

It only overflows once every 49.7 days

If your system has been running for a while, the tick count value will eventually overflow and be restarted at zero. Because it returns a Long value, this should only happen once every 49.7 days. This is unlikely to happen (after all, Windows would have to go nearly two months without a single reboot), so I didn't bother to include code to handle this condition.

SELECTING OBJECTS USING THE DXGRAPHICS CLASS

Because I went to all the trouble to display objects that have been selected, I guess I need to add some code that will allow someone to select an object in the mall. This code has two parts. The MouseDown event in the Form object, which detects when someone presses a mouse button, and the HitObject method in DXGraphics.

DETECTING A MOUSE CLICK

This MouseDown event should be old hat to most Visual Basic programmers. It's fired whenever someone pushes the mouse button while over a control on a form. Listing 6.7 processes this event. This event relies on a module level variable called SelectedObject, which contains an object pointer to the currently selected object on the screen. If no object is selected, SelectedObject is set to Nothing.

LISTING 6.7   FORM1.PICTURE1_MOUSEDOWN

```
Private Sub Picture1_MouseDown(Button As Integer, _
    Shift As Integer, X As Single, Y As Single)

If Not SelectedObject Is Nothing Then
    SelectedObject.mType = TexturedMesh

End If

Set SelectedObject = dx.HitObject(X / Screen.TwipsPerPixelX, _
    Y / Screen.TwipsPerPixelY)

If Not SelectedObject Is Nothing Then
    SelectedObject.mType = SelectedMesh

End If

End Sub
```

The routine begins by resetting the currently selected object to Nothing. Then it calls the HitObject method after converting X and Y from twips to pixels. If the HitObject method returns a pointer to a valid DXObject object, set the mType property to SelectedMesh.

CHECKING EACH 3D OBJECT

The HitObject routine (see Listing 6.8) uses a For Each loop to iterate through the entire collection of objects. Then for each individual object, it calls the HitAnObject routine see if the object has a face that might contain those coordinates. If it finds a match, it returns a reference to that particular object and exits the routine. If no match is found, the routine returns Nothing.

PART

I

CH

6

LISTING 6.8 DXGRAPHICS.HITOBJECT

```
Public Function HitObject(X As Single, _
    Y As Single) As DXObject

Dim o As DXObject

For Each o In DXobs
    If HitAnObject(o, X, Y) And _
            o.oType <> dxobjectmall Then
        Set HitObject = o
        Exit Function

    End If

Next o

Set HitObject = Nothing

End Function
```

Note that I specifically will not return a reference to a Mall object. Because the shopping mall is always loaded first, you will never be able to select a store because the stores are totally contained within the mall. Thus, clicking on a store is the same as clicking on the mall.

CHECKING A PARTICULAR OBJECT

The biggest problem with determining if a particular object contains the specified X- and Y-coordinates is translating those coordinates into a line in 3D space. After I know the line in 3D space, it is a relatively simple matter to determine if the line intersects the 3D object. However, to complicate the situation, the coordinates stored in the 3D object's mesh assume that the object is at the center of the 3D world.

So the first step in this process is to move the origin of the world to the origin of the 3D object. The code to do this is the same code that you used to draw the object in the Render method.

LISTING 6.9 DXGRAPHICS.HITANOBJECT

```
Private Function HitAnObject(o As DXObject, _
    X As Single, Y As Single) As Boolean

Dim vIn As D3DVECTOR
Dim vNear As D3DVECTOR
Dim vFar As D3DVECTOR
Dim vDir As D3DVECTOR
Dim viewport As D3DVIEWPORT8
Dim hit As Long
Dim faceindex As Long
Dim retu As Single
Dim retv As Single
```

LISTING 6.9   CONTINUED

```
Dim dist As Single

Dim matTemp As D3DMATRIX
Dim matNewWorld As D3DMATRIX
Dim matTrans As D3DMATRIX

D3DXMatrixIdentity matTemp
D3DXMatrixRotationY matTemp, o.Rotation
D3DXMatrixMultiply matTemp, matWorld, matTemp
D3DXMatrixTranslation matTrans, -o.Location.X, _
    -o.Location.Y, -o.Location.Z
D3DXMatrixMultiply matNewWorld, matTemp, matTrans

d3dDevice.GetViewport viewport

vIn.X = X
vIn.Y = Y

vIn.Z = 1
D3DXVec3Unproject vNear, vIn, viewport, matProj, _
    matView, matNewWorld

vIn.Z = -100
D3DXVec3Unproject vFar, vIn, viewport, matProj, _
    matView, matNewWorld

D3DXVec3Subtract vDir, vNear, vFar

d3dx.Intersect DXmshs(o.MeshFilename).Mesh, vFar, _
    vDir, hit, faceindex, retu, retv, dist

HitAnObject = (hit = 1)

End Function
```

Then, create a vector using the X and Y pixel coordinates and assuming a Z-coordinate of 1. After that use the d3DXVec3Unproject routine to convert the vector into the new world space where the object is at the center. This defines the the vNear vector. Repeat the process using the same X and Y values, but using a Z value of –100 to define the vFar cector.

The resulting vectors describe a line through the world space. However, if you subtract the vNear vector from the vFar vector, you create a directional vector which, when combined with the vFar vector, indicates which direction the line is going.

After all this you can call the Intersect method to determine if the specified line (using the vFar and vDir vectors) crosses that particular mesh. This method returns five individual values. Hit contains a one if the line interests the mesh, or zero if it doesn't. Faceindex contains the number of the face that the line passes through. Retu and retv contain the relative coordinates within the face where the line crosses. (These values range between zero and one.) Finally, the value in dist contains the relative distance from vFar to the place where the line intersected the face.

PART

I

CH

6

The very last step of this routine converts the hit value to a Boolean value by comparing it to one. Thus if hit equals one, the function will return True, otherwise the function will return False.

RUNNING THE PROGRAM

After all of this work, you're going to want to test the program. Running the program simply involves loading the files from the \VBGame\Chapter06 directory into Visual Basic and pressing the F5 function key. The form should be displayed fairly quickly, followed shortly after that by the shopping mall (see Figure 6.2). Note that the actual time depends largely on the speed of your processor and your video card. The faster your processor, the faster you'll see the display.

Figure 6.2
Displaying the shopping mall with the Chapter 6 version of the program.

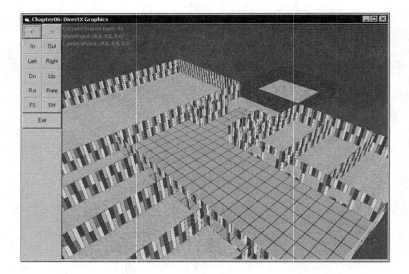

The program contains a set of buttons along the side of the DirectX display. The arrows at the top allow you to spin the mall along the Y-axis in 45° chunks. Below those buttons are the In and Out buttons, which control the zoom, while the Left, Right, Dn, and Up buttons scroll the mall to the left, right, down and up.

The Rst button is used to reset the view to the default view because it is fairly easy to zoom or position the mall so you can't find it. The Rate button controls whether the current frame rate, viewpoint, and camera information is displayed in the upper-left corner of the screen.

The FS button places the mall into full screen mode. To return to windowed mode press the Escape key. The SM button allows you to select a mesh. Clicking SM the first time will select the anchor store, while pressing it after that will select each of the objects in the DXObjects collection until you reach the end of the collection, where it will start over by selecting the shopping mall.

Finally, the Exit button will return you to Visual Basic. If you click the mouse on a particular store, it will be highlighted as shown in Figure 6.3.

Figure 6.3
Selecting the anchor store in the shopping mall.

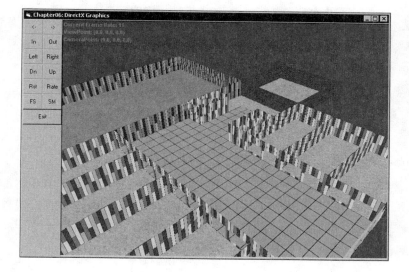

FINAL THOUGHTS

This chapter included a lot of mathematics. Fortunately, you don't really need to know how all of it works—you can just use the code as is and leave the math for the serious game programmers.

One problem with the approach used in this chapter to generate the graphics is that it is relatively slow, due to the number of simple meshes being displayed. A better technique would be to massage the raw mesh information into a handful of large objects and then display it. The big drawback to this is the amount of code and mathematics that are required to do it. It would take away from the basics learned in this chapter.

PART

I

CH

6

SIMULATING REALITY

RANDOM NUMBERS AIN'T RANDOM

In this chapter

There are many different kinds of computer games, and nearly all of them rely on random numbers to provide a degree of unpredictability. Without random numbers, you could always beat the game by following a predetermined list of actions. Even non-computer based games rely on random numbers to make them interesting. For instance, nearly all board games use dice, spinners, or shuffled cards to determine a player's move.

But while the ability to create random numbers is important in most games, they are critical for a simulation game. This chapter explores some of the fundamentals of random numbers and how they are used in a simulation game.

DEFINING A RANDOM NUMBER

A random number is a value that can't be accurately predicted ahead of time. For example, you can create a sequence of random numbers by rolling a pair of dice. Because you never know exactly which number will appear on the cubes until they stop, each number is truly random. (Of course, if you can accurately predict which number will appear, drop me an e-mail note and we'll plan a trip to Las Vegas!)

You can't look at a random number in isolation. Instead, you have to look at a series of random numbers. Otherwise you'll never be able to determine if numbers are truly random.

The first thing you want to look for in the series of number is a sequence of numbers that repeats itself. In other words, the following series of numbers are not random because the numbers 5, 3, 2, 4 are repeated in the sequence. Also because the sequence ends with 2, you would expect the next number to be 1.

5, 3, 2, 4, 1, 4, 1, 6, 5, 3, 2, 4

However, given a large enough series of random numbers, there may be some sequences that repeat by accident like this:

5, 3, 2, 4, 1, 4, 1, 6, 5, 3, 2, 4, 4, 2, 5, 1, 3, 6, 5

The main thing to worry about is that after 20, 50, or even a million numbers, is if the entire sequence of numbers will start over again. If the sequence of numbers repeats then the sequence of numbers isn't truly random.

RANDOM NUMBERS AND COMPUTERS

The ability to create random numbers on a computer is extremely important to a computer game. Imagine how fun it would be to play Solitaire if it dealt the same hand every time. Likewise, Minesweeper would be equally boring. The challenge in most games comes from the fact that the result of an action can't be predicted.

While generating random numbers with dice is easy, generating random numbers with a computer is hard. The only way for a computer to generate a random number is by following a set of instructions. However, the mere fact that the random number is created by following a set of instructions means you can accurately predict the random number if you know the algorithm and the sequence of numbers that proceeded the most recent value.

While this statement sounds implausible, consider this. Each instruction in the algorithm is a discrete mathematical operation that returns a specific value for a specific set of inputs. This means that the entire list of instructions will return a specific value for any given set of inputs. Which means that the final result is not random.

Even if you include an input value from the system timer, the sequence of random numbers will repeat at some point. Remember that the algorithm will take the same amount of time to compute a random number for a given set of inputs. Thus sooner or later you will encounter a situation where the timer value repeats, which in turn will eventually lead to a repeating sequence of random numbers. (Also remember that the resolution of the timer in Windows 2000 is about 10 milliseconds and in Windows 9x is about 55 milliseconds, which means that it is highly likely that the value of the timer won't change from one call to the next anyway.)

So while it is impossible for the computer to generate a true random number, it's possible for a computer to generate a number that can be used in place of a random number for most types of programs. This is known as a *pseudorandom number*.

As long as the sequence of pseudorandom numbers is sufficiently short, you can't tell the difference between the pseudorandom numbers and a sequence of true random numbers. In practice, this isn't a problem with most random number generators.

A pseudorandom number is created by performing a sequence of mathematical operations using an initial seed value. The new pseudorandom number is then saved as the seed value for the next pseudorandom number. Using this technique, you can generate a sequence of pseudorandom numbers.

If you use the same seed value each time, you will get the same sequence of random numbers. This can be both desirable and undesirable at the same time. If you are debugging a program that uses random numbers, you may want to use the same series of random numbers, which will make it easier to find a bug in your program.

On the other hand, using the same sequence of random numbers means that your program will always work the same way, which means that the same deck of cards will be dealt each time in Solitaire or the same mines will be laid in Minesweeper.

To avoid this problem, you need to choose a random value for the seed. One of the best ways to get a random value for the seed is to use the system's timer. Ideally, you should use that part of the timer that is the most rapidly changing, such as the Timer function in Visual Basic or the GetTickCount Win32 API routine I used in the DXGraphics class to compute frame rate.

Note

Pseudo complex to me too

Rather than type "pseudorandom number" throughout the rest of the book, I'm going to refer to pseudorandom numbers simply as random numbers. Because any computer-generated random number must be a pseudorandom number, there isn't a strong reason to continue to use the term. Besides, spelling pseudorandom correctly each time is too hard on the poor author.

CREATING RANDOM NUMBERS

There is branch of probability and statistics devoted to creating random numbers on a computer. A lot of research has been done in this area over the years.

One simple technique for creating random numbers is known as the *mid-square method*. This method starts with a four-digit seed value and squares it. This will create a number with up to eight digits. You extract the middle four digits to create the random number.

The problem with the mid-square method is that some seed values will lead to a sequence of numbers that aren't really random. For instance, consider a seed value of 0010. Its eight digit square is 0000010, and the extracted four-digit random number value is 0000. When this value is used as the next seed value, you'll return yet another random number value of 0000. So once you get a random number of 0000, your sequence of random numbers will always return 0000.

A better algorithm is shown in Listing 7.1. This is known as a *linear congruential generator*. It uses a seed like the mid-square method to create a new random number. It multiplies the seed by a large number and adds a constant to it. Then it performs a Mod operation using another large number that happens to be a power of 2 (2^{31} to be exact). The result is still a fairly large number, which is used as the seed for the next random number. Finally the number is divided by that same power of two to create a random number in the range of 0.0 and 1.0.

LISTING 7.1   FORM1.MYRND

```
Private Function MyRnd() As Single

Dim r As Double

r = (314159269 * MyRndSeed + 453806245)

r = r - Int(r / 2147483648) * 2147483648

MyRndSeed = r

MyRnd = CSng(r / 2147483648)

End Function
```

The key is to pick the appropriate values to fit into the algorithm. This is something best left to the statisticians who study random numbers.

Note

Timers aren't random

It may have occurred to you that you could simply use the system's timer as a random number generator. The problem with this approach is twofold. First, the timer is always increasing, making the full value useless as a random number. Second, even if you used only a portion of the timer's value, you'd run into a more subtle problem. If your program frequently requests random numbers, the difference between any two random numbers would be a function of the amount of time between calls to get the current value of the time. Because this value would be relatively constant, the random numbers would follow a similar pattern each time you ran your program, no matter what initial seed you used, which defeats the purpose of using random numbers in the first place.

RANDOM NUMBERS AND VISUAL BASIC

Fortunately, Visual Basic programmers don't have to create their own random number generators. Visual Basic includes a fairly good random number generator, which is more than adequate for this program.

RANDOMIZE AND RND

The Visual Basic random number generator has two parts, a statement called Randomize, which initializes the random number's seed to the specified value, and a function called Rnd, which returns the random number.

The Randomize statement takes an optional parameter which is used to initialize the random number generator. If no value is supplied, an initial value derived from the system's timer will be used.

The Rnd function is used to return the next random number in the sequence. The value of the random number is always less than one and greater than or equal to zero.

Rnd has one optional parameter. If you specify a value of zero, Rnd will return the current random number. If you specify a negative value, Rnd will return a random number using the specified value as a seed. If you specify a positive value, or omit the parameter, Rnd will return the next random number in the sequence based on the current seed value.

To create a repeatable sequence of random numbers, you must first call Rnd with a negative value before you do anything else. If you call Randomize, you must specify a value. However, a call to Randomize isn't required. Calling Randomize without specifying a value will reinitialize the seed and you'll lose your repeatable sequence. If you call Randomize and then call Rnd with a negative value, the effect of the Randomize statement is lost.

PART

II

CH

7

GENERATING RANDOM NUMBERS WITH RND

I created the program shown in Figure 7.1 to help you understand how Randomize and Rnd work. You can find source code for the program on the book's CD-ROM, in the \VBGame\Chapter07\RandomList directory. This program allows you to enter an initial seed for the Randomize statement and an initial seed value for Rnd. Clicking the Generate button will generate the first 12 random numbers in the sequence.

Figure 7.1
Generating random numbers.

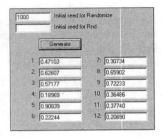

The code for this program is shown in Listing 7.2. It begins by checking the Text1 text box to determine how to execute the Randomize statement. If the text box is empty, the Randomize statement is called without a parameter. If the value in Text is numeric, I convert it to a Single and use it in the Randomize statement. If the value isn't numeric, I skip the Randomize statement totally.

LISTING 7.2   FORM1.COMMAND1_CLICK

```
Private Sub Command1_Click()

Dim r As Single
Dim i As Long

If Len(Text1.Text) = 0 Then
   Randomize

Else If IsNumeric(Text1.Text) Then
    Randomize CSng(Text1.Text)

End If

If Len(Text2.Text) = 0 Then
    r = Rnd(100)

Else
    r = Rnd(CSng(Text2.Text))

End If

For i = 1 To 12
   Display(i) = FormatNumber(Rnd(), 5)

Next i

End Sub
```

Then if there is a value in the `Text2` text box, I'll convert the value to a `Single` and use it as an argument to `Rnd` to create the first random number. Otherwise, I call `Rnd` with a value of `100` to create the first random number.

From running this program, you should see that passing a negative seed value to `Rnd` generates a repeatable sequence of random numbers, while passing a positive value returns a different sequence of numbers each time. Also, the `Randomize` statement isn't all that important, as long as you throw away the first random number you create.

ROLLING DICE

The simple program shown in Figure 7.2 demonstrates how to create random numbers—it enables you to roll either a single die or a pair of dice. The program allows you to enter the number of times the dice will be rolled and specify an initial seed value. You also have a choice of using Visual Basic's random number generator or the one shown in Listing 7.1.

Figure 7.2
Rolling dice electronically.

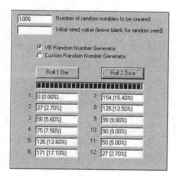

Once you enter this information, you can click the Roll 1 Die button to roll a single die or you can click the Roll 2 Dice button to roll two dice. If you enter a relatively large number for the number of times to roll the dice, you may have to wait while the program runs through the calculations, so I added a progress bar immediately below the buttons to show that the program is working.

After the calculations are finished, the results are shown below the progress bar. Beside each number is displayed the number of times that particular number was thrown and the relative percentage of the total.

Since the logic for both buttons is similar, I'm only going to talk about the logic to roll one die. You can load the sample project in `VBGame\Chapter07\Dice` to see how it works. I begin the program by declaring some local variables and calling the `ClearScreen` subroutine to clear all of the display text boxes (see Listing 7.3).

LISTING 7.3 FORM1.COMMAND1_CLICK

```
Private Sub Command1_Click()

Dim i As Long
Dim die(6) As Long
Dim r As Long
Dim l As Long

ClearScreen

If Len(Text2.Text) = 0 Then
    If Option1.Value Then
        Randomize

    Else
        MyRandomize

    End If

Else
    If Option1.Value Then
        Randomize CLng(Text2.Text)

    Else
        MyRndSeed = CLng(Text2.Text)

    End If

End If

For i = 1 To 6
    die(1) = 0

Next i

ProgressBar1.Value = 0

l = CLng(Text1.Text)

For i = 1 To l
    If Option1.Value Then
        r = Int(Rnd() * 6) + 1

    Else
        r = Int(MyRnd() * 6) + 1

    End If

    die(r) = die(r) + 1

    If i Mod 100 = 0 Then
        ProgressBar1.Value = i / l * 100

    End If

Next i
```

LISTING 7.3   CONTINUED

```
For i = 1 To 6
   Display(i).Text = FormatNumber(die(i), 0) & _
      " (" & FormatPercent(die(i) / 1, 2) & ")"

Next i

ProgressBar1.Value = 100

End Sub
```

The routine begins by checking the Text2 to see if the user entered a seed value. If not, the routine calls either Randomize or MyRandomize, depending on which random number generator the user selected based on Option1.Value.

Next, each element of the Die array is set to zero and the Value property of ProgressBar1 is set to zero as well. Then I convert the value in Text1 to a long value that I'll use as the limit in the For loop. Notice that I didn't bother to verify that the values in either Text1 or Text2 are numeric before converting them. That's because this is strictly a test program and not intended to be used by someone who isn't using it correctly.

The main processing is done in this For loop. Based on the value of Option1 I generate a random number using either Rnd or MyRnd. I use the scaling technique discussed earlier to ensure that the random number is an integer in the range from one to six. Then I increment the appropriate entry in Die. Every 100 rolls, I update the value of the progress bar to show the current status.

At the end of the loop, I use a For loop and with calls to FormatNumber and FormatPercent to display the value for each value of Die. Then I set the value of ProgressBar1 to 100 to ensure that the progress bar shows that the process is completed if someone chooses a value for 1 that doesn't end with 00.

RANGES OF RANDOM NUMBERS

The range of a random number can either be discrete or continuous. Discrete random numbers are generally represented by a collection of integer values such as the numbers on a die. A continuous random number is represented by all of the floating-point values between two specified limit values.

Rnd generates a continuous random number that is always less than one and greater than or equal to zero. However, it is often useful to generate a random number with a range that may be larger or smaller. Also, you may want to create a random number that can represent distinct values such as those on a pair of dice or a deck of cards.

SCALING CONTINUOUS RANDOM NUMBERS

You can multiply a random number by a constant and the result will still be a random number. Likewise you can add a constant to a random number and it will still be random. These operations have the effect of merely scaling the range.

PART

II

CH

7

For instance, if you want a continuous random number that ranges from zero to 10, you can multiple Rnd by 10 like this:

```
NewRandomNumber = Rnd() * 10
```

If you need a random number that ranges between one and two, you can simply add one to the value of Rnd like this:

```
NewRandomNumber = Rnd() + 1
```

You can combine these operations together to create a random number in the range from one to 10 like this:

```
NewRandomNumber = (Rnd() * 9) + 1
```

A general function that returns a scaled continuous random number is shown in Listing 7.4. This routine takes three optional parameters: Max, which contains the maximum value to be returned; Min, which contains the minimum value to be returned; and Seed, which supplies a seed value to the Rnd function.

LISTING 7.4   RANDOMNUMBER.RAND

```
Public Function Rand(Optional Max As Variant, _
    Optional Min As Variant, Optional Seed As Variant)
    As Single

Dim Range As Single
Dim Offset As Single

Range = 1
Offset = 0

If Not IsMissing(Max) Then
    Range = Max

End If

If Not IsMissing(Min) Then
    Range = Range - Min
    Offset = Min

End If

If IsMissing(Seed) Then
    Rand = Rnd() * Range + Offset

Else
    Rand = Rnd(Seed) * Range + Offset

End If

End Function
```

The routine begins by initializing Range and Offset to one and zero respectively. If a value for Max is supplied, I save it as the Range. If a value for Min is supplied, I recompute Range and set the value for Offset. Finally I compute a random number that is multiplied by Range and is then added to Offset. If the Seed value is supplied, I pass that to Rnd; otherwise, Rnd is called without any parameters.

CREATING DISCRETE RANDOM NUMBERS

It's very easy to convert a continuous random number to a discrete random number. You simply scale the continuous random number to the range you want and then use the Int function to truncate the fractional part of the number, like this:

```
MyRandomNumber = Int(Rnd()*6) + 1
```

You can easily use Rnd to create a random number that represents the result of rolling a single die. First you multiply Rnd by six, generating numbers that range from zero to less then six. If you take the Int of this value you will end up with one of these integers: 0, 1, 2, 3, 4, or 5. Finally you add one to the result to scale the results to these integers: 1, 2, 3, 4, 5, or 6.

You can also call the Rand function from Listing 7.4 to compute this random number by using the following line of code:

```
MyRandomNumber = Int(Rnd(7,1))
```

The trick here is remembering that Rand (as well as Rnd) will never return the maximum value of the range (7 for Rand and 1 for Rnd).

DISTRIBUTION OF RANDOM NUMBERS

Random numbers can also be categorized as having a uniform distribution or a non-uniform distribution depending on how frequently various values appear in the sequence. Rnd returns a sequence of random numbers with a uniform distribution. This means that the numbers it will generate have an equal probability of appearing. However, there are many cases where having a random number with a non-uniform distribution is important also.

UNIFORM DISTRIBUTION

If you were to roll a single die 600 times, you would expect to roll about 100 ones, 100 twos, etc. While you won't roll exactly 100 of each of the numbers on the die, each count should be relatively close to 100. Thus rolling a single die has a uniform distribution.

Another way of saying this is that each of the numbers on the die is equally likely to appear. The probability of any particular number appearing is one out of six, which is 1/6 or 16.67%.

NON-UNIFORM DISTRIBUTION

While most random number generators will return uniform random numbers, sometimes you have to work with non-uniform distributions. For instance, if you roll a pair of dice, the resulting set of numbers is no longer uniform. Instead you have the distribution shown in Table 7.1.

TABLE 7.1   ROLLING A PAIR OF DICE RESULTS IN A NON-UNIFORM DISTRIBUTION OF RANDOM NUMBERS

Value	Number of Combinations	Probability	Combinations
2	1	2.78%	1,1
3	2	5.56%	1,2; 2,1
4	3	8.33%	1,3; 2,2; 3,1
5	4	11.11%	1,4; 2,3; 3,2; 4,1
6	5	13.89%	1,5; 2,4; 3,3; 4,2; 5,1
7	6	16.67%	1,6; 2,5; 3,4; 4,3; 5,2; 6,1
8	5	13.89%	2,6; 3,5; 4,4; 5,3; 6,2
9	4	11.11%	3,6; 4,5; 5,4; 6,3
10	3	8.33%	4,6; 5,5; 6,4
11	2	5.56%	5,6; 6,5
12	1	2.78%	6,6

From this example, you can see that adding two uniform discrete random numbers together creates a non-uniform discrete random number. If you experimented, you would find that you can use many different approaches to create non-uniform discrete random numbers. The key is to ensure that you always end up with an integer value at the end of your operations.

You can also create non-uniform continuous random numbers by adding two uniform continuous random numbers together. You can also apply nearly any mathematical formula to a uniform continuous random number to generate a non-uniform continuous random number. Techniques that involve logarithms and exponentials create useful distributions like those shown in Figure 7.3.

CREATING DISCRETE NON-UNIFORM RANDOM NUMBERS

Although using mathematics to create non-uniform discrete random numbers is relatively simple, I use a weighted number technique that enables me to define a series of values and their relative weights using the following Type definition.

```
Public Type RandomDistribution
    Value As Single
    Weight As Single
    Probability As Single

End Type
```

In your application program you need to define an array of RandomDistribution with a lower bound that starts with zero and with an upper bound that contains the last valid piece of data. Based on the sum of the weights, I can compute the relative probability for each value by computing the total of all the individual Weights and computing the cumulative probability value for each weight (see Listing 7.5).

Figure 7.3
Creating non-uniform random numbers mathematically.

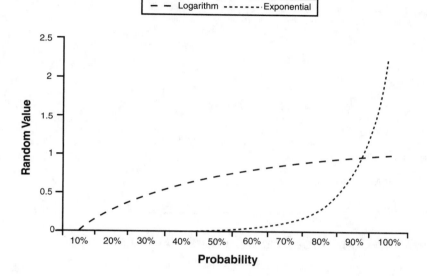

LISTING 7.5   RANDOMNUMBER.NORMALIZEDISTRIBUTION

```
Public Sub NormalizeDistribution_
    (dist() As RandomDistribution)

Dim i As Long
Dim s As Single
Dim w As Single

s = 0
For i = 0 To UBound(dist)
    s = s + dist(i).Weight

Next i

w = 0
For i = 0 To UBound(dist)
    w = w + dist(i).Weight
    dist(i).Probability = w / s

Next i

End Sub
```

After the cumulative probability values have been computed, I can easily call the DRand routine in Listing 7.6 to return a discrete random number. This routine simply computes a random number and scans through the supplied array until it finds a Probability value that exceeds the random number. Then it returns the Value associated with the index.

LISTING 7.6   RANDOMNUMBER.DRAND

```
Public Function DRand(dist() As _
   RandomDistribution) As Single

Dim i As Long
Dim r As Single

r = Rnd()
i = 0
Do While (r > dist(i).Probability) _
      And (i < UBound(dist))
  i = i + 1

Loop

DRand = dist(i).Value

End Function
```

CREATING CONTINUOUS NON-UNIFORM RANDOM NUMBERS

You can use a similar technique as used by DRand (see Listing 7.6) to create continuous random numbers using the same RandomDistribution type and the same NormalizeDistribution routine.

Rather than returning the first Value that has a Probability greater than the random number, the CRand routine computes a uniform random using the interval between this Value and the previous Value (see Listing 7.7).

LISTING 7.7   RANDOMNUMBER.CRAND

```
Public Function CRand(dist() As RandomDistribution) As Single

Dim i As Long
Dim r As Single

r = Rnd()

i = 0
Do While (r > dist(i).Probability) And (i < UBound(dist))
   i = i + 1

Loop

If i = 0 Then
   CRand = Rand(dist(i).Value)
```

LISTING 7.7   CONTINUED

```
Else
    CRand = Rand(dist(i).Value, dist(i - 1).Value)

End If

End Function
```

If this seems confusing, consider the diagram in Figure 7.4. If `Rnd` computes a value for `r` of `0.2`, it falls into the interval `0.1` to `0.7`, which means that `CRand` will return a uniform random number in the range of `10` to `20`.

Figure 7.4
Returning a uniform random number between two values in the distribution.

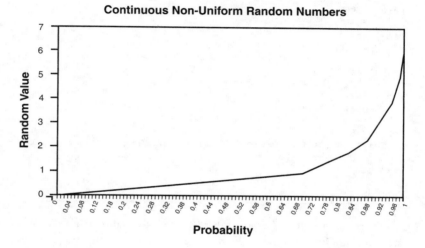

Continuous Non-Uniform Random Numbers

CREATING NON-UNIFORM RANDOM NUMBERS

The code for the non-uniform random number generators can be found on the CD-ROM in the `\VBGame\Chapter07\RandNumbers` directory. Along with the code shown earlier, I wrote a simple program that will generate a collection of random numbers based on a series of weights and values you specify (see Figure 7.5).

The program allows you to enter a set of six weights and values. You can specify the number of random numbers to be generated in the Count fields. Then clicking Discrete or Continuous will normalize the distribution and display the random numbers on the right.

Clicking the Discrete button triggers the `Command1_Click` event shown in Listing 7.8. This routine begins by calling the `Normalize` routine to load the values into the `dist` module level variable. Next, I clear the value displayed in the `Text1` text box and extract the number of random numbers to be generated from the `Text2` text box. Finally, I use a `For` loop to call `DRand` and append the results to the text box.

Figure 7.5
Generating non-uniform random numbers using DRand and CRand.

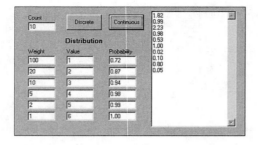

LISTING 7.8   FORM1.COMMAND1_CLICK

```
Private Sub Command1_Click()

Dim i As Long
Dim j As Long

Normalize

Text1.Text = ""
j = CLng(Text2.Text) - 1

For i = 0 To j
   Text1.Text = Text1.Text & FormatNumber(DRand(dist)) & vbCrLf

Next i

End Sub
```

The Normalize routine (see Listing 7.9) copies the values from the Weight and Val control arrays on the form and saves them in the dist array. I call NormalizeDistribution to initialize the cumulative probability distribution values stored in Probability. I use another For loop to display the newly computed probability values into the Distrib control array.

LISTING 7.9   FORM1.NORMALIZE

```
Private Sub Normalize()

Dim i As Long

For i = 0 To 5
   dist(i).Weight = CSng(Weight(i).Text)
   dist(i).Value = CSng(Val(i).Text)
   dist(i).Probability = 0

Next i

NormalizeDistribution dist

For i = 0 To 5
   Distrib(i).Text = FormatNumber(dist(i).Probability)
```

LISTING 7.9   CONTINUED

```
Next i

End Sub
```

FINAL THOUGHTS

Random numbers are used in games to make the behavior of an object or character unpredictable. In a 3D shooting game, you might use a random number to choose how the alien begins its attack. While a random number would enable you to choose from one of several different attacks, a uniform random number means that each attack would be equally likely. A better option would be to create a random number that forces one attack option to be typical, with other attack variations being less likely. This means that the player would be expecting one particular gambit, making it harder to defend from the other variations.

SIMULATING REALITY

In this chapter

Life is complicated. Many times it's way too complicated to really understand, so often the best way to understand it is to make it nice and simple. This is the fundamental idea behind a simulation. A simulation is nothing more than a way to use a few key indicators to predict what will happen over time.

INTRODUCING SIMULATIONS

Simulations are simply computer programs that attempt to model a small portion of part of the real world. People use simulations for many purposes, such as modeling the stock market, the economy, or the weather. You can simulate many things. Even the program that rolled the dice in Chapter 7, "Random Numbers Ain't Random," is considered a simulation.

Simulation games also attempt to model the world, though the world modeled by the game is often different from the one we live in. But even though the worlds may be different, a simulation game is still a simulation and the same techniques used to build simulations still apply.

SIMULATIONS AND MODELS

A model is a way to describe how something works in the real world. It takes a series of inputs, performs some processing, and returns some output. In the case of the dice program, the input is a request to roll the dice. The processing involves rolling simulated dice and collecting statistics on each outcome. Displaying the result is merely a matter of copying the statistics to various elements on the screen.

Most models are much more complicated than rolling a pair of dice, but they follow the same basic structure: input, process, and output (see Figure 8.1).

Figure 8.1
A simulation consists of a series of inputs, a model that processes the inputs, and a set of outputs that describe the results of the simulation.

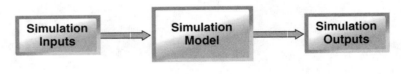

When building a simulation model, you are limited in the number of inputs you can process as well as the overall complexity of the model. This is a function of sheer computing power. For instance even the largest computers have trouble processing weather models due to the huge amount of data. Given enough time, the weather models can reasonably predict the weather, but when you need an accurate forecast for tomorrow, what good is a model that won't finish processing until next week?

Just because a model isn't as complex as the real-world situation you're trying to simulate doesn't mean it can't be accurate. It all depends how accurate you need the results to be.

When modeling the weather, you don't need to know the exact amount of snow that will fall. Knowing whether to expect one inch of snow or eight inches is good enough.

One way to simplify the model is to limit the number of inputs into the model and to simplify them as much as possible. Less data to work with means less processing will be needed inside the model.

TYPES OF SIMULATIONS

There are three basic classifications that can be applied to simulations—static or dynamic, deterministic or stochastic, and discrete or continuous.

A *static simulation* is one that represents what is happening at a single point in time. What happened in the past has no impact on what will happen in the future. Rolling dice is an example of a static simulation. A *dynamic simulation* is one where the model adjusts based on what has happened while the simulation is running. A stock market simulation is a good example of a dynamic simulation. The model must remember changes in stock prices over time to forecast future stock prices.

A *deterministic simulation* is one in which the inputs directly determine the output. A *stochastic simulation* uses random numbers to account for factors that can't be accurately predicted. Most simulations are stochastic because most factors can only be predicted within a certain range or follow a certain pattern.

A *discrete simulation* is one where the model processes a series of events over time, while a *continuous simulation* processes data in a continuous stream over time. For instance, if you're trying to model the stock market using a discrete simulation, you would have to model each and every trade. In a continuous simulation of the stock market, you would try to build and solve a set of mathematical equations that describes how the market rises and falls.

You should view discrete simulators and continuous simulators as a range, not as specific types of simulators. Most simulators have aspects that are continuous and discrete and the one classification or the other is usually assigned based on what type plays a larger role in the simulation.

PARTS OF A SIMULATION MODEL

Every simulation is composed of a number of fundamental pieces. These pieces correspond directly to things in the real world that the simulation is attempting to model.

CLIENTS, SERVERS, AND QUEUES

Most simulations are viewed as a collection of clients and servers. A server is an object that provides a resource that a client consumes. Consider a vendor in a shopping mall's food court. People arrive at the vendor to purchase some food, while workers at the food vendor supply the food. The workers are known as *servers*, while the customers are known as *clients*.

If the food vendor isn't busy, a customer can walk right up to the vendor and order food. The time the customer shows up at the counter is known as the *arrival* time. The time spent waiting for the food is known as the *service* time. Once the customer has received the food, he leaves the vendor to eat the food. This is known as the customer's *departure* time.

If the food vendor is busy, the customer may have to wait in line for the next available server (see Figure 8.2). This line is known as a *queue*. A queue is a first-in, first-out device that ensures that the customers are processed in the order that they arrived. As new customers arrive, they enter at the end of the queue. When a server gives the food to the customer, the customer at the head of the queue will step up to place an order.

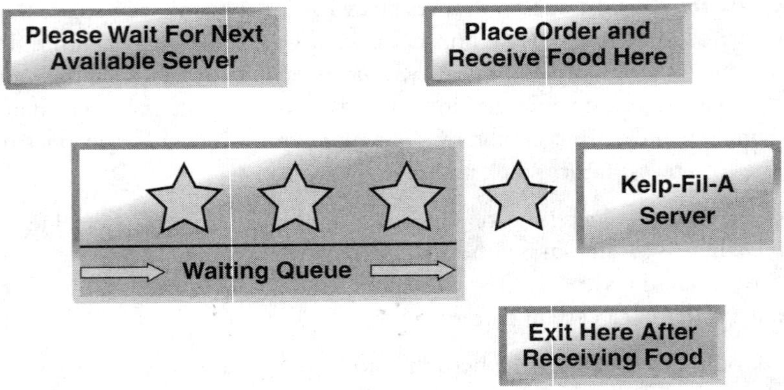

Figure 8.2
Customers wait in line to order and receive food.

WAIT AND SERVICE TIMES

The time the client spends at the server is known as the *service time*. This time varies based on the actual transactions the customer performs. In our example, ordering more food (or placing a special order) increases the amount of service time.

Service times are generally computed from one or more random numbers. If you're modeling a real life application, you can measure the actual service times for the clients. Then you can summarize these observations over time to build a distribution table that can be used by a non-uniform random number.

The time the customer spends waiting in line is known as *wait time*. This time depends on the number of customers ahead of him and how long it takes the server to fill his order. The time the customer is in the system is known as the *total time* and it's computed by adding the wait time to the service time.

ARRIVAL RATES

The frequency with which the clients arrive at the server is known as the *arrival rate*. In most simulations the arrival rate will vary over time. This makes sense in our example because you would expect to see more customers around lunch time and dinner time than in between.

Like service times, arrival rates are usually controlled by a non-uniform random number generator. This makes it easy to vary the arrival rate over time.

If you take the inverse of the arrival rate, you get the amount of time between clients. When the average amount of time between clients arriving is less than the average service time, the clients will generally not have to wait for the server. However, if the clients arrive quicker than they can be served, the server can't keep up and a queue is needed to ensure that the customers are serviced in the proper order.

MULTIPLE SERVERS AND QUEUES

So far, this discussion has assumed that there was only one person behind the counter to handle customer orders. However, there is no reason why you can't have multiple servers. As each server finishes with a client, he will serve the next client in the queue (see Figure 8.3).

Figure 8.3
Customers wait for the first available server.

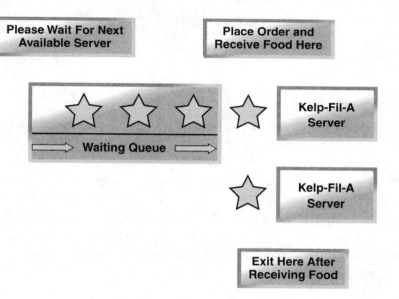

Likewise, you can use multiple queues in your simulation, either multiple queues for a single server or multiple queues for multiple servers. Realistically, unless there are constraints on which queue a client will enter, multiple queues will not process requests any faster than a single queue (see Figure 8.4).

If you do apply constraints on which clients may enter a queue, multiple queues may be useful. For example, the express lane in a supermarket limits the number of items a customer may purchase. This means that the customers in the express lane will have a shorter wait time due to the shorter service times for each customer than the rest of the customers waiting in other lines.

Figure 8.4
Each server has his
own queue.

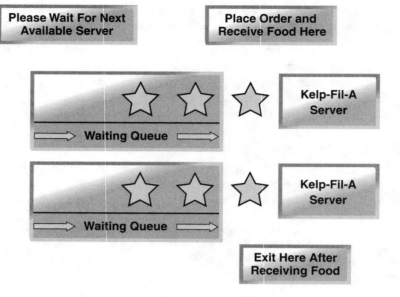

COMPLEX SIMULATIONS

Up to this point, I've talked mostly about a single queue or set of queues that feed a single server or set of servers. However, most simulations use these components in more complex arrangements.

In the example, each server at the food court vendor took the order and supplied the food. While this is true for some food court vendors, others use a more complex organization where some people take orders while others fill them (see Figure 8.5).

This approach is typical of most simulations. The client moves from one queue and server, onto the next queue and server and so forth until the all of the processing is complete for that particular client.

OTHER VARIATIONS ON QUEUES

In the queues I've discussed so far, once you've entered, you can't leave. In many situations, that's not realistic. For instance, someone may decide not to purchase a slice of pizza at the food court because the line is too long. Of course determining a queue is too long is a very subjective process and will vary from client to client. However this is something easily modeled with yet another random number.

Likewise, a client may leave a queue before reaching the front because she waited too long. After all, if you're waiting in a slow line in a food court, the pizza in the next booth with a short line may be more attractive than the taco for which you've been waiting for the past 15 minutes.

Figure 8.5
Using multiple servers and queues to streamline operations.

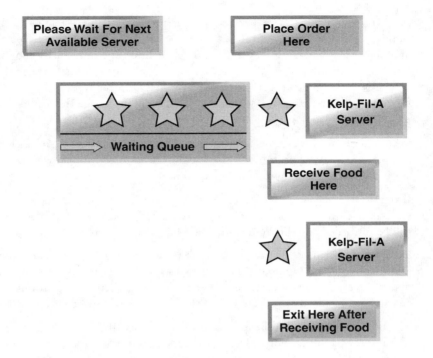

In a truly dynamic simulation, you may add and delete servers as necessary. After all, a food court vendor or store will schedule staff to ensure that there are extra people available to handle peak demands.

THE MASTER CLOCK

Most simulations track how things change over time. The master clock is a way to track how time changes in the simulation. There are two basic approaches to keeping track of time, an incremental clock or an event-driven clock.

INCREMENTAL CLOCK

An *incremental clock* is similar to a timer that fires an event periodically. The collection of objects in the simulation are examined for any actions that need to take place at that particular time. Once those actions are completed, the simulation waits until the next time the timer fires.

Understanding an incremental clock is easy if you tie the clock to the computer system's clock. Then as the clock changes in the system, so does the clock in the simulation. Of course there isn't a need to have the clocks run at the same speed. For each second in the system clock, your incremental clock may jump a minute, an hour, or a day, depending on how quickly you want the simulation to progress.

Note that that you don't have to link the master clock to the system clock. You can run your simulation independently of the system clock. When you finish processing the actions for one time interval, you can begin processing the next time interval. While this is nice, it causes problems in games where the number of actions processed in each time interval increases as the game progresses. The player may be faced with a runaway situation where time in the game passes so fast that they can't build or change the game's environment.

Tying the system clocks to the master clock has many advantages in computer games since the speed of the clock in the simulation is constant. Because most simulations grow more complex as the game progresses, more actions need to be handled with each tick of the clock. More actions require more computing power.

If you do tie your master clock to the system's clock, you need to ensure that you can complete all of the simulation's processing between ticks of the clock. If you can't, some actions will be discarded and the simulation won't be accurate.

For instance, assume that each second of the system's clock corresponds to one minute in the simulation and the simulation takes two seconds to process all of the actions for each tick of the clock. You either have to give up processing half of the actions in the simulation or you have to change the incremental clock so that is fires once every two seconds.

The best solution is a hybrid approach, where you use the system's clock to control the speed of the game and only increment the master clock when all actions have been completed. This prevents the game from running too fast at the start of the game, and ensures that you don't discard actions later in the game to keep up with the system clock.

This approach also has the advantage of adapting easily to a wide range of computers. If your simulation needs two seconds of processing on a 500MHz computer late in the game, it may need only one second on a 1.0GHz computer and close to a half of a second on a 2.0GHz machine. The only way to ensure that the game is playable on all of these computers is to loosely tie both clocks together.

EVENT-DRIVEN CLOCK

An *event-driven clock* is similar to the increment clock in that a set of actions will be processed when the clock ticks, but it differs in that each tick of the clock represents a different amount of time.

The best way to think of an event-driven clock is to imagine a calendar. During an event, other events can be scheduled for particular dates and times. Once all of the actions have been processed, the clock will jump to the next scheduled event. This means that the simulation skips over all of the time between the now finished event and the next scheduled event.

The advantage of this type of clock is that it's more efficient than incremental clocks. You don't waste time by processing events where there are no actions.

Event-driven clocks are easy to program as long you are comfortable with a clock that might advance by a few days on one tick and a few minutes in the next tick.

Event-driven clocks can be a real problem in a game for the same reasons that incremental clocks can be a problem—if not much is happening in the game, the player will watch time rush by. When the game gets bogged down, time will seem to creep.

I frequently use event-driven clocks when I only care about the results of the simulation. The faster the simulation runs, the faster I get my results.

SIMULATION STATISTICS

Simply moving clients around from one server to another is not a complete simulation. You will want to collect statistics and other information while the simulation is running. This information will be helpful in tuning the simulation to get the results you want.

Perhaps the most important statistic in a simulation is the number of people served. This provides a way to understand how busy your simulation is over time. A lot of clients implies that a lot of work is being done.

Along with the number of clients served, you may want to track the amount of time used in the simulation, both real time and simulated time. This is especially important when you need to balance the complexity of the simulation with the amount of time the simulation consumes.

Another interesting statistic to monitor is the maximum number of clients in a queue. While having a few clients in a queue is acceptable, having too many can lead to problems. The best way to correct the problem is to reduce the arrival rate of the clients or add more servers to process the clients.

Of course, as you develop the simulation, you'll need to track other information. In the case of a store, you may want to track net income from the customers served to help determine if the store is profitable.

PROGRAMMING SIMULATIONS

Programming a simulation is really easy as long as you remember that everything is built around the master clock. This means the main part of the simulation is a subroutine that performs the work for each tick of the master clock. You can call this routine from either a timer event or a loop that increments the master clock.

To demonstrate these concepts, I've built a simple simulation program (see Figure 8.6) that tracks customers as they visit the Kelp-Fil-A shop in Swim Mall's food court. You can input the number of customers expected each hour and the distribution of how long each customer needs for service. You can choose to run the simulation directly or run it off the timer. When the simulation is complete, it will display selected statistics captures while it was run.

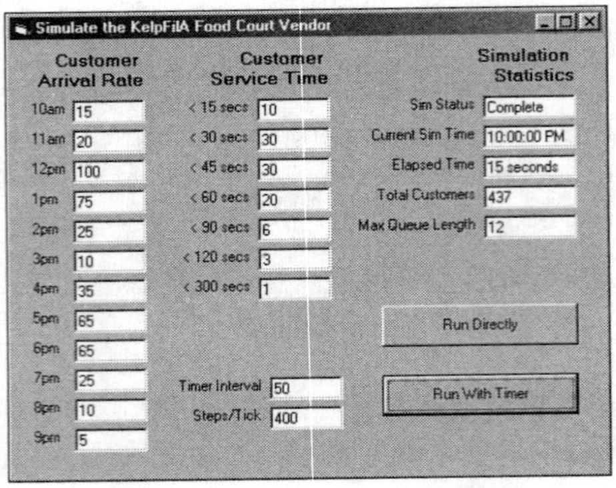

Figure 8.6
Running the Kelp-Fil-A
simulation.

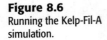

Kelp-Fil-A has many of the common parts of a normal simulation, including random number generators, queues, and a master clock that controls the activity in the simulation. I also like to create a class for each client or server in the simulation. In this case, there are classes for both the store and each person who visits the store.

RANDOM NUMBER GENERATORS

Random number generators are very critical to stochastic simulations because the random numbers are the source of the simulation's unpredictability. It is important to be able to create both discrete and continuous random numbers with various distribution patterns.

This simulation makes use of the CRand and Rand functions created in Chapter 7, "Random Numbers Ain't Random," as well as the NormalizeDistribution subroutine to prepare the data for CRand.

QUEUES

The most common data structure associated with a simulation is the queue. There are many different ways to implement a queue. The approach I choose for this program uses an array that expands and contracts as items are added and removed from the queue.

The Queue class exposes four properties and methods. The properties include Length and MaxLength, while the methods include Add and Front. Internally I use an array with undefined bounds like this:

```
Private xQueue() As Object
```

Then I redimension it when I create an instance of the Queue object so that it has exactly one element, Redim xQueue(0).

ADDING AN OBJECT TO THE QUEUE

The Add method inserts an object into the array at one position past the current upper bound of the array (see Listing 8.1). To do this, use the ReDim statement with the Preserve keyword. Then save the maximum length of the queue in the MaxLength property.

LISTING 8.1   QUEUE.ADD

```
Public Sub Add(Item As Object)

Dim l As Long

l = UBound(xQueue) + 1
ReDim Preserve xQueue(l)

Set xQueue(l) = Item

If UBound(xQueue) > MaxLength Then
    MaxLength = UBound(xQueue)

End If

End Sub
```

RETRIEVING THE FRONT OBJECT FROM THE QUEUE

Retrieving an object from the queue is merely a matter of determining if the queue isn't empty, returning the object reference, and moving all of the objects one position closer to the front in the queue (see Listing 8.2).

LISTING 8.2   QUEUE.FRONT

```
Public Function Front() As Object

Dim i As Long

If UBound(xQueue) > 0 Then
    Set Front = xQueue(1)

    For i = 2 To UBound(xQueue)
        Set xQueue(i - 1) = xQueue(i)

    Next i

    ReDim Preserve xQueue(UBound(xQueue) - 1)

Else
    Set Front = Nothing

End If

End Function
```

When looking at this code, you should note a few things. First, if the upper bound of the xQueue array is zero, the queue is empty. I never store anything in this first element of the array. Second, the process of physically copying the elements down one position is inefficient for long queues. As long as the length of the queue is relatively short, it won't be a problem. A more efficient approach is to use a static sized array with pointers to the first and last items in the queue. However, you risk overflowing the queue if you attempt to store one more element in the queue than the array will hold.

PEOPLE IN THE MALL

The `Person` object is a very simple class, consisting primarily of these four public variables:

```
Public Name As String
Public ArriveTime As Date
Public ServeTime As Long
Public DepartTime As Date
```

`Name` contains a simple random value that really isn't used in the simulation as it currently stands. It's primarily useful when you want to track an individual's activity by using `Debug.Print` statements by adding the `Debugger` class for more sophisticated tracing.

The other three variables reflect the time the person arrived at the queue, the amount of time required to serve the person once they reach a server, and the time that the person has been served. All of these variables contain values relative to the master clock.

THE KELP-FIL-A STORE

Like the `Person` class, the `Store` class is also relatively simple. It contains these three public variables:

```
Public WaitQueue As Queue
```

```
Public ActivePerson As Person
```

```
Public Customers As Long
```

`WaitQueue` is simply the waiting queue associated with the store. Rather than creating a method in the `Store` class, I choose to keep it simple and just expose the `Queue` directly. This makes some of the code in the main body of the simulation slightly longer, but clearer, as you soon see.

`Customers` contains the current total of customers who have been served by the store. This value is updated via the class's `Serve` method and displayed when the simulation is complete.

The `ActivePerson` variable hold an object pointer to the `Person` object, which represents the current person being served by the store.

To keep things simple, limit the store to a single queue and a single server. This may or may not be realistic in real life, but it is realistic enough for this simple simulation.

RUNNING THE SIMULATION

Now that I've covered all of the assorted pieces of the simulation, let's look at its main body (see Listing 8.3). It's deceptively simple. The `InitSim` routine does all of the work necessary to run the simulation, while the `EndSim` routine displays the statistics collected during the simulation's execution.

LISTING 8.3   FORM1.COMMAND1_CLICK

```
Private Sub Command1_Click()

InitSim

Do While MasterTime < SimEndMasterTime
   StepSim  .

Loop

EndSim

End Sub
```

The StepSim routine is called once for each simulated second. It is responsible for incrementing the master clock as well as simulating one second's worth of time at the Kelp-Fil-A shop.

> **Tip**
>
> **A one line fix**
>
> As with any relatively complex program, you need to know where to look to get the best return when optimizing your program. For all practical purposes, you can ignore the code in the InitSim and EndSim routines. They will not have a big impact on performance. You should focus your attention on the StepSim routine and the loop that controls it. While testing the program, I had coded CDate("9:59:59pm") instead of using the SimEndMasterTime variable in the loop. Switching to a variable instead of converting the constant value for each step of the simulation reduced the runtime of the simulation to one third of the original runtime. Remember that the InitSim and EndSim routines are called only once, while the StepSim routine is called more than 40,000 times. Thus any improvement you can make in the StepSim routine may make a much bigger improvement than you think.

INITIALIZING THE SIMULATION

Initializing the simulation is pretty simple (see Listing 8.4). I begin by defining ServDist as a RandomDistribution(6) at the module level and then loading it with the appropriate values. Note that I initialize the Value parts with individual statements because I don't permit the user to change the values, only the Weights.

LISTING 8.4   FORM1.INITSIM

```
Private Sub InitSim()

Dim i As Long

ServDist(0).Value = 15
ServDist(1).Value = 30
ServDist(2).Value = 45
```

LISTING 8.4   CONTINUED

```
ServDist(3).Value = 60
ServDist(4).Value = 90
ServDist(5).Value = 120
ServDist(6).Value = 300

For i = 0 To 6
    ServDist(i).Weight = CSng(ServeTime(i).Text)

Next i

NormalizeDistribution ServDist

For i = 0 To 11
    ArrDist(i) = CSng(ArrivalRate(i).Text)

Next i

Set KelpFilA = New Store
MasterTime = CDate("10:00am")
TimeToCreateNextPerson = CDate("10:00am")
SimEndMasterTime = CDate("9:59:59pm")
Text4.Text = "Running"
StartTime = Now

End Sub
```

After normalizing the distribution, initialize a simple array (ArrDist) to hold the average number of people that will show up at Kelp-Fil-A each hour. These values will be used to determine when the next customer will show up.

Finally, create a new Store object and initialize various variables. The MasterTime variable holds the current time for the simulation. The TimeToCreateNextPerson variable holds the time the next person should be created. This assumes that the first person will show up at the store exactly at 10 a.m., which is not very realistic considering the taste of a Kelp-Fil-A sandwich. However, you always need a first customer and it really doesn't matter that much in the overall simulation.

The SimEndMasterTime contains the time just before the mall closes. So at 9:59:59 p.m., the mall is still open, while the mall is closed at 10:00:00 p.m. and any customers remaining are instantly thrown out. StartTime holds the current external time, which will be used later to compute the total number of seconds to run the simulation.

A SECOND IN THE SIMULATION

The StepSim routine performs all of the tasks that occur during one simulated second of the store (see Listing 8.5). It begins by calling the OkToCreateNewPerson function to see if a person should arrive at the shop. If so, create a new Person object and initialize ArriveTime with the current simulation time and create a random service time using the CRand function. Then I add the person to the end of the shop's wait queue.

LISTING 8.5   FORM1.STEPSIM

```
Private Sub StepSim()

Dim P As Person

If OKToCreateNewPerson(MasterTime) Then
   Set P = New Person
   P.ArriveTime = MasterTime
   P.ServeTime = CLng(CRand(ServDist))
   KelpFilA.WaitQueue.Add P

End If

If Not KelpFilA.ActivePerson Is Nothing Then
   If KelpFilA.ActivePerson.DepartTime < MasterTime Then
      Set KelpFilA.ActivePerson = Nothing

   End If

End If

If KelpFilA.ActivePerson Is Nothing Then
   If KelpFilA.WaitQueue.Length > 0 Then
      Set KelpFilA.ActivePerson = KelpFilA.WaitQueue.Front
      KelpFilA.ActivePerson.DepartTime = _
         DateAdd("s", KelpFilA.ActivePerson.ServeTime, MasterTime)
      KelpFilA.Serve

   End If

End If

UpdateMasterTime

End Sub
```

Next, determine if Kelp-Fil-A is currently serving someone. If it is, the `ActivePerson` property will contain a valid `Person` object. I can see if the person is finished by comparing their departure time with the master clock. If it's past their departure time, I set the `ActivePerson` object to `Nothing`.

Afterwards, check to see if the `ActivePerson` object is `Nothing`, which means I can select the next person from the queue, assuming there is one. Use the queue's `Front` method to return a reference to the `Person` object and assign it to the `ActivePerson` property. Then compute their departure time by adding the number of seconds in the `ServeTime` property to the current value of the master clock. Then execute the `KelpFilA.Serve` to perform any tasks related to serving the customer.

After handing all of the details about the simulation, call the `UpdateMasterTime` subroutine to update the master clock.

CREATING A CUSTOMER

The OKToCreateNewPerson function returns True if a new customer should arrive (see Listing 8.6). The module level variable, TimeToCreateNextPerson, holds the arrival time of next person. When the simulation starts, it holds the exact time the mall opens, so the first time this routine is called, it will return True.

LISTING 8.6   FORM1.OKTOCREATENEWPERSON

```
Private Function OKToCreateNewPerson(d As Date) As Boolean

Dim l As Single
Dim r As Single

If MasterTime >= TimeToCreateNextPerson Then
    OKToCreateNewPerson = True
    r = 3600 / (ArrDist(Hour(MasterTime) - 10))
    l = r * (Rand(2, 0))
    TimeToCreateNextPerson = DateAdd("s", l, MasterTime)

Else
    OKToCreateNewPerson = False

End If

End Function
```

Whenever the OKToCreateNewPerson function returns True, it also calculates the time the next person should be created. It does this by converting the average number of customers expected in a given hour into the average number of seconds between customers. Next, it multiplies this value by a uniform random number in the range of zero to two. This returns a value that can be as little as one half the average time or twice the average time between customers. Finally it adds this value to the current value of the master clock to create a new value for TimeToCreateNextPerson.

> **Note**
>
> **It's good enough for now**
>
> To make this simulation interesting, I wanted to add a little randomness to the arrival time of the customers. From a true simulation perspective, you would probably want a more interesting distribution for arrival times. However, for a game program, this is more than sufficient.

UPDATING THE MASTER CLOCK

Each tick of the master clock merely adds another second to the current time, but updating the clock is also a good place to capture some data about how the simulation is running. Listing 8.7 determines if the clock is exactly on the hour. If so, you compute the difference between the real starting time and the present time to compute the elapsed time since the simulation has started and display the information on the form. Then you can display the current value of the master clock, the number of customers that have been served by Kelp-Fil-A, and the maximum people that had to wait in line for their Kelp-Fil-A sandwich. Finally, after all that, add one second to the master clock.

LISTING 8.7   FORM1.UPDATEMASTERTIME

```
Private Sub UpdateMasterTime()

If Minute(MasterTime) = 0 And Second(MasterTime) = 0 Then
   Text1.Text = FormatNumber(DateDiff("s", StartTime, Now), 0) & " seconds"
   Text3.Text = FormatDateTime(MasterTime, vbLongTime)
   Text2.Text = FormatNumber(KelpFilA.Customers, 0)
   Text5.Text = FormatNumber(KelpFilA.WaitQueue.MaxLength, 0)
   DoEvents

End If

MasterTime = DateAdd("s", 1, MasterTime)

End Sub
```

DISPLAYING FINAL STATISTICS

After the simulation is complete, display the same statistics that were displayed in the UpdateMasterTime routine, and also update the form to say that the simulation is complete (see Listing 8.8).

LISTING 8.8   FORM1.ENDSIM

```
Private Sub EndSim()

Text1.Text = FormatNumber(DateDiff("s", StartTime, Now), 0) _
   & " seconds"
Text3.Text = FormatDateTime(MasterTime, vbLongTime)
Text4.Text = "Complete"
Text2.Text = FormatNumber(KelpFilA.Customers, 0)
Text5.Text = FormatNumber(KelpFilA.WaitQueue.MaxLength, 0)

Set KelpFilA = Nothing

End Sub
```

RUNNING THE SIMULATION WITH A TIMER

Running the simulation with a timer requires a different mindset to create the code. This code relies on the standard Timer control that comes with Visual Basic. When you set the timer's Enabled property to True, Windows will automatically fire the Timer event based on the value you specify in the timer's Interval property.

The downside to using the timer is that the resolution of the timer in a Windows 95/98/Me system is about 55 milliseconds. This means that the timer event will be called no more than

18 times per second, which could be a big problem if you try to run only one second during each tick of the clock. If you specify a value for Interval that is not a multiple of 55 milliseconds, it will be automatically rounded up to the next highest multiple of 55 on Windows 95/98/Me systems.

Tip

Windows 2000 is better

Timers on a Windows 2000 system are rounded to multiples of 10 milliseconds.

The way I worked around this problem was to allow you to specify the number of times StepSim should be called during each clock tick (see Listing 8.9). Store this value in the module level variable StepsPerTick. I also allowed you to specify the timer's interval value on the form. Finally, setting Enabled to True will start the timer.

LISTING 8.9   FORM1.COMMAND2_CLICK

```
Private Sub Command2_Click()

InitSim

Timer1.Interval = CLng(Text6.Text)
StepsPerTick = CLng(Text7.Text)
Timer1.Enabled = True

End Sub
```

The timer event is handled by the code in Listing 8.10. Because you don't use a loop to determine when the simulation is finished, you must disable the timer if SimEndMasterTime is greater than MasterTime. If it isn't, then simply call the StepSim routine the specified number of times using a For statement.

LISTING 8.10   FORM1.TIMER1_TIMER

```
Private Sub Timer1_Timer()

Dim i As Long

If MasterTime < SimEndMasterTime Then
   For i = 1 To StepsPerTick
      StepSim
   Next i

Else
   Timer1.Enabled = False
   EndSim

End If

End Sub
```

FINAL THOUGHTS

I enjoy building simulations. As long as you have the proper tools like random number generators and a way to manage queues, it isn't very difficult. Of course, a simulation isn't a game—I doubt that anyone would buy a game that looks like the program from this chapter.

It's possible to take a simulation and use it as the basis for a game, but it is important to remember that a simulation used in a game need not be accurate. It only needs to look accurate. After all, I haven't seen many fish swimming through my local shopping mall.

SIMULATING THE MALL

To simulate a shopping mall, you need to take an extremely complex environment and reduce its complexity so that it can be simulated. Not only that, the simulation needs to run alongside a CPU-intensive 3D graphics program that displays the results of the simulation. To complicate the matter even further, the simulation must be sufficiently challenging to control so as to make the game fun.

UNDERSTANDING THE SIMULATION

A shopping mall must provide a place where a large number of customers may visit stores to satisfy their needs while making their experience pleasant so that they will return in the future. The job of the mall's manager is to satisfy that goal, while at the same time making the mall a profitable business.

Unlike a store that derives its income from selling goods to satisfy a customer's needs, a shopping mall's income is dependent on the stores within the shopping mall making a good profit. If the collection of stores isn't successful, the mall will fail. However, with the right collection of stores, a mall can be wildly successful.

When creating a simulation for the mall there are a number of pieces that must be included in the simulation. Obviously, you need to simulate customers and stores. Things like the other malls in the neighborhood and the bank (which keeps track of money earned and loaned) also need to be included in the simulation. Then all of these pieces need to be integrated into a single entity known as the game.

In a database application, it is fairly easy to build a series of independent pieces and then tie them together near the end of the project, but a simulation generally isn't built that way. Instead, skeleton versions of the various pieces are created and pulled together to form the simulation. Each of these pieces are enhanced to add new functions as the complete simulation is finished.

One interesting side effect of this approach to building a program means that the program is never really finished. You may stop adding features for various reasons, but it doesn't mean that you can't improve the simulation over time. For instance, one of the most common reasons for not adding new features in a simulation is that the simulation is too slow or displaying graphics takes too much time. As faster computers become more popular, you can go back and increase the complexity of the simulation or the graphics or both.

BUILDING THE SIMULATION FRAMEWORK

The logical place to start building the simulation is to create a framework to run the simulation. The framework must be integrated into the existing program to take advantage of the facilities that already exist, yet run independently of the rest of the program.

RUNNING THE SIMULATION

There are two ways the simulation could be added to the game. The simplest way is to modify the PlayGame routine in Form1 to call a simulation step before you update the display. However, I prefer to use a timer control to fire the simulation step. It allows the render logic to run independently of the simulation so that the render logic can display as many frames as possible, while the simulation will chug away at the same rate whether you're running on a slow CPU or a very fast CPU. Listing 9.1 enables the timer control just before the rendering loop is started.

LISTING 9.1   FORM1.PLAYGAME

```
Sub PlayGame()

Timer1.Interval = 100
Timer1.Enabled = True

Do While GameActive
    dx.Render
    DoEvents

Loop

End Sub
```

I chose a value of 100 milliseconds as a nice balancing point. This means that the timer will fire approximately 10 times per second. While the timer event is active, nothing else can run, including any rendering code, so it is important to keep this value rather small.

> **Note**
>
> **Resolution #55**
>
> The timer in Windows Me and 98 systems has a resolution of 55 milliseconds. Specifying a value of less than 55 means that the timer will still fire every 55 milliseconds. In Windows XP and 2000, the resolution of the timer is about 10 milliseconds.

The timer routine consists of the following line of code, which allows the simulation to progress exactly one step.

```
GameObj.Step
```

STEPPING THE SIMULATION

The Step method in the Game class controls the simulation from the game perspective. It is responsible for creating customers and sending them to the appropriate mall. It is also responsible for controlling the speed of the game by updating the master clock. This routine uses these global variables.

```
Global MasterClock As Date
Global TicksPerStep As Long
Global Speed As Long
```

MasterClock keeps track of the current date and time in the simulation. Speed contains the number of seconds that pass in the simulation for each tick of the timer, which in turn controls the pace of the game.

TicksPerStep holds the current number of ticks that were required to run the last step of the simulation. This value is important because it allows you to determine if the simulation is taking too long relative to the timer's interval. If value exceeds the timer's interval, the call to dx.Render routine will be delayed until the simulation step has finished, which will negatively impact frame rate. For best results, this value should be no more than one half of the timer's interval.

The Game.Step method (see Listing 9.2) contains the logic that drives the game. It begins by saving the current tick count into the local variable Start. If the mall is open, it computes the starting time for the next step by adding the value in Speed to the value in MasterClock.

LISTING 9.2   GAME.STEP

```
Public Sub Step()

Dim c As Customer
Dim d As Date
Dim i As Long
Dim l As Long
Dim Start As Long

Start = GetTickCount

If IsMallOpen Then
    d = DateAdd("s", Speed, MasterClock)

    Set c = GetCustomer
    Do While MasterClock < d
       If Not c Is Nothing Then
          If (c.Needs And Mall.Needs) Or (c.FoodNeeds And Mall.FoodNeeds) Then
                MallObj.MallCustomers.PriorityAdd c, c.MallArrive

          End If
       End If
       Set c = GetCustomer

    Loop
    MasterClock = d

Else

    MasterClock = DateAdd("s", 1800, MasterClock)

End If

MallObj.Step

TicksPerStep = GetTickCount - Start

End Sub
```

Then the routine creates a new customer by calling the GetCustomer function. This function returns the information about the next customer. If the Customer object is Nothing, the customer went to a competitor's mall. If the Customer object is not Nothing, the Needs and FoodNeeds properties contain information about the customer's needs. Finally, GetCustomer will update the master clock to reflect the time the customer was created. (I'll discuss the details of this function in Chapter 10, "Simulating Customers," along with all of the other related information about how customers are processed in the game.)

If GetCustomer returns a valid object, then the code checks to see if the mall satisfies at least one of the customer's needs. Then it adds the customer to a queue within the Mall class for later processing. Unlike the first-in, first-out queue I used in the last chapter, I've modified the Queue class to keep the information in the queue in an order based on a priority value (arrival time of the customer). Then when items are retrieved from the queue, the item with the highest priority (lowest time value) will be retrieved.

PART

II

CH

9

After adding the customer to the queue the routine gets another customer and repeats this process, until the arrival time of the customer is greater than the start of the next time interval. Then the master clock value is restored to the start of the next time interval.

If the mall is closed, simply advance the clock by 30 minutes (1,800 seconds) to help pass the time more quickly. Because customers can only arrive when the mall is open, this value can be relatively large. Although I could have just jumped to the time the mall opens the next day, I felt that stepping quickly through the midnight hours gave a nicer feel for the game and leaves enough time for the player to pause the game between the time the mall closes for the night and reopens the next morning.

At the end of the routine, call the Mall.Step method to allow the mall to process the customers in the queue, plus any other actions related to the mall. Then compute the total time to execute this routine by getting a new value for tick count and subtracting the original starting tick count.

Note

Multiplayer in mind

Although generating customers could have been handled in the Mall class, it makes more sense to handle it in the Game class if you plan to implement a multiplayer game. One player's computer would become the game's server and generate customers for each of the other players. These customers would be sent to their computers using DirectPlay where they would be received and processed as if they were created by the local Game class.

STEPPING INSIDE THE MALL

The Mall.Step routine (see Listing 9.3) is called each time the timer ticks. Its job is to coordinate all the activities within the mall. There are basically four types of processing required inside the mall, which are the processing represented by the change of time in the master clock, plus those events that occur at the end of the day, the end of the month, and the end of the year.

LISTING 9.3   MALL.STEP

```
Public Sub Step()

If DateValue(MasterClock) <> Yesterday Then
   StepDay

   If Day(MasterClock) = 1 Then
      StepMonth

      If Month(MasterClock) = 1 Then
         StepYear

      End If

   End If

   Yesterday = DateValue(MasterClock)

End If

StepTick

End Sub
```

The routine begins by determining if the day has changed. It then will call StepDay to perform the end of day processing.

After processing the end of day logic, check to see if it is the end of the month by looking for the first day of the month. Then do a similar test for the end of the year by looking for the first month. Because the code has already determined that the master clock is on the first day of a month, it is safe to merely see if it is the first month of the year. Next after processing the end of day, month, and year reset the variable Yesterday to contain today's date.

Finally, after handling all of the other processing, it is time to handle the normal second-by-second operation of the mall by calling the StepTick routine.

The StepDay, StepMonth, and StepYear routines are very similar. Listing 9.4 shows the code for StepYear. This logic is aimed at allowing each of the different types of stores to perform their processing by calling their appropriate EndYear method. After all of the stores have been processed, the mall can perform its own end of year processing by calling the EndYear subroutine.

LISTING 9.4   MALL.STEPYEAR

```
Private Sub StepYear()

Dim a As Anchor
Dim f As Food
Dim s As Store

For Each a In Anchors
```

LISTING 9.4   CONTINUED

```
    a.EndYear

Next a

For Each f In Foods
    f.EndYear

Next f

For Each s In Stores
    s.EndYear

Next s

EndYear

z
```

CONTROLLING SIMULATION SPEED

The global variable Speed contains the number of seconds that the master clock will advance with each tick. For normal gameplay, a value of 300 gives nice results. To make the game easier to play, allow the player to choose from values of 60, 120, 300, 600, 900, and 1,800 seconds. The larger the number the faster the simulation will progress.

Listing 9.5 shows the code I use to allow the user to change the speed of the simulation. It merely chooses a new value for Speed based on the current value. After Speed reaches 1,800 seconds, I set Speed to zero and disable the timer to pause the game.

LISTING 9.5   FORM1.COMMAND13_CLICK

```
Private Sub Command13_Click()

Select Case Speed

Case 0
    Speed = 60
    Timer1.Enabled = True

Case 60
    Speed = 120

Case 120
    Speed = 300

Case 300
    Speed = 600

Case 600
    Speed = 900
```

LISTING 9.5 CONTINUED

```
Case 900
   Speed = 1800

Case 1800
   Speed = 0
   Timer1.Enabled = False

End Select

End Sub
```

COMMUNITIES AND COMPETITORS

Customers are attracted to the mall from the communities surrounding the mall. Collectively these communities are known as the mall's neighborhood.

BUILDING A COMMUNITY

A neighborhood is a two-dimensional grid that is controlled by initialization information. Each cell in the grid is known as a *community*. A community is a structure that looks like this:

```
Type Community
   Name As String
   Satisfaction As Single
   X As Long
   Y As Long
   Population As Single

End Type
```

Name is an optional attribute that associates a name with the community. Satisfaction describes the community's overall satisfaction with the mall. This value is affected by advertising and other actions taken by the player and is used as the initial satisfaction value for a customer. X and Y are the coordinates of the community in the grid, while Population contains the number of people in that particular community.

The community information is stored in a one-dimensional array as follows. It is kept in the Global.BAS module to make it easily accessible from anywhere in the program.

```
Global Communities() As Community
```

The primary reason I chose to use a one-dimensional array is that it makes it easy to convert the Population information into a RandomDistribution. Thus, I can generate customers randomly according to the overall population distribution. Another advantage of this approach is that you only have to define communities that exist in the grid. This give you the option to easily make a sparsely populated neighborhood.

```
Global PopulationDistribution() As RandomDistribution
```

The information is stored in the saved game file (see Listing 9.6). Because satisfaction isn't specified, a value of zero will be assumed.

LISTING 9.6   SELECTED TEXT FROM THE SWIMMALL.SMG FILE

```
Community\Mall\x=6
Community\Mall\y=5
Community\1\x=1
Community\1\y=1
Community\1\population=1000
Community\2\x=1
Community\2\y=2
Community\2\population=50
Community\3\x=1
Community\3\y=3
Community\3\population=300
```

The second key value in each entry in the .SMG file either represents a characteristic of the player's mall or the index in the Communities array. The routine to load this information is shown in Listing 9.7. It is called from the existing SetData routine in the Game class whenever the Community keyword is found.

LISTING 9.7   GAME.SETCOMMUNITY

```
Private Sub SetCommunity(Key1 As String, Key2 As String, _
   Key3 As String, Data As String)

Dim i As Long

If IsNumeric(Key2) Then
   i = CLng(Key2)

   If i > UBound(Communities) Then
      ReDim Preserve Communities(i)

   End If

   Select Case Key3
      Case "x"
         Communities(i).X = CSng(Data)

      Case "y"
         Communities(i).Y = CSng(Data)

      Case "name"
         Communities(i).Name = Data

      Case "population"
         Communities(i).Population = CSng(Data)

      Case Else
         GameDebugger.WriteLine _
            "Illegal community key value: " & Key1 & "/" & Key2

   End Select
```

LISTING 9.7 CONTINUED

```
ElseIf Key2 = "mall" Then
    Select Case Key3
        Case "x"
            Mall.CommunityX = CSng(Data)

        Case "y"
            Mall.CommunityY = CSng(Data)

        Case Else
            GameDebugger.WriteLine _
                "Illegal mall community key value: " & Key1 & "/" & Key2

    End Select

Else
    GameDebugger.WriteLine _
        "Unknown community data value: " & Key1 & "/" & Key2 & " = " & Data

End If

End Sub
```

This routine takes advantage of the ReDim Preserve statement to adjust the bounds of the Communities array to accept as many elements as supplied in the initialization file. The rest of the code uses a big Select statement to identify the appropriate part of the key value and then updates the mall information accordingly.

After all of the information in the saved game file has been loaded, the following block of code is executed in the PostGameLoadProcessing routine located in the Game class:

```
ReDim PopulationDistribution(UBound(Communities) - 1)
For i = 1 To UBound(Communities)
    PopulationDistribution(i - 1).value = i
    PopulationDistribution(i - 1).weight = Communities(i).Population

Next i

NormalizeDistribution PopulationDistribution
```

This code adjusts the size of the PopulationDistribution array (which is a RandomDistribution array) in the Game class. It then copies the Population element into the Weight property and sets the Value element to the community's index value. Note that the lowest index value in the Communities array is 1, while elements in the RandomDistribution array start with 0. Finally, call NormalizeDistribution to compute the Weight values used by the DRand function.

FOSTERING COMPETITION

Having competitors for the player's mall is important because they draw potential customers away from the player's mall. Because there is only a limited set of customers, the success of the player's mall depends on how many of these customers go to the player's mall when compared to the competitor's malls. To properly simulate the competitor's malls it is necessary to track some of the same key indicators for each competitor as I do for the mall itself. This is done using the `Competitor` type as shown below.

```
Type Competitor
    Name As String
    Satisfaction As Single
    X As Long
    Y As Long
    Needs As NeedTypes
    FoodNeeds As FoodNeedTypes
    CustomerCount As Long

End Type
```

The competitors are stored in this global array, which is loaded using code similar to the code used to load the communities. Listing 9.8 contains some of the information from the `SwimMall.SMG` initialization file.

```
Global Competitors() As Competitor
```

LISTING 9.8   SELECTED TEXT FROM THE SWIMMALL.SMG FILE

```
Competitor\1\name=The Underwater Kingdom Mall
Competitor\1\x=1
Competitor\1\y=1
Competitor\1\satisfaction=0
Competitor\1\needs=-1
Competitor\1\foodneeds=-1
Competitor\2\name=The Mall in Atlantis
Competitor\2\x=2
Competitor\2\y=10
Competitor\2\satisfaction=-0.1
Competitor\2\needs=-1
Competitor\2\foodneeds=-1
```

The X and Y values identify the location of the community where the competitor is located, while `Satisfaction` determines the initial satisfaction level for the mall. In this example both `Needs` and `FoodNeeds` are set to –1. This implies that these competitors will fulfill every possible need for a customer (see Chapter 10, "Simulating Customers," for more information about customers and their needs).

INITIALIZING THE SIMULATION

Like the graphics components of the game, the simulation relies heavily on information from external files to set key values within the simulation. Some of these values represent the current state of the simulation such as the master clock and the amount of cash in the bank.

KEY MALL INDICATORS

Every simulation has a few key indicators that track how the simulation is running. In Swim Mall, these indicators include the following:

- **MasterClock** contains the current date and time in the simulation.
- **Satisfaction** is a value ranging between –1 (poor) and +1 (excellent) that indicates how the customers perceive the mall. A value of zero is average.
- **Difficulty** contains a difficulty factor that is used to modify a customer's satisfaction. If the value is greater than 1, customer satisfaction is increased, making the game easier to play. A value between 0 and 1 will decrease customer satisfaction making the game harder to play.
- **Cash** contains the amount of money needed to cover expenses.
- **Loans** contains the amount of money that the mall has borrowed from the bank. The interest is payable at the end of each month, while the principle must be explicitly paid by the player.
- **Inflation** contains the average inflation index, which will vary from month to month and have a negative impact on the cost of operating the mall.
- **CustomerCount** contains the total number of customers who have made a trip to any of the shopping malls in this game.
- **MallCustomers** contains the total number of customers who have visited the player's mall. A similar value is kept for each of the competitor's malls.

These values are declared as global variables, meaning that they can be accessed from anywhere in the program. They are also kept in the saved game file, so that you can restore their state whenever a game is loaded.

Satisfaction and the master clock information is important enough that I included it on the screen in the rendering routines. The other information is available on the `MallInfo` form, which I'll cover later in this chapter.

LOADING MALL HOURS

Another part of initializing the mall is setting when the mall is open and closed. This information is also kept in the saved game file and defined with statements like the following:

```
Schedule\default\open=10
Schedule\default\close=22
Schedule\Sunday\open=12
Schedule\Sunday\close=18
```

This information is loaded into these arrays:

```
Public MallOpen(6) As Date
Public MallClose(6) As Date
```

To make things easier, use a key2 value of default to set the default operating hours for the mall. After setting the default opening and closing times, you can follow it with any exceptions. In this case, the mall is open from 10 a.m. to 10 p.m. each day except for Sunday, when the mall is only open from noon until 6 p.m.

The IsMallOpen routine (see Listing 9.9) returns True if the master clock contains a time between the opening and closing times in the mall. This routine determines the day of the week by using the Weekday function and then uses that value as a subscript into the MallOpen and MallClose arrays containing the mall's schedule.

LISTING 9.9   GAME.ISMALLOPEN

```
Public Function IsMallOpen() As Boolean

Dim w As Long

w = Weekday(MasterClock) - 1

IsMallOpen = (TimeValue(MasterClock) > MallOpen(w)) And _
    (TimeValue(MasterClock) < MallClose(w))

End Function
```

MONITORING THE MALL

There is a lot of information generated while the mall simulation is running. To understand how things are running in the mall, I added a form called MallInfo that displays some of the key indicators for the mall (see Figure 9.1).

Figure 9.1
The MallInfo form displays general information about the player's mall.

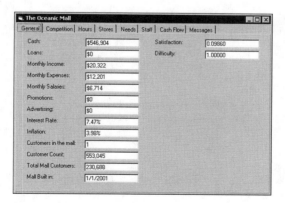

This form relies on the SSTab control to organize data, otherwise the form would need far more real estate. When the form is loaded, it enables a timer control that fires every 500 milliseconds. In the timer event, I call the DisplaySummary routine shown in Listing 9.10.

LISTING 9.10   MALLINFO.DISPLAYSUMMARY

```
Private Sub DisplaySummary()

Dim i As Long
Dim j As Long
Dim l As ListItem
Dim a As Anchor
Dim f As Food
Dim s As Store

Me.Caption = GameObj.Name
Text1.Text = FormatCurrency(Cash, 0)
Text2.Text = FormatCurrency(Loans, 0)
Text3.Text = FormatCurrency(MonthlyIncome, 0)
Text4.Text = FormatCurrency(MonthlyExpenses, 0)
Text5.Text = FormatCurrency(MonthlySalary, 0)
Text6.Text = FormatCurrency(Promotions, 0)
Text7.Text = FormatCurrency(Advertising, 0)
Text8.Text = FormatPercent(InterestRate, 2)
Text9.Text = FormatPercent(Inflation, 2)
Text10.Text = FormatNumber(GameObj.Mall.MallCustomers.Length, 0)
Text11.Text = FormatNumber(CustomerCount, 0)
Text12.Text = FormatNumber(MallCustomerCount, 0)
Text13.Text = FormatDateTime(MallBuilt, vbShortDate)
Text14.Text = FormatNumber(Satisfaction, 5)
Text15.Text = FormatNumber(Difficulty, 5)

ListView1.ListItems.Clear
Set l = ListView1.ListItems.Add(1, "x0", GameObj.Name)
l.SubItems(1) = FormatNumber(MallCustomerCount, 0)
l.SubItems(2) = FormatNumber(Satisfaction, 5)

For i = 1 To UBound(Competitors)
    Set l = ListView1.ListItems.Add(i + 1, "x" & FormatNumber(i, 0), _
        Competitors(i).Name)
    l.SubItems(1) = FormatNumber(Competitors(i).CustomerCount, 0)
    l.SubItems(2) = FormatNumber(Competitors(i).Satisfaction, 5)

Next i

For i = 0 To 6
    OpenTime(i).Text = FormatDateTime(MallOpen(i), vbLongTime)
    CloseTime(i).Text = FormatDateTime(MallClose(i), vbLongTime)

Next i

ListView2.ListItems.Clear
i = 0
For Each a In GameObj.Mall.Anchors
    i = i + 1
    Set l = ListView2.ListItems.Add(i, "x" & FormatNumber(i, 0), a.Name)
    l.SubItems(1) = "Anchor"
    l.SubItems(2) = FormatNumber(a.X, 0) & ", " & FormatNumber(a.Z, 0)
    l.SubItems(3) = FormatCurrency(a.TotalSales, 0)
    l.SubItems(4) = FormatCurrency(a.TotalProfit, 0)
```

LISTING 9.10   CONTINUED

```
    l.SubItems(5) = FormatNumber(a.TotalCustomers, 0)

Next a

For Each f In GameObj.Mall.Foods
    i = i + 1
    Set l = ListView2.ListItems.Add(i, "x" & FormatNumber(i, 0), f.Name)
    l.SubItems(1) = "Food Vendor"
    l.SubItems(2) = FormatNumber(f.X, 0) & ", " & FormatNumber(f.Z, 0)
    l.SubItems(3) = FormatCurrency(f.TotalSales, 0)
    l.SubItems(4) = FormatCurrency(f.TotalProfit, 0)
    l.SubItems(5) = FormatNumber(f.TotalCustomers, 0)

Next f

For Each s In GameObj.Mall.Stores
    i = i + 1
    Set l = ListView2.ListItems.Add(i, "x" & FormatNumber(i, 0), s.Name)
    l.SubItems(1) = "Store"
    l.SubItems(2) = FormatNumber(s.X, 0) & ", " & FormatNumber(s.Z, 0)
    l.SubItems(3) = FormatCurrency(s.TotalSales, 0)
    l.SubItems(4) = FormatCurrency(s.TotalProfit, 0)
    l.SubItems(5) = FormatNumber(s.TotalCustomers, 0)

Next s

j = 1
For i = 0 To 29
    Needs(i).Value = IIf(GameObj.Mall.Needs And j, 1, 0)
    j = j * 2

Next i

j = 1
For i = 0 To 16
    FoodNeeds(i).Value = IIf(GameObj.Mall.FoodNeeds And j, 1, 0)
    j = j * 2

Next i

ListView3.ListItems.Clear
For i = 1 To UBound(Staff)
    Set l = ListView3.ListItems.Add(i, "x" & FormatNumber(i, 0), Staff(i).Name)
    Select Case Staff(i).StaffType
        Case Janitor
            l.SubItems(1) = "Janitor"

        Case Security
            l.SubItems(1) = "Security"

        Case Clerk
            l.SubItems(1) = "Clerk"

        Case Else
```

LISTING 9.10 CONTINUED

```
            l.SubItems(1) = "Unknown"

    End Select

    l.SubItems(2) = FormatCurrency(Staff(i).Salary, 0)

Next i

ListView4.ListItems.Clear
For i = 1 To UBound(RunningExpenses)
    Set l = ListView4.ListItems.Add(i, "x" & _
        FormatNumber(i, 0), _
        FormatDateTime(RunningExpenses(i).Date, vbShortDate))
    l.SubItems(1) = FormatCurrency(RunningExpenses(i).MonthlyIncome, 0)
    l.SubItems(2) = FormatCurrency(RunningExpenses(i).MonthlyExpenses, 0)
    l.SubItems(3) = FormatCurrency(RunningExpenses(i).Profit, 0)
    l.SubItems(4) = FormatCurrency(RunningExpenses(i).Cash, 0)
    l.SubItems(5) = FormatCurrency(RunningExpenses(i).Salaries, 0)
    l.SubItems(6) = FormatCurrency(RunningExpenses(i).Insurance, 0)
    l.SubItems(7) = FormatCurrency(RunningExpenses(i).Supplies, 0)
    l.SubItems(8) = FormatCurrency(RunningExpenses(i).Utilities, 0)
    l.SubItems(9) = FormatCurrency(RunningExpenses(i).Taxes, 0)
    l.SubItems(10) = FormatCurrency(RunningExpenses(i).Interest, 0)
    l.SubItems(11) = FormatCurrency(RunningExpenses(i).Promotions, 0)
    l.SubItems(12) = FormatCurrency(RunningExpenses(i).Advertising, 0)

Next i

End Sub
```

This routine merely copies data to the form in the assorted text boxes, check boxes, and ListView controls. I'm not very concerned about the efficiency of this routine because it is more of a debugging aid than a feature of the game. I've set each of the ListView controls into report mode, which makes it easy to display this kind of tabular data.

Note that for each competitor, including the mall itself (see Figure 9.2), the Competition tab displays its name, the number of customers that have shopped at the mall, and the satisfaction rating for each mall.

Figure 9.2
Information about each competitor is displayed on the Competition tab.

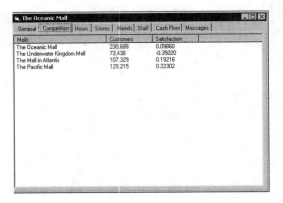

The `ListView2` control is displayed on the Stores tab and contains a summary of the information kept for each store (see Figure 9.3). You can see the total number of customers who have visited each store, plus the total sales and profit that were generated by their visits. You'll see how this information is generated in Chapter 11, "Simulating Stores and Money."

Figure 9.3
The Stores tab displays useful information about each store in the player's mall.

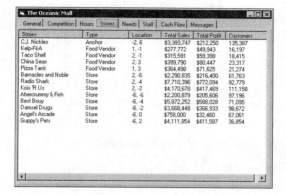

The Needs tab (see Figure 9.4) displays a series of checkboxes that identifies which needs are fulfilled by the mall as a whole. Obviously part of the game involves trying to attract a mix of stores that offer as many needs as possible.

Figure 9.4
The Needs tab lists all possible needs and identifies how well the player's mall meets them.

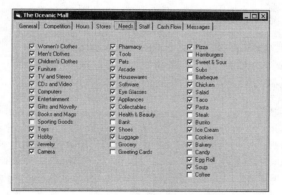

The Staff tab (see Figure 9.5) lists information about all of the mall's employees, including their name, the type of job they hold, and their monthly salary.

The Cash Flow tab (see Figure 9.6) displays a monthly summary of the mall's income and expenses. This is a fairly complex form with a lot of information. Chapter 11 contains the details of how these numbers are generated.

Figure 9.5
The Staff tab lists all of the employees at the mall.

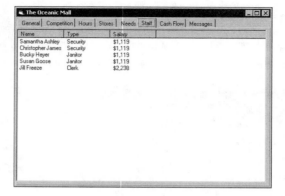

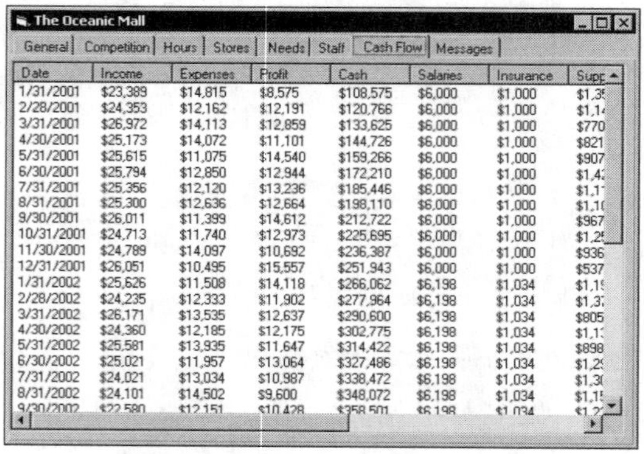

Figure 9.6
The Cash Flow tab contains a monthly summary of the mall's income and expenses.

FINAL THOUGHTS

This chapter discusses the core issues related to the simulation. It talked about how to control the rate of execution by controlling how quickly value of the master clock changes and how to use the Timer control to separate the simulation from the graphics engine. I also discussed priority queues and showed how to modify the Queue class from Chapter 8, "Simulating Reality," without affecting how programs that used the previous version worked.

In terms of the game, I covered how to load information about the simulation from the saved game file and discussed how to simulate the malls that compete with the player's mall. I also showed how to display information about the mall in real time. This technique is very useful for debugging the simulation.

One limitation of the simulation is the approach I've used for implementing priority queues. Using an array is not a very efficient approach, especially when you have more than a handful of items in the queue. The main drawback is the linear search to find where to place the item into the queue.

I took advantage of the fact that most of the items added to the queue would be added at the end, by starting my search from the end of the queue rather than the front. However, even this approach is extremely CPU intensive. A better approach would be to store the items in the queue with a tree structure. This way you could minimize the amount of time required to find the appropriate place to store the new item.

PART

II

CH

9

SIMULATING CUSTOMERS

In this chapter

Customers are the key to Swim Mall. Attracting them to the stores in the mall is critical for a successful shopping mall. Although most people have a number of different reasons for choosing a shopping mall, Swim Mall simplifies these reasons into three things: needs, distance, and satisfaction. Needs are a functional way of describing why the customer want to go to a mall. Distance represents the relative distance the customer has to travel to a mall. Satisfaction represents how much the customer likes a particular mall.

Once the customer is at the mall, the simulation has to decide where to send the customer and whether the customer should make a purchase while she is there. Depending on the customer's experience in the mall the overall satisfaction of the mall changes, which is why it's important to keep the customer happy.

THE CUSTOMER CLASS

The Customer class contains the information about a single customer including name (Name), the reasons he wants to go shopping (Needs and FoodNeeds), where he comes from (Community, CommunityX, and CommunityY) and how he feels about the mall (Satisfaction). This information is used to choose which mall he wants to shop at and the individual stores within the mall he wants to visit (see Listing 10.1).

LISTING 10.1   PROPERTIES OF THE CUSTOMER CLASS

```
Public Name As String

Public FoodNeeds As FoodNeedTypes
Public Needs As NeedTypes
Public NeedCount As Long

Public Satisfaction As Single
Public Community As Long
Public CommunityX As Long
Public CommunityY As Long

Public NextAction As ActionTypes
Public Store As Object
Public StoreArrive As Date
Public StoreDepart As Date
Public MallArrive As Date
Public MallDepart As Date
```

In addition to these items, a number of pieces of information are used to track when and where the customer is in the mall. The NextAction property describes the customer's next action within the mall. ArriveAtMall means that the customer arrives at the mall at the value stored in MallArrive. ArriveAtStore implies that the customer arrives at the store referenced by Store based on the value StoreArrive. DepartStore indicates that the customer leaves the store at the time stored in DepartStore. Finally DepartMall means that the customer has finished shopping and leaves the mall at the time stored in MallDepart.

CUSTOMER NEEDS

Customer needs fall into two main categories, *general needs* and *food needs*. General needs are met by going to a regular store or an anchor store. They represent items such as clothes, furniture, computers, and toys (see Listing 10.2).

LISTING 10.2   CUSTOMER.NEEDTYPES

```
Public Enum NeedTypes
    WomensClothes = &H1&          ' 0 - 0000 0001
    MensClothes = &H2&            ' 1 - 0000 0002
    ChildrensClothes = &H4&       ' 2 - 0000 0004
    Furniture = &H8&              ' 3 - 0000 0008
    TVStereo = &H10&              ' 4 - 0000 0010
    MusicCDVideoTapes = &H20&     ' 5 - 0000 0020
    Computers = &H40&             ' 6 - 0000 0040
    Entertainment = &H80&         ' 7 - 0000 0080
    GiftsNovelty = &H100&         ' 8 - 0000 0100
    BooksMagazines = &H200&       ' 9 - 0000 0200
    SportingGoods = &H400&        '10 - 0000 0400
    Toys = &H800&                 '11 - 0000 0800
    Hobby = &H1000&               '12 - 0000 1000
    Jewelry = &H2000&             '13 - 0000 2000
    Camera = &H4000&              '14 - 0000 4000
    Pharmacy = &H8000&            '15 - 0000 8000
    Tools = &H10000               '16 - 0001 0000
    Pets = &H20000                '17 - 0002 0000
    Arcade = &H40000              '18 - 0004 0000
    Housewares = &H80000          '19 - 0008 0000
    Software = &H100000           '20 - 0010 0000
    EyeGlasses = &H200000         '21 - 0020 0000
    Appliances = &H400000         '22 - 0040 0000
    Collectables = &H800000       '23 - 0080 0000
    HealthBeauty = &H1000000      '24 - 0100 0000
    Bank = &H2000000              '25 - 0200 0000
    Shoes = &H4000000             '26 - 0400 0000
    Luggage = &H8000000           '27 - 0800 0000
    Grocery = &H10000000          '28 - 1000 0000
    GreetingCard = &H20000000     '29 - 2000 0000
    Food = &H40000000             '30 - 4000 0000
End Enum
```

Although I used an enum type to describe the needs, I chose to assign a specific value for each need. An enum stores its information as a Long value. This means that you can assign values to each of the 32 bits. I took advantage of this fact and carefully assigned a numeric value to each name that represents a particular bit in the Long value.

This technique allows you to quickly compare two sets of needs using the And operator. In Visual Basic, And is a bit-wise operator, which will And each pair of bits together (for example, a bit is True, only with both bits in the And operation are True). Thus, you can quickly determine with a single operation if a store meets any of the customer's needs.

Although you can use all 32 bits, I limited myself to only the first 30 bits (0–29) to describe a customer's needs. I did this because Visual Basic doesn't support bit-shift operators and multiplying a Long value where bit 30 is True by two causes an overflow and aborts the program.

However, I found another way to use bit 30. I call it the food bit. This bit is set to True whenever any of the bits in the FoodNeeds field are set.

Note

Long and short chaos

When declaring constants in this fashion, Visual Basic assumes that the constant is 16 bits if the number can be stored in 16 bits (less than or equal to 32,767 decimal/&H8FFF hex). To prevent this problem, you need to append an ampersand (&) to the end of the value to ensure that Visual Basic treats it as a 32 bit value.

FOOD NEEDS

Food needs are met by going to a food court vendor, with each individual need representing a specific type of food (see Listing 10.3). Unlike NeedTypes I chose to define fewer needs because there would be fewer vendors in the food court than in the rest of the mall. This makes meeting a customer's food needs simpler.

LISTING 10.3   CUSTOMER.FOODNEEDTYPES

```
Public Enum FoodNeedTypes
    Pizza = &H1&              ' 0 - 0000 0001
    Hamburgers = &H2&         ' 1 - 0000 0002
    SweetSour = &H4&          ' 2 - 0000 0004
    Subs = &H8&               ' 3 - 0000 0008
    Barbeque = &H10&          ' 4 - 0000 0010
    Chicken = &H20&           ' 5 - 0000 0020
    Salad = &H40&             ' 6 - 0000 0040
    Taco = &H80&              ' 7 - 0000 0080
    Pasta = &H100&            ' 8 - 0000 0100
    Steak = &H200&            ' 9 - 0000 0200
    Burrito = &H400&          '10 - 0000 0400
    IceCream = &H800&         '11 - 0000 0800
    Cookies = &H1000&         '12 - 0000 1000
    Bakery = &H2000&          '13 - 0000 2000
    Candy = &H4000&           '14 - 0000 4000
    EggRoll = &H8000&         '15 - 0000 8000
    Soup = &H10000            '16 - 0001 0000
    Coffee = &H20000          '17 - 0002 0000

End Enum
```

Each of the food needs represents a specific type of food, including related foods. For instance, Hamburgers also implies that the customer would purchase French fries and a beverage. The only exception to this rule is Coffee. This value recognizes the fact that there are several popular coffee chains that serve exotic coffee without necessarily serving any other type of food.

COUNTING NEEDS

Listing 10.4 contains a utility routine that counts the number of needs that a customer has. I took advantage of the fact that I can use an enum value in place of a Long and created a single routine called CountBits that counts the number of needs in a NeedsType or FoodNeedsType expression.

LISTING 10.4   GLOBAL.COUNTBITS

```
Public Function CountBits(n As Long) As Long

Dim c As Long
Dim i As Long
Dim X As Long

c = 0
X = 1
For i = 0 To 29
    If n And X Then
        c = c + 1

    End If

    X = X * 2

Next i

CountBits = c

End Function
```

PART
II
CH
10

This routine uses the variable c to hold the number of needs found, and the variable X to hold a mask value that you can use to extract a single bit. When X is equal to 1, you can use the And operator to determine if bit zero is set. If bit 0 is 1, n And X returns a non-zero value. If bit 0 is 0, n And X returns 0. Because Visual Basic assumes that a value of 0 is False and any other value is True, I can use a simple If statement to decide whether to add 1 to the count or not.

Note

Not in C++

In C++ you can declare a variable to be unsigned, so multiplying 2^{30} by 2 does not generate an overflow. However multiplying 2^{31} by 2 does generate an overflow because you have run out of bits to hold the number.

To examine the next bit all you have to do is to multiply x by 2. However, this technique has a major limitation; eventually if you multiply by 2 you get an overflow. This happens when you have just tested bit 30 and want to multiply x by 2 to test the last bit. It turns out that the last bit is the sign bit in a 32-bit Long number, so 2^{30} is the largest possible number you can manipulate using a Long value.

The For loop in Listing 10.4 has the problem where it would multiply the number after I test the bit (x = x * 2). Although I could have included code to prevent this situation, I decided to only define bits 0–29 for a customer's needs and leave the ugly kludge out of the code.

WHEN DO CUSTOMERS ARRIVE?

Before I can create a customer, I need to determine how often a customer decides to visit the mall. You can't use a simple random number because most shopping malls have more customers on Saturday than any other day of the week. Likewise, most malls see a surge of customers around lunch time and dinner time during the week.

I handle this by creating a two-dimensional array that contains the number of customers who are expected to arrive during each hour the mall is open. The first dimension is the day of the week, which ranges from 0–6, while the second dimension is the hour of the day. This information is specified in the saved game file as shown in Listing 10.5.

LISTING 10.5   SELECTED DATA FROM THE SWIMMALL.SMG FILE

```
Arrival\Sunday\10=10
Arrival\Sunday\11=50
Arrival\Sunday\12=50
Arrival\Sunday\13=75
Arrival\Sunday\14=50
Arrival\Sunday\15=50
Arrival\Sunday\16=25
Arrival\Sunday\17=10
Arrival\Monday\10=10
Arrival\Monday\11=25
Arrival\Monday\12=50
Arrival\Monday\13=25
Arrival\Monday\14=25
Arrival\Monday\15=25
Arrival\Monday\16=25
Arrival\Monday\17=35
Arrival\Monday\18=50
Arrival\Monday\19=50
Arrival\Monday\20=25
Arrival\Monday\21=10
```

Each element of the array is initialized to zero during the Class_Initialize event when the Game object is created. Then the code shown in Listing 10.4 is used to load the actual values from the initialization file. Because the array is always initialized to zero, only the non-zero values of the array need be specified in the initialization file.

The SetArrival routine (see Listing 10.6) is called from the SetData routine each time an Arrival keyword is found. SetArrival merely parses the information and stores it in the appropriate part of the CustomerArrival array.

LISTING 10.6   GAME.SETARRIVAL

```
Private Sub SetArrival(Key2 As String, Key3 As String, Data As String)

Select Case Key2
   Case "Sunday"
      CustomerArrival(0, CLng(Key3)) = CSng(Data)

   Case "Monday"
      CustomerArrival(1, CLng(Key3)) = CSng(Data)

   Case "Tuesday"
      CustomerArrival(2, CLng(Key3)) = CSng(Data)

   Case "Wednesday"
      CustomerArrival(3, CLng(Key3)) = CSng(Data)

   Case "Thursday"
      CustomerArrival(4, CLng(Key3)) = CSng(Data)

   Case "Friday"
      CustomerArrival(5, CLng(Key3)) = CSng(Data)

   Case "Saturday"
      CustomerArrival(6, CLng(Key3)) = CSng(Data)

   Case Else
      GameDebugger.WriteLine "Unknown arrival value: " & _
         Key2 & " \ " & Key3 & " = " & Data

End Select

End Sub
```

CREATING CUSTOMERS

The MakeCustomer function (see Listing 10.7) returns an initialized customer object. It starts by adding 1 to the number of customers created, and then it creates an empty customer object and initializes the Name property with the customer number.

LISTING 10.7   GAME.MAKECUSTOMER

```
Private Function MakeCustomer() As Customer

Dim c As Customer
Dim i As Long
Dim n As Single
Dim r As Single

CustomerCount = CustomerCount + 1
```

LISTING 10.7   CONTINUED

```
Set c = New Customer
c.Name = "Customer " & FormatNumber(CustomerCount, 0)

c.NextAction = ArriveAtMall
n = CustomerArrival(Weekday(MasterClock) - 1, Hour(MasterClock))
r = 3600 / n
MasterClock = DateAdd("s", Int(Rand(r * 2, 1)), MasterClock)
c.MallArrive = MasterClock
c.MallDepart = 0

c.Community = DRand(PopulationDistribution)
c.CommunityX = Communities(c.Community).X
c.CommunityY = Communities(c.Community).Y

c.FoodNeeds = 0
c.Needs = 0

r = Int(Rand(10, 1))
For i = 1 To CLng(r)
   c.Needs = c.Needs Or NeedsArray(Int(Rand(30, 0)))

Next i

If Hour(MasterClock) > 11 And Hour(MasterClock) < 1 Then
   c.Needs = c.Needs Or Food

ElseIf Hour(MasterClock) > 17 And Hour(MasterClock) < 19 Then
  c.Needs = c.Needs Or Food

ElseIf Rand(4) < 1 Then
   c.Needs = c.Needs Or Food

End If

If c.Needs And Food Then
   r = Rand(3, 1)
   For i = 1 To CLng(r)
      c.FoodNeeds = c.FoodNeeds Or NeedsArray(Int(Rand(18, 0)))

   Next i

End If

c.NeedCount = CountBits(c.Needs) + CountBits(c.FoodNeeds)

Set MakeCustomer = c

End Function
```

Next, I set the NextAction property to ArriveAtMall and compute when the customer should arrive at the mall. I extract the number of customers per hour from the CustomerArrival array using the Weekday function to get the day of the week and the Hour function to get the hour of the day. Note that I have to subtract 1 from the value returned by the Weekday function since Weekday returns a value of 1 for Sunday, while the array uses a subscript of 0 for Sunday.

Once you have the number of customers per hour value in the variable n, you can translate that into the number of seconds between customers by dividing 3600 (seconds in an hour) by n, which I store in the variable r. Then use this value to create a random number in the range of 1 to r * 2, which contains the number of seconds to be added to the master clock, which is the time that this customer arrives at the mall.

After this, pick a community for the customer using the PopulationDistribution created in Chapter 9, "Simulating the Mall." Note that I'll also save the X and Y values for the community in the customer object.

Generating needs is a little tricky because I use a single bit to represent each need and Visual Basic lacks the facilities to manipulate bits that are found in C and C++. However, that isn't a major problem here. First I know that a variable defined as an enum can be interchanged with a Long. So, I defined a 32-element array called NeedsArray where each element in the array holds a value with one bit set that corresponds to the position in the array. Then I initialize it using the following code in the Class_Initialize event.

```
j = 1
For i = 0 To 29
   NeedsArray(i) = j
   j = j * 2

Next I
NeedsArray(30) = &H40000000
NeedsArray(31) = &H80000000
```

Back in the MakeCustomer routine, set both Needs and FoodNeeds to zero. Then create a random number in the range of 1 to 10 that determines the number of needs you want to set in Needs. Then use a For loop to add the needs. Generate a random number in the range of 0 to 29 and then Or the corresponding element from the NeedsArray to the Needs property. This always sets that particular bit associated with the need, even if the same need is later generated in the same loop.

Note that the Food bit is really bit 30. This bit is not set by the above loop that processes the bits in NeedsArray. This is because the Food need is unique. When this bit is set, generate a set of random foods for the customer. Set this bit if the master clock indicates that it is lunchtime or dinner time. However, because people eat at other times, I'll generate a random number between 0 and 4. If the value is less than 1, I'll also set the bit.

Once the bit is set, generate three random foods using the same technique you used earlier. Then count the total number of bits set in Needs and FoodNeeds and save the value into the NeedCount property. Finally, return the customer object to the calling routine.

PICKING THE BEST MALL

Now that you can create a customer, you need to determine the mall that the customer goes to. The Step routine (see Listing 9.2 in Chapter 9) calls the GetCustomer routine to return the next customer for this mall. If GetCustomer returns a valid customer object, Step adds it to the mall's queue for processing. If GetCustomer returns Nothing, the customer went to another mall.

To pick the best mall, take key information for each mall and compute a rating for the mall. This information includes the percentage of needs met, distance to the mall, and the customer's satisfaction with the mall. After evaluating this information, the customer then goes to the mall with the highest rating. If the mall happens to be a competitor to the player's mall, update the competitor's information to reflect the choice.

The GetCustomer routine (see Listing 10.8) begins by getting a customer object from the MakeCustomer routine. Then redimension an array called MallRating to be the same size as the Competitors array. Because the first competitor is stored in element 1, you can use element 0 to store information about the player's mall.

LISTING 10.8 GAME.GETCUSTOMER

```
Public Function GetCustomer() As Customer

Dim c As Customer
Dim i As Long
Dim j As Long

Dim MallNeeds As Single
Dim cn As Single
Dim cd As Single
Dim mn As Single
Dim md As Single
Dim s As Single

Dim MallRating() As Single

Set c = MakeCustomer

ReDim MallRating(UBound(Competitors))

mn = CSng(CountBits(c.Needs And Mall.Needs) + _
    CountBits(c.FoodNeeds And Mall.FoodNeeds)) / _
    CSng(c.NeedCount)

md = Sqr((c.CommunityX - Mall.CommunityX) * _
    (c.CommunityX - Mall.CommunityX) + _
    (c.CommunityY - Mall.CommunityY) * _
    (c.CommunityY - Mall.CommunityY))

MallRating(0) = Satisfaction + mn - (md / 15) + _
    Communities(c.Community).Satisfaction + Rand(1)

For i = 1 To UBound(Competitors)
    cn = CSng(CountBits(c.Needs And Competitors(i).Needs) + _
        CountBits(c.FoodNeeds And Competitors(i).FoodNeeds)) / _
        CSng(c.NeedCount)

    cd = Sqr((c.CommunityX - Competitors(i).X) * _
        (c.CommunityX - Competitors(i).X) + _
```

LISTING 10.8   CONTINUED

```
            (c.CommunityY - Competitors(i).Y) * _
            (c.CommunityY - Competitors(i).Y))

      MallRating(i) = Competitors(i).Satisfaction + cn - _
         (cd / 15) + Rand(1)

   Next i

   j = 0
   For i = 0 To UBound(Competitors)
      If MallRating(i) > MallRating(j) Then
         j = i

      End If

   Next i

   If j = 0 Then
      Set GetCustomer = c

   Else
      Competitors(j).CustomerCount = Competitors(j).CustomerCount + 1
      s = Rand(2, -2)
      s = IIf(s > 1, 1, IIf(s < -1, -1, s))

      Competitors(j).Satisfaction = Competitors(j).Satisfaction + _
         s * Abs(1 - Competitors(j).Satisfaction) / 1000
      Set GetCustomer = Nothing

   End If

   End Function
```

The next step is to compute the number of needs met by the player's mall. This is done by And'ing the player's mall needs with those generated for the customer and then using the CountBits function to count the number of True bits. I can divide the sum of these values by the NeedCount property to determine the percentage of needs that are met by the mall.

Next compute the distance to the mall by computing as the square root of the square of the distances in the X and Y directions.

The rating for the player's mall is computed by starting with the mall's satisfaction rating and adding the percent of needs met. Then divide the distance to the mall by 15 and subtract it from the rating. Next add the customer's community satisfaction with the mall. Finally add a floating-point random value ranging between 0 and 1, just to account for some intangible random factor. All of the values in this equation range have a maximum value of 1, so dividing the distance by 15 simply scales the value so that it doesn't overwhelm the other numbers.

After you've computed the rating for the player's mall, repeat the same process for each of the competing malls. Then you can scan through the list of results looking for the index of the mall with the highest rating, which is stored in the variable j. If j is zero, this means that the player's mall was selected and you can simply return the customer object in c.

If the player's mall is not selected, you have to update the competitor's satisfaction rating, and keep track of any other statistics for the competitor.

PRIORITY QUEUES

In Chapter 8, "Simulating Reality," I introduced the idea of a queue, which works like a pipe. You can put items in one end and take them out of the other end. This means that the first item placed in the queue is the first item removed from the queue.

While queues are a useful tool for buffering requests for processing, the rule that ensures the first item added to the queue is the first item processed is a big limitation. Sometimes it's necessary to process the items in the queue in a different order. The best way to do this is by using a priority queue.

A priority queue is similar to a regular queue, except that the items in the queue are stored in order based on a priority value. Typically, when a new item is added to the queue, it is stored in the appropriate place in the queue.

RESTRUCTURING THE QUEUE

In the Queue class in Chapter 8, the items in the queue were stored in a simple array of type Object. Adding a priority value means you have to hold the priority value as well as an object pointer. This is easily accomplished using the following definitions:

```
Private Type QStuff
   Data As Object
   Priority As Variant

End Type

Private xQueue() As QStuff
```

This change means that you have to adjust the code to reference the Data attribute when you try to access the object pointer from the array like I did in the Add method (see Listing 10.9).

LISTING 10.9   QUEUE.ADD

```
Public Sub Add(item As Object)

Dim l As Long

l = UBound(xQueue) + 1
ReDim Preserve xQueue(l)

Set xQueue(l).Data = item

If UBound(xQueue) > MaxLength Then
```

LISTING 10.9 CONTINUED

```
    MaxLength = UBound(xQueue)

End If

End Sub
```

ADDING ITEMS TO THE QUEUE

Although the old Add method continues to work, it doesn't assign a priority value for anything it adds to the queue. So you can add the PriorityAdd method to add new items to the queue as well as the PriorityPeek method to return the priority of the first item in the queue.

The PriorityAdd routine (see Listing 10.10) takes two parameters, the item to be added and the priority of the item (pri). The first step is to increase the size of the array by 1 to allow the new item to be inserted somewhere.

LISTING 10.10 QUEUE.PRIORITYADD

```
Public Sub PriorityAdd(item As Object, pri As Variant)

Dim i As Long
Dim l As Long

l = UBound(xQueue) + 1
ReDim Preserve xQueue(l)

i = l - 1

Do While i > 0 And xQueue(i).Priority > pri
    xQueue(i + 1) = xQueue(i)
    i = i - 1

Loop

Set xQueue(i + 1).Data = item
xQueue(i + 1).Priority = pri

If UBound(xQueue) > MaxLength Then
    MaxLength = UBound(xQueue)

End If

End Sub
```

Next start with the last element in the array and scan backwards until you find an element whose Priority value is less than or equal to pri. If Priority is greater than pri, move the element one place toward the end of the array and try again. When you finally find the place to insert the new item, simply insert it into the queue and update the maximum length of the queue like I did with the original Add method.

I also added a `PeekPriority` priority routine (see Listing 10.11) to the `Queue` class that makes it easy to examine the priority value of the first item in the queue without removing it from the queue. This routine comes in handy in Chapter 11, "Simulating Stores and Money," when I start pulling customers from the queue.

LISTING 10.11   QUEUE.PEEKPRIORITY

```
Public Function PeekPriority() As Variant

Dim i As Long

If UBound(xQueue) > 0 Then
    PeekPriority = xQueue(1).Priority

Else
    PeekPriority = Empty

End If

End Function
```

SIMULATING THE CUSTOMER IN THE MALL

Simulating a customer in the shopping mall involves keeping track of every customer in the mall, the next activity the customer will perform, and when the activity will be performed. The easiest way to implement this is by using a finite state machine.

DESIGNING A FINITE STATE MACHINE

A finite state machine is a relatively simple yet powerful concept. It's essentially a roadmap for making decisions and describing actions within a computer program. In Figure 10.1, you see a diagram that describes how the customer moves through the mall.

Figure 10.1
A finite state machine describes how a customer moves through a mall.

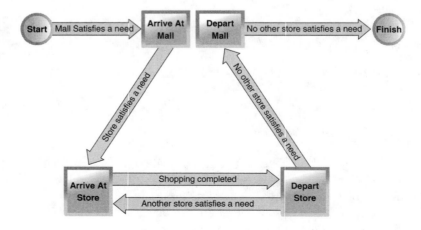

Each state describes a set of activities that should be performed using the customer. One of the activities is determining the next state the customer will be sent to. The objects in the finite state machine have a memory so that as they move from state to state the information in the object changes. This allows decisions made by the finite state machine to be based on this memory.

Each finite state machine has a distinct start point and finish point. In this case, customers go from start to the Arrive At Mall state whenever the mall satisfies their needs. Customers leave the Arrive At Mall state for a store when there is a store that meets their needs.

Once in a store, customers go to the Depart Store state when they have finished shopping at the store. Their needs may or may not have been met by the store.

At the Depart Store state, the other stores in the mall are examined and if another store that satisfies the customer's needs is found, the customer is placed back at the Arrive At Store state. If no other stores exist that satisfy the customer's needs or all of the customer's needs have been satisfied, the customer is sent to the Depart Mall state.

In the Depart Mall state, customers are on their way out of the mall. Once the processing related to the Depart Mall state is finished, the customers are removed from the system.

IMPLEMENTING THE FINITE STATE MACHINE

The `Game.Step` method adds customers into the `MallCustomers` queue, while the `Mall.StepTick` routine (see Listing 10.12) controls how the customer moves from store to store in the mall. It begins by using the `PeekPriority` routine to return the priority value associated with the first customer in the queue. Then it uses a loop to process each customer in the queue whose priority value is less that the current value of the master clock.

LISTING 10.12   MALL.STEPTICK

```
Public Sub StepTick()

Dim X As Single
Dim c As Customer
Dim s As Object
Dim t As Date

t = MallCustomers.PeekPriority
Do While (t < MasterClock) And MallCustomers.Length > 0
   Set c = MallCustomers.Front
   Select Case c.NextAction

   Case ArriveAtMall
      MallCustomerCount = MallCustomerCount + 1
      TodaysCustomers = TodaysCustomers + 1
      Set c.Store = FindStore(c.Needs, c.FoodNeeds)
      c.StoreArrive = DateAdd("s", Int(Rand(60)), c.MallArrive)
      c.NextAction = ArriveAtStore
      MallCustomers.PriorityAdd c, c.StoreArrive

   Case ArriveAtStore
```

LISTING 10.12 CONTINUED

```
        c.Store.ArriveStore c
        c.StoreDepart = c.Store.ComputeDepartTime(c)
        c.NextAction = DepartStore
        MallCustomers.PriorityAdd c, c.StoreDepart

    Case DepartStore
        c.Store.DepartStore c
        Set c.Store = FindStore(c.Needs, c.FoodNeeds)
        If Not c.Store Is Nothing Then
            c.StoreArrive = DateAdd("s", Int(Rand(60)), c.StoreDepart)
            c.StoreDepart = c.Store.ComputeDepartTime(c)
            c.NextAction = ArriveAtStore
            MallCustomers.PriorityAdd c, c.StoreDepart

        Else
            c.NextAction = DepartMall
            c.MallDepart = DateAdd("s", Int(Rand(60)), c.StoreDepart)
            MallCustomers.PriorityAdd c, c.MallDepart

        End If

    Case DepartMall
        If Not (c.Needs Or Not c.FoodNeeds) Then
            X = CountBits(c.Needs) + CountBits(c.FoodNeeds)
            c.Satisfaction = c.Satisfaction - Rand(2 * X / c.NeedCount)

        End If

        c.Satisfaction = c.Satisfaction - Abs(c.Satisfaction * _
            (Year(MasterClock) - Year(MallBuilt)) / 20)
        c.Satisfaction = c.Satisfaction * Difficulty
        c.Satisfaction = IIf(c.Satisfaction > 1, _
            1, IIf(c.Satisfaction < -1, -1, c.Satisfaction))
        Satisfaction = Satisfaction + ((c.Satisfaction - Satisfaction) _
            * Abs(1 - Satisfaction)) / 1000

    Case Else
        MallDebugger.WriteLong "Invalid action value", c.NextAction

    End Select

    t = MallCustomers.PeekPriority

Loop

End Sub
```

Within this loop, retrieve the first customer from the queue and select the appropriate action based on the value in the NextAction property. If there are no customers in the queue, exit the loop and the subroutine.

If the customer's next action is ArriveAtMall, increment the mall's customer count and the number of customers in the mall today. Then find a store that meets the customer's needs and save a reference to it in the customer's Store property. Next, allow the customer a random amount of time to get to the store and add him back to the customer queue.

After the customer arrives at the store, call the store's ArriveStore method to process the customer. The store's ComputerDepartTime method is used to determine when the customer leaves the store and adds the customer back into the priority queue.

When it is time for the customer to leave the store, use the store's DepartStore method to process the customer. Then use the FindStore method to see if another store meets any of the customer's needs. If this method returns a valid object reference, compute how long it takes the customer to reach the store and add her back into the priority queue. These are the same steps that I went through when the customer first arrived at the mall. If the FindStore returns Nothing, set NextAction to DepartMall and add the customer back into the queue.

The final case is to handle what happens when the customer is ready to leave the mall. The first step is to see if all the customer's needs have been satisfied. If not, subtract a random number based on the percent of customer needs not satisfied from the customer's Satisfaction property. Then factor the age of the mall into the customer's satisfaction and also scale the result by the Difficulty factor. Finally, adjust the mall's Satisfaction based on the customer's Satisfaction value in such a way to make it harder to improve the satisfaction level as the satisfaction level approaches 1.

Although the Case Else clause should never be executed, I included it just to be on the safe side. This will trap any errors that may happen if I accidentally use a wrong value for NextAction. Finally, use the PeekPriority method to get the arrival time of the next customer in the queue and repeat the loop over again until all of the customers' arrival times are less than the current value of the master clock.

FINAL THOUGHTS

Finite state machines are a useful concept when building most kinds of games, even non-computer games. For instance, most of the popular board games can be considered finite state machines. You roll the dice and land on a square that provides a set of instructions that modify the information about your game piece, such as collecting money or providing a reward. Sometimes the instructions include switching the piece to another state directly.

In the case of Swim Mall, the finite state machine is relatively simple, but in the case of a game like Quake, the machine is very complex. Each room or location offers a particular state from which the player can perform one or more separate tasks.

If you want to put time and effort into improving how Swim Mall works, this is an ideal place to start. You can make simple changes like changing how customers are created to provide a real name for the customer instead of a names like Customer 3,142. One way to do it would be to add a pair of string arrays, one containing first names and the other containing last names. Then create a pair of RandomDistribution arrays containing weights for each of the names. Then it is a simple matter of using the DRand function to select a first name and last name and concatenate them together. All of the necessary information could be loaded from the saved game file or another file using the Swim File format.

Another change you might want to make is to incorporate a level of difficulty variable that modifies the Satisfaction values for both the mall and the competitors' malls to make the game easier or harder. This change would directly affect how the best mall is chosen, and thus determine the percentage of customers who go to the player's mall versus the competitors' malls.

CHAPTER **11**

SIMULATING STORES AND MONEY

In this chapter

So far I've shown you how to manage the simulation, and simulate the mall's competitors and the customers. This leaves only the discussion about how to simulate the stores in the mall and how their rent is spent to maintain the mall.

STORES AND NEEDS

There are three basic types of stores in Swim Mall: anchors, food court vendors, and regular stores. Food court vendors can only meet the customer's food needs that are kept in FoodNeeds. This limitation is pretty obvious. Since when have you seen a food court vendor sell a stove or a pair of running shoes?

Regular stores can only meet the customer's general needs, which are kept in Needs. This limitation is not so obvious, but most regular stores in a mall have a highly focused product line. Very few stores sell both women's clothing and pet supplies.

Anchor stores do not have this restriction. They can fulfill both regular needs and food needs. This is because it is quite common for a large department store to have a small food area inside of the store where a customer can purchase some food. Some of the higher end anchors might even have a small restaurant tucked away in the corner of the store.

STORING STORE INFORMATION

Listing 11.1 contains a list of the module level variables related to the simulation. Some of these variables you've used in other modules, like the Needs and FoodNeeds variables, which identify which customer needs are satisfied by this particular store. The others are used to track information about how the store is operating or are loaded with the store to determine how the store works.

LISTING 11.1   FORM1.COMMAND12_CLICK

```
Public Needs As NeedTypes
Public FoodNeeds As FoodNeedTypes

Public CustomersInStore As Long
Public TodaysCustomers As Long

Public TodaysSales As Single
Public MonthlySales As Single
Public YearToDateSales As Single

Public ProbabilityOfSale As Single
Public ProfitMargin As Single
Private xSaleDistribution() As RandomDistribution
Public MonthlyProfit As Single
Public YearToDateProfit As Single
```

LISTING 11.1   CONTINUED

```
Public PercentageSalesRent As Single
Public BaseRent As Single

Public MinTimeInStore As Long
Public MaxTimeInStore As Long
Public MaxCustomers As Long
```

CustomersInStore is simply a counter that indicates the total number of customers in the store at any one time, while TodaysCustomers counts the total number of customers that have visited the store in the current day.

TodaysSales is a running total of all the purchases made by customers in the current day. At the end of the day it is added to the MonthlySales value and the YearToDateSales value.

Whether the customer makes a purchase or not is determined by the ProbabilityOfSale value. The closer this value is to one, the greater the probability that the customer makes a purchase. The xSaleDistribution array contains a RandomDistribution that describes a weighted probability that the customer makes a sale.

The store's profit is computed by multiplying TodaysSales by the ProfitMargin and adding the result to the MonthlyProfit variable and the YearToDateProfit variable.

The store's rent is based on the total sales for each month. The mall gets a percentage of the store's sales (PercentageSalesRent). However, the player also has the capability to impose a minimum rent, which the store must pay to the mall even if the store's sales weren't up to their expectations.

Finally two variables, the MinTimeInStore and the MaxTimeInStore, determine how long the customer stays in the store, while MaxCustomers determines how many customers can be in the store before the next customer gets frustrated and leaves immediately. All three values are loaded from the store's initialization file.

PART
II
CH
11

CUSTOMERS AND STORES

There are four main functions involving customers and stores. The FindStore function locates a store that meets the customer's needs. Then the ArriveStore function is triggered for each customer that arrives at a store, while the ComputeDepartTime function is used to determine when the DepartStore method is triggered for the customer.

FINDING A STORE

The FindStore function (see Listing 11.2) returns a store within the mall that meets at least one of the specified needs. While I could have programmed it to pick the first store that satisfied at least one need, it would tend to send the customers to the first store in the list. This would make the first store in the mall the most successful, which is not desirable.

LISTING 11.2 MALL.FINDSTORE

```
Public Function FindStore(n As NeedTypes, _
   fn As FoodNeedTypes) As Object

Dim c As Long
Dim i As Long
Dim j As Long

c = Stores.Count
j = Int(Rand(c + 1, 1))

For i = j To c
   If n And Stores(i).Needs Then
      Set FindStore = Stores(i)
      Exit Function

   End If

Next i

For i = 1 To j - 1
   If n And Stores(i).Needs Then
      Set FindStore = Stores(i)
      Exit Function

   End If

Next i

c = Foods.Count
j = Int(Rand(c + 1, 1))

For i = j To c
   If fn And Foods(i).FoodNeeds Then
      Set FindStore = Foods(i)
      Exit Function

   End If

Next i

For i = 1 To j - 1
   If fn And Foods(i).FoodNeeds Then
      Set FindStore = Foods(i)
      Exit Function

   End If

Next i

c = Anchors.Count
j = Int(Rand(c + 1, 1))

For i = j To c
   If (n And Anchors(i).Needs) Or _
         (fn And Anchors(i).FoodNeeds) Then
```

LISTING 11.2   CONTINUED

```
        Set FindStore = Anchors(i)
        Exit Function

    End If

Next i

For i = 1 To j - 1
    If (n And Anchors(i).Needs) Or _
            (fn And Anchors(i).FoodNeeds) Then
        Set FindStore = Anchors(i)
        Exit Function

    End If

Next i

Set FindStore = Nothing

End Function
```

Next, I thought about directing the customer to the store that fulfilled the most needs from a customer. I discarded that approach because a customer would almost always be sent to an anchor store simply because anchor stores generally satisfy the most needs. This would leave very few needs for other stores in the mall to satisfy.

To get around these problems, I decided to check for stores in the following order: regular stores, food court stores, and anchor stores. This approach ensures that the regular stores and food court vendors aren't starved for customers. Then within each category of store, I would randomly select the starting point in the list of stores and return the store that matches the needs.

The easiest way to do this is to get the number of stores in a particular category by using the collection's Count property. Then generate a random number in the range of 1 to the count. Note that you have to specify Count + 1 in the call to Rand because Rand does not return a random number that is equal to the upper bound.

Loop through the collection of items starting with this initial value and increment the loop counter until you reach the last item in the collection. If you find a match, return an object reference to the store and exit the function immediately.

If the loop terminates without a match, repeat the process starting with the first store in the collection and continuing on until you reach the store just before the starting point. Again if you find a match, return the store.

If, after checking all possible stores, food court vendors, and anchors, you don't find a match for the customer's needs, return a value of Nothing to indicate that there isn't a store in the mall that satisfies any of these needs.

ARRIVING AT A STORE

When a customer arrives at a store, these statements are executed to capture statistics that will be used later:

```
CustomersInStore = CustomersInStore + 1
TodaysCustomers = TodaysCustomers + 1
```

COMPUTING THE DEPARTURE TIME

Computing when the customer leaves the store is handled by the DepartStore method. The ComputeDepartTime routine (see Listing 11.3) starts by checking to see if the store is too crowded. If there are more people in the store than the MaxCustomers variable that was loaded for the store, the function returns a value of zero. This allows the customer to be placed at the head of the queue so that they may immediately leave the store.

LISTING 11.3   STORE.COMPUTEDEPARTTIME

```
Public Function ComputeDepartTime(c As Customer) As Date

If CustomersInStore > MaxCustomers Then
    ComputeDepartTime = 0

Else
    ComputeDepartTime = DateAdd("s", Rand(MaxTimeInStore, _
        MinTimeInStore), c.StoreArrive)

End If

End Function
```

If the store isn't crowded, a random number of seconds between the MinTimeInStore and MaxTimeInStore values is added to the current value of the master clock and returned as the value of the function.

DEPARTING A STORE

Most of the work associated with a customer occurs when she leaves a store. The DepartStore routine (see Listing 11.4) determines if the customer makes a purchase and updates the statistics accordingly. It also adjusts the customer's satisfaction level, which eventually affects the mall's overall satisfaction rating.

LISTING 11.4   STORE.DEPARTSTORE

```
Public Sub DepartStore(c As Customer)

Dim p As Single

If c.StoreDepart = 0 Then
    c.Satisfaction = c.Satisfaction - Rand(1)

Else
```

LISTING 11.4   CONTINUED

```
    p = CountBits(c.Needs And Needs) / c.NeedCount

    If Rand() < ProbabilityOfSale Then
        TodaysSales = TodaysSales + CRand(xSaleDistribution)
        c.Satisfaction = c.Satisfaction + Rand(1.5, -0.5) * p

    Else
        c.Satisfaction = c.Satisfaction + Rand(1, -1) * p

    End If

End If

c.Needs = c.Needs And Not Needs
CustomersInStore = CustomersInStore - 1

End Sub
```

This routine begins by seeing if the customer arrived at the store when there were too many people in it. This is determined when the customer's StoreDepart property is set to zero. Rather than allowing the customer to purchase something, the customer immediately exits the store with his satisfaction rating randomly decreased.

Assuming that the customer isn't annoyed, determine the relative percentage of the needs met by this store. Then generate a random number between zero and one and compare it to the ProbabilityOfSale value to see if the customer purchases something before leaving. If the random number is less then the ProbabiltyOfSale, the store makes a sale. The amount of the sale is computed using the CRand function and sale distribution information loaded from the store's initialization file. Next add the value of the sale to TodaysSales. Then adjust the customer's satisfaction by adding a random value between 1.5 and –0.5 that is scaled by the percentage of needs met by the store.

If the customer didn't purchase anything, the routine adjusts the customer's satisfaction using the same technique, though the range of possible values is shifted to 1 to –1. (A customer who purchases something is more likely to be satisfied than one who doesn't.) Finally, remove the needs met by this store from the customer's needs and decrement the number of customers in the store.

HOUSEKEEPING FOR THE STORE

At the end of each day, month, and year, the simulation engine calls the EndDay, EndMonth, and EndYear methods for each store in the mall. This is where the store updates its statistics and performs other tasks.

ENDING THE DAY

At the end of each day, the EndDay method (see Listing 11.5) is called to clean up after the days work. Add today's sales to the monthly total. Then update the monthly profit using today's sales and the ProfitMargin value from the store's initialization file.

LISTING 11.5 STORE.ENDDAY

```
Public Sub EndDay()

MonthlySales = MonthlySales + TodaysSales
MonthlyProfit = MonthlyProfit + TodaysSales * ProfitMargin

TotalSales = TotalSales + TodaysSales
TotalProfit = TotalProfit + TodaysSales * ProfitMargin
TotalCustomers = TotalCustomers + TodaysCustomers

TodaysSales = 0
TodaysCustomers = 0

End Sub
```

Next compute running totals for sales, profit, and customers the same way. Finally, zero out TodaysSales and TodaysCustomers, so the store is ready before the next day's customers.

ENDING THE MONTH

When the simulation reaches the end of the month, simply clear the variables used to hold monthly statistics for the store using these statements.

```
MonthlySales = 0
MonthlyProfit = 0
```

DISPLAYING INFORMATION FOR A STORE

In Chapter 6, "Displaying 3D Graphics," I talked about how to select a store in the mall by clicking on the store. This technique resulted in the SelectedObject variable holding an object pointer to the appropriate store object. This makes it really easy to pop up a window containing information about that particular object (see Listing 11.6).

LISTING 11.6 FORM1.COMMAND12_CLICK

```
Private Sub Command12_Click()

If Not SelectedObject Is Nothing Then
    StoreInfo.Show 0

Else
    MsgBox "Please select an object in the mall."

End If

End Sub
```

The `StoreInfo` form (see Figure 11.1) contains information about a store. Because a store contains a lot of detailed information, I use a tabbed control to keep the size of the form small relative to the information it displays.

Figure 11.1
The `StoreInfo` form displays information about the currently selected store.

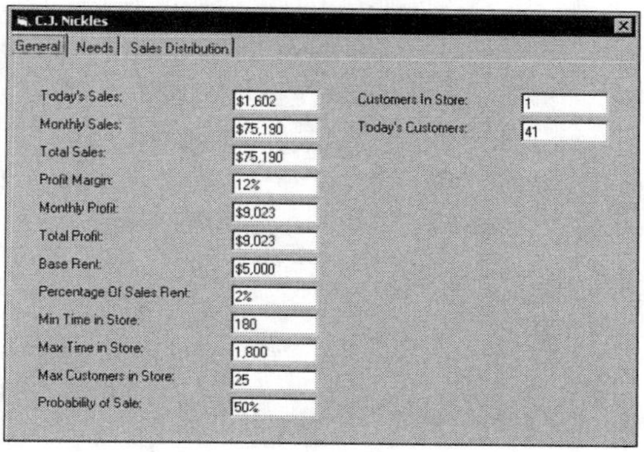

All of the information displayed on the form is read-only, meaning that changing any of the values on the form does absolutely nothing. In the `Form_Load` event, enable a timer control that calls `DisplaySummary` routine every half second. The `DisplaySummary` routine gets information from the store's object and displays it in the various text boxes on the form. With a half second refresh time, you can watch as various events take place in the simulation.

In the `DisplaySummary` routine (see Listing 11.7), verify that `SelectedObject` contains a valid object reference and then use a `With` statement to make the corresponding `Store`, `Anchor`, or `Food` object the default object. Remember that the `SelectedObject` points to the `DXObject` corresponding to the mesh on the screen. The `SimObject` property provides a link to the simulation object that corresponds to the mesh.

LISTING 11.7 STOREINFO.DISPLAYSUMMARY

```
Private Sub DisplaySummary()

Dim i As Long
Dim j As Long

If Not SelectedObject Is Nothing Then
    With SelectedObject.SimObject
        Me.Caption = .Name
        Text1.Text = FormatCurrency(.TodaysSales, 0)
        Text2.Text = FormatCurrency(.MonthlySales, 0)
        Text3.Text = FormatCurrency(.TotalSales, 0)
        Text4.Text = FormatPercent(.ProfitMargin, 0)
        Text5.Text = FormatCurrency(.MonthlyProfit, 0)
        Text6.Text = FormatCurrency(.TotalProfit, 0)
        Text7.Text = FormatCurrency(.BaseRent, 0)
        Text8.Text = FormatPercent(.PercentageSalesRent, 0)
        Text9.Text = FormatNumber(.MinTimeInStore, 0)
        Text10.Text = FormatNumber(.MaxTimeInStore, 0)
        Text11.Text = FormatPercent(.ProbabilityOfSale, 0)
        Text12.Text = FormatNumber(.CustomersInStore, 0)
```

LISTING 11.7   CONTINUED

```
            Text13.Text = FormatNumber(.TodaysCustomers, 0)

            For i = 1 To .SaleDistributionSize
                DistValue(i - 1).Text = FormatCurrency (.SaleDistributionValue(i), 2)
                DistWeight(i - 1).Text = FormatNumber(.SaleDistributionWeight(i), 5)

            Next i

            For i = .SaleDistributionSize To 7
                DistValue(i).Text = ""
                DistWeight(i).Text = ""

            Next i

            j = 1
            For i = 0 To 29
                Needs(i).Value = IIf(.Needs And j, 1, 0)
                j = j * 2

            Next i

            j = 1
            For i = 0 To 16
                FoodNeeds(i).Value = IIf(.FoodNeeds And j, 1, 0)
                j = j * 2

            Next i

        End With

    Else
        Me.Caption = ""
        Text1.Text = ""
        Text2.Text = ""
        Text3.Text = ""
        Text4.Text = ""
        Text5.Text = ""
        Text6.Text = ""
        Text7.Text = ""
        Text8.Text = ""
        Text9.Text = ""
        Text10.Text = ""
        Text11.Text = ""
        Text12.Text = ""
        Text13.Text = ""

        For i = 0 To 29
            Needs(i).Value = 0

        Next i

        For i = 0 To 16
            FoodNeeds(i).Value = 0

        Next i
```

LISTING 11.7   CONTINUED

```
    For i = 0 To 7
        DistValue(i).Text = ""
        DistWeight(i).Text = ""

    Next i

End If

End Sub
```

After the default object has been set up, merely copy and format various values to the text fields on the form. I make use of control arrays to simplify some of the code.

If `SelectedObject` doesn't point to a valid object, clear all of the fields on the form. This ensures that the form doesn't have any invalid data if the user were to select an invalid object in the mall.

MANAGING THE MALL'S MONEY

While satisfaction attracts customers to the mall, the thing that keeps the mall alive is income. The sole source of income for the mall is the rent it charges the stores. If the rent is too high, the stores can't make a profit and will eventually be forced to close. If the rent is too low, the mall won't take in enough money to pay for necessary expenses such as security guards and utilities.

COLLECTING RENT

Each type of store (`Anchor`, `Food`, and `Store`) pays a percentage of its income as rent, with a minimum amount guaranteed. Default values are supplied in the initialization file, but the player is allowed to change these value as desired. The `GetRent` method (see Listing 11.8) computes the amount of rent that is paid to the mall and subtracts the amount of rent from the store's profit.

LISTING 11.8   STORE.GETRENT

```
Public Function GetRent() As Single

Dim r As Single

r = MonthlySales * PercentageSalesRent
If r < BaseRent Then
    r = BaseRent

End If

TotalProfit = TotalProfit - r

GetRent = r

End Function
```

This routine computes the rent by multiplying the `MonthlySales` for the store by the `PercentageSalesRent` value. If this value is less then the `BaseRent`, use that value instead. Next, subtract the rent from the total profit value and return the rent as the value of the function. Note that I don't worry about subtracting the rent from the `MonthlyProfit` figure because the store's `EndMonth` method is called immediately after the rent is collected (refer to "Ending the Month" earlier in this chapter).

ENDING THE MONTH FOR THE MALL

The end of month processing for the mall involves updating a number of variables and then computing the mall's expenses. This code is buried in the mall's `EndMonth` method (see Listing 11.9), which is called after processing the `EndMonth` method for each of the stores in the mall.

LISTING 11.9   MALL.ENDMONTH

```
Private Sub EndMonth()

Dim i As Long
Dim m As Long
Dim r As Single
Dim u As Long

r = Rand(0.005, -0.005)

Inflation = Inflation + r
If r > 0 Then
    InterestRate = InterestRate + Rand(0.005, -0.0025)

Else
    InterestRate = InterestRate - Rand(0.005, -0.0025)

End If

MonthlySalary = 0
For i = 1 To UBound(Staff)
    MonthlySalary = MonthlySalary + Staff(i).Salary

Next i

m = Month(Yesterday)
u = UBound(RunningExpenses) + 1
ReDim Preserve RunningExpenses(u)

RunningExpenses(u).Date = Yesterday
RunningExpenses(u).MonthlyIncome = MonthlyIncome
RunningExpenses(u).Salaries = MonthlySalary
RunningExpenses(u).Insurance = BaseExpenses(m).Insurance
RunningExpenses(u).Supplies = BaseExpenses(m).Supplies * Rand(1.5, 0.5)
RunningExpenses(u).Utilities = BaseExpenses(m).Utilities * Rand(1.5, 0.5)
RunningExpenses(u).Taxes = TaxRate / 12 * MonthlyIncome
```

LISTING 11.9 CONTINUED

```
RunningExpenses(u).Interest = InterestRate / 12 * Loans
RunningExpenses(u).Advertising = Advertising
RunningExpenses(u).Promotions = Promotions

MonthlyExpenses = RunningExpenses(u).Salaries + _
    RunningExpenses(u).Insurance + _RunningExpenses(u).Supplies + _
    RunningExpenses(u).Utilities + RunningExpenses(u).Taxes + _
    RunningExpenses(u).Interest + RunningExpenses(u).Advertising + _
    RunningExpenses(u).Promotions

Cash = Cash + MonthlyIncome - MonthlyExpenses

RunningExpenses(u).MonthlyExpenses = MonthlyExpenses
RunningExpenses(u).Profit = MonthlyIncome - MonthlyExpenses
RunningExpenses(u).Cash = Cash

Advertising = 0
Promotions = 0

End Sub
```

The first step in closing out the month is to adjust the inflation rate. I compute a random number whose value is somewhere between 0.5% and –0.5%. This value is then added to Inflation.

Because interest rates are generally tied to inflation, update the interest rate differently depending on whether inflation is going up or down. If inflation is going up (r > 0), add a random number in the range of 0.5% to –0.25%, while I subtract a similar value if inflation is going down. This means that interest rates tend to rise when inflation is going up, while interest rates tend to fall when inflation is going down.

Next use a simple For loop to compute the monthly salary for all of the employees and save the result in MonthlySalary.

The RunningExpenses array holds the details that are displayed on the Cash Flow tab of the MallInfo form. Its structure is shown in Listing 11.10. Each element of the array corresponds to one month's worth of information. This information is stored in the Date attribute. The actual value stored is the last day of the month, which comes from the variable Yesterday.

LISTING 11.10 GLOBAL.EXPENSETYPE

```
Type ExpenseType
    Date As Date
    Taxes As Single
    Utilities As Single
    Insurance As Single
    Supplies As Single
```

LISTING 11.10   CONTINUED

```
    MonthlyIncome As Single
    MonthlyExpenses As Single
    Profit As Single
    Cash As Single
    Salaries As Single
    Promotions As Single
    Advertising As Single
    Interest As Single

End Type
```

MonthlyIncome and Salaries are simply copied over from variables that already hold this information. Likewise Advertising and Promotions hold the actual amounts spent in the current month.

Taxes are computed by multiplying MonthlyIncome by the value in TaxRate, while Interest is computed by multiplying the total amount the player has borrowed (Loans) by 1/12 of InterestRate. (Remember that the value in InterestRate is an annualized value, so 1/12 represents the monthly rate.)

The remaining values (Insurance, Supplies, and Utilities) are based on parameters loaded from the saved game file. These parameters are stored using a simplified version of the ExpenseType structure called BaseExpensesType that contains only these three values. The array BaseExpenses has one entry for each month of the year. This permits you to vary these values over the year to make the simulation more realistic. For example, you may choose to increase Utilities in the winter and summer to account for extra usage for heating and air conditioning.

The values in the BaseExpenses array are multiplied by a random number to account for normal fluctuations in demand. This value is chosen from the range of 1.5 to 0.5, which means that the actual value could be as little as 50% of the base value to as high as 150% of the base product. Insurance, however has a constant value that is recomputed at the end of each year.

After the monthly expenses are computed, add them together and store the result in MonthlyExpenses. Then adjust the amount of Cash by adding the income and subtracting the expenses. With these values, you can then save this summary information into the RunningExpenses array.

Finally, zero out the Advertising and Promotions variables to make the ready for the following month.

ENDING THE STORE'S YEAR

To account for the effect of inflation, each store raises its prices at the end of the year. Because the prices are determined by the xSaleDistribution array, it is a simple matter to

loop through the array and update the Value property. Rather than simply using the inflation rate, add a random value in the range of +2% to –2% (see Listing 11.11). This may
make a marginally profitable store really profitable or force it into bankruptcy.

LISTING 11.11   STORE.ENDYEAR

```
Public Sub EndYear()

Dim i As Long

For i = 1 To UBound(xSaleDistribution)
   xSaleDistribution(i).Value = xSaleDistribution(i).Value * _
      (1 + Inflation + Rand(0.02, -0.02))

Next i

End Sub
```

Because I'm not touching either the Probability or the Weight attributes, there is no need
to normalize the distribution again.

ENDING THE MALL'S YEAR

Like the stores, I also factor inflation into the mall's operation (see Listing 11.12). In this
case, I give each staff member an automatic salary increase based on the inflation rate. It is
up to the player to provide other increases or bonuses during the year.

LISTING 11.12   MALL.ENDYEAR

```
Private Sub EndYear()

Dim i As Long
Dim r As Single

For i = 1 To UBound(Staff)
   Staff(i).Salary = Staff(i).Salary * (1 + Inflation)

Next i

r = BaseExpenses(i).Insurance * (1 + Inflation + Rand(0.02, -0.02))
For i = 1 To 12
   BaseExpenses(i).Insurance = r
   BaseExpenses(i).Supplies = BaseExpenses(i).Supplies * _
      (1 + Inflation + Rand(0.02, -0.02))
   BaseExpenses(i).Utilities = BaseExpenses(i).Utilities * _
      (1 + Inflation + Rand(0.03, 0.01))

Next i

End Sub
```

Because the cost of insurance doesn't vary from month to month, I compute that outside the loop and then simply assign that value inside the loop. However, for `Supplies` and `Utilities`, I add a random factor to the inflation rate. I use a range of ±2% for `Supplies`, while `Utilities` outpace inflation by somewhere between 1% and 3%.

FINAL THOUGHTS

In a game like Swim Mall, the player can only do a limited amount of things to attract people to the mall. Hopefully, attracting additional customers to the mall makes the stores more profitable, which in turn makes the mall more profitable. The player can't change many of the basic characteristics of the stores, which are fixed by the game designer. Thus the player must carefully choose the stores that are placed in the mall to minimize competition.

If there was a high degree of overlap between the stores, the mall is less attractive to potential customers. Also this means a customer stops at fewer stores, which means less money is spent by each customer. This directly affects each store's income and indirectly the mall's income.

When playing the game, it is important to remember that the mall doesn't own the stores. Thus the mall never receives any income directly from the customer. The only income in this game comes from the rent collected from the stores. However in real life, the mall has several other sources of income. For instance, the mall receives an income stream from any pay telephones in the mall. The same goes for ATM machines, vending machines, and other devices scattered through the mall.

Adding mall objects that generate revenue is an easy-to-implement change within the game's framework. All you have to do is to add code to compute the income for each mall object and add it to the `MallObject` class. Then you need to place the appropriate hooks in the `Mall` class to add the income to the mall.

PART III

MAKING THE GAME FUN

CHAPTER 12

CONTROLLING THE MALL WITH DIRECTINPUT

In this chapter

At this point, you have seen how to combine 3D graphics with a simulation to form the core foundation of a computer game. However, Swim Mall has relied on conventional Visual Basic controls to monitor the activities in the mall. While this approach is reasonable for some games, I choose to replace the collection of command buttons and text boxes along with their associated events with a completely new user interface that uses DirectInput.

EXPLORING DIRECTINPUT

Like Direct3D, DirectInput provides programmers with a low level interface to the hardware devices it supports. DirectInput supports a wide range of specialized gaming devices such as joysticks, steering wheels, rudder pedals, and other specialized gaming controls, and it provides a low-level interface to access the computer's keyboard and mouse.

Because this is a low-level interface, it bypasses the normal Windows features and works directly with the device drivers. This allows DirectInput to support a wide range of devices, including those not directly supported by Windows.

The low-level access also means that DirectInput doesn't offer some of the features you may take for granted. For instance, while you gain the capability to identify the individual keys on the keyboard, such as Right Shift key and the Num Lock key, you lose some features, like automatically applying the Shift key to create an uppercase letter and holding down a key to automatically repeat the character.

USING DIRECTINPUT

Initializing DirectInput involves creating an instance of the `DirectInput` object, determining the devices that are available, and creating a `DirectInputDevice` object for each device you wish to use. Then you need to configure each device and acquire it for your use.

When you configure the devices, you need to consider how these devices will interact with Windows. Although a joystick isn't a critical input device to Windows, the keyboard and mouse are. So in addition to configuring each device, you need to determine the level of cooperation. Basically this boils down to two value situations, whether your game is willing to let another program have access to the input device and whether your game will continue to receive data from the input device even though another program is active. Implementing this level of cooperation may involve making some Win32 API calls to disable or enable some basic Windows functions, in addition to making the appropriate calls to DirectInput.

After the program is running, you need to monitor the devices for input. This means that you need to either frequently check them to see if the device has any input or you need to define an event that DirectX will trigger each time a device has input for you to process.

Finally, when the game is over, you need to properly destroy the devices. Note that you may also have to undo any changes you made to Windows when you initialized the devices.

INTEGRATING DIRECTINPUT INTO SWIM MALL

In Swim Mall I decided to separate the actual input collection from the input processing. This approach is less efficient than it could be, but by isolating these two elements I was able to focus on developing the code for one input device at a time. This simplified debugging immensely.

I defined a global object called dxi, which contains an instance of the DXInput class. This class contains all of the code necessary to interface with the keyboard and mouse.

When dxi is initialized, it creates a DirectXEvent8 event handler and links it to the game's main form. Then any input activity detected by DirectInput will trigger the event handler in the Form object. The event handler in the Form object calls methods in the DXInput class to process the input and make the information available (see Figure 12.1).

Figure 12.1
The player uses the mouse and keyboard to control the game's execution.

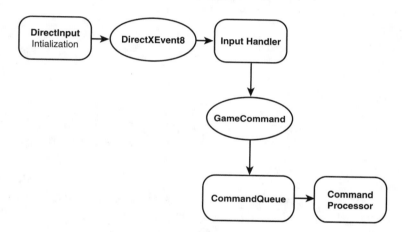

INITIALIZING DIRECTINPUT

I use a large number of module level variables to manage DirectInput, as shown in Listing 12.1. CommandQueue holds the list of commands that the Game object will process. DXInput, DXKeyboard, and DXMouse hold object references for DirectInput and the devices that are used in the game. EventHandle is used to identify the proper input handler for DirectInput. The DXDebugger property holds an object reference to the debugger object used throughout the project.

LISTING 12.1   SELECTED MODULE-LEVEL DEFINITIONS IN DXGRAPHICS FOR DIRECTINPUT

```
Public CommandQueue As Queue

Private DXInput As DirectInput8
Private DXKeyboard As DirectInputDevice8
```

PART

III

CH

12

Listing 12.1 Continued

```
Private DXMouse As DirectInputDevice8
Private EventHandle As Long

Private LastKeyboardState(255) As Byte
Private KeyboardCode(255, 2) As String
Public InputBuffer As String
Public KeyboardTextMode As Boolean

Public MouseX As Long
Public MouseY As Long
Public MouseZ As Long
Private MouseButton0 As Boolean
Private MouseButton1 As Boolean
Private MouseButton2 As Boolean
Private MouseButton0Click As Boolean
Private MouseButton0DoubleClick As Boolean
Private OldMouseX As Long
Private OldMouseY As Long
Private OldMouseZ As Long
Private MouseButton0Time As Long
Private MouseButton0ClickTime As Long

Private DXDebugger As Debugger
```

LastKeyboardState and KeyboardCode help translate keyboard scan codes into ASCII characters. Setting KeyboardTextMode to True will save input characters into InputBuffer.

The Mouse properties store information about the current state of the mouse. MouseX, MouseY, and MouseZ store the current location of the mouse pointer, while OldMouseX, OldMouseY, and OldMouseZ store the previous position. MouseButton0, MouseButton1 and MouseButton2 store information about the state of the buttons on the mouse. The remaining properties are used to differeniate between a mouse click and double click and will be explained in more detail in the section titled "Tracking the Mouse" later in this chapter.

INITIALIZING DIRECTINPUT

The InitDXInput routine (see Listing 12.2) creates the environment necessary to handle the player's input using DirectInput. It begins by creating an instance of the DirectInput object using the dx property from the DXGraphics object to reference the root DirectX object.

Listing 12.2 DXInput.InitDXInput

```
Public Function InitDXInput() As Long

Dim diprop As DIPROPLONG

Set DXInput = dx.dx.DirectInputCreate
If DXInput Is Nothing Then
    DXDebugger.WriteDXErr "DirectInputCreate failed ", Err

End If
```

LISTING 12.2   CONTINUED

```
Set DXKeyboard = DXInput.CreateDevice("GUID_SysKeyboard")
If DXKeyboard Is Nothing Then
    DXDebugger.WriteDXErr "Create DXInput keyboard failed ", Err

End If

Set DXMouse = DXInput.CreateDevice("GUID_SysMouse")
If (DXMouse Is Nothing) Or (Err.Number > 0) Then
    DXDebugger.WriteDXErr "Create DXInput mouse failed ", Err

End If

SetCursorPos Form1.Left / Screen.TwipsPerPixelX, Form1.Top / _
    Screen.TwipsPerPixelY

MouseX = 0
MouseY = 0
MouseZ = 0
MouseButton0 = False
MouseButton1 = False
MouseButton2 = False

DXKeyboard.SetCommonDataFormat DIFORMAT_KEYBOARD
DXMouse.SetCommonDataFormat DIFORMAT_MOUSE

DXKeyboard.SetCooperativeLevel Form1.hWnd, _
    DISCL_NONEXCLUSIVE Or DISCL_BACKGROUND
DXMouse.SetCooperativeLevel Form1.hWnd, _
    DISCL_FOREGROUND_EXCLUSIVE Or DISCL_FOREGROUND

diprop.lHow = DIPH_DEVICE
diprop.lObj = 0
diprop.lData = 48

DXMouse.SetProperty "DIPROP_BUFFERSIZE", diprop

EventHandle = dx.dx.CreateEvent(Form1)
DXMouse.SetEventNotification EventHandle
DXKeyboard.SetEventNotification EventHandle

DXKeyboard.Acquire
If Err.Number > 0 Then
    DXDebugger.WriteDXErr "Can't acquire keyboard", Err

End If

DXMouse.Acquire
If Err.Number > 0 Then
    DXDebugger.WriteDXErr "Can't acquire mouse", Err

End If

SetKeyboardCodes

DXDebugger.WriteErr "InitDXInput complete: ", Err
```

LISTING 12.2 CONTINUED

```
InitDXInput = Err.Number

End Function
```

After I have a `DirectInput8` object, I use it to create devices for the default keyboard and the default mouse. Note that I use string values `GUID_SysKeyboard` and `GUID_SysMouse` when I create the devices. Normally each device supported by DirectInput has its own GUID that you need to specify to uniquely identify an input device.

A GUID stands for Globally Unique Identifier, which is merely a 128 bit value that is guaranteed to be unique. It is typically used anytime you want to associate a unique value with an item, which in this case is an input device. Each possible input device other than the keyboard and mouse will have a GUID associated with it.

Note

Check before you create

Usually you should use the `DirectInput8.GetDIDevices` method to get a complete list of DirectInput devices available on the player's system. I decided that because each system should have both a keyboard and a mouse, I didn't have to bother. However, I must use the `GetDIDevices` method if I wanted to support a joystick or other gaming control.

After creating objects for the keyboard and mouse, I use the Win32 API call `SetCursorPos` to move the cursor to the upper-left corner of the game's window. Then I initialize the mouse's position (`MouseX`, `MouseY`, and `MouseZ`) to zero and initialize the state of each mouse button (`MouseButton0`, `MouseButton1` and `MouseButton2`) to `False` (meaning that the button is not pressed).

Note

A three-dimensional mouse—NOT!

A typical mouse represents a two dimensional position on the screen using an X and Y coordinate. However, the wheel found on many mice is treated by DirectInput as a third dimension, hence I keep track of this using the `MouseX` variable. Most wheels also have the capability to be clicked, which means that in addition to having three axes, they also have three mouse buttons.

Then I specify the format that should be used to return information from the device. In this case, I specify the appropriate parameters for the keyboard and mouse. Although this step may not seem necessary for these simple devices, remember that DirectInput is very flexible in terms of the types of devices it can handle. In theory you could create a joystick that appeared like a mouse or make your mouse look like a joystick using this capability.

After determining the data the devices should return, you have to specify how each device will interact with Windows using the SetCooperativeLevel method. This method has a single parameter, which accepts two values that have been put together with the Or operator. The first value determines the type of access your program has to the device. You can specify either exclusive (DISCL_EXCLUSIVE) or nonexclusive (DISCL_NONEXCLUSIVE), plus you can specify whether your program can use the device only in the foreground (DISCL_FOREGROUND) or in both the foreground and background (DISCL_BACKGROUND).

Typically you should specify DISCL_NONEXCLUSIVE OR DISCL_BACKGROUND for a keyboard, meaning that you are willing to share the keyboard with any other application, but you don't have to reacquire the device each time another application has the focus.

However, for the mouse, I like to use DISCL_EXCLUSIVE OR DISCL_FOREGROUND. When you specify these values, DirectInput restricts the mouse pointer to the window associated with your application. The game player can't move the mouse outside this area. Instead he must use Alt+Tab or some other keyboard control to switch control to another window. At the same time, while your game is in the foreground, the normal Windows cursor is disabled, which makes it easier for you to create your own cursor using DirectX graphics.

> **Tip**
>
> ### A Win32 API shortcut
>
> If you choose not to specify DISCL_EXCLUSIVE Or DISCL_FOREGROUND as the cooperative level for a mouse you can still hide the Windows cursor by calling the Win32 API routine ShowCursor. This routine takes a single parameter, which indicates whether to show the cursor or hide it. However, you should use this routine carefully because Windows keeps track of the number of times you show and hide the cursor. If your program hides the cursor one more time than it shows it, your program will end without a visible cursor. The only way to restore the cursor is to write a program that calls ShowCursor and run it over and over again until you see the cursor.

By default, when DirectInput receives a piece of input, it makes it available to your program. If your program can't process the input quick enough, the input will be lost. To prevent this from happening to mouse movements, I decided to allow DirectInput to buffer the mouse movements. So, in the next block of code, I fill in the parameters for a DIPROPLONG structure that instructs DirectInput to buffer as many as 48 separate mouse events. Of course this makes processing mouse data somewhat more complicated as you'll see later in this chapter in the "Tracking the Mouse" section.

After all the devices are set up, I use the DirectX8 object from DXGraphics to create a DirectXEvent8. This event must exist in the Form object and you must include some special code that I'll talk about in the next section to define and handle the event. However, to enable it, all you have to do is to create the event and then use the SetEventNotification method for each device to instruct the device to fire the event whenever the device has input to be processed.

After all this work to prepare the device, you simply use the Acquire method to allow your program to begin receiving input from the device. Then call the SetKeyboardCodes routine to initialize the keyboard codes that will automatically be decoded by this object. Assuming that everything worked properly, the initialization routine will return a value of zero to the routine that called it.

HANDLING DIRECTINPUT EVENTS

To receive DirectInput events, you need to include the following statement immediately after the Option Explicit statement in the Form object and before any other statements:

```
Implements DirectXEvent8
```

This statement allows the Form object to inherit the characteristics of the DirectXEvent8 object. In this case, the only thing I want to use is the DirectXEvent8_DXCallback event (see Listing 12.3). This event is fired each time DirectInput has some data to be processed. In this case, I merely call the InputKeyboardEvent and InputMouseEvent methods of the DXInput object to process the input from keyboard and mouse.

LISTING 12.3   FORM1.DIRECTXEVENT8_DXCALLBACK

```
Public Sub DirectXEvent8_DXCallback(ByVal eventid As Long)

dxi.InputKeyboardEvent
dxi.InputMouseEvent

End Sub
```

Tip

Option Explicit should be required

If you forgot to include an Option Explicit statement at the beginning of each module, you should run to your computer and do it now! This statement is arguably the most important statement in the Visual Basic language. It requires you to define a variable or constant before you use it. When developing any complex program, especially one that uses DirectX or the Win32 API, this statement helps to ensure that everything is defined before it is used. Then if you start your program with Run, Start With Full Compile while in the Visual Basic development environment, you can quickly find and fix undefined constants and variables before your program crashes.

COLLECTING KEYSTROKES

Keyboards on a PC do not return a character that can be processed directly by the computer. Instead, each key on the computer is assigned a unique identifier known as a scan code. Normally Windows will automatically translate the scan code into the appropriate character. However, DirectInput merely returns the scan code. It is up to you to translate the scan code into a value useful for your program.

To support this translation process, I've defined these module-level variables to hold key information between calls to the InputKeyboardEvent. The LastKeyboardState array holds the state information from the last keyboard event. KeyboardCode is used to translate scan codes into an ASCII character. When KeyboardTextMode is True, characters are collected into InputBuffer. Otherwise characters are treated as commands and executed immediately.

```
Private LastKeyboardState(255) As Byte
Private KeyboardCode(255, 2) As String
Public InputBuffer As String
Public KeyboardTextMode As Boolean
```

The InputKeyboardEvent routine (see Listing 12.4) is called whenever a DirectX event occurs. The routine begins by calling the GetDeviceStateKeyboard method to get the information about the keys pressed that may have triggered this event.

LISTING 12.4   DXINPUT.INPUTKEYBOARDEVENT

```
Public Sub InputKeyboardEvent()

Dim i As Long
Dim DXKeyboardState As DIKEYBOARDSTATE
Dim DXMouseState As DIMOUSESTATE

DXKeyboard.GetDeviceStateKeyboard DXKeyboardState
If Err.Number <> 0 Then
    DXDebugger.WriteErr "Can't get keyboard state info:", Err

End If

If KeyboardTextMode Then
    If DXKeyboardState.Key(DIK_BACKSPACE) = &H80 And _
        LastKeyboardState(DIK_BACKSPACE) = 0 Then
        If Len(InputBuffer) > 0 Then
            InputBuffer = Left(InputBuffer, Len(InputBuffer) - 1)

        End If

    ElseIf DXKeyboardState.Key(DIK_RETURN) = &H80 And _
        LastKeyboardState(DIK_RETURN) = 0 Then
        KeyboardTextMode = False

    Else
        InputBuffer = InputBuffer & ToAscii(DXKeyboardState.Key)

    End If

Else
    For i = 0 To 255
        If DXKeyboardState.Key(i) = 128 And DXKeyboardState.Key(i) <> _
            LastKeyboardState(i) Then
            KeyBoardStateChange i

        End If

    Next i
```

LISTING 12.4 CONTINUED

```
End If

For i = 0 To 255
    LastKeyboardState(i) = DXKeyboardState.Key(i)

Next i

End Sub
```

The information about each key pressed for this event is stored in the `Key` property. You can access the state of each key by using the scan code as a subscript into the array. Because scan codes range from 0 to 255, you can specify scan code directly by using the appropriate DirectInput constant or you can simply check each individual element in the array to see all of the keys that were pressed.

`Key` returns a `Byte` value whose high order bit reflects the state of that particular key. If the high order bit is 1, the key was pressed; otherwise, the key wasn't pressed. Because the high order bit of a `Byte` is really just 2^7, you can compare the value to either `128` or `&h80`.

After getting the keyboard state data, I decide how to process it based on `KeyboardTextMode`. If this value is `True`, I translate the scan codes into characters and append them to `InputBuffer`.

Translating scan codes into an ASCII character is harder than it looks. Simply knowing that a key is pressed doesn't mean that someone has entered a new character. It is possible that the player has held the key down for several events. In this case it is necessary to know whether the key was pressed the last time this event was triggered. If the key wasn't pressed last time, but was pressed this time, a key was pressed and should be processed. Thus I need to verify that the key's state was changed in this state by comparing the value in `LastKeyboardState` with the value in `Key`.

Using this technique, I check to see if the backspace key was pressed. If it was, I delete the last character from `InputBuffer`. Of course I need to ensure that there is at least one character in the buffer before I delete it; otherwise, Visual Basic will trigger a nasty runtime error.

Next I see if the player has pressed the Return key. I use the Return key to signal the end of the buffered input processing. All this requires is setting `KeyBoardTextMode` to `False`.

If the key pressed wasn't the Backspace key or the Enter key, I translate the scan code into an ASCII character using the `ToAscii` function.

If I'm not saving characters into `InputBuffer`, I will process the character immediately. I loop through all possible key numbers and see if the key was pressed and check to see if the key wasn't pressed the last time this event was triggered. If the key wasn't pressed the last time and it is pressed this time, I call the `KeyBoardStateChange` routine to process this particular key. Finally, I save the current `Key` value into `LastKeyboardState`, so I can compare it to the value in `Key` the next time this routine is called.

CONVERTING SCAN CODES TO ASCII

The trick to the `ToAscii` routine is the `KeyboardCode` array. This is a two-dimensional array where the first dimension corresponds to the scan code and the second element corresponds to the state of the Shift keys. This array is initialized using statement like this in the `SetKeyboardCodes` routine.

```
KeyboardCode(DIK_A, 0) = "a"
KeyboardCode(DIK_A, 1) = "A"
```

The `ToAscii` routine (see Listing 12.5) looks through the array to find a key that was pressed and uses the current index as an index into the `KeyboardCode` array along with the current state of the Shift keys.

LISTING 12.5   DXINPUT.TOASCII

```
Private Function ToAscii(Key() As Byte) As String

Dim i As Long
Dim s As String

For i = 0 To 255
    If (Key(i) = &H80) And (LastKeyboardState(i) = 0) Then
        If (Key(DIK_LSHIFT) Or Key(DIK_RSHIFT)) = &H80 Then
            s = KeyboardCode(i, 1)

        Else
            s = KeyboardCode(i, 0)

        End If

    End If

Next i

ToAscii = s

End Function
```

If the scan code corresponds to a character that should be processed, `KeyboardCode` will return the appropriate character; otherwise, `KeyboardCode` will return an empty string.

TRACKING THE MOUSE

The processing required for the mouse is much more complex than the keyboard because the input data is buffered; each mouse axis movement or button click must be extracted from the buffer and processed independently. After the data is extracted for a particular axis or button, it requires further processing to make it easy to use.

Like the keyboard, the mouse buttons represent a particular state either up or down. This forces you to detect clicks and double-clicks in your input handler. Also, axis data represents the amount that the mouse has moved since the last piece of data. This means that the input

PART

III

CH

12

handler must process these relative values to determine where the cursor should be placed on the screen.

Because this information has to be tracked between events, I use a collection of module variables (see Listing 12.6) to hold the current state of the mouse. The absolute screen location is kept in the variables MouseX, MouseY, and MouseZ, while button information is kept in MouseButton0 (the left mouse button is pressed), MouseButton0Click (the left mouse button is clicked), and MouseButton0DoubleCLick (the left mouse button is double-clicked).

LISTING 12.6   MOUSE-RELATED MODULE-LEVEL VARIABLES FOR DXGRAPHICS

```
Public MouseX As Long
Public MouseY As Long
Public MouseZ As Long
Private MouseButton0 As Boolean
Private MouseButton1 As Boolean
Private MouseButton2 As Boolean
Private MouseButton0Click As Boolean
Private MouseButton0DoubleClick As Boolean
Private OldMouseX As Long
Private OldMouseY As Long
Private OldMouseZ As Long
Private MouseButton0Time As Long
Private MouseButton0ClickTime As Long
```

I also track the previous values in the MouseX, MouseY, and MouseZ values in OldMouseX, OldMouseY, and OldMouseZ so that the program can later determine how the mouse has moved since the last input.

Listing 12.7 shows the code for the InputMouseEvent. This routine begins by declaring a few local variables used for processing data and then it disables error checking. Then it uses the GetDeviceData method to get data that has been buffered. If this routine fails, you should assume that the mouse was taken away from the game and must be reacquired before you can process any input data. Setting GetMouse to True will allow the Form object's MouseMove event to determine when to reacquire the mouse.

LISTING 12.7   DXINPUT.INPUTMOUSEEVENT

```
Public Sub InputMouseEvent()

Dim i As Long
Dim MouseItems As Long
Dim MouseData(48) As DIDEVICEOBJECTDATA
Dim MouseTick As Long

On Error Resume Next
MouseItems = DXMouse.GetDeviceData(MouseData, 0) - 1
If Err.Number <> 0 Then
    GetMouse = True
    Exit Sub

End If
```

LISTING 12.7 CONTINUED

```
On Error GoTo 0

OldMouseX = MouseX
OldMouseY = MouseY
OldMouseZ = MouseZ

MouseTick = MouseData(0).lSequence
MouseButton0Click = False
MouseButton0DoubleClick = False

For i = 0 To MouseItems
    If MouseData(i).lSequence <> MouseTick Then
        MouseStateChange
        MouseTick = MouseData(i).lSequence

    End If

    Select Case MouseData(i).lOfs
        Case DIMOFS_X
            MouseX = MouseX + MouseData(i).lData * 2
            If MouseX < 0 Then
                MouseX = 0

            ElseIf MouseX > dx.Width - 16 Then
                MouseX = dx.Width - 16

            End If

        Case DIMOFS_Y
            MouseY = MouseY + MouseData(i).lData * 2
            If MouseY < 0 Then
                MouseY = 0

            ElseIf MouseY > dx.Height - 32 Then
                MouseY = dx.Height - 32

            End If

        Case DIMOFS_Z
            MouseZ = MouseZ + MouseData(i).lData
            If MouseZ < -1000 Then
                MouseZ = -1000

            ElseIf MouseZ > 1000 Then
                MouseZ = 1000

            End If

        Case DIMOFS_BUTTON0
            MouseButton0 = MouseData(i).lData And &H80
            If MouseButton0 Then
                ' button down
                MouseButton0Time = MouseData(i).lTimeStamp
```

LISTING 12.7   CONTINUED

```
            ElseIf ((MouseData(i).lTimeStamp - MouseButton0ClickTime) < 400) Then
                'button up, already have a click, button up in time for double-click
                MouseButton0Click = False
                MouseButton0DoubleClick = True
                MouseButton0Time = 0
                MouseButton0ClickTime = 0

            ElseIf (MouseData(i).lTimeStamp - MouseButton0Time) < 200 Then
                'button up, button up late for double-click,
                    'button up in time for single-click
                MouseButton0Click = True
                MouseButton0DoubleClick = False
                MouseButton0Time = 0
                MouseButton0ClickTime = MouseData(i).lTimeStamp

            Else
                'button up, no previous click, too late for click or double-click
                MouseButton0Click = False
                MouseButton0DoubleClick = False
                MouseButton0Time = 0
                MouseButton0ClickTime = 0

            End If

        Case DIMOFS_BUTTON1
            MouseButton1 = MouseData(i).lData And &H80

        Case DIMOFS_BUTTON2
            MouseButton2 = MouseData(i).lData And &H80

    End Select

Next i

MouseStateChange

End Sub
```

The mouse data returned by the GetDeviceData method is stored in the MouseData array with the number of items in the array stored in MouseItems. The MouseData is a DIDEVICEOBJECTDATA structure that contains four key items. lOfs contains the part of the mouse that is associated with the data value stored in lData. The lSequence and lTimeStamp values hold information about when the data was collected. These values will be identical for all of the information collected in a single mouse event. lSequence is merely a sequential number associated with each event, while lTimeStamp returns a value that can be compared with the GetTickCount Win32 API call.

Before I process the data from the MouseData array, save the current values for MouseX, MouseY, and MouseZ into OldMouseX, OldMouseY, and OldMouseZ, respectively. Next, I set the variable MouseTick to the lSequence value from the first element in the array. Then I set both MouseButton0Click and MouseButton0DoubleClick to False.

After this setup I start a `For` loop that processes all of the buffered input. The first step is to determine if the current data value is part of the current sequence of data as recorded in `MouseTick`. If it isn't, I call the `MouseStateChange` routine to process the data I've already recorded.

To process the data in a single element of the array, I use a `Select` statement using the value in the `lOfs` property to determine the type of data.

If the data comes from a mouse movement on the X-axis, I simply multiply the value by 2 and add it to the value already in `MouseX`. Because the value in `MouseX` is used to position the cursor on the screen, I verify that the new value is in the range of 0 to `Width` - 16. The reason the upper bound is not simply `Width` is that I don't want the cursor to totally disappear. Because the width of the cursor is 32 pixels, using 16 pixels means that half of the cursor will be visible.

Note

The magic number two

The reason I multiplied the raw value returned by the mouse driver by two was an attempt to make the mouse appear more responsive to me. Although I used a value of two, you may want to create a sensitivity option in your game that can be adjusted by the player. While this isn't as important in this type of game, it can make a big difference to someone playing a first person shooter with a mouse.

I repeat this process for the Y-axis, substituting the `Height` property for the `Width` property. I also do something similar to the Z-axis (the wheel on a wheel mouse); however, because I don't have a height or width associated with this axis, I merely ensure that the value stays in the range from –1000 to +1000.

Handling the mouse buttons is more complex than the axis due to the need to determine when a click or double-click occurs. A click occurs when the user presses a mouse button and releases it within 200 milliseconds. A double-click occurs when someone clicks the mouse a second time within 400 milliseconds of the first click. The variable `MouseButton0Time` tracks the elapsed time for a single click, while the variable `MouseButton0ClickTime` tracks the elapsed time for a double-click.

Like the keys on the keyboard, when a mouse button is pressed, the data item associated with it will have the high order bit set. So I will set `MouseButton0` to `True` when the high order bit in `lData` equals `&h80`.

Then I'll set up a complex `If` statement to determine how to process the mouse button. If someone pressed the mouse button (`MouseButton0` is `True`), I'll save time that the data was collected in the `MouseButton0Time` variable. Because this test traps all button presses, any other `ElseIf` statement can assume that the mouse button was released.

Next, I'll try to determine if the player double-clicked the mouse by subtracting the time for the current button release with the value in `MouseButton0DoubleClick`. If this value is less than 400 milliseconds, I know that I have a double-click event. So I set the `MouseButton0Click` to `False` and `MouseButton0DoubleClick` to `True` and set both `MouseButton0Time` and `MouseButton0ClickTime` to zero.

If I don't have a double-click event, I may have a single click. This means I should subtract `MouseButton0Time` from the `lTimeStamp` value associated with the current data element and see if the result is less than 200 milliseconds. If this is true, I need to set `MouseButton0Click` to `True`, `MouseButton0DoubleClick` to `False`, and set `MouseButton0Time` to zero. Then I set `MouseButton0ClickTime` to the value in `lTimeStamp` to mark the beginning time for the double-click event.

Finally, if none of the previous conditions apply, I know that the user has pressed the mouse and released it more than 200 milliseconds later, so neither a single-click or double-click has occurred and I need to set both `MouseButton0Click` and `MouseButton0DoubleClick` to `False` and `MouseButton0Time` and `MouseButton0ClickTime` to zero.

> **Note**
>
> ### Clicks and double-clicks
>
> All this code makes you appreciate some of the nice things that Visual Basic does for you automatically. The values of 200 milliseconds and 400 milliseconds were chosen because they were comfortable to me. You may want to allow the player to adjust these values like the mouse sensitivity value.

The other two buttons can be handled in the same way as button zero; however, I decided that there wasn't much of a need to trap single- and double-clicks for these buttons. So I merely detected when these mouse buttons were pressed for use later. I end this routine by calling the `MouseStateChange` event to apply the cumulative effect of the mouse events to the game.

MOUSE RECOVERY

Whenever the mouse loses input, usually caused when the player switched to another program while running the game, an error will occur when I try to get the data from the device and I'll set `GetMouse` to `True`. This means that the next time the program detects any mouse movement, I need to reacquire the mouse to properly process mouse input.

To detect when the mouse is returned to the program, I use the `MouseMove` event in the `Form` object containing the game's display. When this event occurs, the following code is executed:

```
If GetMouse Then
    dxi.ReaquireMouse

End If
```

The `ReacquireMouse` method in `DXInput` merely calls the `Acquire` method for the device associated with the mouse like this.

```
On Error Resume Next
DXMouse.Acquire
```

The `On Error Resume Next` statement merely ignores any errors. This process may be repeated several times before the mouse will begin working normally. However, this will happen so fast that the player will never notice it.

ENDING DIRECTINPUT

It is important that you properly terminate any program that uses DirectInput, especially if you acquire the mouse in exclusive foreground mode. Listing 12.8 shows the steps I use to make sure that the program ends properly. First I unacquire both the keyboard and the mouse devices and then I set both devices to `Nothing` to ensure that all of the resources they control are released. Finally I set `DXInput` to `Nothing` to terminate DirectInput nicely.

LISTING 12.8   DXINPUT.TERMDXINPUT

```
Public Sub TermDXInput()

DXKeyboard.Unacquire
DXMouse.Unacquire

Set DXKeyboard = Nothing
Set DXMouse = Nothing
Set DXInput = Nothing

End Sub
```

PART

III

CH

12

FINAL THOUGHTS

One of the difficult things about using DirectInput with your application is debugging your DirectInput code. If it doesn't work properly, you may not be able to do much with your program, including exiting it properly. The best advice I can give you is to save your program often and be ready to kill Visual Basic and your program if necessary. You may also have to reboot your computer if you try using the `ShowCursor` Win32API routine. However, once you have a working DirectInput routine, you should be in relatively good shape at least from a debugging perspective.

The real question is whether using DirectInput is worth all of the time and effort. In Swim Mall, which uses only the keyboard and mouse, DirectInput doesn't offer many benefits. You can use the `MouseMove` event in the `Form` object to follow the cursor around on the screen. You can hide the Windows cursor using the `ShowCursor` Win32 API routine and use the same techniques I'll cover in the next chapter to create your own cursor. You can even use the `MouseDown` and `MouseUp` events to manage clicks and double-clicks.

However, if you plan to use joysticks or other gaming devices or if you need to identify the Shift, Ctrl, or Alt keys as unique input values then your only option is to use DirectInput. The KeyDown and KeyUp events will not trap these keys as unique keys. They only come into play with one of the other keys. Because these keys are typically larger than the other keys on the keyboard, they are desirable to use for games that require the player to move, aim, and shoot with the keyboard.

CHAPTER **13**

COMMANDING THE GAME

In this chapter

Translating the input into commands and executing the commands is a key part of the game. Likewise providing feedback about the commands to the player is also important. Feedback can take the form of custom cursors on the screen and various types of pop-up messages displayed on the screen. This chapter builds on the work done in the previous chapter with DirectInput and finishes the basic user interface by running commands.

RUNNING THE GAME

Before I dig into the code, I want to discuss how the new user interface works. In past versions of the program, the user interface used standard Visual Basic command buttons to perform the most common tasks.

MOVING AROUND THE MALL

There are three controls the player can use to change how the mall is displayed. First, the player can move the mall from front to back or side to side. Second, the player can rotate the mall around its center. Finally, the player can zoom in and out to look at a detail in the mall or see more of the mall.

In most simulation computer games, the player is allowed to only rotate the game surface in increments of 90 degrees. This limitation comes from the fact that most games are developed using a 2D engine. By creating four different views for each object, the developer can let the player see different sides of the object. Since Swim Mall uses a true 3D engine, it is a trivial matter to rotate the mall any amount you want.

To make the interface really easy to use, I choose to let the user right-click on the screen with the mouse to perform these operations. When the player clicks the right mouse button, the cursor will be changed to tell the player how he can change the screen's view. After the cursor has changed, the player just drags the mouse to see a different view of the mall.

The screen is divided vertically into three areas. Clicking the right mouse button while the mouse pointer is in the left quarter of the screen allows the user to rotate the mall. Move the cursor up and the mall will rotate counterclockwise, while moving the cursor toward the bottom of the window will rotate the mall in a clockwise direction. The user can also press the Page Down key to rotate the mall clockwise, while Page Up rotates the mall in the other direction.

If the player clicks the right mouse button while in the right quarter of the screen, dragging the mouse down will zoom in on the position at the center of the display. Dragging the mouse up causes the display to zoom out.

Clicking the right button while in the middle half of the screen allows the player to move the mall up, down, left, and right in the same direction as the mouse. Moving the mall can also be accomplished by using the cursor keys.

When combined with similar free-form zoom and move controls, it's real easy to get lost on the screen. Therefore it is important to have a way to return to the default setting. Pressing the Home key restores the mall to its default display.

CONTROLLING SPEED

The simulation speed is controlled by pressing the function keys F9 through F12. F9 sets the speed to zero, effectively pausing the game. F10 is the normal simulation speed of 300 seconds per tick, while F11 and F12 set the simulation speed to 900 and 1,800 seconds per tick, respectively.

SELECTING STORES

The player can select a store by clicking on it. Double-clicking on a store will display an pop-up message containing some key statistics. The pop-up can be cleared by clicking on the OK button or by pressing Esc.

USING MENU COMMANDS

Pressing the Esc key will display the pop-up menu. Currently the only options on this menu are Return to Game and Quit. You simply type the first letter of the command to execute the command. Pressing Esc a second time without selecting a command will cause the menu to disappear.

RUNNING COMMANDS

DirectInput detects the keys that are pressed on the keyboard and the movement and button clicks on the mouse and make the information available for other routines in the DXInput class to process. These routines are responsible for translating the input values into game commands and sending them to the Game class for execution. This process is illustrated in Figure 13.1.

The input handler creates a GameCommand object that contains the information about the command the user just issued. This command is passed to the game engine for execution via a Queue object, which ensures that the game player's input is not lost no matter what is going on at the time and it also ensures that the input is processed in the order it was entered.

The game engine will extract information from the queue and execute it in the command processor. The command processor is called just before the screen is rendered and it will execute all of the commands in the queue.

Also associated with the game is a state. Each state describes the collection of commands that can be executed. You can view this graphically as a finite state machine (see Figure 13.2). Each ellipse describes a particular state in the game. In this diagram there are only four states: Normal, Menu, Quit, and OK. Commands are drawn as a rectangle. When you are in a particular state, you have a list of commands that can be executed. After executing a command, you are returned to a particular state.

For instance, to quit the game, the player must first hit the Esc key to select an Options menu. Then from the Options menu, the player must select the Quit command. Then another message box will be displayed asking the player if he really wants to quit. If the user responds yes, the game will end; if the user responds no, the game will return to the normal state.

PART

III

CH

13

Figure 13.1
The GameCommand object passes commands from the DXInput object to Game object for execution.

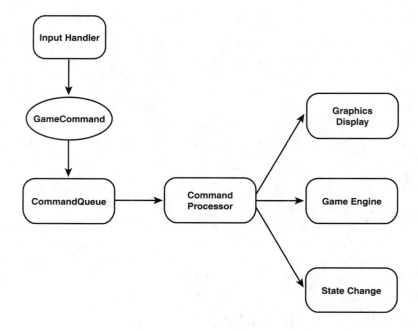

Figure 13.2
The paths taken for command execution can be viewed as a finite state machine.

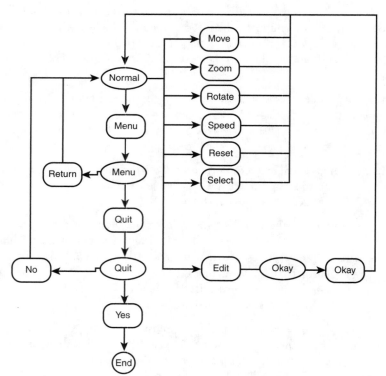

MANAGING GAME STATE

The game state is maintained in the variable GameState, which is declared in the Global module. GameState uses the enumerated data type GameStateEnum, which is shown here:

```
Public Enum GameStateEnum
    UnknownState
    MenuState
    NormalState
    OkayState
    QuitState

End Enum
```

Note

For the future

While there are only four states at this point in the development process, other states will be added as the game evolves. These states will process new commands that will be added to the game.

There are four main states for the game. NormalState is the normal operating state for the game. The player can move, zoom and rotate the mall to examine what is happening. Some commands will change the game state to a different state.

In MenuState, the player has told the game to display the main menu of options. From this menu, the player can select two options, to return to the game or to quit the game. As new features are added to the game, more options will be added to the menu.

OkayState is used when a pop-up message is displayed and the game must wait for the player to read it and click on OK, while QuitState is used when the player has asked to end the game.

NEW GRAPHIC FUNCTIONS

To replace the old Visual Basic interface used through Chapter 11, I need two new types of graphics. The first is a replacement for the standard Windows cursor. The new cursor not only will serve as a pointer for selecting objects in the game, but it will also communicate information to the user about how they are using the mouse.

To choose a cursor, simply set the DXGraphics.Cursor property to the number of the cursor you want to display. The game currently supports a maximum of 16 cursors chosen from a bitmap image, as shown in Figure 13.3.

Another useful tool is the capability to show a pop-up display. You can use pop-ups to communicate information to the user and to request a response. Pop-up displays come in three different flavors. A YesNo pop-up display allows you to display a single line of text and request that the user enters either Yes or No. An Okay pop-up can display several lines of information. To close the display, the player must click on the OK button. Menus are also considered a type of pop-up display and work the same way.

Figure 13.3
Cursors are extracted from the Cursors.BMP file.

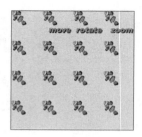

To use the pop-up display, set DXGraphics.PopupMessage to the type of graphic you want to use. In this version of the program, the possible values include the following:

- None—No pop-up message will be displayed.
- Menu—Display the pop-up menu.
- Okay—Display the okay message.
- YesNo—Display the yes/no message (see Figure 13.4).

The DXGraphics.PopupMessageText property is used to display whatever text you desire on top of a pop-up message. This allows you to use the yes/no message when quitting the game (see Figure 13.4), or for any other situation you desire.

One interesting feature of the pop-up message facility is the capability to detect hotspots on the screen. When the mouse pointer passes over a hot spot, the value DXGraphics.PopupMessageHotSpot is changed to reflect the specific location on the menu. For instance, if the cursor passes over the OK button on an OK message, PopupMessageHotSpot will be set to 1 and the button will be highlighted.

Figure 13.4
The YesNo display allows you to display a line of text in addition to the yes and no buttons.

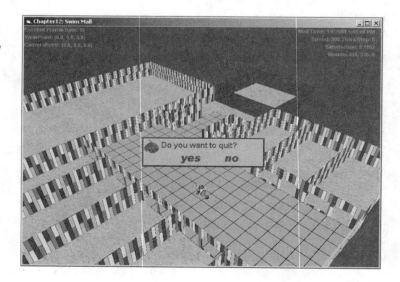

CREATING COMMANDS

The GameCommand class (see Listing 13.1) exists solely to pass information from the input devices to the game's engine. It consists of an enumerated type called Command, which describes the basic function to be performed. Along with the command is a series of attributes that provide additional information for the command.

LISTING 13.1   GAMECOMMAND CLASS

```
Public Enum CommandEnums
    UnknownCommand
    EditCommand
    MenuCommand
    Movecommand
    NoCommand
    OkayCommand
    QuitCommand
    ReturnToGameCommand
    ResetViewCommand
    RotateCommand
    SelectCommand
    SpeedCommand
    YesCommand
    ZoomCommand

End Enum

Public Command As CommandEnums
Public dx As Single
Public dy As Single
Public rotate As Single
Public speed As Long
Public Zoom As Single
Public X As Long
Public Y As Long
```

It's important to note that none of the commands will use all of the attributes. The different names exist simply to associate the proper data type with the proper property and to clearly identify the type of information being supplied.

Tip

Unknown command

When using enumerated types it is often useful to make the first entry represent either an unknown value or a default value. Enumerated types are stored as an Integer or Long value. The individual values are assigned numbers starting with zero. By calling the first value in the list unknown allows you to easily detect situations where someone declared a variable using the enumerated type and forgot to assign it a value.

To make adding the GameCommand object to the CommandQueue easier, I created the AddCommand routine in Listing 13.2. It creates a new GameCommand object and sets the various properties

PART

III

CH

13

in the object based on the parameters supplied to the routine. The key to making this easy is that I've used the Optional keyword for all of the parameters except for the command I'm adding. This means that they can be omitted and a meaningful default value can be used.

LISTING 13.2 DXINPUT.ADDCOMMAND

```
Private Sub AddCommand(cmd As CommandEnums, Optional dx As Single = 0, _
    Optional dy As Single = 0, Optional rotate As Single = 0, _
    Optional speed As Long = 0, Optional X As Long = 0, _
    Optional Y As Long = 0, Optional Zoom As Single = 0)

Dim c As GameCommand

Set c = New GameCommand
c.Command = cmd
c.dx = dx
c.dy = dy
c.rotate = rotate
c.speed = speed
c.X = X
c.Y = Y
c.Zoom = Zoom
CommandQueue.Add c

End Sub
```

Note

Expanding commands

The GameCommand class was designed to be easily expanded; however, you must use care when expanding the AddCommand routine. Because all of the parameters are referenced by position, any new parameters must be added at the end of the parameter list or you will cause serious problems with the existing code that uses this routine.

CONVERTING KEYBOARD INFORMATION INTO COMMANDS

Converting keyboard information into a GameCommand requires the use of a big Select statement (see Listing 13.3). The Select statement uses the GameState variable to determine which types of commands should be processed. Any commands generated by the keyboard that don't fit into the current game state are ignored.

LISTING 13.3 DXINPUT.KEYBOARDSTATECHANGE

```
Private Sub KeyBoardStateChange(k As Long)

Select Case GameState
    Case NormalState
        Select Case k
            Case DIK_ESCAPE
```

LISTING 13.3   CONTINUED

```
                AddCommand MenuCommand

        Case DIK_HOME, DIK_NUMPAD7
            AddCommand ResetViewCommand

        Case DIK_LEFT, DIK_NUMPAD4
            AddCommand Movecommand, -0.5, 0.5

        Case DIK_RIGHT, DIK_NUMPAD6
            AddCommand Movecommand, 0.5, -0.5

        Case DIK_UP, DIK_NUMPAD8
            AddCommand Movecommand, 0.5, 0.5

        Case DIK_DOWN, DIK_NUMPAD2
            AddCommand Movecommand, -0.5, -0.5

        Case DIK_PRIOR, DIK_NUMPAD9
            AddCommand RotateCommand, , , -0.05

        Case DIK_NEXT, DIK_NUMPAD3
            AddCommand RotateCommand, , , 0.05

        Case DIK_INSERT, DIK_NUMPAD0
            AddCommand ZoomCommand, , , , , , 0.05

        Case DIK_DELETE, DIK_DECIMAL
            AddCommand ZoomCommand, , , , , , , -0.05

        Case DIK_F9
            AddCommand SpeedCommand, , , , 0

        Case DIK_F10
            AddCommand SpeedCommand, , , , 300

        Case DIK_F11
            AddCommand SpeedCommand, , , , 900

        Case DIK_F12
            AddCommand SpeedCommand, , , , 1800

    End Select

Case MenuState
    Select Case k
        Case DIK_ESCAPE
            AddCommand ReturnToGameCommand

        Case DIK_Q
            AddCommand QuitCommand

        Case DIK_R
            AddCommand ReturnToGameCommand

    End Select
```

PART

III

CH

13

LISTING 13.3 CONTINUED

```
   Case QuitState
      Select Case k
         Case DIK_N
            AddCommand NoCommand

         Case DIK_Y
            AddCommand YesCommand

         Case DIK_RETURN And dx.PopupMessageHotSpot = 1
            AddCommand YesCommand

         Case DIK_RETURN And dx.PopupMessageHotSpot = 2
            AddCommand NoCommand

      End Select

   Case OkayState
      Select Case k
         Case DIK_ESCAPE
            AddCommand OkayCommand

         Case DIK_RETURN And dx.PopupMessageHotSpot = 1
            AddCommand OkayCommand

      End Select

End Select

End Sub
```

The variable k that is passed to this routine from the InputKeyboardEvent routine contains the scan code corresponding to the input character. These scan codes match the series of DIK constants defined in CONST_DIKEYFLAGS.

Remember that the scan codes represent a single key on the keyboard. Modifiers such as Shift, Ctrl, and Alt are not factored into the scan code. Num Lock and Caps Lock have no effect either. If a key is duplicated on the main keyboard area and the keypad, each key has a unique scan code. Thus the scan code for 1 on the main keyboard is DIK_1, while the scan code for 1 on the keypad is DIK_NUMPAD1.

The routine begins by handling Normal state. If the player presses the Esc key, the routine will add the MenuCommand to the command queue. If the person presses the home key either on the edit section of the keyboard or the numeric keypad, I'll add the ResetViewCommand to the command queue.

If the player presses any of the arrow keys, either on the arrow section of the keyboard or the numeric keypad, I'll move the mall in the appropriate direction by 0.5 units in the X and Z directions. Note that to move the mall more than this relatively small value, the player must press the arrow keys multiple times. The logic used in the previous chapter that was used to capture a keystroke doesn't include a repeat key function.

Note

Why or Z?

Remember the mall's floor is drawn along the X- and Z-axes, while the Y-axis describes the height above the mall's floor. When moving the mall, all you need to do is consider the X and Z components. The Y component will always remain constant; thus only the two values are sufficient to describe how to move the mall around on the screen.

The same technique I used to move the mall around is used to handle RotateCommand and ZoomCommand.

Pressing F9 will set the simulation speed to zero, thus pausing the game. F10 runs the game at normal speed, 300 seconds per tick of the simulation clock, while F11 and F12 will set the speed to 900 and 1,800 seconds per tick respectively.

While in the MenuState, pressing the Esc key will return the player back to the game. Pressing R will also return the player back to the game. Pressing Q will add QuitCommand to the queue.

The QuitState is a little more complex. Pressing Y will execute the Yes command, while pressing N will execute the No command. Pressing the Enter key on the main keyboard (DIK_RETURN) has no effect unless the cursor is over a hot spot. Hot spot 1 is over the Yes button, so pressing Enter means the same thing as pressing Y. Pressing Enter while over hot spot two has the same effect as pressing N.

OkayState is similar to the Quit state, except that pressing Esc will clear the display and well as pressing Enter while the mouse is over the OK button.

CONVERTING MOUSE INFORMATION INTO COMMANDS

Information generated by the mouse is handled in the same fashion as the keyboard. However, while the keyboard routine merely has to handle a single character that has been input, the MouseStateChange routine (see Listing 13.4) is far more complex due to the number of different input values that can be generated by the mouse.

LISTING 13.4   DXINPUT.MOUSESTATECHANGE

```
Private Sub MouseStateChange()

Select Case GameState
   Case NormalState
      If MouseButton1 And dx.Cursor = 0 Then
         If MouseX < dx.Width / 4 Then
            dx.Cursor = 2

         ElseIf MouseX > 3 * dx.Width / 4 Then
            dx.Cursor = 3

         Else
```

PART
III

CH

13

LISTING 13.4   CONTINUED

```
            dx.Cursor = 1

        End If

    ElseIf Not MouseButton1 Then
        dx.Cursor = 0

    End If

    If MouseButton0DoubleClick Then
        AddCommand EditCommand, , , , , MouseX, MouseY

    ElseIf MouseButton0Click Then
        AddCommand SelectCommand, , , , , MouseX, MouseY

    ElseIf (dx.Cursor = 2) And (OldMouseY < MouseY) Then
        AddCommand RotateCommand, , , 0.05

    ElseIf (dx.Cursor = 2) And (OldMouseY > MouseY) Then
        AddCommand RotateCommand, , , -0.05

    ElseIf (dx.Cursor = 3) And (OldMouseY > MouseY) Then
        AddCommand ZoomCommand, , , , , , , 0.01

    ElseIf (dx.Cursor = 3) And (OldMouseY < MouseY) Then
        AddCommand ZoomCommand, , , , , , , -0.01

    ElseIf (dx.Cursor = 1) Then
        AddCommand Movecommand, _
            (MouseX - OldMouseX) / 25 - MouseY - OldMouseY) / 25, _
            -(MouseX - OldMouseX) / 25 - (MouseY - OldMouseY) / 25

    End If

Case QuitState
    If dx.PopupMessageHotSpot = 1 And MouseButton0 Then
        AddCommand YesCommand

    ElseIf dx.PopupMessageHotSpot = 2 And MouseButton0 Then
        AddCommand NoCommand

    End If

Case OkayState
    If dx.PopupMessageHotSpot = 1 And MouseButton0 Then
        AddCommand OkayCommand

    End If

End Select

End Sub
```

In the NormalState case, I begin by seeing if the player has pressed the right mouse button (MouseButton1 = True) and if the default cursor is being displayed (dx.Cursor = 0). If both conditions are true, the player wants to move, rotate, or zoom the image on the screen.

If the mouse pointer is in the left quarter of the screen, I'll set the cursor to 2, which displays the rotate cursor. If the mouse pointer is on the right quarter of the screen, I'll set the cursor to 3 to display the zoom cursor. Finally, if the mouse is in the middle half of the screen, I set the cursor to 1, which will display the move cursor.

Now that the proper cursor is displayed, I need to determine what type of command the player issued. A double-click adds an EditCommand to the queue, with the absolute location of the mouse. A single-click will add a SelectCommand to the queue also specifying the absolute location of the mouse.

After checking for clicks and double-clicks, I need to see if the player wants to change her view of the mall. If Cursor is 2, the player wants to rotate the mall. To determine which direction to rotate the mall, I compare the OldMouseY position with MouseY. If OldMouseY is less than MouseY, this means that the player moved the mouse toward the bottom of the screen and I'll rotate the mall counterclockwise by 0.05 radians or roughly three degrees. If the OldMouseY is greater than MouseY, it means that the player moved the cursor up and I'll rotate the mall the same amount in the other direction.

Note that if the mouse hasn't moved (that is, OldMouseY = MouseY), I'll do nothing. If you were tempted to see if the mouse moved down and simply use an Else statement to handle the other condition, you will wind up with a situation where the mall will rotate if the player simply clicks the right mouse button. The mall should only rotate if the player moves the mouse.

Next I'll execute similar code to handle the zoom function. Again remember you shouldn't zoom if the player doesn't move the mouse.

Moving the mall is a little bit more complex as you can see when I handle the condition where the cursor has a value of one. Although I can handle the move in a single statement, I need to compute how far the mall should move in a particular direction. Because the camera is placed at 45 degrees between the X and Z axes, I have to convert the horizontal and vertical mouse movements into changes of distance along each axis.

Note

Weird constants

The constants I used for rotating, zooming, and movement were chosen because they felt comfortable to me. In a commercial game, you would probably want to allow the players to control these values so that they can tweak the sensitivity of the controls themselves.

While in the QuitState, the only legal commands that can be generated by a mouse are clicking on the hot spots for the Yes and No buttons. In the same vein, the only legal mouse command occurs while the mouse is clicked while over the OK button. In these cases, all I need to do is to add the appropriate command to CommandQueue.

EXECUTING COMMANDS

Before we added the DirectInput logic, we basically had two tasks running independently of each other in the game. The main rendering loop simply displayed the graphics associated with the game, while the simulation engine ran independently of the rendering loop.

Now we've added a third independent task that collects commands and adds them to CommandQueue. However, executing the commands from the command queue shouldn't be handled as an independent task. It should be integrated into the main game loop to minimize conflicts with the other tasks.

MODIFYING THE MAIN LOOP

Integrating the command processor into the game is very simple. I just add a call to the RunCommands method in the PlayGame routine in the main form (see Listing 13.5). Note that I added it ahead of the rendering routine so that any changes of the graphics will be immediately displayed. This really doesn't make much of a difference in most systems; however, it will make a difference on systems with a really low frame rate.

LISTING 13.5   FORM1.PLAYGAME

```
Sub PlayGame()

Timer1.Interval = 100
Timer1.Enabled = True

Do While GameActive
    GameObj.RunCommands
    dx.Render
    DoEvents

Loop

End Sub
```

RUNNING COMMANDS

The real work of executing the commands in the CommandQueue is done by the RunCommands method of Game class (see Listing 13.6). This routine uses a Do loop to pull each command from the command queue and then pass the command to a subroutine associated with a particular game state to execute the command.

LISTING 13.6   GAME.RUNCOMMAND

```
Public Sub RunCommands()

Dim c As GameCommand
```

LISTING 13.6   CONTINUED

```
Do While dxi.CommandQueue.Length > 0
    Set c = dxi.CommandQueue.Front
    Select Case GameState
        Case NormalState
            RunNormal c

        Case QuitState
            RunQuitting c

        Case MenuState
            RunMenu c

        Case OkayState
            RunOkay c

    End Select

Loop

End Sub
```

RUNNING COMMANDS IN THE OKAY STATE

The RunOkay routine (see Listing 13.7) is the simplest of the four routines called from the RunCommands method because it merely has to handle a single command. If it sees an OkayCommand, all it has to do is to switch the game's state to normal and set the currently displayed pop-up message to None.

LISTING 13.7   GAME.RUNOKAY

```
Private Sub RunOkay(c As GameCommand)

Select Case c.Command
    Case OkayCommand
        GameState = NormalState
        dx.PopupMessage = None

End Select

End Sub
```

RUNNING COMMANDS IN THE NORMAL STATE

Processing commands for the NormalState (see Listing 13.8) is a bit more complex than OkayState, but the same technique applies. A Select statement is used to determine which command should be executed and then the code associated with the command will be executed.

LISTING 13.8   GAME.RUNNORMAL

```
Private Sub RunNormal(c As GameCommand)

Select Case c.Command
  Case MenuCommand
     GameState = MenuState
     dx.PopupMessage = Menu
     dx.PopupMessageText = vbCrLf & "Quit" & vbCrLf & "Return"

  Case MoveCommand
     dx.View c.dx, 0, c.dy

  Case RotateCommand
     dx.rotate c.rotate

  Case ZoomCommand
     dx.Zoom c.Zoom

  Case ResetViewCommand
     dx.ResetView

  Case SelectCommand
     If Not SelectedObject Is Nothing Then
        SelectedObject.mType = TexturedMesh

     End If

     Set SelectedObject = dx.HitObject(c.X, c.Y)

     If Not SelectedObject Is Nothing Then
        SelectedObject.mType = SelectedMesh

     End If

  Case EditCommand
     If Not SelectedObject Is Nothing Then
        GameState = OkayState
        dx.PopupMessage = Okay
        With SelectedObject.SimObject
           dx.PopupMessageText = .Name & vbCrLf & _
              "Today's sales: " & FormatCurrency(.TodaysSales, 0) & _
              vbCrLf & _
              "Monthly sales: " & FormatCurrency(.MonthlySales, 0) & _
              vbCrLf & _
              "Total sales: " & FormatCurrency(.TotalSales, 0)

        End With

     End If

  Case SpeedCommand
     If c.speed = 0 Then
        Form1.Timer1.Enabled = False
        speed = 0

     ElseIf speed = 0 Then
```

Listing 13.8   Continued

```
        Form1.Timer1.Enabled = True
        speed = c.speed

    Else
        speed = c.speed

    End If

End Select

End Sub
```

Most of the commands are relatively straightforward. They either involve switching the game from one state to another or calling one of the graphics methods to display a message or change the player's view of the mall.

The processing for `MenuCommand` is typical of most of the commands. I change the game state to `MenuState`, set `PopupMessage` to `Menu`, and set `PopupMessageText` to the list of text to be displayed on the menu.

`MoveCommand` is even simpler because I just have to call the `dx.Move` method with the appropriate values from the `GameCommand` object.

When processing the `SelectCommand` I remove the highlighting from any object in the mall that is already selected by assigning `TexturedMesh` to `mType`. Then I can use the `HitObject` method to determine which object intersects the line projected through the mall using the cursor's current X and Y position. If I find an object, I need to set `mType` to `SelectedMesh`.

Although the processing for the `EditCommand` looks complicated, it really isn't. Because this result of this command is to display a pop-up message with information about the currently selected object, I switch the game state to `OkayState` and select the `Okay` pop-up message. Then I use the `With` statement to access `SimObject` property so that I can get the information about the particular `Store`, `Anchor`, or `Food` object. This isn't absolutely necessary, but it does save a bunch of typing in the next statement, where I assign a long, multiline string with the store's statistics to `PopupMessageText`.

The `SpeedCommand` is somewhat interesting in that I need to disable the timer whenever I set `Speed` to zero and reenable it whenever it is disabled and I assign a non-zero value to `Speed`.

Displaying 2D Information

DirectX includes several techniques for displaying 2D data on the screen. I'm going to show you two different techniques here, one to draw the cursor on the screen and the other to draw the pop-up menus.

Cursors are implemented using a `D3DXSprite`, while menus are implemented using the `CopyRects` method. Both techniques are based upon the fact that Direct3D renders the image onto a flat surface, which in turn is displayed on your screen. The data is simply copied onto the same flat surface without any of the calculations that would be necessary if you were to create a plane with the appropriate texture.

DRAWING A CURSOR

As you previously saw in Figure 13.3, cursors are selected from a 4 by 4 grid. The total size of the image is 256 pixels by 256 pixels, so each cursor occupies a 64 pixels by 64 pixels piece of the raw image.

This image is stored in this texture, which is declared at the start of the DXGraphics module:

```
Private dxCursorTexture As Direct3DTexture8
```

And the image is loaded using this statement from the InitDXCursor routine.

```
Set dxCursorTexture = d3dx.CreateTextureFromFileEx(d3ddevice, _
    App.Path & "\cursors.bmp", 256, 256, D3DX_DEFAULT, 0, _
    D3DFMT_UNKNOWN, D3DPOOL_MANAGED, D3DX_FILTER_POINT, _
    D3DX_FILTER_POINT, &HFF00FFFF, ByVal 0, ByVal 0)
```

The primary difference between this particular statement and the other times I loaded a texture is the constant, &HFF00FFFF. This constant specifies that the color &H00FFFF (cyan) is treated as transparent. Thus when you go to display the cursor, you'll see only the cursor and not the surrounding background image.

Note

Clearly transparent

One of the problems with creating using transparent backgrounds is that the image will occasionally display a glowing edge that appears to be the same color as the background. In reality the color is not quite the same color as the transparent background. It is typically caused when you edit your image with antialiasing enabled. Antialiasing blends the edges of the image with the surrounding color so that the edge appears to be less pixilated. So when you blend the edge with the background color, you end up with some pixels that are part image color and part background color. Then when you remove the background color as part of the transparency process, you're stuck with the blended pixels. Although I originally didn't like the effect with these cursors, I found that the contrasting color make the cursor more visible and I decided to leave it that way.

Once the cursor is loaded into the texture, the rendering routine actually places the cursor on the screen. The following declarations are included at the start of Render and will be used by the cursor display logic.

```
Dim CursorSprite As D3DXSprite
Dim CursorSource As RECT
Dim CursorScaling As D3DVECTOR2
Dim CursorTranslation As D3DVECTOR2
```

Listing 13.9 contains a partial listing of DXGraphics.Render, which includes the statements necessary to draw the cursor on the screen.

LISTING 13.9 DXGRAPHICS.RENDER (PARTIAL LISTING)

```
CursorSource.Top = (Cursor \ 4) * 64
CursorSource.Bottom = CursorSource.Top + 63
CursorSource.Left = (Cursor Mod 4) * 64
CursorSource.Right = CursorSource.Left + 63

CursorTranslation.X = dxi.MouseX
CursorTranslation.Y = dxi.MouseY

CursorScaling.X = 1
CursorScaling.Y = 1

Set CursorSprite = d3dx.CreateSprite(d3ddevice)
CursorSprite.Draw dxCursorTexture, CursorSource, _
    CursorScaling, CursorScaling, 0, CursorTranslation, &HFFFFFFFF

d3ddevice.EndScene
```

Before you can draw the cursor on the screen, you need three pieces of information. First, you need to define the pixel location of where the information is coming from. This is stored in a RECT type, which defines the four corners of the rectangle.

To convert the cursor number into a RECT, you need to find the Top and Left values for the cursor you want to display. The Bottom and Right properties can be computed from the Top and Left properties by adding 63. (Remember that the cursor is a 64×64 square.)

The Top position is computed by doing an integer division of Cursor and 4. Thus for Cursor values of 0, 1, 2, and 3, Top will have a value of 0, for Cursor values of 4, 5, 6, and 7, Top will have a value of 1, and so forth. When multiplied by 64, this value will give the proper vertical pixel location.

The Left position is computed by computing the remainder of Cursor and 4 using the Mod operator. This means that for Cursor values of 0, 4, 8, and 12 will have a Left value of 0; for Cursor values of 1, 5, 9, and 13, Left will have a value of 1. Multiplying this value by 64 will give the appropriate horizontal pixel location.

Note

C++ rules!?!?!?

One of the advantages of programming in C++ is the capability to directly manipulate the bits in a number. In Visual Basic, I need to use an integer division and a multiplication to perform the same task that C++ programmers can perform with an and operation and a shift operation. The and operation and shift operation are much faster than the integer division and multiplication that a VB programmer must use. While these calculations will not noticeably slow done this particular game because they are only executed one per frame, it is little tricks like this that allow C++ programmers to do more work on the same computer than a VB programmer.

After computing which part of the cursor's texture you need to extract, you then need to specify where on the screen you want to draw the cursor. CursorTranslation holds the X and Y pixel location on this screen and it easily copied from the MouseX and MouseY properties.

The scaling factor describes how the texture will be stretched or shrunk when drawn on the screen. A value of 1 means that the image should be drawn exactly as extracted from the texture.

Next, create a new D3DXSprite object using the CreateSprite method. Then you can use the Draw method to copy the bits from the texture to the screen. Note that I use CursorScaling twice. The first time indicates the scaling factor, while the second time indicates the center of rotation. Because I'm not rotating the cursor (the zero in the Draw method), I just reused this value a second time.

The &HFFFFFFFF specifies the color modulation value. It is important to use this particular value to draw the cursor using the transparent background and to show all colors as they are in the original .BMP file.

After all this work, the cursor will be displayed in a new position on the screen each time, depending on the current position of the mouse. One drawback to this technique is that the cursor is drawn only as fast as the frame rate of the game. If you have a frame rate below 10 frames per second, the cursor will be very jumpy, much like the rest of the graphics.

DRAWING A POP-UP MESSAGE

Using sprites is a nice high-level approach to displaying 2D information on top of 3D information. However, I decided to show you a lower-level approach to drawing 2D data. This approach uses the Direct3Dsurface8 object to hold the information you want to display and then you can simply copy the information from the predefined surface to the rendering surface that Direct3D uses to create your view of the game.

At the module, level I declare this surface object, which I'll use to hold the image I want to display:

```
Private OkaySurface As Direct3DSurface8
```

Then as part of the InitDXMessages routine, I'll load the surface from a .BMP file using these statements. The first statement creates a new surface object and saves it in OkaySurface. You have to specify the surface size, which in this case is 256 by 256 pixels. It also must use the same display format at the rendering surface. This information is found in d3dDispMode.Format.

```
Set OkaySurface = d3ddevice.CreateImageSurface(256, 256, d3dDispMode.Format)
d3dx.LoadSurfaceFromFile OkaySurface, ByVal 0, ByVal 0, _
    App.Path & "\okay.bmp", ByVal 0, D3DX_DEFAULT, &HFF00FFFF, ByVal 0
```

After the surface is ready, you can use the LoadSurfaceFromFile method to copy the surface from a .BMP file (see Figure 13.5). Note that the image for the OK pop-up contains two copies of the OK pop-up. The top part of the image is the normal display, while the bottom part contains the display that is shown when the cursor is over the hot spot.

Figure 13.5
The OK pop-up image contains two images, one for normal display and one that is displayed when the cursor is over the hot spot.

I use the default values for most of the parameters because I'm simply loading the bits. You can also specify `Rects` for both source and destination that will allow you to load part of the image onto part of the surface and stretch the image to fit properly using one of several different filtering techniques.

One change that you need to make from the earlier versions of the program involves telling the Direct3D device that you will want to write to its rendering surface. This is done by specifying `D3DPRESENTFLAG_LOCKABLE_BACKBUFFER` for the `d3dWindow.flags` property in the `InitDXDevice` routine. Without this change you can't copy the bits to the rendering surface.

```
d3dWindow.flags = D3DPRESENTFLAG_LOCKABLE_BACKBUFFER
```

With these additions to the `DXGraphics` class, you merely need to add the code in `Render` to decide which surface you want to render and execute the appropriate code. In this case, I choose to call a separate routine due to the amount code.

Listing 13.10 contains the code to display the OK message. The routine begins by declaring a `Direct3Dsurface8` object and some `RECT` variables. Then I use the `GetRenderTarget` to get an object pointer to the actual rendering surface.

LISTING 13.10   DXGRAPHICS.DRAWOKAYMESSAGE

```
Private Sub DrawOkayMessage()

Dim ds As Direct3DSurface8

Dim center As RECT
Dim part As RECT
Dim TextRect As RECT

Set ds = d3ddevice.GetRenderTarget

center.Top = Height / 2 - 64
center.bottom = Height / 2 + 64
center.Left = Width / 2 - 128
center.Right = Width / 2 + 128

If dxi.MouseX > center.Left + 64 And _
    dxi.MouseX < center.Left + 192 And _
    dxi.MouseY > center.Top + 100 And _
    dxi.MouseY < center.Top + 128 Then
  PopupMessageHotSpot = 1
```

PART

III

CH

13

LISTING 13.10   CONTINUED

```
    part.Top = 128
    part.Left = 0
    part.bottom = 255
    part.Right = 255
    d3ddevice.CopyRects OkaySurface, part, 1, ds, center

Else

    PopupMessageHotSpot = 0
    part.Top = 0
    part.Left = 0
    part.bottom = 127
    part.Right = 255
    d3ddevice.CopyRects OkaySurface, part, 1, ds, center

End If

TextRect.Top = Height / 2 - 60
TextRect.Left = Width / 2 - 80
TextRect.bottom = Height / 2 + 20
TextRect.Right = Width / 2 + 115
d3dx.DrawText BigGameFont, &HFF0000FF, PopupMessageText, _
    TextRect, DT_TOP Or DT_LEFT

End Sub
```

Next I compute the location of the destination rectangle. Because I want to display the OK message in the center of the screen, I can compute the Top value by dividing Height by two and subtracting one half of the height of the OK message image. I use the same technique to compute the rest of the values for the destination. Note that the height of the OK message is 128 pixels, while its width is 256.

Next I use a long If condition to determine when the mouse is over the hot spot. If it is over the hot spot, I set the PopupMessageHotSpot variable to 1. Then I specify the bottom half of the source image using the part variable. I use the CopyRects method to copy the rectangle from the source surface to the destination surface. Finally, if the cursor isn't over the hot spot, I copy the top half of the image to the rendering surface.

> **Note**
>
> **Rendering rectangles**
>
> Although I only copy a single rectangle in this routine, you can copy multiple rectangles in a single operation. Simply create arrays of RECT for both the source and destination rectangles and replace the 1 in the call with the number of rectangles in the array. This approach is faster than calling CopyRects for each rectangle you want to copy.

The code at the end of this routine is used to display the text from the PopupMessageText string onto the screen. I simply define the area that I want to write to on the screen and use the `DrawText` method to display the text. Note that you can incorporate carriage return and line feeds into the string to display multiple lines of text within the rectangle.

FINAL THOUGHTS

Isolating the command processing from the input processing and the graphics display makes for a much cleaner design. It gives you more flexibility as you add more and more commands to the game as well as supporting other devices besides the mouse and keyboard.

The technique of using sprites and `CopyRects` allows you to simplify some of your programming. However, these facilities are not without their own limitations. For instance, one limitation of sprites is that you must use a texture. While some video cards support textures as large as 1,024×1,024, most video cards only support 256×256 textures. Also textures must be square and must be a power of 2. Thus you can use textures like 32×32, 64×64, 128×128, and so on. This can be a big limitation if you want to display big images or odd-sized images.

The `CopyRects` approach is not without its problems. Although a surface object can be any size, both surfaces must be identical in format. This may cause problems if your rendering surface doesn't support transparent pixels, which is common in many computers. Thus you can't create a menu that uses transparent pixels.

Another limitation of the `CopyRects` approach is that DirectX will lock the rendering surface while you are writing to it. This can adversely impact performance. If you need to do a lot of copying to the rendering surface, you may want to copy the information on another surface and then copy all of this information from the intermediate surface to the rendering surface.

These problems are merely things you need to keep in mind while building your game. DirectX is a toolbox and every tool is not perfect for every job. However, DirectX gives you several different ways to accomplish the same thing, so you can pick the one that is most appropriate to your application.

CHAPTER 14

ATTENTION, SHOPPERS

In this chapter

A computer game is not complete unless it has sound effects. Sound effects provide audible clues to the player that something has happened. Sounds can also help set the tone and mood of the game. This chapter explores how you can integrate sounds into Swim Mall using DirectX Audio and how you can create your own sounds using Cool Edit.

SOUNDS IN THE MALL

While a siren will let you know that you're being chased by a police car in a driving simulation, and hearing rapid gunfire from behind you let's you know you have to turn around and kill the evil alien behind you, Swim Mall doesn't rely on sounds in quite the same way.

Although using sounds to provide audible clues is useful in Swim Mall, the player doesn't benefit from them in the same way as in many other games. Therefore I decided to incorporate two types of sounds. First I decided to include an MP3 player, simply to provide some background music for the game. I like to think of it as elevator music for the mall. Second, I decided to use short sound clips as various events happen in the mall.

INTRODUCING DIRECTX AUDIO

DirectX Audio is a term that spans several different parts of DirectX—DirectSound, DirectMusic, and DirectShow. Though they each appear to represent a separate technology, under the covers all three are closely related.

Originally DirectSound and DirectMusic were targeted at two different needs. DirectSound focused on playing prerecorded digitized audio clips, while DirectMusic targeted developers that wanted to compose and play digital music. In DirectX 8, these tools have been blended together, though both the DirectMusic and DirectSound APIs remain.

Originally known as ActiveMovie, DirectShow is distinct from both DirectSound and DirectMusic, though it makes use of their services as well as some of the DirectX graphical services. It became a part of DirectX starting with version 8. Of the three sets of APIs, DirectShow is the easiest to exploit in this game.

One of the most useful features in DirectShow is the capability to play nearly any type of sound or music file transparently. This means that you can use MP3s, MIDIs, or .WAV files interchangeably without worrying about how to handle the specific file format.

> **Note**
>
> **Undocumented DirectShow**
>
> DirectShow is not included with the DirectX documentation for Visual Basic. It is included with the C++ version of the documentation. Note that not all of the features that are listed in the C++ documentation work under Visual Basic. However, those features are well marked, so you can easily avoid them.

INTEGRATING SOUNDS INTO SWIM MALL

In keeping with the philosophy that each functional area of the program should be isolated as much as possible from the other areas of the program, all of the audio code is stored in the DXAudio class. Because Swim Mall needs two kinds of sounds, background music and foreground alerts, the DXAudio supports the concept of foreground sounds and background music.

Foreground sounds are relatively short sound clips that alert the player to a condition in the game. It is important that the sounds be long enough so that the player can recognize the sound, but short enough that they aren't annoying. While a foreground sound is played, the volume for the background music is cut in half to let the player hear the sound clearly.

The background music is designed to play continuously while the game is active. When one song finishes, another will start. Songs are chosen at random from a list of files stored in the DXAudio object.

For the most part, once DXAudio is initialized and the music files are loaded you don't have to worry about it. The background music will continue to play automatically. The player has keyboard controls that can pause the music or switch to the next background song, and the player can control the overall volume.

Note

The music files are missing

While I would like to have distributed some music files for this game, there are many copyright issues that prevent me from doing so. If no music files are found in the Media directory, then no background music will be played during the game. Therefore I suggest that you create some of your own by using Cool Edit 2000. The registered version can easily copy songs from any music CD you own to your hard disk using the MP3 format. Simply open the music CD as if it were a data CD and load the desired track from the CD into Cool Edit. Then simply save the Cool Edit waveform as an .MP3 file into the Media directory.

INITIALIZING DXAUDIO

Listing 14.1 contains the module level variables that are used for the DXAudio class. The FilgraphManager object is the basis for all of the DirectShow functions used in this program. One instance of this object controls the foreground sound, while another controls the background sound.

LISTING 14.1   DXAUDIO MODULE-LEVEL VARIABLES

```
Private BackgroundMediaControl As FilgraphManager
Private ForegroundMediaControl As FilgraphManager
Private BackgroundBasicAudio As IBasicAudio
Private ForegroundBasicAudio As IBasicAudio
```

LISTING 14.1   CONTINUED

```
Private BackgroundMediaEvent As IMediaEvent
Private ForegroundMediaEvent As IMediaEvent
Private BackgroundStatus As Long
Private ForegroundStatus As Long
Private BackgroundIsPaused As Boolean
Private BackgroundVolumeLevel As Long

Private BackgroundFileList() As String

Private DXDebugger As Debugger
```

The `IBasicAudio` object has the capability to control the volume and the left/right balance of a sound. The `ImediaEvent` is used to determine whether a sound clip is currently playing. The current status value is stored in the `ForegroundStatus` and `BackgroundStatus` variables.

The `BackgroundIsPaused` variable is `True` when the background sound file is paused, while the `BackgroundVolumeLevel` holds the normal volume level. The list of music files is stored in `BackgroundFileList`. Finally, my old friend `DXDebugger` is available to record errors and other status information in the game's log file.

The `InitDXAudio` routine does very little work, as you can see in Listing 14.2. All of the module level variables are initialized, except that `BackgroundVolume` variables are initialized when a sound is played. The `Redim` is necessary to ensure that the array contains at least one element, so I can test the array's upper bound. Then I set the `BackgroundVolume` level to zero before returning a zero to the calling routine.

LISTING 14.2   DXAUDIO.INITDXAUDIO

```
Public Function InitDXAudio() As Long

ReDim BackgroundFileList(0)
BackgroundVolume = 0

InitDXAudio = 0

End Function
```

The `InitDXAudio` is called from the `Form` object using the `InitAudio` routine (see Listing 14.3). Along with creating and initializing the `DXAudio` object, this routine also calls the `AddDirectory` method to load the music files found in the game's `Music` directory. Then it calls `AddDirectory` a second time to load the files from the `AlternateMusicDirectory`.

LISTING 14.3   FORM1.INITAUDIO

```
Function InitAudio() As Long

Set dxa = New DXAudio
Set dxa.DebugObject = GameDebugger
```

LISTING 14.3   CONTINUED

```
InitAudio = dxa.InitDXAudio
dxa.AddDirectory App.path & "\Music"
dxa.AddDirectory AlternateMusicDirectory

End Function
```

> **Tip**
>
> **I have my own music files**
>
> If you already have a directory that contains your own music files, you can include the `MusicDirectory` statement in the `SwimMall.SMG` file (for example, `MusicDirectory=c:\My Documents\My Music`). The files in the specified directory will be added to any files found in the game's `Music` directory when the saved game file is processed. This statement is picked up in the `Game` class and the directory is saved in the global variable `AlternateMusicDirectory`.

PLAYING BACKGROUND MUSIC

Background music is chosen randomly from the list of files added to the `DXAudio` object using the `AddDirectory` method. After the files are loaded, you can start the background music with the `StartBackground` method, while the `StopBackground` method will stop the music from playing. The `PauseBackground` method will temporarily pause the background music, while the `ResumeBackground` method resumes the music from where it was paused. Finally the `BackgroundVolume` method can be used to increase or decrease the volume by the specified amount.

LOADING THE BACKGROUND MUSIC FILES

Before I can play background music, I need to load the music files into memory. I do this using the `AddFile` and `AddDirectory` methods. The `AddFile` method (see Listing 14.4) is very simple. It merely extends the `BackgroundFileList` by a single element and adds the filename to the end of the array.

LISTING 14.4   DXAUDIO.ADDFILE

```
Public Sub AddFile(path As String)

ReDim Preserve BackgroundFileList(UBound(BackgroundFileList) + 1)
BackgroundFileList(UBound(BackgroundFileList)) = path

End Sub
```

The `AddDirectory` method (see Listing 14.5) is a little more interesting in that it uses the `FileSystemObject` to get a `Folder` object, which contains all of the files in the directory. Once I have the `Folder` object, I use a `For Each` loop to retrieve each of the files in the

PART

III

CH

14

folder. If the file is a supported sound file, I use the `AddFile` method to add it to the array; otherwise, I'll check the next file.

LISTING 14.5   DXAUDIO.ADDDIRECTORY

```
Public Sub AddDirectory(path As String)

Dim fso As FileSystemObject
Dim folder As folder
Dim f As File
Dim t As String

Set fso = New FileSystemObject
Set folder = fso.GetFolder(path)

For Each f In folder.Files
    t = Right(f.Name, 4)
    If t = ".WAV" Or t = ".MP3" Or t = ".MID" Then
        AddFile f.path

    End If

Next f

Set f = Nothing
Set folder = Nothing
Set fso = Nothing

End Sub
```

Note

What about .AU and other types of sound files?

DirectSound is extremely flexible in terms of the sound files it will play. I chose to limit the files supported by this game to `.WAV`, `.MP3`, and `.MID` because I thought they were the most popular. However, you can easily modify the `If` statement to include any other types of sound files you want to use.

STARTING THE BACKGROUND MUSIC

After the list of files has been added using the `AddFile` or `AddDirectory` methods, all it takes to begin playing background music is to call `StartBackground`. `StartBackground` begins by ensuring that there is at least one file in the `BackgroundFiles` array. If there is at least one, it creates a new instance of the `FilgraphManager`.

LISTING 14.6   DXAUDIO.STARTBACKGROUND

```
Public Sub StartBackground()

If UBound(BackgroundFileList) > 0 Then
    Set BackgroundMediaControl = New FilgraphManager
```

LISTING 14.6   CONTINUED

```
On Error Resume Next
BackgroundMediaControl.RenderFile BackgroundFileList _
    (Rand(UBound(BackgroundFileList), 1))
If Err.Number = 0 Then
    Set BackgroundBasicAudio = BackgroundMediaControl
    Set BackgroundMediaEvent = BackgroundMediaControl

    BackgroundBasicAudio.Volume = BackgroundVolumeLevel
    BackgroundMediaControl.Run

Else
    Set BackgroundMediaControl = Nothing

End If

End If

End Sub
```

With the new instance of the `FilgraphManager`, I can load a music file with the `RenderFile` method. If `RenderFile` has an error, I'll trap it and set `BackgroundMediaControl` to `Nothing`.

If the music file loaded properly, I set two other object pointers (`BackgroundBasicAudio` and `BackgroundMediaEvent`) to point to `BackgroundMediaControl`. This has the effect of exposing additional properties of the `FilgraphManager` object, but be careful. You now have to destroy all three references to the `FilgraphManager` object in order to destroy the object. Just setting `BackgroundMediaEvent` to `Nothing` leaves the other two pointers intact, and as a result the `FilgraphManager` object will not be destroyed.

Next I set the volume level using the `Volume` property of the `BackgroundBasicAudio` object. `Volume` ranges from –10,000 to 0, with zero being the loudest and –10,000 being the softest. This value is in decibels times 100, so setting the volume to –300 means that it would sound one half as loud as if you set to the volume to zero.

| Note |

Playing it too loud?

Sound is generally measured in decibels. Decibels use a logarithmic scale where an increase of three decibels doubles the apparent loudness of the sound, while a decrease of three decibels cuts the apparent loudness in half.

The game's volume level is relative to the Windows Volume Control (see Figure 14.1). The `Volume` property is subject to the Wave Volume slider, and then subject to the main Volume Control and finally subject to the volume control on the speakers (if present). So setting `Volume` to zero doesn't mean that the game's sound will be blasting, but that it is putting out the standard volume level subject to the normal Windows volume controls.

PART

III

CH

14

Figure 14.1
The Windows Volume Control mixes and controls all of the sounds generated by the computer.

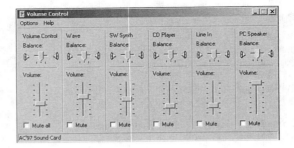

After the volume is set, using the Run method will start the background music playing. Aside from periodically checking the state of BackgroundMediaControl, the code necessary to play music is complete.

STOPPING THE MUSIC

The easiest way to stop the background music is by issuing the Stop method BackgroundMediaControl as shown in Listing 14.7. After the Stop method completes, I destroy all of the objects related to the BackgroundMediaControl.

LISTING 14.7   DXAUDIO.STOPBACKGROUND

```
Public Sub StopBackground()

If Not BackgroundMediaControl Is Nothing Then
    BackgroundMediaControl.Stop
    Set BackgroundBasicAudio = Nothing
    Set BackgroundMediaEvent = Nothing
    Set BackgroundMediaControl = Nothing

End If

End Sub
```

PAUSING THE BACKGROUND MUSIC

Pausing the background music is even easier than stopping it because I don't have to worry about destroying the objects associated with it (see Listing 14.8). However, I must keep track of the paused state of the music in the BackgroundIsPaused module level variable. This prevents any problems that might result from calling this routine twice.

LISTING 14.8   DXAUDIO.PAUSEBACKGROUND

```
Public Sub PauseBackground()

If (Not BackgroundMediaControl Is Nothing) And Not BackgroundIsPaused Then
    BackgroundIsPaused = True
    BackgroundMediaControl.Pause
```

LISTING 14.8   CONTINUED

```
End If

End Sub
```

RESUMING THE BACKGROUND MUSIC

After pausing the background music, the ResumeBackground method of the DXAudio class (see Listing 14.9) picks the current song from where it was paused. Note that the Run method from the FilgraphManager is also used here.

LISTING 14.9   DXAUDIO.RESUMEBACKGROUND

```
Public Sub ResumeBackground()

If (Not BackgroundMediaControl Is Nothing) And BackgroundIsPaused Then
    BackgroundIsPaused = False
    BackgroundMediaControl.Run

End If

End Sub
```

SETTING THE BACKGROUND MUSIC'S VOLUME

The BackgroundVolumeLevel module level variable stores the normal volume level that is used to play music. The BackgroundVolume method shown in Listing 14.10 verifies that the game is playing background music and then adds the specified value to the BackgroundVolumeLevel. Then it ensures that the new level is in the range from –10,000 to 0. Finally it sets the current background volume level using the Volume property of the BackgroundBasicAudio object.

LISTING 14.10   DXAUDIO.BACKGROUNDVOLUME

```
Public Sub BackgroundVolume(vol As Long)

If Not BackgroundMediaControl Is Nothing Then
    BackgroundVolumeLevel = BackgroundVolumeLevel + vol
    If BackgroundVolumeLevel < -10000 Then
        BackgroundVolumeLevel = -10000

    ElseIf BackgroundVolumeLevel > 0 Then
        BackgroundVolumeLevel = 0

    End If

    BackgroundBasicAudio.Volume = BackgroundVolumeLevel

End If

End Sub
```

PART

III

CH

14

FOREGROUND SOUNDS

The same basic technique to play background music is also used to play foreground sounds (see Listing 14.11). The major difference is that the name of the audio file is specified when the routine is called.

LISTING 14.11 DXAUDIO.PLAYFOREGROUND

```
Public Sub PlayForeground(AudioFile As String)

If Len(Dir(AudioFile)) > 0 Then
    Set ForegroundMediaControl = New FilgraphManager

    On Error Resume Next
    ForegroundMediaControl.RenderFile App.Path & "\Media\" & AudioFile
    If Err.Number = 0 Then
        Set ForegroundBasicAudio = ForegroundMediaControl
        Set ForegroundMediaEvent = ForegroundMediaControl

        ForegroundBasicAudio.Volume = BackgroundVolumeLevel
        If Not BackgroundMediaControl Is Nothing Then
            BackgroundBasicAudio.Volume = BackgroundBasicAudio.Volume - 300

        End If

        ForegroundMediaControl.Run

    Else
        Set ForegroundMediaControl = Nothing

    End If

End If

End Sub
```

To ensure that the foreground sound is heard, I cut the current volume level for the background music in half, while the sound is being played. To do this I simply assign a value that is 300 units (3 decibels) less than the current volume level for the background music. When the foreground sound is finished, I restore the normal volume level.

Note that I only permit one sound to be played at a time. If this routine is called before the first sound is finished, it will be ignored. I briefly considered queuing the requests and playing them back in order, but decided that it would be more confusing for the user to hear the sound long after the event that triggered the sound occurred.

To play a sound anywhere in the game, simply insert a line of code like this:

```
dxa.PlayForeground "Welcome.wav"
```

POLLING FOR MUSIC

One limitation of using DirectShow in Visual Basic is that your Visual Basic program can't receive DirectShow events. The only practical option you have is to periodically check the status of both the foreground and background sounds. Then when the polling routine determines the background music has finished, it can switch to the next song and when the foreground sound has finished, it can restore the current volume level.

The easiest way to poll the background and foreground sounds is to create another timer on the game's main form to have it call a polling method in DXAudio. In this case, I felt that using a timer with a one second interval was sufficient. The only potential problem with this approach is that changing songs or restoring the volume could happen as long as a second after the sound finished. I felt this was more than acceptable.

Listing 14.12 shows the DXAudio.Poll method. It begins by ensuring that BackgroundMediaControl exists and then uses the BackgroundMediaEvent.WaitForCompletion method to determine the current status of the sound. The first parameter specifies the amount of time to wait before returning to the calling program, while the second parameter contains the current status. Because I want to return quickly, I specified a wait time of 0.

LISTING 14.12   DXAUDIO.POLL

```
Public Sub Poll()

On Error Resume Next

If Not BackgroundMediaControl Is Nothing Then
    BackgroundMediaEvent.WaitForCompletion 0, BackgroundStatus
    If BackgroundStatus <> 0 Then
        StopBackground
        StartBackground

    End If

End If

If Not ForegroundMediaControl Is Nothing Then
    ForegroundMediaEvent.WaitForCompletion 0, ForegroundStatus
    If ForegroundStatus <> 0 Then
        StopForeground

    End If

End If

End Sub
```

If the current status is zero, it means that a sound is playing, while a value of one means that the sound has finished. In the case of the background music, this means that I need to switch to the next song. Because the laziest way to do this is to call the StopBackground method followed by the StartBackground method, that's exactly what I did.

PART

III

CH

14

It turns out that once you have rendered a sound or music file using a `FilgraphControl` object, you can't render another file. Because I already have code that destroys the objects and re-creates them, I decided to take the lazy way out and simply use them rather than rewrite the code again.

In the case of a foreground sound, I simply have to destroy the objects and rest the volume level of the background music if it's playing. Calling `StopForeground` does precisely this.

CREATING SOUNDS

Learning how to play sounds in Visual Basic is only half the battle to add sounds to your game. The other half is finding or creating the sounds that you want to use in your game.

SOUND FORMATS

Like image files, sound files come in a variety of different types and formats. Here is a short list of some of the more popular sound formats you are likely to encounter.

- **.AIFF** files are similar to .WAV files, but are typically used by Apple Macintosh computers.

- **.AU** files are popular for Unix-based computers. You'll find a lot of them when you search for sound files on the Internet. Note that these files are often of poor quality, which may not sound good in your game.

- **.MID** files (usually called MIDI files) contain a series of musical notes that are designed to be played back through the sound card. These files can't hold voice information. The music contained in these files is often very simple—like someone playing a tune on a piano. However, unlike other types of sound files, MIDI files are usually very short, usually in the thousands of bytes rather than megabytes of space typically used for .MP3 files and .WAV files.

- **.MP3** files typically contain information extracted from a music CD. These files will be much smaller than a typical .WAV file containing the same data. The space savings is due to the fact that .MP3 files use a technique to remove musically insignificant information from the sound. Unfortunately, this means that .MP3 files don't store voices and other sound very well. You can expect to store a minute's worth of music in a megabyte of disk space.

- **.WAV** files are the most popular sound file format for Windows computers and contain raw digitized sounds. This results in a very large file—on the order of ten megabytes per minute of high-quality, stereo sound. You can store both mono and stereo files in a .WAV file and you can choose various sampling rates, which control the overall quality of the sound.

Note that DirectAudio may not support all of these types of sound files. I recommend you stick with .MID files for MIDI music, .MP3 files for CD-quality music files, and .WAV for everything else. DirectAudio supports all three types of sound files, while Cool Edit supports nearly any type of sound file you may encounter except for MIDI. Generally if you run into a different type of sound file, you can use Cool Edit to convert it to either .MP3 or .WAV format.

FINDING SOUNDS

There are many different ways to get sounds for your game. You can buy sound effect CDs and copy the sounds to your computer or you can search the Internet for the sound files that suit your needs.

However, these techniques have several problems. The biggest problem is finding material that can legally be used. Most of the material you are likely to find is copyrighted and can't be used without permission of the copyright holder.

Another problem with public domain sounds is that they may be created in many different formats. While DirectShow can play most of the popular sound formats, some formats will sound better than others.

Which leads to perhaps the biggest reason of them all. Your sound files should be consistent in quality. Although I don't recommend using poor-quality sounds, if you mix poor-quality sounds with high-quality sounds, the poor-quality sounds will really stand out.

INTRODUCING COOL EDIT 2000

This technique involves finding a particular sound that fits into your game and recording it. You can use a tool in Windows called Sound Recorder (choose Start, Program Files, Accessories, Entertainment, Sound Recorder) to record sounds. This program is very limited in the functions it can perform once the sound is recorded. You really need a professional-quality sound editor like Cool Edit 2000 (see Figure 14.2).

Figure 14.2
Cool Edit 2000 has a graphical interface that makes it easy to edit sound information.

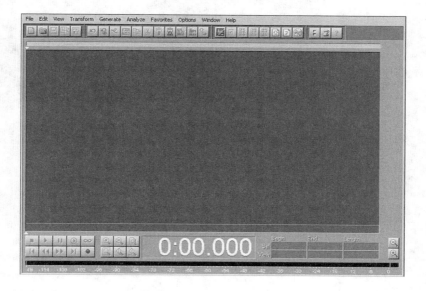

Cool Edit 2000 enables you to record and edit sound files, much like Photoshop enables you to create and edit image files. Also like Photoshop, Cool Edit 2000 enables you to crop sound files to eliminate unwanted sounds, plus it has filters that allow you to transform the sound in many different ways.

> **Note**
>
> **Cool Edit 2000**
>
> In the \CoolEdit directory you will find demo versions of Cool Edit 2000 and its more powerful sibling, Cool Edit Pro. These tools are used by many people including professional game developers to create sound files. I've also added some filters that you can use to add interesting effects to your sounds.

DIGITIZING SOUNDS

A sound can be represented by a waveform. The more complex the sound, the more complex the waveform. Because a waveform is analog, in order to digitize the signal, you must break up the sound into a number of individual samples (see Figure 14.3). Each sample records the amplitude of the signal and saves the information into the sound file. This technique is known as *digitizing* because the sound samples are recorded as digital information.

Figure 14.3
A sound is broken into a fixed number of samples per second.

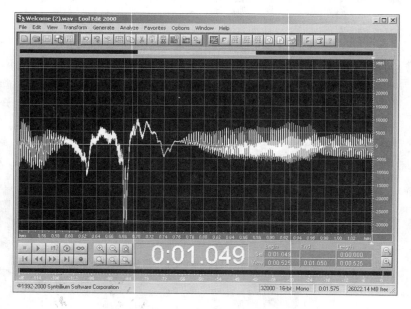

When the sound file is played, each sample is used to re-create the amplitude of the sound for that particular interval, so rather than playing a smooth curve like the original sound, this results in a rather step-like signal. The more samples you take, the smoother the output curve will be and the closer the output sound will be to the original sound.

The number of bits available for recording the amplitude of each sample is also important. Generally you can choose from 8, 16, or 32 bits. Again, the more bits you use for each sample, the more accurate the particular sample will be.

Finally, you have the option to record the sound in either mono or stereo. Mono implies that you are using a single input device or microphone to create a single track of information. Stereo implies that you have two or more input devices or microphones to create two tracks of information.

The theory behind stereo is that you can create a sound that better reflects what you will hear with each ear. Thus you could easily give the impression that the player is hearing a sound that is coming from his left or right or somewhere in between, while a mono sound gives the impression that the sound originates directly in front of the player.

Music CDs are recorded using 44,100 samples per second, with 16 bits for each sample, and use two tracks to record the sounds. These settings are sufficient to represent nearly any sound the human ear can hear. Telephones, on the other hand, typically use 8 bit, mono sound with a sample rate of 8,000 samples per second. This is only sufficient to carry voice over a telephone wire. Playing music using these settings will badly distort or even ignore higher-pitched sounds.

For game programming, you are probably safe using a sample rate of 32,000 samples per second using a resolution of 16 bits. Whether you use stereo or mono is really up to you. If you record your sound using mono and play the sound back using the typical computer's stereo speakers you will hear the same identical sound from each speaker.

Note

Megabytes

CD-quality sound files take up a lot of space. Each minute of CD-quality sound will occupy about 10 megabytes of disk space. Switching from stereo to mono will cut this value in half. Using a sample rate of 32,000 samples per second will reduce the space even more. If you plan on using a lot of CD-quality digitized sounds, be prepared to use lots of disk space.

RECORDING A WAVEFORM

To record a sound file using Cool Edit, select File, New from the main menu in Cool Edit. This will display the New Waveform dialog box (see Figure 14.4). You can then choose the sample rate, the number of channels, and the resolution for your new sound file.

After you create the new sound file, you can manipulate it using Cool Edit. To record a sound click the record button in the transport area in bottom-left corner of the screen. When you are finished recording the sound, you can press the record button again or press the stop button.

Figure 14.4
When you create a
new sound file in
Cool Edit, you need to
define the sound's
characteristics.

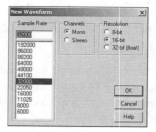

The digitized sound will be shown in the display area. You can press the play button to play back the sound or your can begin the process of editing the sound file to get the sound you really want.

> **Tip**
>
> **My sound is lost**
>
> If you see a flat line after you recorded some sound, you should verify the recording level. Display the Windows Volume Control and choose Options, Properties. Select the Recording radio button and verify that the input source you are using is checked in the Show the Following Volume Controls section of the dialog box and click OK. A window similar to the Windows Volume Control will be displayed, called Recording Control. Make sure that the volume level for your input device is not sitting at the bottom of the slider. This would mean that not enough of a signal is getting through for Cool Edit to record. Also it goes without saying that you should make sure that only the input device you are using should be selected. Otherwise you would get no sound at all.

EDITING A WAVEFORM

After you have recorded a sound, the waveform will be displayed on the screen (see Figure 14.5). Normally Cool Edit will display the waveform in green against a black background. However, you can select some or all of the waveform for processing. Selected areas will be displayed as a blue waveform against a white background.

Cool Edit uses a playback cursor to mark the location in the waveform where playback will begin. The playback cursor is shown as a vertical yellow dotted line against the black background. To place the playback cursor on the waveform, simply position the mouse where you want to place the cursor and click the left mouse button.

After you have placed the playback cursor, clicking play will play the sound starting at the playback cursor and continuing to the end of the waveform.

You can select a part of the waveform by moving the cursor to one end of the area you want to select, clicking the left mouse button, and dragging the mouse over the area you want to select. As you drag the mouse, the selected area will be displayed in blue on white (see Figure 14.6). You can also expand or contract this selected area by moving the mouse to the new end of the selected area and right-clicking the mouse.

Figure 14.5
Cool Edit shows you
the waveform for the
sound you just
recorded.

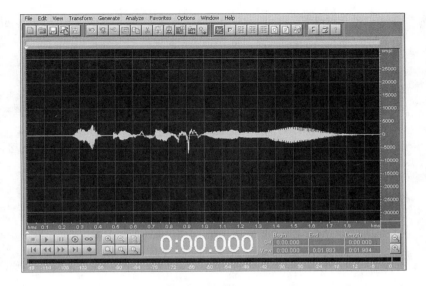

Figure 14.6
You can easily select
an area on the wave-
form using the mouse.

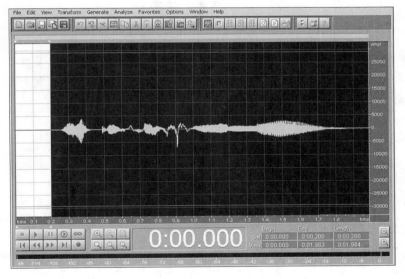

After you have selected part of the waveform, you can press the Del key to remove it from
the waveform or you can also choose Edit, Delete from the main menu to delete it. Note
that when you make a change to the waveform, Cool Edit saves the previous copy so that
you can undo the change by pressing Ctrl+Z.

The most common editing function is deleting unwanted parts of the sound clip. Typically
when you record a sound clip, there will be some extra space at the start and the end of the
clip. You can select and delete this area by using the select and delete functions or you can
select the entire waveform and choose Edit, Trim.

PART

III

CH

14

You can also copy the selected area to the Clipboard by choosing Edit, Copy. Note that Cool Edit maintains five internal Clipboard areas, plus the Windows Clipboard, which you can select by choosing Edit, Set Current Clipboard.

After you have copied material to the Clipboard, you can insert it into the current waveform where the playback cursor is located or in place of the currently selected area. You can also create a new waveform by choosing Edit, Paste to New from the main menu.

You can mix the material into the current waveform by choosing Paste Mix from the main menu. This technique is useful if you want to combine two or more sounds together such as someone speaking while a siren is wailing in the background.

MANAGING WAVEFORM FILES

After you record your waveform, you should save it in case you run into problems. Cool Edit supports many different types of sound file formats; however, there are really only three formats you need to use. The .PCM file format uses no compression and stores the sound in exactly the same format as you used when you initially created the sound file.

While this format takes up a lot of disk space, you can delete any intermediate files you use while working on the waveform and save only the original and final files. However these files normally won't be distributed with your game.

For normal sound files, it's probably best to stick with .WAV files. These files store information using a wide variety of settings for sampling rate, stereo/mono, and resolution. These files don't use compression, so they can get rather large. For CD quality sound (44,100/16 bit/stereo) you can expect to use 10 megabytes of disk space for every minute of sound.

You should use .MP3 files to store music. .MP3 files use a lossy compression algorithm that discards sounds that aren't noticeable so that each minute of music occupies about one megabyte. Although you can record any sound in an .MP3 file, you will get the best results if you are recording music. The compression algorithm was optimized for recording music, not ordinary sounds and voices.

FILTERING SOUNDS

Cool Edit includes a number of different filters and if these aren't enough you can purchase even more filters that you can add to the standard filters. Filters usually work only on the selected part of the waveform; however, if you don't select a part of the waveform, the filter will assume you want to transform the entire waveform.

AMPLIFYING A WAVEFORM

One of the most useful filters allows you to amplify a waveform. This is very useful when you want to normalize the volume. It can be used to make soft sounds louder and loud sounds softer. Choose Transform, Amplitude, Amplify from the main menu to display the Amplify filter (see Figure 14.7).

Figure 14.7
You can easily control the amplitude of the waveform by using the Amplify filter.

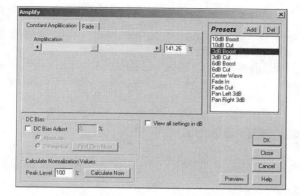

You can apply a number of preset transforms such as a 3dB cut or a 6dB boost, which will cut the volume level in half or increase it by a factor of 4. You can also drag the slider or enter a relative percentage that will control the transform.

REDUCING NOISE

Another useful tool is Noise Reduction (choose Transform, Noise Reduction, Noise Reduction). This tool will analyze your waveform to determine the background noise and then attempt to remove it from the waveform (see Figure 14.8).

Figure 14.8
Using Noise Reduction will make your waveform sound clearer.

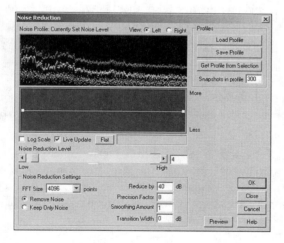

If you plan to use noise reduction, you should record several seconds of silence at the start of your waveform before you begin recording your live material. This provides the filter with information about the background noise and makes it easier for the filter to determine what is noise and what is the real waveform.

SPECIAL EFFECTS

One of the things I enjoy about Cool Edit is the capability to play with echoes. One of my favorite transforms is the Chorus from the Phat Pack plug-in (Transform, Delay Effects, Chorus). This filter applies a series of delays and feedback to achieve various effects (see Figure 14.9). I really enjoy the Flying Saucers preset because of its truly unique effect on the sound.

Figure 14.9
Using Noise Reduction will make your waveform sound clearer.

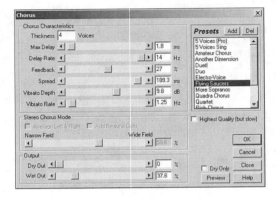

OTHER FILTERS

Cool Edit has too many filters to mention all of them here, but some of them deserve special note. You can use the Stretch filter (Transform, Time/Pitch, Stretch) to play the sound faster or slower. Of course, as you change the speed of the sound, the pitch will also change accordingly.

Another interesting transform is Reverse (choose Transform, Reverse). As you might expect, this filter plays the sound in the reverse order. This is ideal if you want someone to speak backwards, but it's probably more useful to create really unique sounds from rather ordinary ones.

Finally the 3-D Echo Chamber (choose Transform, Delay/Effects, Echo Chamber) creates echoes that simulate different environments. You can make it sound as if the original sound was recorded in a metal room, a basement, an empty parking garage, or a water closet. If you have a Digital Signal Processor on your stereo system, you should have some idea what this will sound like.

FINAL THOUGHTS

Making sounds is fun. You can get interesting sounds from many different places. You could take a tape recorder (or even a camcorder) around your house and town to capture many different sounds. Then you can load them into Cool Edit to tweak them to achieve the sound you want.

Perhaps one of the best sources is an electronic piano that has a large number of voices. These voices can be recorded directly and manipulated to create some really interesting sounds.

Although I didn't discuss how to create MIDI music in this chapter, that is a very good alternative to MP3s for background music. While MIDI files are strictly instrumental, they can be used to set the mood of a game. While the same code that Swim Mall uses to play MP3s will handle a .MID file, you need special tools to capture or compose MIDI music. The primary advantage of MIDI files is that they are very small. A 100-kilobyte file can play for several minutes.

CHAPTER 15

A MAP AND CUSTOMERS

In this chapter

Even though the simulation part of the game is processing customers, the mall isn't very interesting without customers walking (or swimming) around inside. To display a customer in the mall, you need to know where a customer can be in the mall. This information is stored as part of the mall's map.

Also it's time to jump back into trueSpace to draw some customers for the mall. Unlike designing stores, which dealt with lots of flat rectangular surfaces, customers have various shapes that can't be created by simply combining simple objects together.

MAPPING THE MALL

Animating a customer is easy. All you have to do is draw the customer in a different position in the mall each time you render the scene. The trick is determining where each of the customers should be located at any particular time.

There are several different approaches to solving this problem, but all of them revolve around using a map that describes where the customers can go in the mall. Most games use some sort of directed graph that describes how the various places are connected to one another.

In Swim Mall, I decided that a directed graph wasn't worth the extra complexity, so I simply divided the mall into a grid. Each cell in the grid indicates whether the space is free or if an object is over it.

BUILDING THE MAP

To keep the map implementation flexible, I derive as much information as I can from the initialization files related to the mall and stores. This makes it easy to create malls with different sizes.

All the information associated with the map is managed by the Map class. This makes the physical implementation of the map local only to the Map class. Thus I could easily replace how I manage the map without affecting the rest of the application.

DEFINING THE MAP

The Map class implements the map as a two-dimensional grid. Each cell in the grid represents a small square in the mall that can be occupied by only one object at a time. An object can be anything that can block the path of a customer, such as a wall or another customer.

The size of a particular cell is sufficiently large to hold a customer, while it is sufficiently small to allow multiple customers to be in a single store.

The grid is stored as an array called Cells, and it has a type of CellEnum (see Listing 15.1). The CellEnum type describes each of the possible states for a cell in the map.

LISTING 15.1 MAP.CELLENUM

```
Public Enum CellEnum
    UnknownCell
    OpenCell
    BlockedCell
    OpenEntranceCell
    BlockedEntranceCell
    OpenStoreEntranceCell
    BlockedStoreEntranceCell
    OpenStoreCell
    BlockedStoreCell

End Enum
```

I use the normal trick of defining the first value in the enum as an unknown value. This means when I create the array, it will be populated with zeros, which is the same as UnknownCell. Then as long as I search the map for a specific value in a cell, the unknown values will help to prevent a character from moving outside the mall.

Listing 15.2 contains an excerpt from the BasicMall.SMM file. Note that I've added new keywords for Map, Entrance, and Openarea. Also note that there are no new keywords associated with the store information. Details about the store will be retrieved from the appropriate store file.

LISTING 15.2 BASICMALL.SMM

```
Type=Mall
Name=Basic Mall
DXFilename=BasicMall.x
Map\Top=-8
Map\Bottom=4
Map\Left=-7
Map\Right=9
Entrance\1\top=-3.5
Entrance\1\bottom=-3.1
Entrance\1\left=-7
Entrance\1\right=-7
Entrance\2\top=-2.7
Entrance\2\bottom=-2.3
Entrance\2\left=-7
Entrance\2\right=-7
Entrance\3\top=-1.7
Entrance\3\bottom=-1.3
Entrance\3\left=-7
Entrance\3\right=-7
Entrance\4\top=-0.9
Entrance\4\bottom=-0.5
Entrance\4\left=-7
Entrance\4\right=-7
Openarea\1\top=-4
Openarea\1\bottom=0
Openarea\1\left=-7
Openarea\1\right=3
```

LISTING 15.2   CONTINUED

```
Openarea\2\top=0
Openarea\2\bottom=3
Openarea\2\left=0
Openarea\2\right=2
Anchor\1\Width=12
Anchor\1\Depth=6
Anchor\1\X=-2
Anchor\1\Z=6
Anchor\1\Rotation=-180
```

The Map keyword specifies the coordinates of the mall in 3D graphics units. The Top and Bottom coordinates describe the upper and lower bounds along the Z-axis, whereas the Left and Right values describe the bounds along the X-axis (see Figure 15.1).

Figure 15.1
This map is created using the information from the BasicMall.SMM file.

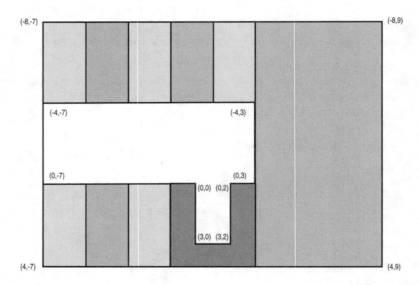

> **Note**
>
> **Keeping it flat**
> Remember that the floor of the mall is displayed along the X- and Z-axes while the Y-axis describes the vertical location of a point relative to the mall's floor.

The Entrance keyword locates the positions where the customer may enter the mall. Because the mall has multiple entrances, multiple Entrance statements are needed. It is important that the second key value in the statement be the same for all of the statements related to a single entrance. This value should also be numeric because it will be used as a subscript into an array that will hold the information.

The store initialization files also use the Entrance statement to determine where the store's entrance is located. Food court vendors, on the other hand, don't really have an entrance to the store proper, but a location relative to the store where the customer can get service.

The Openarea keyword describes the places where customers may walk in the mall. Note that the spaces occupied by the stores are not marked as open areas. This is because the open area in the store depends on the store itself. Note that this particular mall has multiple open areas because you can only describe a rectangle with the Top, Bottom, Left, and Right keywords.

LOADING MAP INFORMATION

Because I process each statement when reading information from a SwimFile file, I simply buffer each piece of information in various arrays and process it after all the information has been loaded in the PostGameLoadProcessing routine in the Mall class (see Listing 15.3).

LISTING 15.3   MALL.POSTGAMELOADPROCESSING

```
Public Function PostGameLoadProcessing()

Dim a As Anchor
Dim f As Food
Dim s As Store
Dim i As Long

Dim top As Single
Dim bottom As Single
Dim left As Single
Dim right As Single

Set MallMap = New Map
Set MallMap.DebugObject = MallDebugger

MallMap.InitMap Mapsize.top, Mapsize.bottom, Mapsize.left, Mapsize.right

For i = 1 To UBound(OpenAreas)
   MallMap.MarkOpenArea OpenAreas(i).top, OpenAreas(i).bottom, _
      OpenAreas(i).left, OpenAreas(i).right, OpenCell

Next i

For i = 1 To UBound(Entrances)
   MallMap.MarkEntrance Entrances(i).top, _
   Entrances(i).bottom, Entrances(i).left, Entrances(i).right, _
   OpenEntranceCell

Next i

For Each s In Stores
   Needs = Needs Or s.Needs

   s.GetEntrance top, bottom, left, right
   MallMap.MarkEntrance top, bottom, left, right, OpenStoreEntranceCell
   s.EntranceX = (top + bottom) / 2
```

Listing 15.3   Continued

```
    s.EntranceY = 0
    s.EntranceZ = (left + right) / 2
    s.GetOpenArea top, bottom, left, right
    MallMap.MarkOpenArea top, bottom, left, right, OpenStoreCell

Next s

For Each f In Foods
    FoodNeeds = FoodNeeds Or f.FoodNeeds
    f.GetEntrance top, bottom, left, right
    MallMap.MarkEntrance top, bottom, left, right, OpenStoreEntranceCell
    f.EntranceX = (top + bottom) / 2
    f.EntranceY = 0
    f.EntranceZ = (left + right) / 2

Next f

For Each a In Anchors
    Needs = Needs Or a.Needs
    FoodNeeds = FoodNeeds Or a.FoodNeeds
    a.GetEntrance top, bottom, left, right
    MallMap.MarkEntrance top, bottom, left, right, OpenStoreEntranceCell
    a.EntranceX = (top + bottom) / 2
    a.EntranceY = 0
    a.EntranceZ = (left + right) / 2
    a.GetOpenArea top, bottom, left, right
    MallMap.MarkOpenArea top, bottom, left, right, OpenStoreCell

Next a

MallMap.DebugMap

Yesterday = DateValue(MasterClock)

End Function
```

In previous chapters this routine existed to compute the needs satisfied by the mall and to initialize the Yesterday variable. Now this routine also takes the map information loaded from the initialization files and passes it along to the Map class.

The first step is to create a new instance of the Map class and use the InitMap to create an empty map using the Top, Bottom, Left, and Right information collected from the mall's initialization file. Next I use the MarkOpenArea method to mark the open areas in the mall using OpenCell. Then I add the entrances to the map using the MarkEntrance method and specify OpenEntranceCell.

In each of the stores, I get the entrance location using the Top, Bottom, Left, and Right values and then call the MarkEntrance method to identify the location of the entrance on the map as an OpenStoreEntranceCell. Then I take the 2D map location and set the appropriate Entrance properties on the store. Finally I use the GetOpenArea method for the store to extract the map coordinates and call the MarkOpenArea method to declare the space inside this rectangle as an OpenStoreCell.

Notice that I only define an entrance for the food court vendors. Because customers are not allowed inside the food court store, there isn't a need to process the open area.

After the map has been completely initialized, I call the `MallMap.DebugMap` method to generate a copy of the map in the `Debug.LOG` file. This will let you easily verify that the map information has been loaded correctly. Remember in the production version of the game, you can comment out the call to `Debugger.Enable` method found in `Form1.InitGame`, so this output will never be generated.

INITIALIZING THE MAP

The `InitMap` routine initializes the map using the 3D coordinate values passed to the routine (see Listing 15.4). The first thing I do is to translate the `Single` values represented by the 3D coordinates into `Long` values that represent indexes into the `Cells` array. I simply multiply the 3D coordinate by the value in `MapScale`. Then I add or subtract one from the value so that there is always one cell that the extends beyond the mall.

LISTING 15.4   MAP.INITMAP

```
Public Sub InitMap(maptop As Single, mapbottom As Single, _
    mapleft As Single, mapright As Single)

Dim i As Long
Dim j As Long
Dim top As Long
Dim bottom As Long
Dim left As Long
Dim right As Long

top = Round(maptop * MapScale) - 1
bottom = Round(mapbottom * MapScale) + 1
left = Round(mapleft * MapScale) - 1
right = Round(mapright * MapScale) + 1

ReDim Cells(top To bottom, left To right)

For i = top To bottom
    For j = left To right
        Cells(i, j) = UnknownCell

    Next j

Next i

End Sub
```

I did this mostly to place an outer bound around the mall. Because these cells should never be initialized, the mall will be surrounded with a collection of `UnknownCell` cells. This will help to prevent subscripting errors due to rounding and other potential problems.

Note that I take advantage of Visual Basic's capability to specify a lower bound for an array. This means that I don't have to add an offset to each subscript supplied to the array because the array can directly handle negative coordinate values.

After I've computed the dimensions for the array, I use the Redim statement to change the size of the Cells array. Then I explicitly set each element of the array to UnknownCell to ensure that the array is properly initialized.

MARKING AREAS

The MarkOpenArea routine (see Listing 15.5) takes the opposing corners of rectangle that will be changed in the mall's map to the specified cell type. Unlike the InitMap routine, this routine shrinks the open area by a single cell along each edge of the rectangle to ensure that the open area doesn't overlap a wall.

LISTING 15.5 MAP.MARKOPENAREA

```
Public Sub MarkOpenArea(maptop As Single, mapbottom As Single, _
    mapleft As Single, mapright As Single, typ As CellEnum)

Dim i As Long
Dim j As Long

Dim top As Long
Dim bottom As Long
Dim left As Long
Dim right As Long

top = Round(maptop * MapScale) + 1
bottom = Round(mapbottom * MapScale) - 1
left = Round(mapleft * MapScale) + 1
right = Round(mapright * MapScale) - 1

For i = top To bottom
   For j = left To right
      Cells(i, j) = typ

   Next j

Next i

End Sub
```

The MarkEntrance routine (see Listing 15.6) is also similar to MarkOpenArea, but this time I don't adjust the size of the rectangle before I assign the specified cell type to the Cells array.

LISTING 15.6 MAP.MARKENTRANCE

```
Public Sub MarkEntrance(maptop As Single, mapbottom As Single, _
    mapleft As Single, mapright As Single, typ As CellEnum)
```

LISTING 15.6   CONTINUED

```
Dim i As Long
Dim j As Long

Dim top As Long
Dim bottom As Long
Dim left As Long
Dim right As Long

top = Round(maptop * MapScale)
bottom = Round(mapbottom * MapScale)
left = Round(mapleft * MapScale)
right = Round(mapright * MapScale)

For i = top To bottom
   For j = left To right
      Cells(i, j) = typ

   Next j

Next i

If typ = OpenEntranceCell Then
   i = UBound(MallEntrances) + 1
   ReDim Preserve MallEntrances(i)
   MallEntrances(i).x = (top + bottom) / 2
   MallEntrances(i).y = (left + right) / 2

End If

End Sub
```

At the end of the routine, I save the entrance information into the MallEntrances array. This provides a quick way to find the entrances for the mall. This will prove useful later, when it comes time to find a place for a customer to arrive at the mall.

DEBUGGING THE MAP

Getting the map right is very important, which is why I included the DebugMap method in the Map class (see Listing 15.7). It simply prints a copy of the map used in the game to the debug log with a table of values that helps you identify the meaning of each number in the map.

LISTING 15.7   MAP.DEBUGMAP

```
Public Sub DebugMap()

Dim i As Long
Dim j As Long
Dim t As String

MapDebugger.WriteLine "Begin Map Info -------------------------"
MapDebugger.WriteLong "Unknown cell", UnknownCell
```

LISTING 15.7   CONTINUED

```
MapDebugger.WriteLong "Open cell", OpenCell
MapDebugger.WriteLong "Blocked cell", BlockedCell
MapDebugger.WriteLong "Open entrance cell", OpenEntranceCell
MapDebugger.WriteLong "Blocked entrance cell", BlockedEntranceCell
MapDebugger.WriteLong "Open store entrance cell", OpenStoreEntranceCell
MapDebugger.WriteLong "Blocked store entrance cell", BlockedStoreEntranceCell
MapDebugger.WriteLong "Open store cell", OpenStoreCell
MapDebugger.WriteLong "Blocked store cell", BlockedStoreCell

For i = LBound(Cells, 1) To UBound(Cells, 1)
    t = ""
    For j = LBound(Cells, 2) To UBound(Cells, 2)
        t = t & FormatNumber(Cells(i, j), 0)

    Next j

    MapDebugger.WriteLine t

Next i

MapDebugger.WriteLine "End Map Info ---------------------------"

End Sub
```

CREATING CUSTOMERS

To have a customer walking through the mall, you first must have a customer that you can display. This means that you need to create a mesh for each unique customer you want to display. In a practical sense, you don't want to create hundreds of meshes for the hundreds of customers that will visit your mall. Instead, creating a handful of customer meshes is sufficient and you can simply reuse them as needed to display all of the customers in your mall.

Note

Programming and Art

Creating 3D art in trueSpace isn't easy for most programmers. Most books that provide a series of steps for creating a 3D object present the steps like this: Choose New Scene from the main menu; Select a particular tool from the toolbox; Use tool to create the art; Choose Save Object from the main menu.

CREATING SKIN AND BONES

The easiest way to design a fish is to think of a fish as a skeleton composed of a series of ellipses that has a skin stretched over them. This is exactly what these steps do.

1. Start trueSpace and create a new scene.

2. Select the Drawpanel tool and create a drawpanel aligned along the Y-axis. Use the object info window to adjust the location of the drawpanel to 0,0,0 (see Figure 15.2).

Figure 15.2
Adding a drawpanel to
a trueSpace scene.

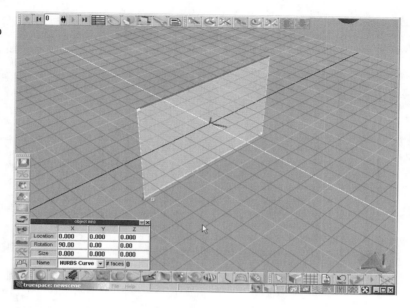

3. Select the Ellipse tool and draw an ellipse on the drawpanel. Then use the Object Info to adjust the X and Y size of the ellipse to 0.3 and 0.4 and the location of the ellipse to 0,0,0 (see Figure 15.3).

Figure 15.3
Drawing an ellipse on
the drawpanel (note
the extreme zoom to
make the ellipse more
visible).

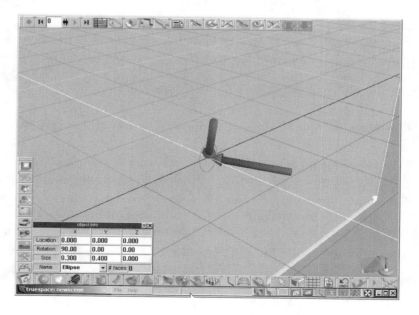

4. Right-click the ellipse to display the series of points that are used to draw the ellipse. Drag the topmost point straight up a little bit. Move the points on each side of the top-most point closer together. Repeat the same for the bottommost points. Your distorted ellipse should look something like the one shown in Figure 15.4.

Figure 15.4
Distorting your ellipse.

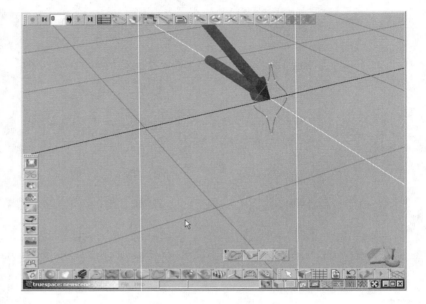

5. Use the copy tool to clone the distorted ellipse and then use the Object Info window to change the Y location property to 0.1. Repeat the process a second time but use a Y location of 0.2 (see Figure 15.5).

6. Create the head of the fish (see Figure 15.6) by adding an ellipse with a Y location of 0.3 and X and Y sizes of 0.1 and 0.3 and then adding a second ellipse with a Y location of 0.4 and X and Y sizes of 0.05 and 0.1. Remember that the X rotation value should be 90 as with the previous ellipses.

7. Create the tail of the fish by adding four more ellipses whose Y location, X size, and Y size values are (–0.1, 0.1, 0.2), (–0.2, 0.05, 0.1), (–0.3, 0.01, 0.3), and (–0.4, 0.01, 0.05).

8. Finally, use the Skin Surface tool to add skin to your skeleton. After choosing the tool, click on each of the ellipses you just created starting from one end or the other. Then right-click to indicate to trueSpace that you've selected all of the shapes that should be enclosed by the skin. The result should look like the fish shown in Figure 15.7 (or at least close enough for this game).

Figure 15.5
Creating multiple distorted ellipses.

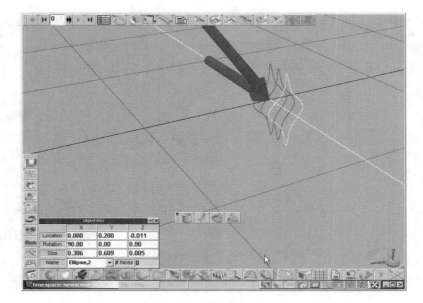

Figure 15.6
Creating the head of the fish.

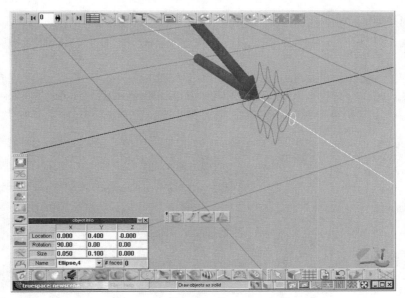

Figure 15.7
Skinning your fish.

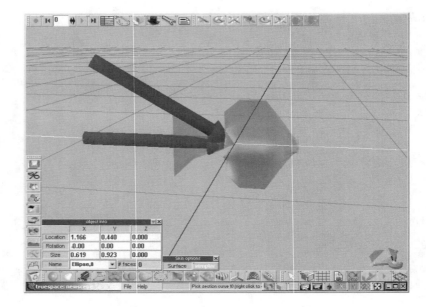

COLORING THE EYES

At this point you now have something that resembles a fish. To complete this fish, you need to give the fish a little color and add some eyes. Both are relatively simple processes.

To add the color, simply click the Material Editor icon to display the Material Editor window. Then click on the color button to display the Color window. Choose a color you like and then click on the paint object button to paint your fish (see Figure 15.8).

Figure 15.8
Adding color to your fish.

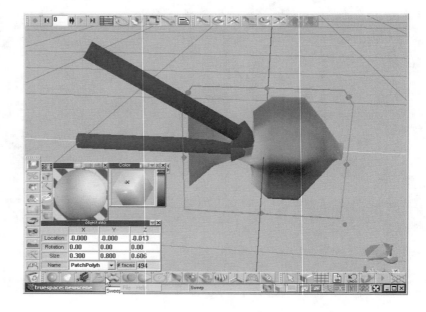

After coloring your fish, you can add an eye by following these steps.

1. While you have the Color window open, select the color you want to use for your eyes. In this case, I choose black.

2. Add a sphere to your scene by clicking on the Sphere tool and dragging the cursor around in a blank area of the screen (see Figure 15.9).

Figure 15.9
Creating the first eye for the fish.

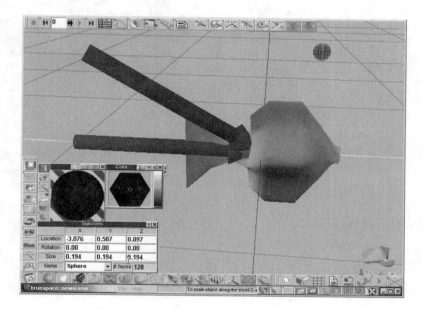

3. Resize the eye using the Object Tool so that the X, Y, and Z size values 0.03.

4. Move the eye onto your fish. You can either use the Object Tool to drag the fish to an appropriate spot or you can use the Object window with these location values (0.03, 0.3,0.1). Note that if you use the Object Tool, be sure to move your view of the fish to ensure that the eye intersects the fish mesh.

5. Repeat the previous step for the other eye using the location value (–0.03, 0.3, 0.1). You fish will now look like the one in Figure 15.10.

SAVING YOUR FISH

To finish your fish, you need to glue the eyes into the head and then save the final mesh to the Customers directory.

1. Select the fish body by using the Object Tool.

2. Select the Glue As Sibling tool and click each eye to combine the eyes with the fish mesh.

3. Choose File, Save As, Object from the main menu and save the mesh using a file type of DirectX .x. Remember to check the ASCII Text check box.

Figure 15.10
Viewing your new fish
with eyes.

FINAL THOUGHTS

Having some sort of map that keeps track of the objects in the mall is important to adding animation to the game. Without a map, you could have customers walking through walls and running into each other. The technique I used here is very simplistic when compared to most commercial games. However, it is reasonably efficient and it does meet the needs of Swim Mall.

Designing interesting customers is also important. It is an important part of making the game interesting to play. The more customers you can create the better, since using a single character structure can get rather boring.

If you are artistically challenged like I am, there are sources on the Internet where you can purchase 3D models for a reasonable price. In some cases, you may be able to find them for free. Before you include art generated elsewhere in your game, make sure that you can redistribute the art. Also, make sure that the models are designed for real-time display. A large number of models are designed for non–real-time applications. While these models often have a lot of detail, trying to display them in real-time can adversely impact your frame rate. Try to look for objects with fewer than 1,000 triangles or polygons for the best performance.

CHAPTER 16

WALKING THROUGH THE MALL

In this chapter

After creating the customers and a map of the mall, all that is left is to add some code to draw the customers and then change their locations in the mall.

DRAWING CUSTOMERS

Drawing customers involves adding code in several different places throughout the program. First the meshes containing the customers need to be loaded into memory. Then information in the Customer objects will be updated to contain the information that reflects their graphical representation. Finally the DXGraphics.Render routine is modified to display the customers in the mall.

The meshes that represent the customers are stored in the Customers directory. As new customers are created, they will be randomly assigned one of the meshes. Each customer will also hold the 3D coordinates where they are located in the mall. Then after the mall and stores are drawn in the rendering routine, each of the customers in the mall will be drawn at their current location.

LOADING CUSTOMER MESHES

In the InitGraphics routine I added a block of code that scans the Customers directory and loads all of the customer meshes (see Listing 16.1). This routine starts by creating a new instance of the FileSystemObject. Then it gets a Folder object that contains information about the files in the Customers directory.

LISTING 16.1   FORM1.INITGRAPHICS (PARTIAL LISTING)

```
Set fso = New FileSystemObject
Set folder = fso.GetFolder(App.path & "\Customers")
v.x = 0
v.y = 0
v.Z = 0
ReDim CustomerMeshes(0)
For Each fi In folder.Files
   t = right(fi.Name, 2)
   If t = ".X" Then
      i = UBound(CustomerMeshes) + 1
      ReDim Preserve CustomerMeshes(i)
      CustomerMeshes(i) = fi.Name
      dx.LoadMeshFromDisk App.path & "\Customers", fi.Name, _
         v, 0, DXObjectCustomer, Nothing, fi.Name

   End If

Next fi

Set fi = Nothing
Set folder = Nothing
Set fso = Nothing
```

Next a D3DVECTOR is initialized to contain zeros for each value. This vector will specify the default location for all of the customers. It really doesn't matter what value is used here because this value will be overridden when the customer is drawn on the screen. `CustomerMeshes` is then redimensioned to zero so I can add mesh names later.

Then a `For Each` loop goes through all of the files in the folder. Each file is checked for a file type of `.X`. When a `.X` file is found, the filename is added to the end of the `CustomerMeshes` array and use the `LoadMeshFromDisk` method to add the file to the collection of meshes in `DXGraphics`.

CUSTOMER CHANGES

To manage the graphical information for a customer, I've added a number of new properties to the `Customer` class (see Listing 16.2). `DXFilename` contains the name of the mesh associated with the customer.

PART

III

CH

16

LISTING 16.2   MODULE-LEVEL DECLARATIONS FOR CUSTOMER (PARTIAL LISTING)

```
Public DXFilename As String
Public x As Single
Public y As Single
Public z As Single
Public Rotation As Single
Public DestinationX As Single
Public DestinationY As Single
Public DestinationZ As Single
Public CellX As Long
Public CellY As Long
Public DeltaX As Long
Public DeltaY As Long
Public WalkingState As WalkingStateEnum
Public WalkingTime As Long
Public Walkticks As Long
```

The x, y, and z properties describe the current location of the customer in the mall using 3D coordinates. `Rotation` contains the direction that the customer is pointing. Like all rotation values in DirectX, this one is measured in radians–not degrees. The `Destination` properties contain the 3D coordinates of where the customer is headed.

`CellX` and `CellY` contain the current location of the customer in the mall's map. `DeltaX` and `DeltaY` contain values that will be added to the customer's current location for each tick of the walking timer. The `WalkingState` property, along with the `WalkingTime` and `Walkticks` properties, determines how the customer will move through the mall.

The following line of code was added to the `GetCustomer` method in the `Game` object just before the customer object is returned. It merely selects a filename at random from the list of filenames contained in the `CustomerMeshes` array.

```
c.DXFilename = CustomerMeshes(Rand(UBound(CustomerMeshes), 1))
```

CUSTOMER QUEUE CHANGES

One minor change was made to the `Queue` class. I added an `Item` method that returns an object reference to the object in the specified position in the array using this code.

```
Public Function Item(index As Long) As Object

Set Item = xQueue(index).Data

End Function
```

While I named the method `Item` it is not as flexible as the `Item` methods associated with a `Collection` object. This method is merely a kludge that allows me to scan through all of the items in the queue without regard to priority or content.

RENDERING CUSTOMERS

The rendering routine has been updated with the new block of code shown in Listing 16.3. This code loops through the customers in the `MallCustomers` queue using the `Item` method previously discussed. The code is located just before I display any text on the screen.

LISTING 16.3 DXGRAPHICS.RENDER (PARTIAL LISTING)

```
With GameObj.Mall.MallCustomers

    For i = 1 To .Length
        Set c = .Item(i)
        D3DXMatrixIdentity matTemp
        D3DXMatrixRotationY matTemp, c.Rotation
        D3DXMatrixTranslation matTrans, -c.x, -c.y, -c.Z
        D3DXMatrixMultiply matTemp, matTemp, matTrans
        d3ddevice.SetTransform D3DTS_WORLD, matTemp

        With DXmshs(DXobs(c.DXFilename).MeshFilename)
            For j = 0 To .Materials - 1
                d3ddevice.SetTexture 0, DXtexs(.MeshTextures(i)).Texture
                d3ddevice.SetMaterial .MeshMaterials(j)
                .Mesh.DrawSubset j

            Next j

        End With

    Next i

End With
```

> **Note**
>
> **The whole code and nothing but the code**
>
> Rather than repeat the entire Render method here, I decided just to include the relevant subset. You should refer to the version of the game on the CD-ROM in the \VBGame\Chapter16 directory to see the entire routine.

The routine begins by using the `With` statement to simplify access to the customer queue. Then I set up a `For` loop to examine each element in the queue. After getting a local pointer to the current customer, I perform the matrix and transform operations to position the world using the information from the Customer object.

Once the world is in the proper position, I can use the same technique I used earlier in the Render routine to display the mesh. This involves accessing the appropriate mesh and then looping through the appropriate materials and textures for each subset of the mesh. Then, once I've drawn the current customer, I just repeat the process until I've drawn each customer.

WALKING THROUGH THE MALL

Simulating a customer walking through the mall requires some careful planning. The mall operates at several different speeds. But even in the slowest speed, time will pass much faster in the mall than in real life. At its fastest speed, time will pass so fast that a customer may arrive at the mall and depart before they can be displayed on the screen. Thus it's important to take the game's speed into consideration as you compute the customer's location in the mall.

In addition to the speed issue, customers need information about the mall so that they won't walk through walls. While there are several ways to solve this problem, creating a map of the mall is perhaps the easiest. The map splits the mall into a series of cells. Information about each cell will show whether the customer can occupy the cell or will be forced to find another path around the cell.

MANAGING CELLS

Because the map is implemented as an array, I created the GetCell function (see Listing 16.4) as a way to prevent subscripting errors. No matter what values are used as subscripts, the function will always return a proper value. While I could have verified that the subscripts were legal before attempting to reference the array, I decided to let Visual Basic do the work and handle the error condition only when it arises.

LISTING 16.4   MAP.GETCELL

```
Public Function GetCell(x As Long, y As Long) As CellEnum

On Error Resume Next
GetCell = Cells(x, y)
If Err.Number <> 0 Then
   GetCell = UnknownCell

End If

End Function
```

After writing the GetCell routine, I created two other routines that allow me to change the contents of a cell. These are called SetCell (see Listing 16.5) and ResetCell. These routines simply toggle the value of the current location of the customer from open to blocked (SetCell) or from blocked to open (ResetCell).

LISTING 16.5 MAP.SETCELL

```
Public Sub SetCell(c As Customer)

If Cells(c.CellX, c.CellY) = OpenEntranceCell Then
   Cells(c.CellX, c.CellY) = BlockedEntranceCell

ElseIf Cells(c.CellX, c.CellY) = OpenCell Then
   Cells(c.CellX, c.CellY) = BlockedCell

ElseIf Cells(c.CellX, c.CellY) = OpenStoreCell Then
   Cells(c.CellX, c.CellY) = BlockedStoreCell

ElseIf Cells(c.CellX, c.CellY) = OpenStoreEntranceCell Then
   Cells(c.CellX, c.CellY) = BlockedStoreEntranceCell

End If

End Sub
```

FINDING AN ENTRANCE

One of the problems with using an array for a map is that only one customer can occupy a cell at a time. If customers arrive at the mall too quickly, there may be multiple customers for each mall entrance. Rather than allowing multiple customers to occupy a single cell, it is better to direct them to a nearby cell.

This is exactly how the GetOpenMallEntrance routine works (see Listing 16.6). It begins by searching through the MallEntrances array looking for an OpenEntranceCell. If it finds one, it sets the customer's X and Z location properties to entrance's coordinates and set the customer's cell location to the entrance coordinates and return.

LISTING 16.6 MAP.GETOPENMALLENTRANCE

```
Public Sub GetOpenMallEntrance(c As Customer)

Dim i As Long
Dim j As Long

i = 1
Do While i <= UBound(MallEntrances)
   If Cells(MallEntrances(i).x, MallEntrances(i).y) = OpenEntranceCell Then
      c.x = MallEntrances(i).x / MapScale
      c.Z = MallEntrances(i).y / MapScale
      c.CellX = MallEntrances(i).x
      c.CellY = MallEntrances(i).y
      Exit Sub

   End If
```

LISTING 16.6   CONTINUED

```
    i = i + 1

Loop

i = Rand(UBound(MallEntrances), 1)
j = 1
Do While Not GetNearbyOpenCell(c, MallEntrances(i).x, _
        MallEntrances(i).y, j, OpenCell)
    j = j + 1

Loop

End Sub
```

If the first entrance is blocked, then the rest of the entrances are checked. If they all are blocked, then one is picked at random and `GetNearbyOpenCell` is called to find an open cell near the current entrance.

FINDING AN OPEN CELL

The `GetOpenCell` routine searches the cells around the specified location looking for a cell that is open (see Listing 16.7). It begins by checking the current cell to see if it is open. If it is, it sets the customer location information and returns to the calling routine. If the current cell is occupied, it calls `GetNearbyOpenCell` until it finds an open cell.

LISTING 16.7   MAP.GETOPENCELL

```
Public Sub GetOpenCell(c As Customer, x As Long, y As Long)

Dim i As Long

If GetCell(x, y) = OpenCell Then
    c.x = x / MapScale
    c.Z = y / MapScale
    c.CellX = x
    c.CellY = y
    Exit Sub

End If

i = 1
Do While Not GetNearbyOpenCell(c, x, y, i, OpenCell)
    i = i + 1

Loop

End Sub
```

FINDING A NEARBY CELL

The GetNearbyOpenCell function (see Listing 16.8) is a very useful function. It takes both a Customer object and a cell's X and Y coordinates, plus a distance parameter (d) and the type of cell you want to find. The depth parameter specifies the distance from the current cell you want to search. Setting d to 1 means that the eight cells immediately surrounding the specified cell will be searched. Each higher value of d means that the next larger surrounding square will be searched for a cell of the specified type.

LISTING 16.8   MAP.GETNEARBYOPENCELL

```
Public Function GetNearbyOpenCell(c As Customer, x As Long, y As Long, _
    d As Long, t As CellEnum) As Boolean

Dim i As Long
Dim j As Long

For i = x - d To x + d
    If GetCell(i, y + d) = t Then
        c.x = i / MapScale
        c.Z = (y + d) / MapScale
        c.CellX = i
        c.CellY = y + d
        GetNearbyOpenCell = True
        Exit Function

    End If

    If GetCell(i, y - d) = t Then
        c.x = i / MapScale
        c.Z = (y - d) / MapScale
        c.CellX = i
        c.CellY = y - d
        GetNearbyOpenCell = True
        Exit Function

    End If

Next i

For i = y - d + 1 To y + d - 1
    If GetCell(x + d, i) = t Then
        c.x = (x + d) / MapScale
        c.Z = i / MapScale
        c.CellX = x + d
        c.CellY = i
        GetNearbyOpenCell = True
        Exit Function

    End If

    If GetCell(x - d, i) = t Then
        c.x = (x - d) / MapScale
        c.Z = i / MapScale
        c.CellX = x - d
```

LISTING 16.8   CONTINUED

```
        c.CellY = i
        GetNearbyOpenCell = True
        Exit Function

    End If

Next i

GetNearbyOpenCell = False

End Function
```

The routine breaks the search process into four individual steps. Each step is responsible for processing one side of the square. If it finds a cell that matches the value passed to the function, it will immediately update the location information in the `Customer` object, set the value of the function to `True` to indicate a cell was found, and exit the function.

If the routine can't find a cell at the specified distance, it will return `False`. Then it's up to the calling program to determine what action to take. In `GetOpenCell` and `GetOpenMallEntrance` is continued until a valid open cell is found. Of course this might cause a problem if there are more customers in the mall than there are available cells.

Note that I use the `GetCell` function to get the contents of a cell. This is very important because this routine could easily exceed the bounds of the mall.

GUIDING CUSTOMERS

The `Mall.StepTick` routine (see Listing 16.9) provides the overall control for the customers in the mall. Originally this routine simply updated the customer objects that had events taking place during this tick of the simulation clock. Now this routine also handles how each customer walks through the mall.

LISTING 16.9   MALL.STEPTICK

```
Public Sub StepTick()

Dim x As Single
Dim c As Customer
Dim s As Object
Dim t As Date
Dim i As Long

For i = 1 To MallCustomers.Length
    MallMap.MoveCustomer MallCustomers.Item(i)

Next i

t = MallCustomers.PeekPriority
Do While (t < MasterClock) And MallCustomers.Length > 0
    Set c = MallCustomers.Front
```

LISTING 16.9   CONTINUED

```
Select Case c.NextAction
Case ArriveAtMall
   MallCustomerCount = MallCustomerCount + 1
   TodaysCustomers = TodaysCustomers + 1
   Set c.Store = FindStore(c.Needs, c.FoodNeeds)
   c.WalkingTime = Int(Rand(180, 60))
   c.StoreArrive = DateAdd("s", c.WalkingTime, c.MallArrive)
   c.NextAction = ArriveAtStore
   MallMap.GetOpenMallEntrance c
   MallMap.SetCell c
   c.DestinationX = c.Store.EntranceX
   c.DestinationY = c.Store.EntranceY
   c.DestinationZ = c.Store.EntranceZ
   c.WalkingState = WalkToStoreEntrance
   c.Walkticks = c.WalkingTime / speed
   MallCustomers.PriorityAdd c, c.StoreArrive

Case ArriveAtStore
   c.Store.ArriveStore c
   c.StoreDepart = c.Store.ComputeDepartTime(c)
   c.NextAction = DepartStore
   If c.StoreDepart > 0 Then
      c.WalkingState = WalkRandomlyInStore
      c.WalkingTime = DateDiff("s", MasterClock, c.StoreDepart)

   Else
      c.WalkingState = WalkToStoreEntrance
      c.WalkingTime = 0

   End If
   MallCustomers.PriorityAdd c, c.StoreDepart

Case DepartStore
   c.Store.DepartStore c
   Set c.Store = FindStore(c.Needs, c.FoodNeeds)
   If Not c.Store Is Nothing Then
      c.WalkingState = WalkToStoreEntrance
      c.WalkingTime = Int(Rand(60, 20))
      c.StoreArrive = DateAdd("s", c.WalkingTime, MasterClock)
      c.StoreDepart = c.Store.ComputeDepartTime(c)
      c.NextAction = ArriveAtStore
      c.DestinationX = c.Store.EntranceX
      c.DestinationY = c.Store.EntranceY
      c.DestinationZ = c.Store.EntranceZ
      MallCustomers.PriorityAdd c, c.StoreDepart

   Else
      c.NextAction = DepartMall
      c.WalkingState = WalkToMallEntrance
      c.WalkingTime = Int(Rand(180, 60))
      c.MallDepart = DateAdd("s", c.WalkingTime, MasterClock)
      ' select real mall entrance
      c.DestinationX = 0
      c.DestinationY = 0
```

LISTING 16.9   CONTINUED

```
            c.DestinationZ = 0
            MallCustomers.PriorityAdd c, c.MallDepart

        End If

    Case DepartMall
        If Not (c.Needs Or Not c.FoodNeeds) Then
            x = CountBits(c.Needs) + CountBits(c.FoodNeeds)
            c.Satisfaction = c.Satisfaction - Rand(2 * x / c.NeedCount)

        End If

        c.Satisfaction = c.Satisfaction - _
            Abs(c.Satisfaction * (Year(MasterClock) - Year(MallBuilt)) / 20)
        c.Satisfaction = c.Satisfaction * Difficulty
        c.Satisfaction = IIf(c.Satisfaction > 1, 1, _
            IIf(c.Satisfaction < -1, -1, c.Satisfaction))
        Satisfaction = Satisfaction + ((c.Satisfaction - Satisfaction) * _
            Abs(1 - Satisfaction)) / 1000
        MallMap.ResetCell c


    Case Else
        MallDebugger.WriteLong "Invalid action value", c.NextAction

    End Select

    t = MallCustomers.PeekPriority

Loop

End Sub
```

The routine now begins by looping through all the customers in the queue and updating their position in the mall by calling the MoveCustomer method in the Map class.

Then it extracts the first customer in the customer queue and determines how to process it by examining the NextAction property of the Customer object. NextAction can take on four different values: ArriveAtMall, ArriveAtStore, DepartStore, and DepartMall. Each case is handled independently.

When the customer arrives at the mall, the routine performs the same processing as before, but now it chooses a random amount of time ranging from one to three minutes to walk to the store. This is known as WalkingTime. This value is added to the time the customer arrived at the mall to set the proper arrival time at the store.

Next an open entrance at the mall is found for the customer using the Map class's GetOpenMallEntrance method. Then that cell is marked as blocked using the SetCell method. Then the Destination properties of the customer are set to the store's Entrance properties and the customer's WalkingState is set to WalkToStoreEntrance. After that, the number of steps needed to walk to the store based on WalkingTime and Speed is computed. Finally the customer is placed back in the queue.

When the customer arrives at the store (Case ArriveAtStore), compute the depart time for the customer. If the depart time is zero, it means that the customer left the store because it was too crowded and I would set WalkingState to WalkToStoreEntrance. Otherwise, it means that the customer is going to stay in the store for a while, so I need to let them walk around the store randomly (WalkingState = WalkRandomlyInStore) until it is time to leave.

Before the customer leaves the store, the routine searches to see if there is another store that meets the customer's remaining needs. If there is one, the customer's WalkingState is set to WalkToStoreEntrance and same properties that were set the customer first arrived at the mall are also updated.

If there aren't any stores left in the mall that will satisfy the customer's needs, the customer is given between 60 and 180 seconds to leave the mall. Then a mall entrance is selected for the customer to walk to.

Finally, when the NextAction property is DepartMall, there is nothing left to do in this routine because the customer should have finished walking to the mall's exit. Because this clause doesn't add the customer back into the queue, the customer will disappear from the screen the next time it is rendered. However, the customer's map position must be reset; otherwise the position will remain blocked.

WALKING A CUSTOMER

While the Mall.StepTick routine provides the overall guidance, the actual work associated with walking a customer around in the mall is handled by the Map class. The MoveCustomer method calls the appropriate routine based on the customer's WalkingState (see Listing 16.10).

LISTING 16.10   MAP.MOVECUSTOMER

```
Public Sub MoveCustomer(c As Customer)

Select Case c.WalkingState
   Case WalkToStoreEntrance
      WalkToStore c

   Case WalkRandomlyInStore
      WalkInStore c

   Case WalkToMallEntrance
      WalkToMallExit c
End Select

End Sub
```

WALKING TO A STORE

When walking a customer to a store, you need to remember that the customer's position is controlled by the simulation. Thus the value in Speed plays a major factor in how the customer moves.

For instance, if Speed is set to 300 seconds per tick, and the customer has 180 seconds to move from the mall's entrance to the store's entrance, you won't see a smooth movement from one place to another. The customer will appear to jump from one place to another.

However, if Speed is slow, like 5 seconds per tick, you have to try to step the customer from one position to the next evenly.

In the WalkToStore routine (see Listing 16.11), the first thing it checks is to see if the customer has arrived at its destination. If it has, then WalkingState is set to WalkRandomlyInStore if the customer has been walking to the store.

PART

III

CH

16

LISTING 16.11   MAP.WALKTOSTORE

```
Private Sub WalkToStore(c As Customer)

If GetCell(c.CellX, c.CellY) = BlockedStoreEntranceCell Then
    If c.NextAction = ArriveAtStore Then
        c.WalkingState = WalkRandomlyInStore

    End If

ElseIf c.WalkingTime > speed And c.Walkticks > 0 Then
    ResetCell c
    GetRotation c, c.DestinationX - c.x, c.DestinationZ - c.Z
    c.x = c.x + (c.DestinationX - c.x) / c.Walkticks
    c.y = c.y + (c.DestinationY - c.y) / c.Walkticks
    c.Z = c.Z + (c.DestinationZ - c.Z) / c.Walkticks
    c.CellX = c.x * MapScale
    c.CellY = c.Z * MapScale
    c.WalkingTime = c.WalkingTime - speed
    SetCell c

Else
    ResetCell c
    GetRotation c, c.DestinationX - c.x, c.DestinationZ - c.Z
    c.x = c.DestinationX
    c.y = c.DestinationY
    c.Z = c.DestinationZ
    c.CellX = c.x * MapScale
    c.CellY = c.Z * MapScale
    c.WalkingTime = 0
    SetCell c

End If

End Sub
```

Next the routine determines if there is enough time to store by comparing WalkingTime to Speed. If there is at least one more step after this one, the customer is moved one step closer toward the destination. After resetting the current cell location, the GetRotation method is used to determine where the customer should be pointing. Then the customer's 3D position and cell location are updated. Next the amount of walking time left is adjusted. Finally the SetCell method updates the customer's current position in the map.

If this is the last step, the customer is moved directly to the store's entrance using the same steps used earlier; however, the WalkingTime is set to zero because the customer has arrived at the store.

WALKING IN THE STORE

Once the customer has arrived at the store, it is still standing on the entrance and needs to move into the store. Then the customer will walk around randomly until it is time to leave. The WalkInStore routine is responsible for these actions (see Listing 16.12).

LISTING 16.12   MAP.WALKINSTORE

```
Private Sub WalkInStore(c As Customer)

ResetCell c

If c.Walkticks = 0 Then
    c.DeltaX = Rand(1, -1)
    c.DeltaY = Rand(1, -1)
    c.Walkticks = Rand(8, 1)

End If

c.Walkticks = c.Walkticks - 1
c.CellX = c.CellX + c.DeltaX
c.CellY = c.CellY + c.DeltaY

If Not GetCell(c.CellX, c.CellY) = OpenStoreCell Then
    GetNearbyOpenCell c, c.CellX, c.CellY, 1, OpenStoreCell

End If

GetRotation c, c.DeltaX, c.DeltaY
c.x = c.CellX / MapScale
c.Z = c.CellY / MapScale
SetCell c

End Sub
```

This routine begins by resetting the current map cell occupied by the customer. Then I see how many ticks are left in Walkticks. If the value is zero, I choose a new random direction for the customer to walk and a new value for Walkticks.

Next, I subtract one from the number of Walkticks and move the customer in the random direction previously chosen. Then I verify that the new cell is an open store cell. If it isn't, I find a nearby open store cell, though I limit myself to a distance of 1 to prevent the customer walking through a wall to another store.

Finally I set the direction of where the customer should be facing and then update the customer's 3D coordinates. I set the customer's new location in the mall and return to the calling routine.

LEAVING THE MALL

When the customer is ready to leave the mall, the customer will walk to the mall entrance using the same technique that was used to walk the customer to a store (see Listing 16.13). While there is still time left in WalkingTime, the current map cell will be reset and a new location compute for the customer will be computed. Then this new location will be set in the map. Otherwise, the customer will be moved directly to its destination.

LISTING 16.13   MAP.WALKTOMALLEXIT

```
Private Sub WalkToMallExit(c As Customer)

If c.WalkingTime > speed And c.Walkticks > 0 Then
    ResetCell c
    GetRotation c, c.DestinationX - c.x, c.DestinationZ - c.Z
    c.x = c.x + (c.DestinationX - c.x) / c.Walkticks
    c.y = c.y + (c.DestinationY - c.y) / c.Walkticks
    c.Z = c.Z + (c.DestinationZ - c.Z) / c.Walkticks
    c.CellX = c.x * MapScale
    c.CellY = c.Z * MapScale
    c.WalkingTime = c.WalkingTime - speed
    SetCell c

Else
    ResetCell c
    GetRotation c, c.DestinationX - c.x, c.DestinationZ - c.Z
    c.x = c.DestinationX
    c.y = c.DestinationY
    c.Z = c.DestinationZ
    c.CellX = c.x * MapScale
    c.CellY = c.Z * MapScale
    c.WalkingTime = 0
    SetCell c

End If

End Sub
```

ROTATING A CUSTOMER

Although this is probably trivial in the scheme of things, it looks better to have the customer pointing in the direction they are walking. So I created the GetRotation routine to compute which direction the customers should be pointing based on the direction they are moving (see Listing 16.14).

LISTING 16.14   MAP.GETROTATION

```
Private Sub GetRotation(c As Customer, dx As Single, dy As Single)


If dx > 0 Then
    c.Rotation = Atn(dy / dx)

ElseIf dx < 0 Then
    c.Rotation = Atn(dy / dx) + pi

End If

End Sub
```

This routine uses the arctangent function (Atn) to convert the change in the x direction divided by the change in the y direction. Because the Atn function returns valid results only over the range from 0 to pi (0 to 180 degrees), pi is added to the result if the change in the x direction is negative. This means that it will properly handle all possible rotation value in the range of 0 to 2 pi (0 to 360 degrees).

FINAL THOUGHTS

Adding movement to the game is a lot more difficult than it first appears. Not only did I have to create a map and customers, the logic used to maneuver a customer in the mall is reasonably complex.

The code I used here has a number of limitations that would be unacceptable in a commercial game. Customers shouldn't just appear and disappear at random, especially when the simulation is running at higher speeds. Either the customer display should be suppressed at higher speeds or the customers should make a smooth transition to the mall's exit.

Another problem revolves around speed control. Changing the speed of the game while a customer moves will disrupt how they walk from place to place. The effect of speed is only taken into account when the customer is being processed in the StepTick routine. Although this isn't a problem when moving from slow speeds to fast speeds, it can be noticeable when moving from fast speeds to slow.

However, the biggest problem that I see occurs when the customer always takes the most direct path from store to store. This isn't very realistic. A random factor should be included to vary the path taken a little bit. Also it would be nice to have the customer pause in front of various stores along their path to see what the stores have to offer.

Yet displaying the customers isn't really critical to the game itself. Displaying customers is mostly eye candy for the player and makes the game more visually appealing. Consider the cars in the SimCity games. They frequently appear and disappear as they represent only traffic density and not individual commuters, so having an accurate representation for the customers isn't really that important.

FINISHING THE GAME

THE MALL STRAIT JOURNAL

In this chapter

There are many ways to communicate information to a game player in a simulation game. Perhaps the most common is through the use of a newspaper. Another common way to communicate information is through a character that provides advice to the player. A character like this remains hidden most of the time, appearing only when it has something useful to say.

READING THE MALL STRAIT JOURNAL

In Swim Mall a newspaper called the Mall Strait Journal (see Figure 17.1) is used to present information to the player. This paper shows up on the first of each month and contains information about what the mall did during the previous month. Although the newspaper in this game shows only one article at a time, you can page through it and see other articles, including articles from previous editions.

Figure 17.1
Browsing the Mall Strait Journal.

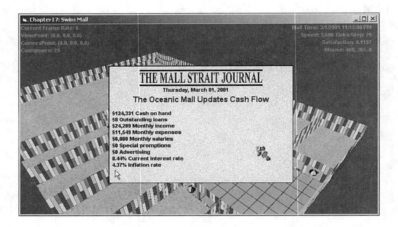

The information that appears in the Mall Strait Journal is stored in a class called MSJ. This class is responsible for both generating and storing all of the newspaper articles.

Displaying the Mall Strait Journal is similar to implementing a menu item. You simply load an image file for the Mall Strait Journal's background from a disk file when you initialize DXGraphics and display it on the screen when you want to display the MSJ. After the background is displayed, it's a simple matter to display the information over the background image.

SAVING NEWS ARTICLES

The MSJ class consists of three main pieces, a routine to add articles to its local storage, a routine to retrieve news articles from its local storage, and routines to generate news articles. A news article consists of three pieces of information, the date the news item was generated, the heading of the article, and the article body.

```
Private Type NewsItem
    NewsDate As Date
    NewsHeading As String
    NewsBody As String

End Type
```

This information is stored in the array `News`, while the `AddNews` method shown in Listing 17.1 is used to add a new entry to the array. This routine simply expands the upper bound of the `News` array to accommodate the next article and saves the article's information into each member of the `NewsItem` type.

LISTING 17.1   MSJ.ADDNEWS

```
Public Sub AddNews(h As String, b As String)

ReDim Preserve News(UBound(News) + 1)

News(UBound(News)).NewsDate = MasterClock
News(UBound(News)).NewsHeading = h
News(UBound(News)).NewsBody = b

End Sub
```

Although this routine accepts the header and body of a news article I don't accept a date parameter. I use the current value of `MasterClock` for the date. This is because the news article always will reflect what is happening in the game at that point in time, just like the news happens in real life.

WRITING NEWS ARTICLES

There are two main methods that the game uses to create news articles. The first method is the `AddStdNews` method, which creates simple news articles and `AddStdReport` which creates more complicated news items.

`AddStdNews` (see Listing 17.2) is merely a big `Select` statement that calls the `AddNews` method with a predefined news article. This approach allows me to isolate all of the news articles in one location, which makes it easy to find and change them later.

LISTING 17.2   MSJ.ADDSTDNEWS

```
Public Sub AddStdNews(NewsItem As Long)

Select Case NewsItem
    Case 0
        AddNews "Welcome to Swim Mall!", "Swim mall is a game that simulates " & _
            "an underwater shopping mall. The object of the game is to " & _
            "attract as many customers to the mall, while keeping their " & _
            "satisfaction high."

    Case 1
        AddNews "New Shopping Mall Opens!", "The Swim Mall shopping mall is " & _
            "now open for business. It features many different stores."
```

LISTING 17.2   CONTINUED

```
End Select

End Sub
```

Note

Resources and languages

Storing news articles in a common location also makes it easier to store the data. Windows resource files are an ideal way to store this type of data. Not only can Windows resource files reduce the amount of code required in the program, it can also make it easier to support alternative languages such as French or Spanish.

The AddStdReport method (see Listing 17.3) is similar to AddStdNews, but differs in that it is used to create monthly reports rather than reporting one-time events.

LISTING 17.3   MSJ.ADDSTDREPORT

```
Public Sub AddStdReport(Rept As Long)

Dim s As String

Select Case Rept
    Case 0
        s = FormatCurrency(Cash, 0) & " Cash on hand" & vbCrLf
        s = s & FormatCurrency(Loans, 0) & " Outstanding loans" & vbCrLf
        s = s & FormatCurrency(MonthlyIncome, 0) & " Monthly income" & vbCrLf
        s = s & FormatCurrency(MonthlyExpenses, 0) & " Monthly expenses" & vbCrLf
        s = s & FormatCurrency(MonthlySalary, 0) & " Monthly salaries" & vbCrLf
        s = s & FormatCurrency(Promotions, 0) & " Special promptions" & vbCrLf
        s = s & FormatCurrency(Advertising, 0) & " Advertising" & vbCrLf
        s = s & FormatPercent(InterestRate, 2) & " Current interest rate" & vbCrLf
        s = s & FormatPercent(Inflation, 2) & " Inflation rate"
        AddNews GameObj.Name & " Updates Cash Flow", s

    Case 1
        s = FormatNumber(CustomerCount, 0, , , vbTrue) & " Total customers" & vbCrLf
        s = s & FormatNumber(GameObj.Mall.MallCustomers.Length, 0, , , vbTrue) & _
            " Maximum customers in the mall" & vbCrLf
        s = s & FormatNumber(Satisfaction, 5) & " Satisfaction" & vbCrLf
        s = s & FormatDateTime(MallBuilt, vbLongDate) & " Date mall opened"
        AddNews GameObj.Name & " Releases Statistics", s

End Select

End Sub
```

GETTING THE NEWS

The GetNews method (see Listing 17.4) returns the parts of the specified news article. The id parameter contains the relative location of the article. A value of zero returns the most recent article, while a value of one returns the previous article, and so forth.

LISTING 17.4   MSJ.GetNews

```
Public Sub GetNews(id As Long, d As String, h As String, b As String)

If id >= 0 And id < UBound(News) Then
    d = FormatDateTime(News(UBound(News) - id).NewsDate, vbLongDate)
    h = News(UBound(News) - id).NewsHeading
    b = News(UBound(News) - id).NewsBody

ElseIf id < 0 Then
    d = ""
    h = "No Newer News"
    b = ""
    id = -1

Else
    d = ""
    h = "No Older News."
    b = ""
    id = UBound(News)

End If

End Sub
```

The routine begins by verifying that id points to a valid entry in the News array. If id is valid, the subscript is computed by subtracting id from the upper bound of the News array. Then the values are saved from the array into each parameter, while taking time to format the date using the FormatDatetime function.

If the value of id is less than zero, it means that the caller attempted to reference an article that is newer than the most current article available. So I'll return an article without a date and body and a header that indicates that there are no newer news articles available. I'll also change id to -1. This ensures that id is never more than one value away from the most current article.

Finally, if id is greater than or equal to the upper bound of the News array, the caller attempted to reference an article older than the oldest one available. So I return a news article indicating that there isn't any older news and set id to the upper bound of the New array.

Note

> **Preserving data**
>
> The technique of storing data in an array by using the upper bound as the newest item means that I never use the zeroth element of the array. When id is equal to the upper bound of the array, Ubound(News) - id will be zero, which means that there isn't any valid data even though the subscript is inside the array.

In the Global module, I use the following statement to declare a new instance of the MSJ object in Mall.PostGameLoadProcessing. Note that News is a global variable so that it can be accessed anywhere in the application.

```
Set News = New MSJ
```

PRINTING THE NEWSPAPER

Once each month, I'll update the newspaper with the latest mall reports and display the most recent edition using the code fragment from the Mall.StepMonth (see Listing 17.5). First the New.AddStdReport method is called to add the monthly reports to the newspaper. Then CurrentNews is set to zero to ensure that the most recent news is displayed. Finally GameState is set to menustate and AddCommand is called to add the MSJCommand command. This simply duplicates the steps that would occur if the user chooses to view the Mall Strait Journal from the main menu.

LISTING 17.5   MALL.STEPMONTH (PARTIAL LISTING)

```
News.AddStdReport 1
News.AddStdReport 0

CurrentNews = 0
GameState = menustate
dxi.AddCommand MSJCommand
```

DISPLAYING THE NEWSPAPER

The image used for the paper was created in Photoshop by creating a new image, 256 pixels high and 384 pixels wide. I picked a background color and added a little noise to it to make it look more realistic. Then I added the letterhead at the top of the image and saved it into the file msj.BMP.

In the DXGraphics.InitDXMessages routine I use these statements to load the newspaper into a Direct3Dsurface8 object:

```
Set MSJSurface = d3ddevice.CreateImageSurface(384, 256, d3dDispMode.Format)
d3dx.LoadSurfaceFromFile MSJSurface, ByVal 0, ByVal 0, App.path & "\msj.bmp", _
    ByVal 0, D3DX_DEFAULT, &HFF00FFFF, ByVal 0
```

Then I use the DrawMSJNews routine in Listing 17.6 to display the newspaper. After declaring some local variables, the routine calls the GetNews method to get the current news item and store the results in some local variables.

LISTING 17.6   DXGRAPHICS.DRAWMSJNEWS

```
Private Sub DrawMSJNews()

Dim ds As Direct3DSurface8
Dim d As String
Dim h As String
Dim b As String

Dim center As RECT
Dim part As RECT
Dim TextRect As RECT

News.GetNews CurrentNews, d, h, b

Set ds = d3ddevice.GetRenderTarget

center.top = Height / 2 - 128
center.bottom = Height / 2 + 128
center.left = Width / 2 - 192
center.right = Width / 2 + 192

part.top = 0
part.left = 0
part.bottom = 255
part.right = 383
d3ddevice.CopyRects MSJSurface, part, 1, ds, center

TextRect.top = center.top + 46
TextRect.left = center.left + 64
TextRect.bottom = center.top + 60
TextRect.right = center.left + 300
d3dx.DrawText GameFont, &HFF000000, d, TextRect, DT_CENTER

TextRect.top = center.top + 64
TextRect.left = center.left + 8
TextRect.bottom = center.top + 96
TextRect.right = center.left + 376
d3dx.DrawText BigGameFont, &HFF000000, h, TextRect, DT_CENTER

TextRect.top = center.top + 96
TextRect.left = center.left + 8
TextRect.bottom = center.top + 252
TextRect.right = center.left + 376
d3dx.DrawText GameFont, &HFF000000, h, TextRect, DT_LEFT Or DT_WORDBREAK

End Sub
```

Next a RECT is defined in the center of the screen where the newspaper will be displayed. Then the surface is copied to the screen using the CopyRects method. After that, the date (d), heading (h), and article body (b) are displayed on the screen using DrawText method.

When I display the article body on the screen, I specify the DT_LEFT or DT_WORDBREAK flags. This means that the text will be aligned with the left edge of TextRect and if a word crosses the right boundary, it will be started on the next line at the left margin. You can also force the text to start on the next line by including &vbCrLf in the text.

FLIPPING THROUGH THE PAGES

Displaying the newspaper will change GameState to msjstate. This allows the KeyBoardStateChange routine (see Listing 17.7) to trap the keystrokes related to the newspaper. In this case, I'll trap the Escape key and use it to close the newspaper, while the B key pages backward through the newspaper and the F key pages forward through the newspaper.

LISTING 17.7 DXINPUT.KEYBOARDSTATECHANGE (PARTIAL LISTING)

```
Case msjstate
   Select Case k
      Case DIK_ESCAPE
         AddCommand MenuCommand

      Case DIK_B
         AddCommand MSJBackupCommand

      Case DIK_F
         AddCommand MSJForwardCommand

   End Select
```

These keystrokes are processed in the Game.RunMSJ routine (see Listing 17.8). This routine clears the pop-up window and sets the game state to normalstate if the user presses Esc. If the user presses a B, CurrentNews is incremented, while a U will decrement CurrentNews. All other input will be ignored.

LISTING 17.8 GAME.RUNMSJ

```
Private Sub RunMSJ(c As GameCommand)

Select Case c.Command
   Case MenuCommand
      GameState = normalstate
      dx.PopupMessage = none

   Case MSJBackupCommand
      CurrentNews = CurrentNews + 1

   Case MSJForwardCommand
      CurrentNews = CurrentNews - 1

End Select

End Sub
```

BORROWING MONEY FROM THE BANK

Swim Mall allows a player to raise funds by borrowing money from the bank. Each month, the interest is computed on the outstanding loan balance and charged to the player. To eliminate the interest payment, the player must repay the money to the bank.

BORROWING MONEY

To implement loans in Swim Mall, I need to implement a way to collect information from the user, which in this case is merely the amount of money the player wants to borrow or repay. This means that I need to display an input box on the screen, which will accept a free form typed value from the player. Then after the value is accepted, it should be applied to the outstanding loan amount. In this case, I'll create a pop-up message where the user can enter a value into the computer similar to a Visual Basic InputBox (see Figure 17.2).

Figure 17.2
Borrowing money requires code in both DXGraphics and DXInput.

The approach I used to implement the input box uses the pop-up message logic from DXGraphics to display the input box and the DXInput keyboard to accept the characters from the keyboard. The overall control is managed by GameState and the related code in the Game class.

INPUTTING STRINGS

Up until this point, any input from the keyboard has been translated into a GameCommand object. Although this is fine for executing commands it really doesn't work for collecting a string of text. In Listing 17.9, you can see the code that is fired each time a key is pressed.

LISTING 17.9   DXINPUT.INPUTKEYBOARDEVENT (PARTIAL LISTING)

```
If KeyboardTextMode Then
   If DXKeyboardState.Key(DIK_BACKSPACE) = &H80 And _
        LastKeyboardState(DIK_BACKSPACE) = 0 Then
      If Len(InputBuffer) > 0 Then
         InputBuffer = left(InputBuffer, Len(InputBuffer) - 1)

      End If

   ElseIf DXKeyboardState.Key(DIK_RETURN) = &H80 And _
        LastKeyboardState(DIK_RETURN) = 0 Then
      AddCommand okaycommand
```

LISTING 17.9   CONTINUED

```
   Else
      InputBuffer = InputBuffer & ToAscii(DXKeyboardState.Key)

   End If

Else
   For i = 0 To 255
      If DXKeyboardState.Key(i) = 128 And _
            DXKeyboardState.Key(i) <> LastKeyboardState(i) Then
         KeyBoardStateChange i

      End If

   Next i

End If
```

Depending on the state of KeyboardTextMode, this fragment will either gather characters and save them into InputBuffer or call KeyBoardStateChange to convert the key press into a GameCommand object. When characters are being gathered into InputBuffer, I allow the player to press the backspace key to remove the last character from the input buffer. When the player presses the enter key, I add the OkayCommand to the command queue. The approach also allows the player to press the left mouse button while over the OK button, which will also add the OkayCommand to the command queue.

Note that after encountering the Enter key, I don't reset KeyboardTextMode. This means that I must reset it in the code that processes the input.

Note

Editing commands

Although this code fragment only processes the Backspace key, you could easily adapt it to handle other keys such as the left and right arrow keys, the Insert key, and the Delete key. You'll need to add a variable that tracks the current location of the cursor because the player can insert characters into the middle of the input buffer. You'll also need to add an insert flag to indicate whether the next typed character should be inserted into the string or replace the next character.

DISPLAYING AN INPUT BOX

Displaying the input buffer is similar to displaying the okay pop-up box, however some extra work is required to display the input buffer and the cursor. The DrawInputBox method (see Listing 17.10) begins by setting center to the area that will be occupied by the input box on the screen.

LISTING 17.10   DXGRAPHICS.DRAWINPUTBOX

```
Private Sub DrawInputBox()

Dim ds As Direct3DSurface8

Set ds = d3ddevice.GetRenderTarget

Dim center As RECT
Dim part As RECT
Dim TextRect As RECT

center.top = Height / 2 - 64
center.bottom = Height / 2 + 64
center.left = Width / 2 - 128
center.right = Width / 2 + 128

If dxi.MouseX > center.left + 64 And dxi.MouseX < center.left + 192 _
    And dxi.MouseY > center.top + 100 And dxi.MouseY < center.top + 128 Then
    PopupMessageHotSpot = 1
    part.top = 128
    part.left = 0
    part.bottom = 255
    part.right = 255
    d3ddevice.CopyRects InputBoxSurface, part, 1, ds, center

Else

    PopupMessageHotSpot = 0
    part.top = 0
    part.left = 0
    part.bottom = 127
    part.right = 255
    d3ddevice.CopyRects InputBoxSurface, part, 1, ds, center

End If

TextRect.top = Height / 2 - 50
TextRect.left = Width / 2 - 80
TextRect.bottom = Height / 2 + 20
TextRect.right = Width / 2 + 115
d3dx.DrawText BigGameFont, &HFF0000FF, PopupMessageText, TextRect, _
    DT_TOP Or DT_LEFT

TextRect.top = Height / 2 - 10
TextRect.left = Width / 2 - 100
TextRect.bottom = Height / 2 + 60
TextRect.right = Width / 2 + 100

If Len(dxi.InputBuffer) <> 0 Then
    d3dx.DrawText BigGameFont, &HFFFF0000, dxi.InputBuffer, TextRect, _
        DT_TOP Or DT_LEFT
    d3dx.DrawText BigGameFont, &HFFFF0000, dxi.InputBuffer, TextRect, _
        DT_TOP Or DT_LEFT Or DT_CALCRECT
    TextRect.left = TextRect.right
    TextRect.right = Width / 2 + 100
```

PART

IV

CH

17

LISTING 17.10   CONTINUED

```
End If

d3dx.DrawText BigGameFont, &HFF000000, "_", TextRect, DT_TOP Or DT_LEFT

End Sub
```

Then the routine determines whether the mouse pointer is over the word Okay on the input box. If the cursor isn't over Okay, the top half of the input box surface is copied to the display. If it isn't, the bottom half of the surface is copied. Next the input prompt that was stored in PopupMessageText is displayed.

The real trick is displaying the characters from the input buffer. If all I had to do was to display the characters, this would be a very simple task. However I also want to display a cursor character in a different color. Because the DrawText method is restricted to a single color, I need to call it twice—once for each color, but I need to know where the text ends from the first call so I can create the appropriate rectangle for the second call.

The DT_CALCRECT flag instructs the DrawText method to adjust the values in the RECT parameter (in this case TextRect) to indicate where the next character should be placed. In this case, because the text spans only a single line, the right value will be modified to point just beyond the last character printed. If you were displaying multiple lines both the right and bottom values will be adjusted to mark the location of the next character.

Including the DT_CALCRECT flag when you call DrawText means that DrawText will not physically render any text. This means that you need to call DrawText twice, the first time to write the text and the second time to compute where the text ended.

In this case, I set up TextRect where I want to display the text, then see if DXI.InputBuffer is empty. If it's not empty, I write the text to the display and adjust TextRect so that the next call will output the cursor in the proper position.

CONTROLLING THE INPUT BOX

When the player wants to borrow money, they choose the main menu and select the Borrow command. This will add LoanBorrowCommand to the command queue, which will be executed in the Game.RunMenu routine with the code from Listing 17.11.

LISTING 17.11   GAME.RUNMENU (PARTIAL LISTING)

```
Case loanborrowcommand
    GameState = borrowstate
    dxi.InputBuffer = ""
    dxi.KeyboardTextMode = True
    dx.PopupMessage = InputBox
    dx.PopupMessageText = "Home much to borrow?"
```

First, set `GameState` to `borrowstate`. Then clear `InputBuffer` and enable `KeyboardTextMode`. Finally, set `dx.PopupMessage` to `InputBox` and ask the player to specify the amount of money she wants to borrow.

Although the input box is displayed on the screen and collecting characters from the player, the game is controlled by the `RunBorrow` routine (refer to Listing 17.12). This routine waits for an `okaycommand` to be generated and then processes the loan request.

LISTING 17.12   DXGRAPHICS.DRAWINPUTBOX

```
Private Sub RunBorrow(c As GameCommand)

Select Case c.Command
    Case okaycommand
        dxi.KeyboardTextMode = False
        GameState = normalstate
        dx.PopupMessage = none
        If IsNumeric(dxi.InputBuffer) Then
            Loans = Loans + CSng(dxi.InputBuffer)
            Cash = Cash + CSng(dxi.InputBuffer)

        Else
            GameState = okaystate
            dx.PopupMessageText = "Invalid loan amount."
            dx.PopupMessage = okay

        End If

End Select

End Sub
```

When the command is received, the routine disables `KeyboardTextMode`. Then it returns `GameState` to `normalstate` and disables the pop-up message. If the value is numeric, it is added to the amount of outstanding loans and to the amount of cash on hand. If the value isn't numeric, pop-up is displayed message letting the user know that the loan amount was invalid.

RAYMOND SPEAKS

The last change to the game that I want to talk about in this chapter revolves around the role of the advisor, Raymond. Raymond provides advice to the player at various points in the game. For example, when the player's cash is running out, Raymond will appear and suggest that the player should borrow some money (see Figure 17.3).

Figure 17.3
Raymond (shown in the upper-left corner of the game's window) welcomes the player to Swim Mall.

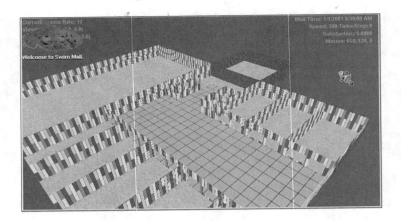

SPEECH SYNTHESIS

To make the user interface more interesting, I decided to have Raymond say his advice to the player. Rather than recording .WAV files for each speech, I decided to use the Microsoft Speech SDK to translate a string of text into sound. Although this sounds complex (yes, the pun was intended), I'm only going to use a small part of the SDK to make Raymond speak.

> **Note**
>
> **On the CD-ROM**
> You can find a complete copy of the Microsoft Speech SDK on the CD-ROM in the \Microsoft directory.

> **Note**
>
> **Speaking clearly**
> The technical term for translating a string into a sound is called *text to speech synthesis*; the technical term for converting words into text is known as *speech recognition*.

STANDARD SPEECHES

Like I did with the MSJ class, I decided to collect all the strings that will be used into a single routine (see Listing 17.13). The Speak method simply selects a standard speech based on the id argument supplied and calls the Say routine, which will display the Raymond image on the screen and convert the text string into speech.

LISTING 17.13   ADVISOR.SPEAK

```
Public Sub Speak(id As Long)

Select Case id
    Case 0
```

LISTING 17.13   CONTINUED

```
      Say "Welcome to Swim Mall. My name is Raymond the Blue " & _
         "Spotted Stingray and I'll help you play the game."

   Case 1
      Say "You are running short of cash. You may want to borrow " & _
         "some money from the bank."

End Select

End Sub
```

MAKING RAYMOND TALK

To use the Microsoft Speech tools, you need to add the speech objects to your program. They can be found in the Microsoft Speech Object Library, which you can select by choosing Project, References from the main menu in Visual Basic.

After the speech library is available, I created a new class called `Advisor`. This class will isolate all the speech synthesis logic, and the text associated with the advisor.

These variables are declared at the start of `Advisor` to track information about the current state of the advisor. `Raymond` is an object pointer to an `SpVoice` object that will be used to speak the words to the player, while `RaymondText` holds the current text being spoken. `RaymondWords` contains the words that have been spoken at a given point in time.

```
Private WithEvents Raymond As SpVoice
Private RaymondText As String
Public RaymondWords As String
```

Note that `Raymond` was declared using the `WithEvents`. This means that you can associate events with the `Raymond` object. These events allow the program to monitor the speech synthesis.

After creating a new instance of the `SpVoice` object, a simple call to the `Speak` method is all that it takes to translate a string of words into speech. The `Say` method in Listing 17.14 accepts a string to be converted into speech. First it saves the string into `RaymondText` and then it uses the `Raymond.Speak` method to say the text aloud.

LISTING 17.14   ADVISOR.SAY

```
Private Sub Say(Text As String)

RaymondText = Text
Raymond.Speak Text, SVSFlagsAsync

End Sub
```

Normally the `Speak` method will block the program until all of the text has been spoken. However, the `SVSFlagsAsync` flag indicates that the `Speak` method should return immediately and process the speech asynchronously.

TRACKING RAYMOND'S SPEECH

When Raymond begins talking, the StartStream event is fired (see Listing 17.15). I use this event to display the Raymond image on the screen and pause the background audio track because text-to-speech synthesizers can be hard to understand.

LISTING 17.15   ADVISOR.RAYMOND_STARTSTREAM

```
Private Sub Raymond_StartStream(ByVal StreamNumber As Long, _
    ByVal StreamPosition As Variant)

dx.ShowRaymond = True
dxa.PauseBackground

End Sub
```

The EndStream event is called when the text-to-speech process is complete (see Listing 17.16). In this case, I merely resume the background audio track and hide Raymond.

LISTING 17.16   ADVISOR.RAYMOND_ENDSTREAM

```
Private Sub Raymond_EndStream(ByVal StreamNumber As Long, _
    ByVal StreamPosition As Variant)

dxa.ResumeBackground
dx.ShowRaymond = False

End Sub
```

The Word event (see Listing 17.17) is fired each time the speech synthesizer has spoken a word. The CharacterPosition and Length arguments point to the word in the text string that is currently being spoken. Rather than saving the list of words that have been spoken, I simply truncate the string after the current word and save it in the RaymondWords property.

LISTING 17.17   ADVISOR.RAYMOND_WORD

```
Private Sub Raymond_Word(ByVal StreamNumber As Long, _
    ByVal StreamPosition As Variant, ByVal CharacterPosition As Long, _
    ByVal Length As Long)

RaymondWords = left(RaymondText, CharacterPosition + Length + 1)

End Sub
```

SHOWING RAYMOND

The last step in this process is to display Raymond on the screen. Rather than load Raymond as a surface and then use CopyRects to copy the image to the screen, I loaded Raymond as a texture and display the image using a D3DXSprite.

The `DrawRaymond` routine (see Listing 17.18) begins by declaring some local variables that will be used in the drawing process. The Raymond texture is 256 pixels by 256 pixels, so I define the `Source RECT` accordingly. Because I don't want to translate the image, I initialize `Translation` to zero. However, The original image looks better if I scale the height and width to 0.3 and 0.5, respectively.

LISTING 17.18   DXGRAPHICS.DRAWRAYMOND

```
Private Sub DrawRaymond()

Dim Sprite As D3DXSprite
Dim Source As RECT
Dim Scaling As D3DVECTOR2
Dim Translation As D3DVECTOR2
Dim TextRect As RECT

Source.top = 0
Source.bottom = 255
Source.left = 0
Source.right = 255
Translation.x = 0
Translation.y = 0
Scaling.x = 0.5
Scaling.y = 0.3

Set Sprite = d3dx.CreateSprite(d3ddevice)
Sprite.Draw dxRaymondTexture, Source, Scaling, Scaling, 0, _
    Translation, &HFFFFFFFF

TextRect.top = 78
TextRect.left = 2
TextRect.bottom = 96
TextRect.right = 128
d3dx.DrawText GameFont, &HFF000000, Raymond.RaymondWords, _
    TextRect, DT_TOP Or DT_RIGHT

TextRect.top = 76
TextRect.left = 0
TextRect.bottom = 96
TextRect.right = 128
d3dx.DrawText GameFont, &HFFFFFFFF, Raymond.RaymondWords, _
    TextRect, DT_TOP Or DT_RIGHT

End Sub
```

Next I create a new `D3DXSprite` object using the `CreateSprite` method, and then I use the `Draw` method to display the sprite on the screen.

Because I can't be sure of the background for the text, I decided to display it using two layers. The letters in the bottom layer are drawn in black, while the top letters are drawn in white. To make them stand out, I offset the two rectangles containing the text by two pixels horizontally and vertically from each other.

Because I want the words to appear when Raymond says them, I extract the text from the `RaymondWords` property and display them right justified within the text's rectangle. By default, the text is displayed as a single line, so the words will appear on the right and scroll to the left. Any words that extend beyond the left edge of the text's rectangle will be automatically truncated.

FINAL THOUGHTS

This chapter explores some refinements to the game. The Mall Strait Journal is a useful way to record what is happening in the game and to keep the player up-to-date with important information. The input box logic enables the player to input a value into the game.

My favorite change was the introduction of Raymond. Raymond's purpose in the game is to pop up occasionally and offer suggestions to the player. However, to make Raymond more interesting, I decided to give him a voice as well as an image. Because recording `.WAV` files for every possible situation is very time-consuming, I decided that using the Microsoft Speech API was a better idea. Because of the modular way I implemented Raymond, I can easily switch to `.WAV` files at some point in the future.

CHAPTER 18

RUNNING THE MALL

In this chapter

With the bulk of the core game already implemented, it's now time to focus on adding controls for the player. Given the complexity of the game, coupled with the fact that both Direct3D and DirectInput don't provide much in the way of high-level interface design tools, adding player-driven functions involves modifying a number of different classes and modules.

BUILDING A COMMAND FRAMEWORK

Adding a new function to Swim Mall involves modifying these modules. The changes range from simple one-line definitions to extensive Select statements.

- **Global**—Defines the various states in the game.
- **GameCommand**—Defines the commands that are used to transition the game from one state to another.
- **DXInput**—Determines the proper command based on the current game state and the input received from the user.
- **Game**—Contains the execution engine that processes commands.

DESIGNING THE FINITE STATE MACHINE

Modifying this many modules can be difficult without a plan for the changes. Fortunately, it's pretty easy to diagram the changes. Whether you use a piece of paper or Visio you'll find it useful to draw a diagram of the states and commands. Figure 18.1 shows why you need a chart for this information.

The chart describes the states and commands used to implement most of the functions under the Store Menu option (see Figure 18.2). The menu itself corresponds to a particular game state, while each command from the menu corresponds to a particular command.

Each state is represented in the diagram by a rectangle with the name of the state inside. A transition from one state to another happens whenever the user enters a command. Typically a command consists of a single DirectInput event, which happens when the player presses a key on the keyboard or uses the mouse. This is shown in the diagram by an arrow with the name of the command.

Figure 18.1
Designing a complex
finite state machine.

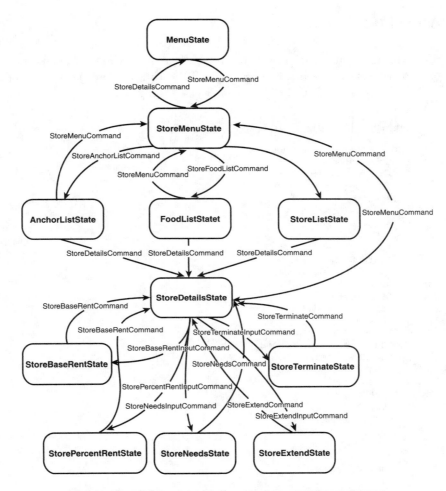

Figure 18.2
Viewing the Store
menu.

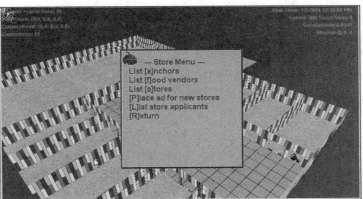

ADDING THE DEFINITIONS

To implement the new menu items, you have to modify the GameCommand class and the Global module. Each new command needs to be added to CommandEnums in the GameCommand class (see Listing 18.1), while each need state needs to be added to GameStateEnum in the Global module (see Listing 18.2).

LISTING 18.1   GAMECOMMAND.COMMANDENUMS

```
Public Enum CommandEnums
    UnknownCommand
    AdAmountCommand
    AdAmountInputCommand
    AdCommand
    AdCancelCommand
    AdRunCommand
    AdStartCommand
    AdStartInputCommand
    AdStopCommand
    AdStopInputCommand
    AdWhereCommand
    CancelCommand
    DistanceCommand
    EditCommand
    LoanBorrowCommand
    LoanBorrowInputCommand
    LoanRepayCommand
    LoanRepayInputCommand
    MenuCommand
    MoveCommand
    msjcommand
    MSJBackupCommand
    MSJForwardCommand
    MusicNextTrack
    MusicTogglePause
    MusicVolumeDown
    MusicVolumeUp
    NoCommand
    OkayCommand
    QuitCommand
    ReturnToGameCommand
    ResetViewCommand
    RotateCommand
    SelectCommand
    SpeedCommand
    StoreAdvertiseCommand
    StoreAnchorListCommand
    StoreApplicantsCommand
    StoreBaseRentCommand
    StoreBaseRentInputCommand
    StoreDetailsCommand
    StoreExtendCommand
    StoreExtendInputCommand
    StoreFoodListCommand
    StoreListCommand
    StoreMenuCommand
```

LISTING 18.1   CONTINUED

```
    StoreNeedsCommand
    StorePercentRentCommand
    StorePercentRentInputCommand
    StoreTerminateCommand
    StoreTerminateInputCommand
    YesCommand
    ZoomCommand

End Enum
```

LISTING 18.2   GLOBAL.GAMESTATEENUM

```
Public Enum GameStateEnum
    UnknownState
    NormalState
    MenuState
    AdAmountState
    AdMenuState
    AdStartState
    AdStopState
    BorrowState
    MSJState
    OkayState
    RepayState
    QuitState
    StoreAnchorListState
    StoreApplicantsState
    StoreBaseRentState
    StoreDetailsState
    StoreExtendState
    StoreFoodListState
    StoreListState
    StoreMenuState
    storeneedsstate
    StorePercentRentState
    StoreTerminateState
    StoreTerminateInputState

End Enum
```

RECEIVING INPUT

The `StoreMenuState` corresponds to the Store menu shown in Figure 18.2. You arrive at this menu from `MenuState`, which corresponds to the game's main menu. The player will choose the Manage Stores menu item by pressing M, which will add the `StoreMenuCommand` to the command queue.

Mapping the keyboard to a command involves a rather lengthy routine called `DXInput.KeyboardStateChange`, which was previously discussed in Chapter 12,

"Controlling the Mall with DirectInput," and Chapter 13, "Commanding the Game." A partial listing of the routine is shown in Listing 18.3. Refer to the CD-ROM source code listing for the complete routine.

LISTING 18.3   DXINPUT.KEYBOARDSTATECHANGE (PARTIAL LISTING)

```
Private Sub KeyBoardStateChange(k As Long)

Dim c As GameCommand

Select Case GameState
    Case NormalState
        Select Case k
            Case DIK_ESCAPE
                AddCommand MenuCommand

        End Select

    Case MenuState
        Select Case k
            Case DIK_M
                AddCommand StoreMenuCommand

            Case DIK_R
                AddCommand ReturnToGameCommand

        End Select

    Case StoreMenuState
        Select Case k
            Case DIK_A
                AddCommand StoreAnchorListCommand

            Case DIK_F
                AddCommand StoreFoodListCommand

            Case DIK_S
                AddCommand StoreListCommand

            Case DIK_P
                AddCommand StoreAdvertiseCommand

            Case DIK_L
                AddCommand StoreApplicantsCommand

            Case DIK_ESCAPE
                AddCommand MenuCommand

            Case DIK_R
                AddCommand MenuCommand

        End Select

End Select

End Sub
```

This routine basically takes a single character as a parameter called k, which represents a keyboard state value and translates it into a command. It begins by setting up a large Select statement whose individual Case clauses check for the various game states. Then within a particular game state, the various keyboard state values are checked. If a match is found, it uses the AddCommand method to add the command to the queue.

For instance, assume that the game is in MenuState. If the M key is pressed, the Select statement associated with MenuState will be executed and the StoreMenuCommand will be added to the command queue using the AddCommand method. If the Z key is pressed, it will be ignored because there isn't a Case clause for it.

RUNNING COMMANDS

Running a particular command is handled by the RunACommand method in the Game class. It consists of a big Select statement that executes a block of code for a specific command (see Listing 18.4). To keep the amount of code to a minimum, I've removed the code associated for all of the commands except the StoreMenuCommand from this routine. You can see the complete code for this routine by looking at the code for this chapter on the CD-ROM.

LISTING 18.4 GAME.RUNACOMMAND (PARTIAL LISTING)

```
Public Sub RunACommand(c As GameCommand)

Dim r As Single

Select Case c.Command

  Case StoreMenuCommand
      GameState = StoreMenuState
      dx.PopupMessage = Menu
      dx.PopupMessageText = "             --- Store Menu ---" & vbCrLf & _
         "List [a]nchors" & vbCrLf & "List [f]ood vendors" & vbCrLf & _
         "List [s]tores" & vbCrLf & "[P]lace ad for new stores" & vbCrLf & _
         "[L]ist store applicants" & vbCrLf & "[R]eturn"

   Case Else
      GameDebugger.WriteLong "Invalid game command: ", c.Command

End Select

End Sub
```

Displaying the Store Menu takes three lines of code. The first switches GameState to StoreMenuState. The second line displays the menu pop-up message, while the third displays the text associated with the pop-up message. This technique is used throughout the game to display simple messages on the screen.

MANAGING STORES

With the framework in place, I want to go though the rest of the finite state machine shown in Figure 18.1. Because I've already covered the entries needed in GameStateEnum and CommandEnums, I'll just show the relevant entries in RunACommand and KeyboardChangeState.

LISTING STORES

The code for the first three commands in the Stores menu are very similar, so I'll focus on the code that is executed for the StoreListCommand. Like the code associated with the StoreMenuCommand, the following code for the StoreListCommand merely creates a new menu that is displayed to the player:

```
Case StoreListCommand
    GameState = StoreListState
    dx.PopupMessage = Menu
    dx.PopupMessageText = MakeStoreList
```

Unlike the code for the StoreMenuCommand, this code calls a subroutine called MakeStoreList (see Listing 18.5) to build the actual menu displayed.

LISTING 18.5 GAME.MAKESTORELIST

```
Private Function MakeStoreList() As String

Dim m As String
Dim s As Store
Dim i As Long

i = Asc("A")
m = "          --- List of Stores ---" & vbCrLf
For Each s In MallObj.Stores
   m = m & "[" & Chr(i) & "] " & s.Name & vbCrLf
   i = i + 1

Next s

MakeStoreList = m & vbCrLf & "[R]eturn to Stores Menu"

End Function
```

The MakeStoreList function begins by getting the ASCII value of the letter A and saving it in the variable i. Next the temporary string m is initialized with the start of the menu.

After that, a For Each loop goes through the collection of stores. The value of I is converted back into a character using the Chr function and append that value, plus the name of the store to the menu list. Finally, the temporary string is returned as the value of the function. This results in a menu (see Figure 18.3) that allows the user to uniquely identify a store using the letters A, B, C, and so on.

Figure 18.3
Listing the stores in
the Oceanic Mall.

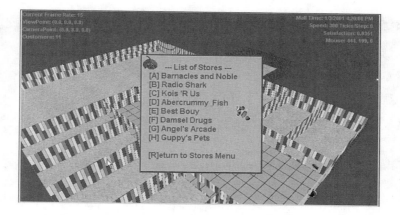

The code in DXInput.KeyboardStateChange that handles the player's input is shown in Listing 18.6. This routine traps the Esc key and the R key and generates a StoreMenuCommand, which will return the player back to the Store menu and StoreMenuState.

LISTING 18.6   DXINPUT.KEYBOARDSTATECHANGE (CASE STORELISTSTATE)

```
Case StoreListState
    Select Case k
        Case DIK_ESCAPE
            AddCommand StoreMenuCommand

        Case DIK_R
            AddCommand StoreMenuCommand

        Case DIK_A
            AddCommand StoreDetailsCommand, , , , , 1, 1

        Case DIK_B
            AddCommand StoreDetailsCommand, , , , , 2, 1

        Case DIK_C
            AddCommand StoreDetailsCommand, , , , , 3, 1

        Case DIK_D
            AddCommand StoreDetailsCommand, , , , , 4, 1

        Case DIK_E
            AddCommand StoreDetailsCommand, , , , , 5, 1

        Case DIK_F
            AddCommand StoreDetailsCommand, , , , , 6, 1

        Case DIK_G
            AddCommand StoreDetailsCommand, , , , , 7, 1

        Case DIK_H
            AddCommand StoreDetailsCommand, , , , , 8, 1
```

LISTING 18.6   CONTINUED

```
      Case DIK_I
         AddCommand StoreDetailsCommand, , , , , 9, 1

      Case DIK_J
         AddCommand StoreDetailsCommand, , , , , 10, 1

      Case DIK_K
         AddCommand StoreDetailsCommand, , , , , 11, 1

      Case DIK_L
         AddCommand StoreDetailsCommand, , , , , 12, 1

   End Select
```

The rest of the keys are mapped to the StoreDetailsCommand. Rather than create a separate command for each key, I decided to use the x and y properties of the GameCommand object to identify the type of store (1 means a store, 2 means a food court vendor, and 3 means an anchor) and the store's relative position in the collection. Thus I can use the y property as an index into the Stores collection to retrieve the information for the store.

DISPLAYING INFORMATION ABOUT A STORE

The StoreDetailsCommand triggers the code in Listing 18.7. Unlike the other Case clauses in RunACommand, this one is relatively complex because of the extra information contained in the GameCommand object.

LISTING 18.7   GAME.RUNACOMMAND (CASE STOREDETAILSCOMMAND)

```
Case StoreDetailsCommand
   Select Case c.y
      Case 0
         GameState = StoreDetailsState
         dx.PopupMessage = Menu
         dx.PopupMessageText = MakeStoreDetailsList

      Case 1
         If c.x <= MallObj.Stores.Count Then
            Set CurrentStore = MallObj.Stores(c.x)
            GameState = StoreDetailsState
            dx.PopupMessage = Menu
            dx.PopupMessageText = MakeStoreDetailsList

         End If

      Case 2
         If c.x <= MallObj.Foods.Count Then
            Set CurrentStore = MallObj.Foods(c.x)
            GameState = StoreDetailsState
            dx.PopupMessage = Menu
            dx.PopupMessageText = MakeStoreDetailsList
```

LISTING 18.7   CONTINUED

```
            End If

        Case 3
            If c.x <= MallObj.Anchors.Count Then
                Set CurrentStore = MallObj.Anchors(c.x)
                GameState = StoreDetailsState
                dx.PopupMessage = Menu
                dx.PopupMessageText = MakeStoreDetailsList

            End If

    End Select
```

There are four possible conditions that need to be handled—the first three represent the three types of stores (anchors, food court vendors, and regular stores), while the fourth is a default condition where the type of store isn't specified.

When the GameCommand contains a reference to a store type (c.x = 1, 2 or 3), The value contained in the y property is checked to ensure that it points to a valid member of the appropriate collection. Then an object reference to the store is saved in the global variable CurrentStore. Finally, GameState is set to StoreDetailsState and display a pop-up menu using the text generated by the MakeStoreDetailsList function.

If c.x contains a value of zero, CurrentStore is assumed to have a valid object pointer to a store and merely create the pop-up menu using the MakeStoreDetailsList function.

The MakeStoreDetailsListFunction (see Listing 18.8) is shared by all three types of stores. It extracts critical information like the store's sales and profit, rent, and number of customers from the object. It also extracts the date the store opened and the date the store's lease is up.

LISTING 18.8   GAME.MAKESTOREDETAILSLISTFUNCTION

```
Private Function MakeStoreDetailsList() As String

Dim m As String
Dim c As Store

m = "         --- " & CurrentStore.Name & " ---" & vbCrLf

m = m & FormatCurrency(CurrentStore.TotalSales, 0) & " / " & _
    FormatCurrency(CurrentStore.TotalProfit, 0) & " sales/profit" & vbCrLf

m = m & FormatCurrency(CurrentStore.BaseRent, 0) & " / " & _
    FormatPercent(CurrentStore.PercentageSalesRent, 2) & " rent" & vbCrLf

m = m & FormatNumber(CurrentStore.TotalCustomers, 0) & " total customers" & vbCrLf

m = m & "Open " & FormatDateTime(CurrentStore.OpenDate, vbShortDate) & " - " & _
    FormatDateTime(CurrentStore.CloseDate, vbShortDate) & vbCrLf
```

LISTING 18.8   CONTINUED

```
MakeStoreDetailsList = m & vbCrLf & "[L]ist Needs" & vbCrLf & _
    "[B]ase rent" & vbCrLf & "[P]ercent of sales rent" & vbCrLf & _
    "[E]xtend lease" & vbCrLf & "[T]erminate lease" & vbCrLf & _
    "[R]eturn to Stores Menu"

End Function
```

Once all of the values from the object have been formatted, I build a short list of menu items that allow the player to list the needs satisfied by the store, to change the base and percentage rent, and to extend or terminate the store's lease. This code is handled by the code fragment shown in Listing 18.9.

LISTING 18.9   DXINPUT.KEYBOARDSTATECHANGE (CASE STOREDETAILSSTATE)

```
Case StoreDetailsState
    Select Case k
        Case DIK_R
            AddCommand StoreMenuCommand

        Case DIK_ESCAPE
            AddCommand StoreMenuCommand

        Case DIK_B
            AddCommand StoreBaseRentInputCommand

        Case DIK_E
            AddCommand StoreExtendInputCommand

        Case DIK_L
            AddCommand StoreNeedsCommand

        Case DIK_P
            AddCommand StorePercentRentInputCommand

        Case DIK_T
            AddCommand StoreTerminateInputCommand

    End Select
```

If the player presses the R or the Esc key, he will be returned to the Store menu to choose another store type. The other keys will add the appropriate command to the command queue for execution.

DISPLAYING A STORE'S NEEDS

Because each store satisfies a different set of needs, it is important for the player to know the needs supplied by a particular store. This is controlled by the StoreNeedsState and the StoreNeedsCommand. This generates a menu item similar to the StoreDetailsCommand, except the MakeStoreNeedsList function (see Listing 18.10) is used to generate the text on the menu.

LISTING 18.10   GAME.MAKESTORENEEDSLIST

```
Private Function MakeStoreNeedsList() As String

Dim i As Long
Dim j As Long
Dim m As String

m = "         --- " & CurrentStore.Name & " ---" & vbCrLf
j = 1
For i = 0 To 29
   If CurrentStore.Needs And j Then
      m = m & CNeedsString(j) & vbCrLf

   End If

j = j * 2

Next i

j = 1
For i = 0 To 18
   If CurrentStore.FoodNeeds And j Then
      m = m & CFoodNeedsString(j) & vbCrLf

   End If

j = j * 2

Next i

MakeStoreNeedsList = m & "[R]eturn"

End Function
```

MakeStoreNeedsList converts the bits stored in the Needs and FoodNeeds properties of the store into text strings using the CFeedsString and CFoodNeedsString functions. The routine begins by initializing a temporary string m with the header that will be displayed on the menu.

Next j is initialized to 1, which will be used as a bit mask to extract the bit corresponding to the specific need. If the extracted bit is 1, the CNeedsString function will convert the relative bit position into the text string that describes the bit. After that the text string is appended to m along with a carriage return line feed that forces the string to continue on the next line.

This process is repeated for each bit in Needs. Then a second loop processes FoodNeeds. Finally a menu item for Return is appended and the temporary string is returned as the value of the function.

The CFoodNeedsString and CNeedsString routines are very similar, differing only in the values of the needs enums accepted and the string returned. Listing 18.11 contains the code used for the CNeedsString routine. As you can see, the routine simply uses a big Select statement, which identifies each possible NeedTypes value and then returns the appropriate text string.

LISTING 18.11   GLOBAL.CNEEDSSTRING

```
Public Function CNeedsString(Data As NeedTypes) As String

Select Case Data
   Case WomensClothes
      CNeedsString = "Women's clothes"

   Case MensClothes
      CNeedsString = "Men's clothes"

   Case ChildrensClothes
      CNeedsString = "Children's Clothes"

   Case Furniture
      CNeedsString = "Furniture"

   Case TVStereo
      CNeedsString = "TV and Stereo"

   Case MusicCDVideoTapes
      CNeedsString = "Music CDs and Video Tapes"

   Case Computers
      CNeedsString = "Computers"

   Case Entertainment
      CNeedsString = "Entertainment"

   Case GiftsNovelty
      CNeedsString = "Gifts and Novelties"

   Case BooksMagazines
      CNeedsString = "Books and Magazines"

   Case SportingGoods
      CNeedsString = "Sporting Goods"

   Case Toys
      CNeedsString = "Toys"

   Case Hobby
      CNeedsString = "Hobby"

   Case Jewelry
      CNeedsString = "Jewelry"

   Case Camera
      CNeedsString = "Camera"

   Case Pharmacy
      CNeedsString = "Pharmacy"
```

LISTING 18.11 CONTINUED

```
   Case Tools
     CNeedsString = "Tools"

   Case Pets
     CNeedsString = "Pets"

   Case Arcade
     CNeedsString = "Arcade"

   Case Housewares
     CNeedsString = "Housewares"

   Case Software
     CNeedsString = "Software"

   Case EyeGlasses
     CNeedsString = "Eyeglasses"

   Case Appliances
     CNeedsString = "Appliances"

   Case Collectables
     CNeedsString = "Collectables"

   Case HealthBeauty
     CNeedsString = "Health Beauty"

   Case Bank
     CNeedsString = "Bank"

   Case Shoes
     CNeedsString = "Shoes"

   Case Luggage
     CNeedsString = "Luggage"

   Case Grocery
     CNeedsString = "Grocery"

   Case GreetingCard
     CNeedsString = "Greeting Card"

End Select

End Function
```

Note

Resource files again

A better approach for translating a need into the equivalent string value would be to use a resource file. This would reduce the total amount of code required to translate the value, while making it easier to translate the game into another language.

TERMINATING A LEASE

The lease for each store expires at a certain point in time. This date varies when the mall is initially created, but can be changed any time by the player through the Extend Lease and Terminate Lease commands (see Figure 18.4).

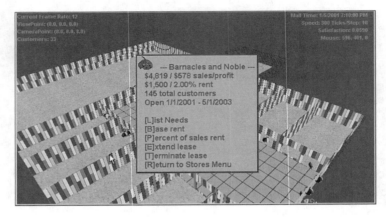

Figure 18.4
Extending and terminating leases.

Both of these commands end up changing a property in the associated store object and use similar code to make the change. In fact, similar code is also used to change the base rent and the percent of sales rent. So I'm only going to discuss the code associated with the terminate command here. You can see the code for the other commands in the source code for game found on the CD-ROM.

HANDLING THE TERMINATE COMMAND

When the player presses T on the store details display, the `StoreTerminateInputCommand` is added to the command queue, which runs the code shown in Listing 18.12.

LISTING 18.12   GAME.RUNACOMMAND (CASE STORETERMINATEINPUTCOMMAND)

```
Case StoreTerminateInputCommand
    GameState = StoreTerminateState
    dxi.InputBuffer = ""
    dxi.KeyboardTextMode = True
    dx.PopupMessage = InputBox
    dx.PopupMessageText = "Store closes on?"
```

This code switches `GameState` to `StoreTerminateState` and sets `dxi.KeyboardTextMode` to `True` to allow the user to enter a string of text. Then it sets the `PopupMessage` property to display an input box and sets `PopupMessageText` to prompt the user to enter the date the store will close. This will display the input box shown in Figure 18.5.

Figure 18.5
Prompting the user for a date using an input box.

When the player has finished entering the date the store will be terminated; then StoreTerminateCommand will be executed. This command runs the code shown in Listing 18.13.

LISTING 18.13   GAME.RUNACOMMAND (CASE STORETERMINATECOMMAND)

```
Case StoreTerminateCommand
    If IsDate(dxi.InputBuffer) Then
        CurrentStore.CloseDate = CDate(dxi.InputBuffer)
        dx.PopupMessageText = CurrentStore.Name & " has been terminated."
        dx.PopupMessage = okay
        GameState = OkayState

    Else
        dx.PopupMessage = okay
        dx.PopupMessageText = "Invalid date."
        GameState = OkayState

    End If
```

The first thing the routine does is to examine the input buffer to see if it contains a valid date. If so, the data is saved in the CloseDate property of the CurrentStore. Then the user is notified that the lease for that store has been terminated. If the date isn't valid, the user will see an error message using an OK box.

CLOSING THE STORE

Just because the store now has a closing date doesn't mean that it will automatically go away when it reaches that day. So I modified the code in the EndDay routine (see Listing 18.14) of each store class (Anchor, Food and Store) to notify the user before the store closes and to do any necessary cleanup work on the day the store closes.

LISTING 18.14   STORE.ENDDAY

```
Public Sub EndDay()

Dim i As Long
Dim j As Long
Dim n As String

MonthlySales = MonthlySales + TodaysSales
MonthlyProfit = MonthlyProfit + TodaysSales * ProfitMargin

TotalSales = TotalSales + TodaysSales
TotalProfit = TotalProfit + TodaysSales * ProfitMargin
TotalCustomers = TotalCustomers + TodaysCustomers

TodaysSales = 0
TodaysCustomers = 0

If DateDiff("d", MasterClock, CloseDate) = 30 Then
    Raymond.Speak 4, Name

End If

If DateDiff("d", MasterClock, CloseDate) = 0 Then
    n = Name & " has closed its doors effective today and it will no " & _
        "longer operate a store in " & GameObj.Name & ". Customers will " & _
        "no longer be able to shop for these products: "
    j = 1
    For i = 0 To 28
        If Needs And j Then
            n = n & CNeedsString(j) & "; "

        End If

        j = j * 2

    Next i

    News.AddNews Name & " Has Closed its Doors", n
    Name = "Vacant"
    Needs = 0
    FoodNeeds = 0
    GameObj.Mall.ComputeMallNeeds
    BaseRent = 0
    PercentageSalesRent = 0
    dxi.AddCommand msjcommand

End If

End Sub
```

The new code begins when I use the DateDiff function to see how many days remain before the store closes. If it's exactly 30, Raymond will speak a message to the player to let them know.

If DateDiff returns zero, a news item is created for the Mall Strait Journal that formally lets the player know that the store is no longer a part of the mall. To ensure that the player knew the customers that the store served, a list of the needs is displayed using logic similar to the code in the MakeStoreNeedsList function. Then the AddNews method is called to post the news to the Mall Strait Journal.

Even though the store is no longer present in the mall, the store object will remain because it also describes the store's physical location in the mall. So the Name property is set to Vacant and the Needs and FoodNeeds properties are zeroed out. Because the store's needs properties have changed, the mall's needs properties are recomputed.

The routine ends by zeroing out the rent properties, otherwise the mall will collect rent from the empty store. Then the dxi.AddCommand is called to display the most recent issue of the Mall Strait Journal. This notifies the player that the store is no longer a part of the mall.

FINAL THOUGHTS

Adding commands and other user interface functions are important for making the game playable. However it involves applying the same techniques over and over again with only minor variations. Although this approach leads to a more stable program, it doesn't really illustrate any new techniques, which is why I didn't discuss all of the details about all of the commands the user can issue to the game. You'll just have to look at the source code on the CD-ROM to see the details of the other commands.

Note that much of the complexity required to implement commands in this game are a direct result of using DirectInput and Direct3D to get user input and display the results. The rest of the complexity is due to the fact that the logic to process the commands runs asynchronously from both the input logic and the display logic. While it would be nice to pause the game each time a player entered a command, it simply isn't practical.

Using the native VB tools like InputBox and MSGBox would make many things easier. Because these tools run independently of the rest of the program, the simulation could continue to run while they are active. The main drawback is that these tools offer a much different look and feel than the game. However, if you want to give your game a strong Windows look and feel (and there is nothing wrong with that), you should consider using these tools to make your life much easier.

THE END OF THE BEGINNING

In this chapter

In this chapter, I want to discuss some details that are needed in Swim Mall, such as the capability to save and load games, plus the capability for the player to enter cheat codes. Also I want to bury an Easter Egg or two for the player to find.

SAVING A GAME

Most simulation games can't be finished in a single session, so it is important to have the capability to save a game in progress and restore it later. Because Swim Mall's initialization information comes from a disk file, adding these features merely involves creating the SwimFile with all of the appropriate information.

GETTING THE FILENAME

When the player presses the F3 key, he or she will be prompted for the name of the file to be used to save the game (see Figure 19.1). The user in turn will enter the filename they want to use.

Figure 19.1
Prompting the player for the save game filename.

Once the player has entered the SaveGameCommand Case will be executed in the Game class (see Listing 19.1). This will call the SaveGame routine using the filename input by the player and the path to the SavedGames directory. If SaveGame returns zero, the game was saved properly and an OK message will be displayed to the player. If SaveGame failed, an error message will be displayed to the player.

LISTING 19.1   GAME.RUNACOMMAND (CASE SAVEGAMECOMMAND)

```
Case SaveGameCommand
    If SaveGame(App.path & "\SavedGames\" & dxi.InputBuffer & ".SMG") = 0 Then
        GameState = OkayState
        dx.PopupMessageText = "Game saved."
        dx.PopupMessage = Okay

    Else
```

LISTING 19.1 CONTINUED

```
        GameState = OkayState
        dx.PopupMessage = "Game was not saved."
        dx.PopupMessage = Okay

    End If
```

WRITING THE SWIMFILE

The SaveGame method runs the save game logic (see Listing 19.2). It records the save game request into the log file and then creates a new instance of a SwimFile.

LISTING 19.2 GAME.SAVEGAME

```
Public Function SaveGame(Filename As String) As Long

Dim GameFile As SwimFile

GameDebugger.WriteLine "Saving game file: " & Filename

Set GameFile = New SwimFile

RC = GameFile.OpenOutFile(Filename)
If RC = 0 Then
    GameFile.PutData "type", , , "Saved Game"
    SaveHeaderInfo GameFile
    SaveAnchorInfo GameFile
    SaveFoodInfo GameFile
    SaveStoreInfo GameFile
    SaveMallInfo GameFile
    SaveArrivalInfo GameFile
    SaveCommunityInfo GameFile
    SaveCompetitorInfo GameFile

    GameFile.CloseFile

End If

GameDebugger.WriteLong "Game save complete.", RC

SaveGame = RC

End Function
```

With the new instance of the SwimFile, I create the output file using the filename provided. Assuming that the open worked properly, I write out the Swim File type line (type=Saved Game), by calling the PutData method.

Next I call a series of subroutines that output various parts of the saved game file. After that I close the file. Finally, I log that the save game routine has finished to the log file and return the return code to the caller.

SAVING GAME INFO

The routines that actually save information to the saved game are fairly similar. They simply make repeated calls to the SwimFile.PutData routine to output the same values that are required to load the game.

In the SaveHeaderInfo routine (see Listing 19.3), you can see that PutData is called to output the appropriate line of information in the SwimFile. Note that PutData only accepts string values, so I have to use the appropriate formatting function to ensure that the data is written to the file properly.

LISTING 19.3   GAME.SAVEHEADERINFO

```
Private Sub SaveHeaderInfo(gf As SwimFile)

Dim i As Long

gf.PutData "Name", , , Name
gf.PutData "Mall", , , Mall.Filename
gf.PutData "Viewpoint", "x", , FormatNumber(dx.GetViewX, 2)
gf.PutData "Viewpoint", "y", , FormatNumber(dx.GetViewY, 2)
gf.PutData "Viewpoint", "z", , FormatNumber(dx.GetViewZ, 2)
gf.PutData "Camera", "x", , FormatNumber(dx.GetCameraX, 2)
gf.PutData "Camera", "y", , FormatNumber(dx.GetCameraY, 2)
gf.PutData "Camera", "z", , FormatNumber(dx.GetCameraZ, 2)
gf.PutData "Zoom", , , "1.0"
gf.PutData "Rotation", , , FormatNumber(dx.GetRotation, 2)

For i = 2 To dxa.GetFileCount
   gf.PutData "MusicDirectory", , , dxa.GetFile(i)

Next i

End Sub
```

CHANGING SWIMFILE

The SwimFile class is already positioned to handle writing data to a saved game file. It really only needs two new routines, one to open the file and one to write the data to the file. The OpenOutFile routine (see Listing 19.4) opens a file in output mode. If the file already exists, its contents will be replaced. If the file doesn't exist a new one will be created.

LISTING 19.4   SWIMFILE.OPENOUTFILE

```
Public Function OpenOutFile(Filename As String) As Long

On Error Resume Next

Set txt = fso.OpenTextFile(Filename, ForWriting, True, TristateUseDefault)

OpenOutFile = Err.Number

End Function
```

The PutData routine (see Listing 19.5) has four parameters, the three keys and the data associated with the keys. The last three parameters are declared as optional simply to make the routine easier to use. Of course, the last parameter isn't really optional, but the Visual Basic syntax requires that the Optional keyboard must be used for every parameter that follows the first one that used it.

LISTING 19.5 SWIMFILE.PUTDATA

```
Sub PutData(Key1 As String, Optional Key2 As String = "", _
    Optional Key3 As String = "", Optional Data As String = "")

Dim t As String

t = Trim(Key1)

If Len(Key2) > 0 Then
    t = t & "\" & Trim(Key2)

End If

If Len(Key3) > 0 Then
    t = t & "\" & Trim(Key3)

End If

t = t & "=" & Trim(Data)

If Len(Trim(Data)) > 0 Then
    txt.WriteLine t

End If

End Sub
```

The routine begins by constructing a temporary string containing the line that will be output to the file. The Trim is used function to remove excessive blanks from each of the values. Then if each key isn't blank, I append it to the temporary string. Finally the value from the data part is appended and output the line only if the Data contains something other then the empty string.

LOADING A SAVED GAME

Swim Mall already has the logic to load a saved game file when the game first starts; however, the logic needs to be updated to allow the player to load a saved game while Swim Mall is running.

STARTING THE GAME

Because nearly all the objects used in the game contain information specific for the particular game, the easiest way to load a new game is to quit the current game, destroy all the

objects, and completely start over again. Because the main body of the game is driven by the
Form_Load event, I've modified the event slightly as shown in Listing 19.6.

LISTING 19.6   FORM.FORM_LOAD

```
Private Sub Form_Load()

Randomize

Me.Show
DoEvents

Set GameDebugger = New Debugger
GameDebugger.Enable

CurrentGame = App.path & "\" & "SwimMall.SMG"
Do While Len(CurrentGame) > 0
    SelectedObj = 1
    GetMouse = False
    GameActive = False

    If InitGame = 0 Then
        PlayGame

    End If

    GameDebugger.WriteLine "PlayGame has finished."

    Set GameObj = Nothing

    Set dxa = Nothing
    dxi.TermDXInput
    Set dxi = Nothing
    Set dx = Nothing

Loop

Unload Me

End Sub
```

The key to making this routine work is a new global variable called CurrentGame. This variable contains the name of the file that will be loaded when the game starts. After the game is loaded, the program will set CurrentGame to an empty string. To start a new game, all I have to do is save the filename for the saved game in CurrentGame and quit the current game.

Form_Load begins by randomizing the random number generator. Then it executes the Show method to force the form to be displayed before the Form_Load event finishes. Next DoEvents is called to pause the program and allow the form to be displayed. A new instance of the Debugger object is created and then enabled. After that, the name of the default SwimFile is stored in CurrentGame.

The Do loop processes each game in turn. Within the loop, I initialize a few key variables and then call the InitGame function to initialize the game, including the initialization required to use DirectX. If InitGame returns a value of zero, PlayGame is called to run the game.

When PlayGame returns, I'll update the game's status in the debug log and destroy all the objects associated with the game, including the objects I use to communicate with DirectX. Finally, when the loop is finished, I use the Unload Me statement to close the form and end the program.

CHOOSING A SAVED GAME

Pressing the F2 key displays a menu using code similar to the other menus used in the game (see Figure 19.2), but this one contains a list of files from the SavedGames directory that can be loaded in place of the current game.

Figure 19.2
Displaying a list of saved games.

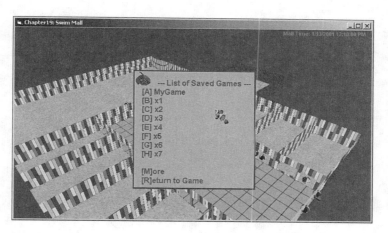

Because it's possible that the player may have more saved games in the SavedGame directory than will fit on a single menu, I grab all the files and store them in a global String array called SavedGameFiles so that the player may view them one page at a time. I also use a variable called SavedGameIndex that points to the first file displayed on the current menu page.

When the code in the LoadGameMenuCommand (see Listing 19.7) is triggered, it uses the same logic to create and display a menu elsewhere in the game. However, before I display the menu, I redimension the SavedGameFiles array to zero, to destroy any previous files that may have been saved in the SavedGameFiles array.

PART

IV

CH

19

LISTING 19.7   GAME.RUNACOMMAND (CASE LOADGAMEMENUCOMMAND)

```
Case LoadGameMenuCommand
    ReDim SavedGameFiles(0)
    GameState = LoadGameState
    dx.PopupMessage = Menu
    dx.PopupMessageText = MakeGameList
```

The actual text of the menu is created by the MakeGameList function shown in Listing 19.8. This routine does two main functions. First, if the upper bound of the SavedGameFiles array is zero, the array is loaded with all of the saved game files from the saved games directory. Then the information will be used to construct a list of the games that can be loaded.

LISTING 19.8   GAME.MAKEGAMELIST

```
Private Function MakeGameList() As String

Dim fso As FileSystemObject
Dim fo As folder
Dim f As File
Dim m As String
Dim t As String
Dim i As Long
Dim j As Long

If UBound(SavedGameFiles) = 0 Then
    Set fso = New FileSystemObject
    Set fo = fso.GetFolder(App.path & "\SavedGames")

    For Each f In fo.Files
        t = right(f.Name, 4)
        If t = ".SMG" Then
            ReDim Preserve SavedGameFiles(UBound(SavedGameFiles) + 1)
            SavedGameFiles(UBound(SavedGameFiles)) = f.Name

        End If

    Next f

    SavedGameIndex = 1
    Set f = Nothing
    Set fo = Nothing
    Set fso = Nothing

End If

i = Asc("A")
m = "          --- List of Saved Games ---" & vbCrLf

For j = SavedGameIndex To SavedGameIndex + 7
    If j <= UBound(SavedGameFiles) Then
        m = m & "[" & Chr(i) & "] " & SavedGameFiles(j) & vbCrLf
        i = i + 1
```

LISTING 19.8   CONTINUED

```
    Else
        m = m & vbCrLf

    End If

Next j

If SavedGameIndex + 7 > UBound(SavedGameFiles) Then
    MakeGameList = m & vbCrLf & "[R]eturn to Game"

Else
    MakeGameList = m & vbCrLf & "[M]ore" & vbCrLf & "[R]eturn to Game"

End If

End Function
```

To save the filenames into the SavedGameFiles array, a new instance of the FileSystemObject is created and used to create a Folder object that represents the files stored in the SavedGames directory. Next a For Each loop is used to examine the collection of files stored in the directory. If a file's extension is .SMG, the filename is extracted and saved in the array. After the list of files has been scanned, SavedGameIndex is set to 1 and the objects used to access the directory are destroyed.

Next generate the menu is generated by choosing the first eight items from the array, starting with the item pointed to by SavedGameIndex. If there are fewer than eight, blank lines are added to take their place. Finally, a check is made to see if there are additional files in the array. If there are, an option to display more files is added followed by the return to game option; otherwise, just the option to return to the game option is added.

When the player presses the M key from the list of saved games, the code in Listing 19.9 will be executed. This command builds the menu just like the one shown in Listing 19.7, but this time 8 is added to the value of SavedGameIndex. Because I didn't redimension the SaveGameFiles array, it won't be reloaded when MakeGameList is called, so the menu will simply contain the next batch of files the player can choose from.

LISTING 19.9   GAME.RUNACOMMAND (CASE LOADGAMEMORECOMMAND)

```
Case LoadGameMoreCommand
    SavedGameIndex = SavedGameIndex + 8
    GameState = LoadGameState
    dx.PopupMessage = Menu
    dx.PopupMessageText = MakeGameList
```

If the player selects a saved game from the menu, the Case clause in Listing 19.10 will be executed. This code simply saves the fully qualified filename in CurrentGame and ends the current game by setting GameActive to False. This will stop the game loop in Form1.PlayGame, which in turn allows the code in Form1.Form_Load to clean up after the current game and reinitialize the new game.

LISTING 19.10   GAME.RUNACOMMAND (CASE LOADGAMECOMMAND)

```
Case LoadGameCommand
    CurrentGame = App.path & "\SavedGames\" & _
        SavedGameFiles(SavedGameIndex + c.x - 1)
    GameActive = False
    dx.PopupMessage = None
```

CHEATING IN SWIM MALL

Every player expects a game to provide them with a way to cheat. Of course, the technique to enter the cheat code and the codes themselves should be not be obvious or it loses some of its appeal to the player.

To enter a cheat code in Swim Mall, the player must type the characters C, H, E, A, and T in sequence while the screen is empty (that is, Raymond and the Mall Strait Journal are hidden and no menus are visible). If the player mistypes a single character, they must start over again. Once the cheat code is entered, an input box will be displayed that allows the player to enter a cheat code.

DETECTING THE CHEAT COMMAND

I choose to keep the code to detect the cheat command buried in the DXInput module to simplify the code. As you might expect, I'm going to use a finite state machine to track each character as it's entered. When I receive the final character, I'll process the command using the same basic techniques I've already shown.

To track the state of the cheat code, I declared this statement at the start of the DXInput module. Then in Listing 19.11, I added the statements for the finite state machine under the Case NormalState. (Note that much of the code in the Case clause was deleted from the listing because it wasn't relevant to this discussion.)

```
Private CheatCodeState As Long
```

LISTING 19.11   DXINPUT.KEYBOARDSTATECHANGE (PARTIAL LISTING)

```
Private Sub KeyBoardStateChange(k As Long)

Dim c As GameCommand

Select Case GameState
    Case NormalState
        Select Case k
            Case DIK_ESCAPE
                AddCommand MenuCommand
                CheatCodeState = 0

'   many case clauses deleted

            Case DIK_C
                CheatCodeState = 1
```

LISTING 19.11   CONTINUED

```
        Case DIK_H
            CheatCodeState = IIf(CheatCodeState = 1, 2, 0)

        Case DIK_E
            CheatCodeState = IIf(CheatCodeState = 2, 3, 0)

        Case DIK_A
            CheatCodeState = IIf(CheatCodeState = 3, 4, 0)

        Case DIK_T
            If CheatCodeState = 4 Then
                AddCommand CheatInputCommand

            End If
            CheatCodeState = 0

        Case Else
            CheatCodeState = 0

    End Select
```

When the game starts, CheatCodeState has a value of zero. When the player presses the C key while in Normal state, CheatCodeState is set to 1, which indicates that the player has pressed the C key.

Pressing the H key causes CheatCodeState to be set to 2, only when CheatCodeState has a value of 1. Otherwise, CheatCodeState will be reset to zero. Thus the only way for CheatCodeState to have a value of 2 is when the player presses both C and H in the proper order.

This process is repeated for the E and A keys. When the player presses the T command, I add the CheatInputCommand to the command queue only when CheatCodeState has a value of 4. Then CheatCodeState is reset back to zero.

Finally, if the game is in NormalState and the player presses a key not defined in one of the Case clauses, CheatCodeState is reset to zero. Note that I also do this after the AddCommand in the Case DIK_ESCAPE clause as well as in all of the Case clauses I deleted in Listing 18.1. This ensures that when the player hits a character that is not part of the cheat command, he has to start over from scratch.

PROCESSING CHEAT COMMANDS

When the cheat command is accepted, the game will display an input box using the code in Listing 19.12.

LISTING 19.12   GAME.RUNACOMMAND (PARTIAL LISTING)

```
Case CheatInputCommand
   GameState = CheatState
   dxi.InputBuffer = ""
   dxi.KeyboardTextMode = True
   dx.PopupMessage = InputBox
   dx.PopupMessageText = "Please enter cheat code."
```

After the user has entered the cheat code, the code associated with `CheatCommand` in RunACommand (see Listing 19.13) will be executed. Because I already include Option Compare Text at the start of the module, I merely need to trim the blanks out of the input buffer to determine which code the player entered.

LISTING 19.13   GAME.RUNACOMMAND (PARTIAL LISTING)

```
Case CheatCommand
   If Trim(dxi.InputBuffer) = "congressperson" Then
      If Cash < 10000 Then
         Cash = Cash + 100000

      Else
         Cash = Cash * 2

      End If
      dx.PopupMessage = Okay
      dx.PopupMessageText = "You now have " & FormatCurrency(Cash, 0)
      GameState = OkayState

   ElseIf Trim(dxi.InputBuffer) = "alan greenspan" Then
      If InterestRate < 1 Then
         InterestRate = InterestRate / 2

      Else
         InterestRate = InterestRate - 1

      End If
      dx.PopupMessage = Okay
      dx.PopupMessageText = "The current interest rate is now " & _
         FormatPercent(InterestRate, 2) & "."
      GameState = OkayState

   ElseIf Trim(dxi.InputBuffer) = "beach boys music" Then
      If Satisfaction < 0 Then
         Satisfaction = Satisfaction + 1

      Else
         Satisfaction = Satisfaction + (1 - Satisfaction) / 2

      End If
      dx.PopupMessage = Okay
      dx.PopupMessageText = "Customer satisfaction is now " & _
         FormatNumber(Satisfaction, 5) & "."
      GameState = OkayState
```

LISTING 19.13   CONTINUED

```
    ElseIf Trim(dxi.InputBuffer) = "income taxes" Then
      If Satisfaction > 0 Then
        Satisfaction = Satisfaction - 1

      End If
      dx.PopupMessage = Okay
      dx.PopupMessageText = "Customer satisfaction is now " & _
        FormatNumber(Satisfaction, 5) & "."
      GameState = OkayState

    ElseIf Trim(dxi.InputBuffer) = "porsche 944" Then
      dx.ShowFrameRate = Not dx.ShowFrameRate
      dx.PopupMessage = None
      GameState = NormalState

    Else
      dx.PopupMessage = Okay
      dx.PopupMessageText = dxi.InputBuffer & " is invalid."
      GameState = OkayState

    End If
```

If the player entered congressperson, the amount of cash they have is increased. If Cash has less then $10,000, $100,000 is added to it. Otherwise, the amount of cash the player can use is doubled.

I do something similar to the interest rate when the player enters the code alan greenspan. If InterestRate is less than 1%, I divide the rate in half; otherwise, I simply subtract 1 from it. This ensures that InterestRate never falls below zero, which could cause problems elsewhere in the game.

Likewise beach boys music increases customer satisfaction at the mall. If Satisfaction is less than zero, I add 1 to the value. Otherwise, I add 1/2 of the remaining possible satisfaction. Again, this prevents Satisfaction from exceeding 1. Income taxes reduces Satisfaction by 1 if Satisfaction is greater than zero; otherwise, I leave it alone.

Finally, I use the cheat code porsche 944 to turn on and off the frame rate information. Because this is primarily a debugging tool the player doesn't really need to see the information. However, some game players find watching debugging tools interesting, so you may find it desirable to expose them.

After each of the cheats are processed, except for porsche 944, I display an Okay message confirming the change. The porsche 944 displays its own confirmation because the frame rate information will appear or be hidden. While I used an Okay box to display the confirmation, you could use anything to let the player know that the cheat worked.

If you don't do this, the player may attempt to execute the cheat command several times, assuming that it didn't work. This can be very frustrating to the player. Even something as simple as a beep would go a long way toward preventing frustration.

HIDING EASTER EGGS

Every game needs a few hidden treasures that the player can find. In Swim Mall, I've hidden a few Easter eggs for you to find. While I'll show you the code that you need to find them, I'm not going to show you the Easter eggs. You'll have to find them for yourself.

SEARCHING FOR EASTER EGGS

Rather than letting the user hit a sequence of keys to find an Easter egg, I decided to use a mouse. Specifically, the player must select a series of stores in the mall in the proper sequence in order to display the Easter egg. Then the player must locate the Easter egg in the mall before they select another store because the Easter egg will be hidden the next time a store is selected.

Although there are many ways to detect the sequence, I decided to limit the code changes to the DXGraphics class to keep it simple. Therefore, in the HitObject routine (see Listing 19.14), I inserted a single line of code to perform the checks. The code simply calls the SetEEStates routine using the name of the object that was selected.

LISTING 19.14   DXGRAPHICS.HITOBJECT

```
Public Function HitObject(x As Single, y As Single) As DXObject

Dim o As DXObject

For Each o In DXobs
   If HitAnObject(o, x, y) And o.oType <> DXObjectMall Then
      Set HitObject = o
      SetEEStates o.SimObject.Name
      Exit Function

   End If

Next o

Set HitObject = Nothing

End Function
```

The SetEEStates routine (see Listing 19.15) works similar to the code I used in the DXInput class to detect a cheat code. I defined a module-level variable called EEggCJState, which keeps track of the Easter egg. Then I use a Select statement in this routine that increments the state each time a store with the appropriate first letter is selected. When all five letters have been selected in the proper order, EEggCJState will have a value of 5 and the Easter egg will become visible.

LISTING 19.15   DXGRAPHICS.SETEESTATES

```
Private Sub SetEEStates(n As String)

Dim t As String

t = left(n, 1)

Select Case EEggCJState
   Case 0
      EEggCJState = IIf(t = "c", 1, 0)

   Case 1
      EEggCJState = IIf(t = "h", 2, 0)

   Case 2
      EEggCJState = IIf(t = "r", 3, 0)

   Case 3
      EEggCJState = IIf(t = "i", 4, 0)

   Case 4
      EEggCJState = IIf(t = "s", 5, 0)

   Case 5
      EEggCJState = 0

End Select

If EEggCJState > 1 Then
   Dxa.PlayForeground "Beep.WAV"

End If

End Sub
```

The next time the player clicks on an object in the mall, EEggCJState is reset to 0, so the player must go through the same sequence each game to uncover the Easter egg.

Finally, the game will beep each time after the second step in the sequence. By beeping only after the second step is selected, the number of beeps is kept to a minimum when a player is merely selecting stores at random, while letting the player know they are on track to find the Easter egg.

Note

Slower is good

If you are having trouble trying to select the stores in the proper sequence, set the game's speed to zero. The game will tend to consume all of the available resources on your computer, which can make the mouse a little sluggish on slower computers. By setting the speed to zero, the number of resources required to run the simulation will be minimized, thus allowing the game to respond a little better to your mouse inputs.

DISPLAYING THE EASTER EGG

The Easter egg in Swim Mall is an image that is hidden somewhere in the mall. Once EEggCJState is set to 5, it is up to the Render method to display it. The partial listing shown in Listing 19.16 shows the code I used to uncover the Easter egg.

LISTING 19.16   DXGRAPHICS.RENDER (PARTIAL LISTING)

```
ElseIf o.mType = TexturedMesh Then
    With DXmshs(o.MeshFilename)
        For i = 0 To .Materials - 1
            d3ddevice.SetMaterial .MeshMaterials(i)

            If .MeshTextures(i) = "cj.bmp" And EEggCJState <> 5 Then
                d3ddevice.SetTexture 0, DXtexs("WhiteBricks.bmp").Texture

            ElseIf Len(.MeshTextures(i) > 0 Then
                d3ddevice.SetTexture 0, DXtexs(.MeshTextures(i)).Texture

            Else
                d3ddevice.SetTexture 0, Nothing

            End If

            .Mesh.DrawSubset i

        Next i
    End With
```

This code doesn't uncover the Easter egg as much as letting the real mesh show through. The real mesh uses a unique texture called CJ.BMP. Unless the Easter egg is active (EEggCJState = 5), a different texture is substituted for CJ.BMP, which ensures that the player can't see the Easter egg.

FINAL THOUGHTS

Although this is the last chapter in this book, it's not the last chapter in the Swim Mall game. The last chapter is really up to you. It is fairly easy to add new stores to the mall. All you have to do is to build some new textures, apply them to one of the existing meshes, and enter the proper information into .SMS file to create a new store.

You could even design a new shopping mall that allows more stores to be placed inside using the techniques discussed in Chapter 3, "Creating 3D Graphics." Adding new customer meshes is another relatively simple task. Simply create the appropriate meshes and copy the meshes and textures to the Customers directory and start the game. They'll be automatically loaded and randomly assigned to each customer that arrives at the mall.

Although these ideas don't involve any code, some others might be even more interesting to implement. For instance, while Swim Mall has three employees, it would be nice to have the capability to hire and fire staff. As the number of customers in your mall grows, you can increase the amount of work they have to do. Likewise if the mall starts losing customers, you may be able to let people go.

There are lots of features still waiting to be added to the game. For instance, the mall could be invaded by a horde of creeping starfish or a giant shark might prowl the hallways discouraging customers from shopping.

Swim Mall contains approximately 10,000 lines of code scattered over 27 classes, 2 modules, and a form file. Compared to high-end commercial games like Black & White that have a million or more lines of code, this is but a drop in the bucket. Of course, Black & White took 25 people more than three years to develop. Fortunately, Swim Mall took much less time and was developed by a single person with occasional assistance from my son, Chris.

I encourage you to play with the code or at least take a look at the code on the CD-ROM. I'm not finished with it and plan to add more code over time. If you find a bug or you have some code you would like me to include with the game, please send it to me at WFreeze@JustPC.com. I also welcome new ideas for the game, questions, and comments about the book. Please check my Web site at http://www.JustPC.com for the latest updates to Swim Mall, plus contests and prizes. Also, if you really liked this book and would like another VB game programming book (perhaps a multiplayer, first-person shooter game with VB.NET), please let me know. I had so much fun writing this game, I'd really enjoy another.

PART

IV

CH

19

INDEX

T

What's on the Disc

The companion CD-ROM contains many useful third-party tools and samples from the book.

Windows 95 Installation Instructions

1. Insert the CD-ROM disc into your CD-ROM drive.
2. From the Windows 95 desktop, double-click the My Computer icon.
3. Double-click the icon representing your CD-ROM drive.
4. Double-click the icon titled START.EXE to run the installation program.

Note

If Windows 95 is installed on your computer and you have the AutoPlay feature enabled, the START.EXE program starts automatically whenever you insert the disc into your CD-ROM drive.

Windows NT Installation Instructions

1. Insert the CD-ROM disc into your CD-ROM drive.
2. From File Manager or Program Manager, choose Run from the File menu.
3. Type `<drive>\START.EXE` and press Enter, where `<drive>` corresponds to the drive letter of your CD-ROM. For example, if your CD-ROM is drive D:, type `D:\START.EXE` and press Enter.

Technical Support from Que

We can't help you with Windows problems or software from third parties, but we can assist you if a problem arises with the CD-ROM itself.

Support: Send e-mail to
`http://www.quepublishing.com/press/Csupport.cfm`.

Mail: Que Publishing
201 West 103rd Street
Indianapolis, IN 46290-1093

Here's how to reach us on the Internet:

World Wide Web: `http://www.quepublishing.com/`

By opening this package, you are agreeing to be bound by the following agreement:

You may not copy or redistribute the entire CD-ROM as a whole. Copying and redistribution of individual software programs on the CD-ROM is governed by terms set by individual copyright holders.

The installer and code from the author(s) are copyrighted by the publisher and the author(s). Individual programs and other items on the CD-ROM are copyrighted or are under GNU license by their various authors or other copyright holders.

This software is sold as is without warranty of any kind, either expressed or implied, including but not limited to the implied warranties of merchantability and fitness for a particular purpose. Neither the publisher nor its dealers or distributors assumes any liability for any alleged or actual damages arising from the use of this program. (Some states do not allow for the exclusion of implied warranties, so the exclusion may not apply to you.)

Note   This CD-ROM uses long and mixed-case filenames requiring the use of a protected-mode CD-ROM driver.